anne frank

ALSO BY SID JACOBSON AND ERNIE COLÓN

Che: A Graphic Biography
After 9/11: America's War on Terror (2001–)
The 9/11 Report: A Graphic Adaptation

anne frank

THE ANNE FRANK HOUSE
AUTHORIZED
GRAPHIC BIOGRAPHY

SID JACOBSON AND ERNIE COLÓN

A Novel Graphic from Hill and Wang

A division of Farrar, Straus and Giroux

NEW YORK

This graphic biography was developed by the authors for Hill and Wang, a division of Farrar, Straus and Giroux, 18 West 18th Street, New York 10011, in collaboration with the Anne Frank House of Amsterdam, the Netherlands

Distributed in Canada by D&M Publishers, Inc.
Printed in the United States of America
Published simultaneously in hardcover and paperback
First edition, 2010

Library of Congress Cataloging-in-Publication Data

Jacobson, Sidney.
  Anne Frank : the Anne Frank House authorized graphic biography / Sid Jacobson and Ernie Colón. — 1st ed.
    p. cm.
  "A novel graphic from Hill and Wang."
  Includes bibliographical references.
  ISBN: 978-0-8090-2684-5 (hardcover : alk. paper)
  ISBN: 978-0-8090-2685-2 (pbk. : alk. paper)
  1. Frank, Anne, 1929–1945—Comic books, strips, etc. 2. Jewish children in the Holocaust—Netherlands—Amsterdam—Biography—Comic books, strips, etc. 3. Jews—Netherlands—Amsterdam—Biography—Comic books, strips, etc. 4. Holocaust, Jewish (1939–1945)—Netherlands—Amsterdam—Biography—Comic books, strips, etc. 5. Amsterdam (Netherlands)—Biography—Comic books, strips, etc. 6. Graphic novels. I. Colón, Ernie. II. Anne Frank House. III. Title.

DS135.N6F73357 2010
940.53'18092—dc22
[B]

2010005776

www.fsgbooks.com

3 5 7 9 10 8 6 4 2

I would like to dedicate this book to my children, Seth and Kathy, who but for the fortune of time and place could have suffered the tragic fate of the young sisters you are about to meet.
—SID JACOBSON

Watching my daughters grow into young women gave me a deep sense of what Anne Frank and her sister Margot missed and what a loss they were to us all. This one is for Amanda, Luisa, and Rebecca.
—ERNIE COLÓN

CONTENTS

anne frank

CHAPTER 1

A Hopeful Beginning

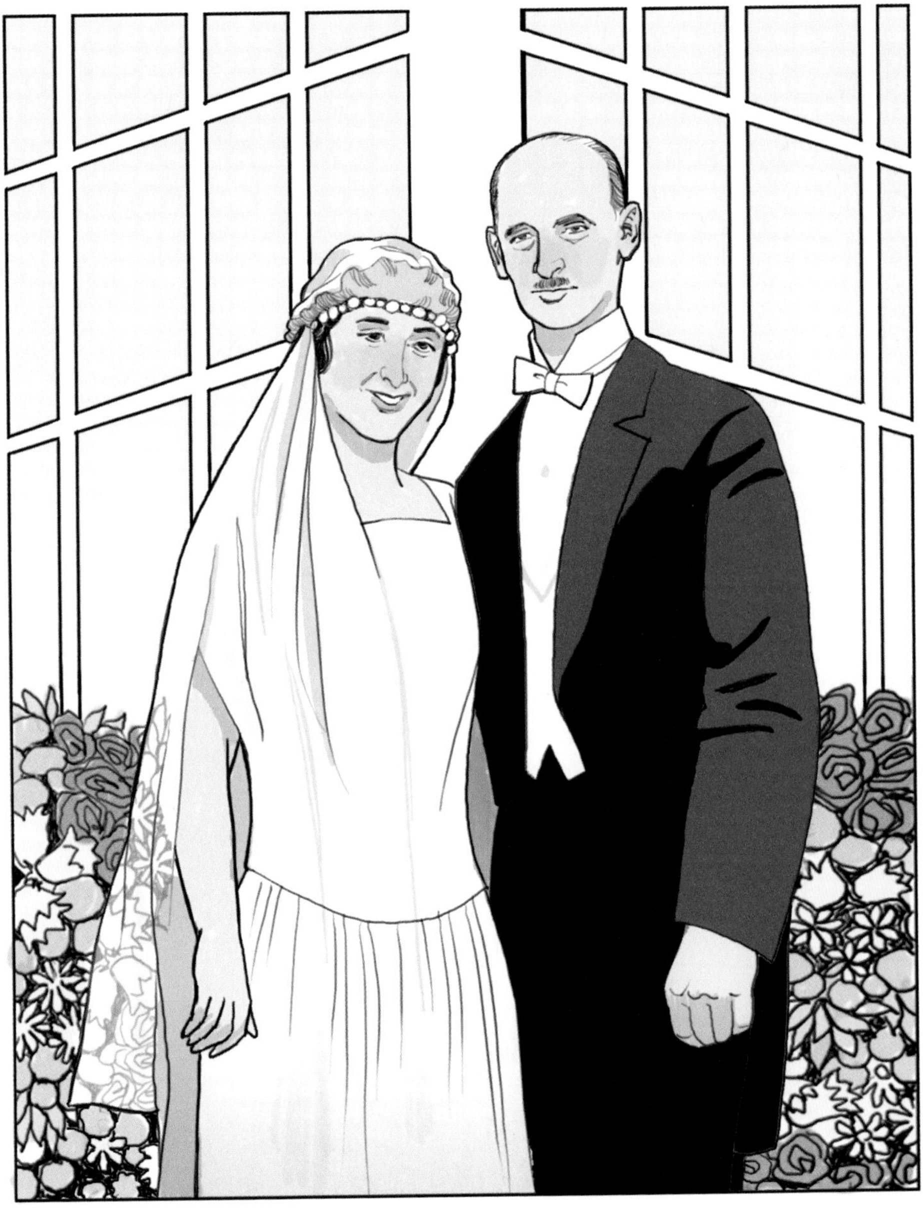

EDITH AND OTTO FRANK, ON THEIR WEDDING DAY, MAY 12, 1925, IN AACHEN, GERMANY

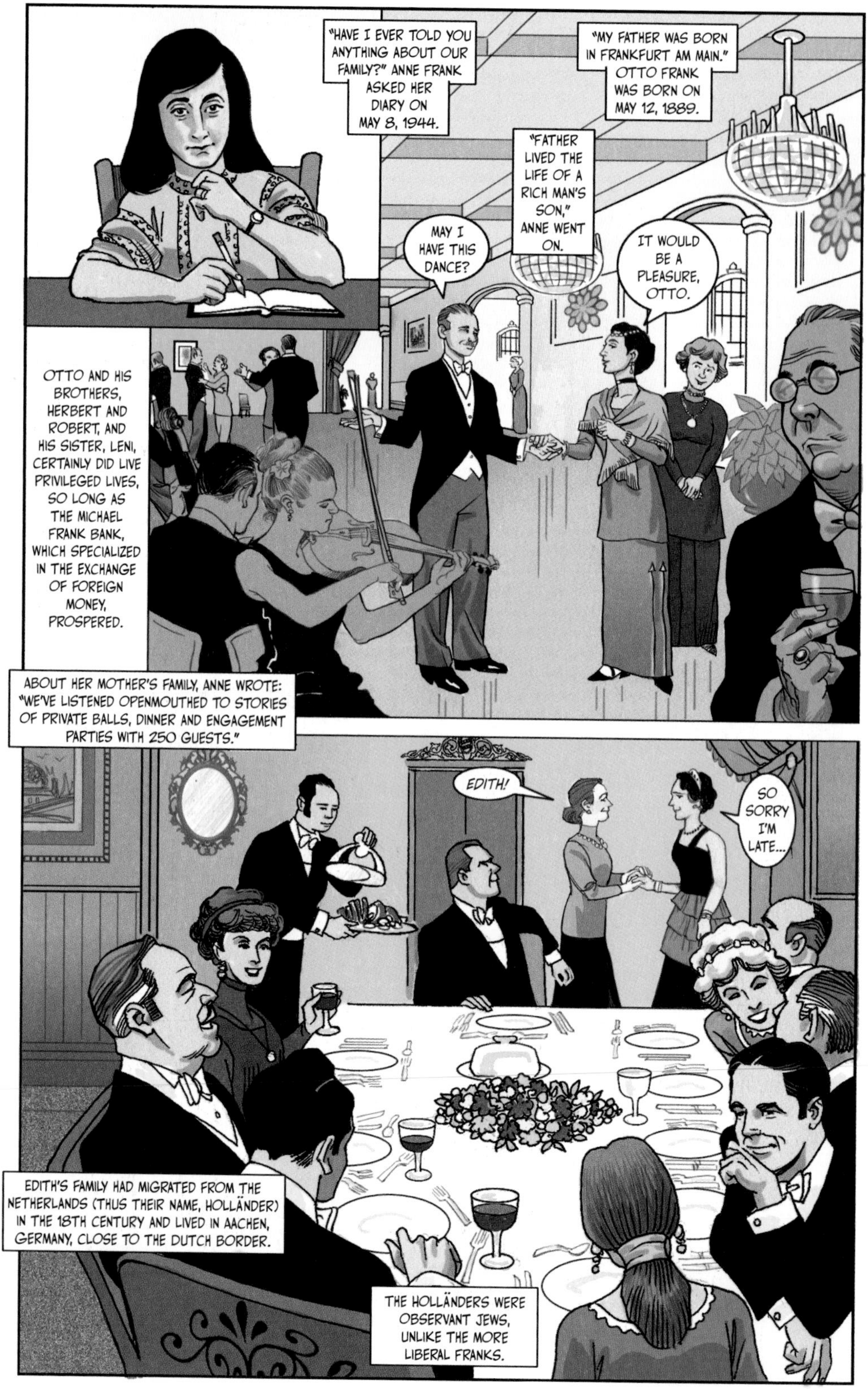
"HAVE I EVER TOLD YOU ANYTHING ABOUT OUR FAMILY?" ANNE FRANK ASKED HER DIARY ON MAY 8, 1944.
"MY FATHER WAS BORN IN FRANKFURT AM MAIN." OTTO FRANK WAS BORN ON MAY 12, 1889.
"FATHER LIVED THE LIFE OF A RICH MAN'S SON," ANNE WENT ON.
MAY I HAVE THIS DANCE?
IT WOULD BE A PLEASURE, OTTO.
OTTO AND HIS BROTHERS, HERBERT AND ROBERT, AND HIS SISTER, LENI, CERTAINLY DID LIVE PRIVILEGED LIVES, SO LONG AS THE MICHAEL FRANK BANK, WHICH SPECIALIZED IN THE EXCHANGE OF FOREIGN MONEY, PROSPERED.
ABOUT HER MOTHER'S FAMILY, ANNE WROTE: "WE'VE LISTENED OPENMOUTHED TO STORIES OF PRIVATE BALLS, DINNER AND ENGAGEMENT PARTIES WITH 250 GUESTS."
EDITH!
SO SORRY I'M LATE...
EDITH'S FAMILY HAD MIGRATED FROM THE NETHERLANDS (THUS THEIR NAME, HOLLÄNDER) IN THE 18TH CENTURY AND LIVED IN AACHEN, GERMANY, CLOSE TO THE DUTCH BORDER.
THE HOLLÄNDERS WERE OBSERVANT JEWS, UNLIKE THE MORE LIBERAL FRANKS.

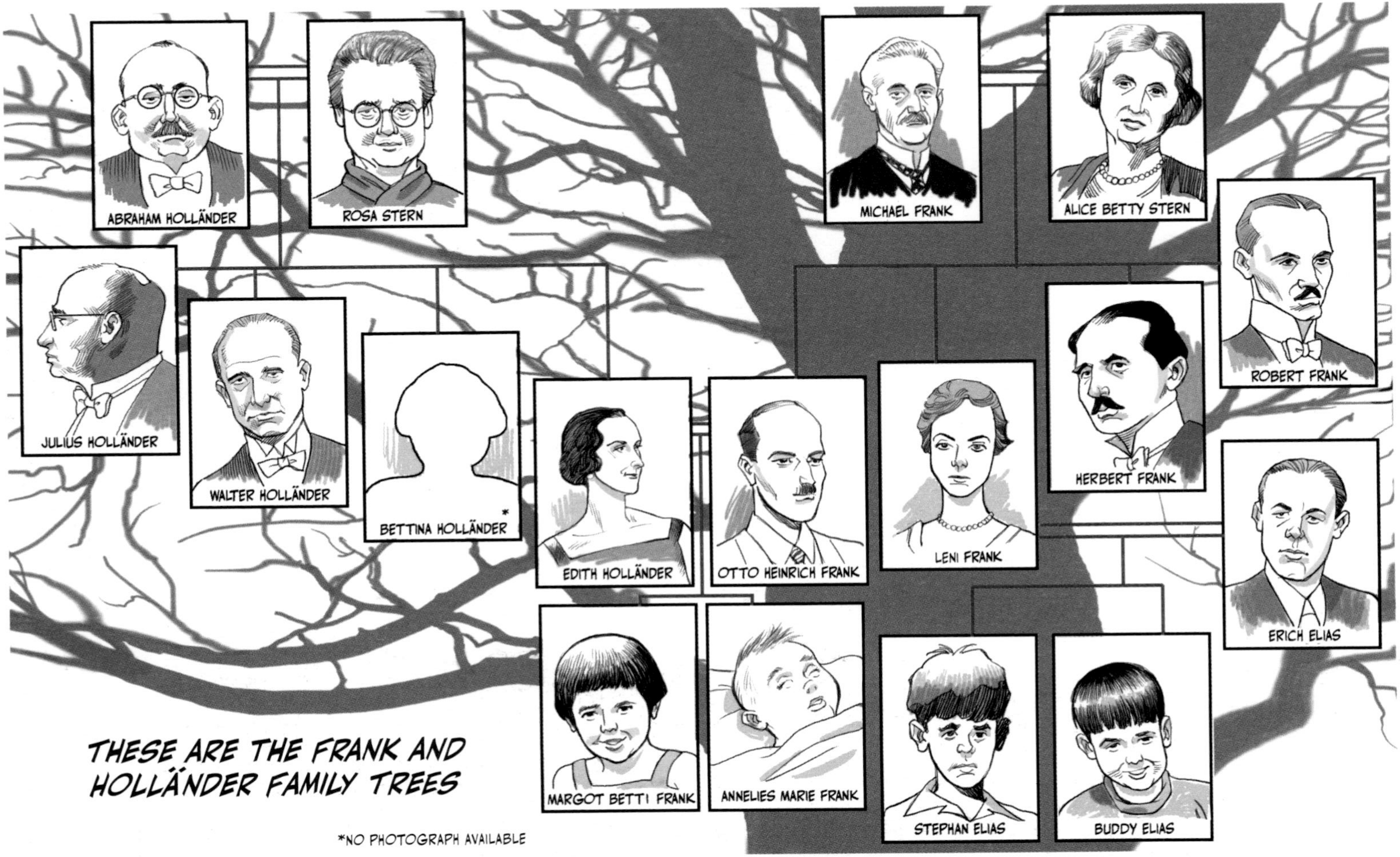
ABRAHAM HOLLÄNDER
ROSA STERN
MICHAEL FRANK
ALICE BETTY STERN
ROBERT FRANK
JULIUS HOLLÄNDER
WALTER HOLLÄNDER
BETTINA HOLLÄNDER*
EDITH HOLLÄNDER
OTTO HEINRICH FRANK
LENI FRANK
HERBERT FRANK
ERICH ELIAS
MARGOT BETTI FRANK
ANNELIES MARIE FRANK
STEPHAN ELIAS
BUDDY ELIAS
THESE ARE THE FRANK AND HOLLÄNDER FAMILY TREES
*NO PHOTOGRAPH AVAILABLE

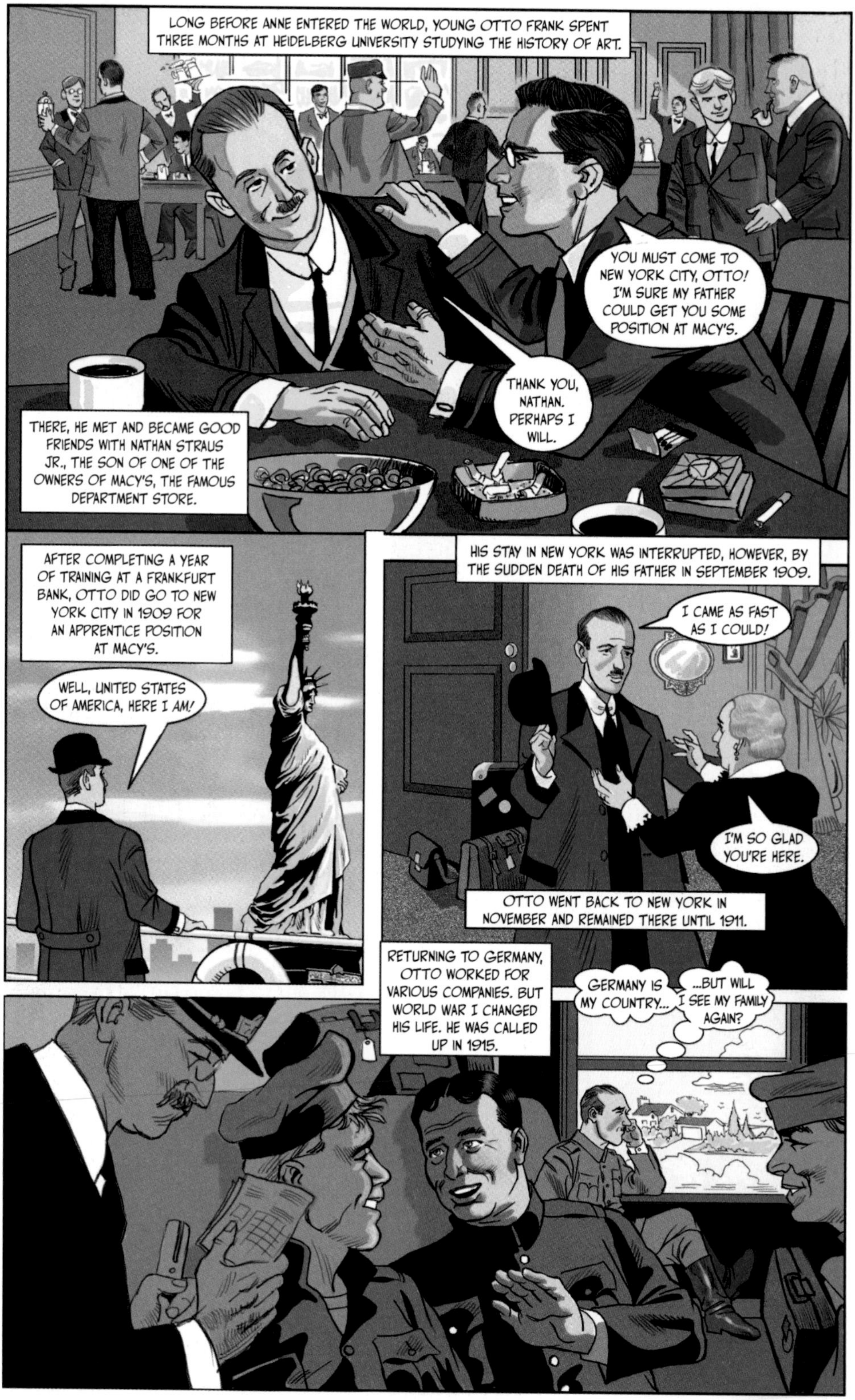

LONG BEFORE ANNE ENTERED THE WORLD, YOUNG OTTO FRANK SPENT THREE MONTHS AT HEIDELBERG UNIVERSITY STUDYING THE HISTORY OF ART.
YOU MUST COME TO NEW YORK CITY, OTTO! I'M SURE MY FATHER COULD GET YOU SOME POSITION AT MACY'S.
THANK YOU, NATHAN. PERHAPS I WILL.
THERE, HE MET AND BECAME GOOD FRIENDS WITH NATHAN STRAUS JR., THE SON OF ONE OF THE OWNERS OF MACY'S, THE FAMOUS DEPARTMENT STORE.
AFTER COMPLETING A YEAR OF TRAINING AT A FRANKFURT BANK, OTTO DID GO TO NEW YORK CITY IN 1909 FOR AN APPRENTICE POSITION AT MACY'S.
WELL, UNITED STATES OF AMERICA, HERE I AM!
HIS STAY IN NEW YORK WAS INTERRUPTED, HOWEVER, BY THE SUDDEN DEATH OF HIS FATHER IN SEPTEMBER 1909.
I CAME AS FAST AS I COULD!
I'M SO GLAD YOU'RE HERE.
OTTO WENT BACK TO NEW YORK IN NOVEMBER AND REMAINED THERE UNTIL 1911.
RETURNING TO GERMANY, OTTO WORKED FOR VARIOUS COMPANIES. BUT WORLD WAR I CHANGED HIS LIFE. HE WAS CALLED UP IN 1915.
GERMANY IS MY COUNTRY...
...BUT WILL I SEE MY FAMILY AGAIN?

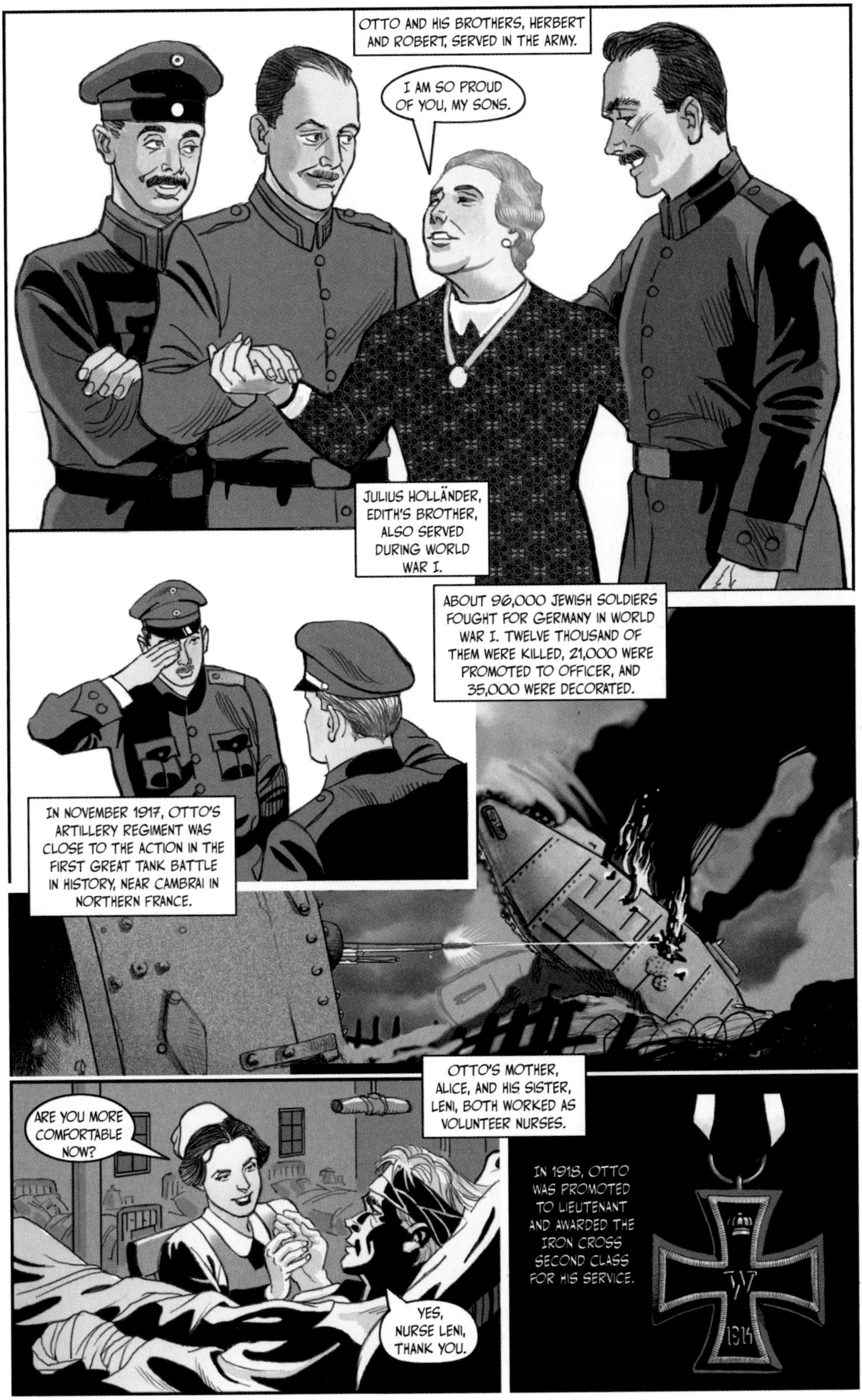
OTTO AND HIS BROTHERS, HERBERT AND ROBERT, SERVED IN THE ARMY.
I AM SO PROUD OF YOU, MY SONS.
JULIUS HOLLÄNDER, EDITH'S BROTHER, ALSO SERVED DURING WORLD WAR I.
ABOUT 96,000 JEWISH SOLDIERS FOUGHT FOR GERMANY IN WORLD WAR I. TWELVE THOUSAND OF THEM WERE KILLED, 21,000 WERE PROMOTED TO OFFICER, AND 35,000 WERE DECORATED.
IN NOVEMBER 1917, OTTO'S ARTILLERY REGIMENT WAS CLOSE TO THE ACTION IN THE FIRST GREAT TANK BATTLE IN HISTORY, NEAR CAMBRAI IN NORTHERN FRANCE.
OTTO'S MOTHER, ALICE, AND HIS SISTER, LENI, BOTH WORKED AS VOLUNTEER NURSES.
ARE YOU MORE COMFORTABLE NOW?
YES, NURSE LENI, THANK YOU.
IN 1918, OTTO WAS PROMOTED TO LIEUTENANT AND AWARDED THE IRON CROSS SECOND CLASS FOR HIS SERVICE.
1914

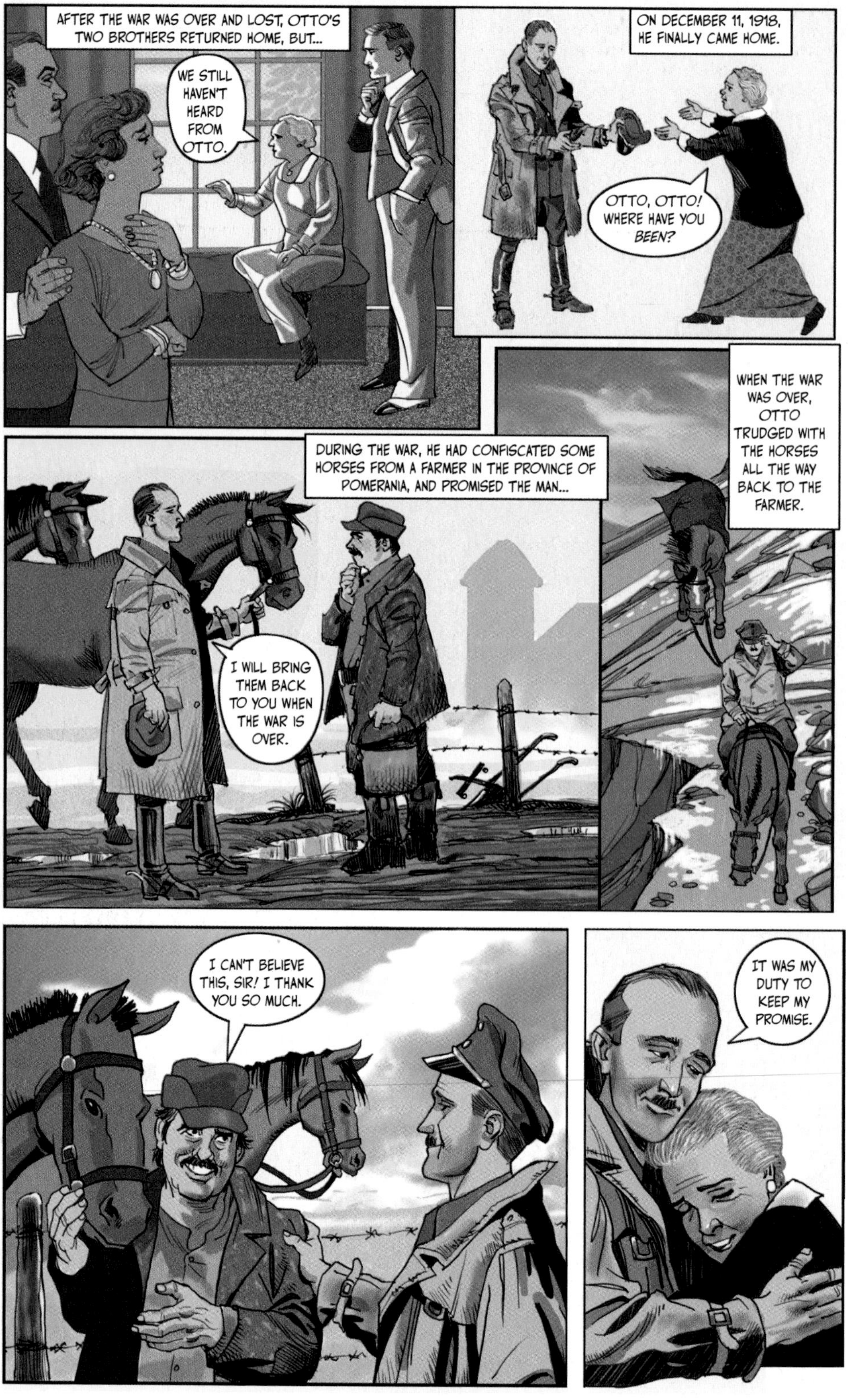
AFTER THE WAR WAS OVER AND LOST, OTTO'S TWO BROTHERS RETURNED HOME, BUT...
WE STILL HAVEN'T HEARD FROM OTTO.
ON DECEMBER 11, 1918, HE FINALLY CAME HOME.
OTTO, OTTO! WHERE HAVE YOU BEEN?
DURING THE WAR, HE HAD CONFISCATED SOME HORSES FROM A FARMER IN THE PROVINCE OF POMERANIA, AND PROMISED THE MAN...
I WILL BRING THEM BACK TO YOU WHEN THE WAR IS OVER.
WHEN THE WAR WAS OVER, OTTO TRUDGED WITH THE HORSES ALL THE WAY BACK TO THE FARMER.
I CAN'T BELIEVE THIS, SIR! I THANK YOU SO MUCH.
IT WAS MY DUTY TO KEEP MY PROMISE.

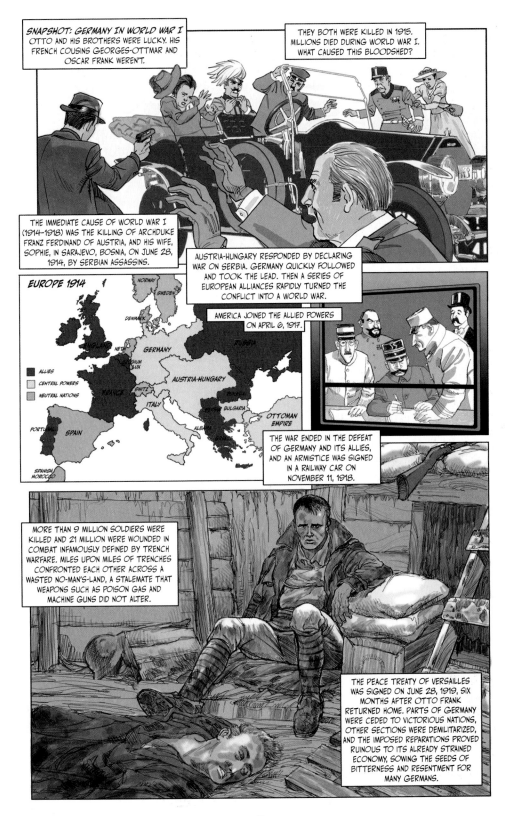

SNAPSHOT: GERMANY IN WORLD WAR I
OTTO AND HIS BROTHERS WERE LUCKY. HIS FRENCH COUSINS GEORGES-OTTMAR AND OSCAR FRANK WEREN'T.

THEY BOTH WERE KILLED IN 1915. MILLIONS DIED DURING WORLD WAR I. WHAT CAUSED THIS BLOODSHED?

THE IMMEDIATE CAUSE OF WORLD WAR I (1914–1918) WAS THE KILLING OF ARCHDUKE FRANZ FERDINAND OF AUSTRIA, AND HIS WIFE, SOPHIE, IN SARAJEVO, BOSNIA, ON JUNE 28, 1914, BY SERBIAN ASSASSINS.

AUSTRIA-HUNGARY RESPONDED BY DECLARING WAR ON SERBIA. GERMANY QUICKLY FOLLOWED AND TOOK THE LEAD. THEN A SERIES OF EUROPEAN ALLIANCES RAPIDLY TURNED THE CONFLICT INTO A WORLD WAR.

AMERICA JOINED THE ALLIED POWERS ON APRIL 6, 1917.

EUROPE 1914

NORWAY
SWEDEN
DENMARK
ENGLAND
NET
GERMANY
RUSSIA
BELGIUM
LUX
FRANCE
SWITZ
AUSTRIA-HUNGARY
ITALY
RUMANIA
BULGARIA
PORTUGAL
SPAIN
ALBANIA
OTTOMAN EMPIRE
SPANISH MOROCCO

ALLIES
CENTRAL POWERS
NEUTRAL NATIONS

THE WAR ENDED IN THE DEFEAT OF GERMANY AND ITS ALLIES, AND AN ARMISTICE WAS SIGNED IN A RAILWAY CAR ON NOVEMBER 11, 1918.

MORE THAN 9 MILLION SOLDIERS WERE KILLED AND 21 MILLION WERE WOUNDED IN COMBAT INFAMOUSLY DEFINED BY TRENCH WARFARE. MILES UPON MILES OF TRENCHES CONFRONTED EACH OTHER ACROSS A WASTED NO-MAN'S-LAND, A STALEMATE THAT WEAPONS SUCH AS POISON GAS AND MACHINE GUNS DID NOT ALTER.

THE PEACE TREATY OF VERSAILLES WAS SIGNED ON JUNE 28, 1919, SIX MONTHS AFTER OTTO FRANK RETURNED HOME. PARTS OF GERMANY WERE CEDED TO VICTORIOUS NATIONS, OTHER SECTIONS WERE DEMILITARIZED, AND THE IMPOSED REPARATIONS PROVED RUINOUS TO ITS ALREADY STRAINED ECONOMY, SOWING THE SEEDS OF BITTERNESS AND RESENTMENT FOR MANY GERMANS.

9

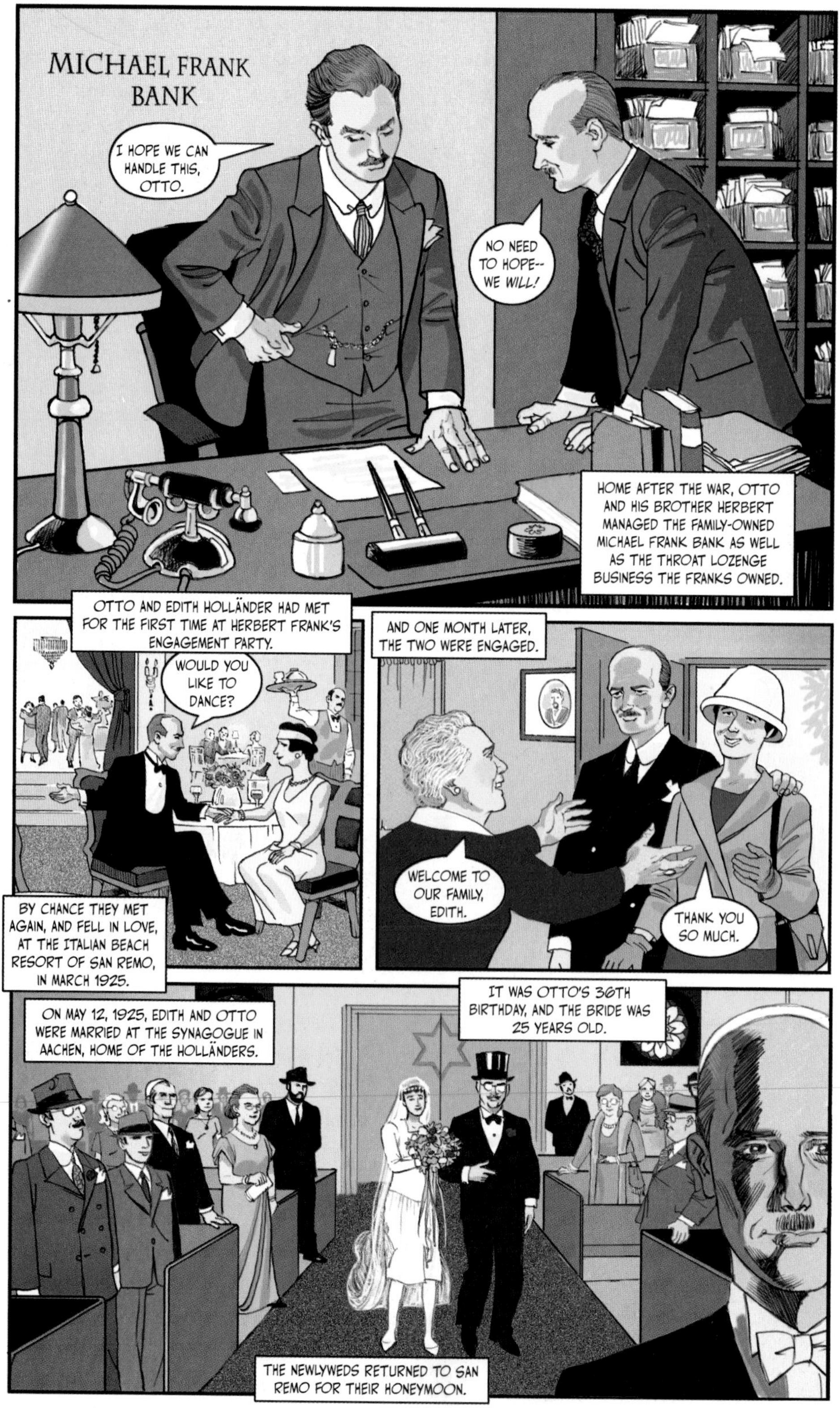
MICHAEL FRANK BANK
I HOPE WE CAN HANDLE THIS, OTTO.
NO NEED TO HOPE-- WE WILL!
HOME AFTER THE WAR, OTTO AND HIS BROTHER HERBERT MANAGED THE FAMILY-OWNED MICHAEL FRANK BANK AS WELL AS THE THROAT LOZENGE BUSINESS THE FRANKS OWNED.
OTTO AND EDITH HOLLÄNDER HAD MET FOR THE FIRST TIME AT HERBERT FRANK'S ENGAGEMENT PARTY.
WOULD YOU LIKE TO DANCE?
BY CHANCE THEY MET AGAIN, AND FELL IN LOVE, AT THE ITALIAN BEACH RESORT OF SAN REMO, IN MARCH 1925.
AND ONE MONTH LATER, THE TWO WERE ENGAGED.
WELCOME TO OUR FAMILY, EDITH.
THANK YOU SO MUCH.
ON MAY 12, 1925, EDITH AND OTTO WERE MARRIED AT THE SYNAGOGUE IN AACHEN, HOME OF THE HOLLÄNDERS.
IT WAS OTTO'S 36TH BIRTHDAY, AND THE BRIDE WAS 25 YEARS OLD.
THE NEWLYWEDS RETURNED TO SAN REMO FOR THEIR HONEYMOON.

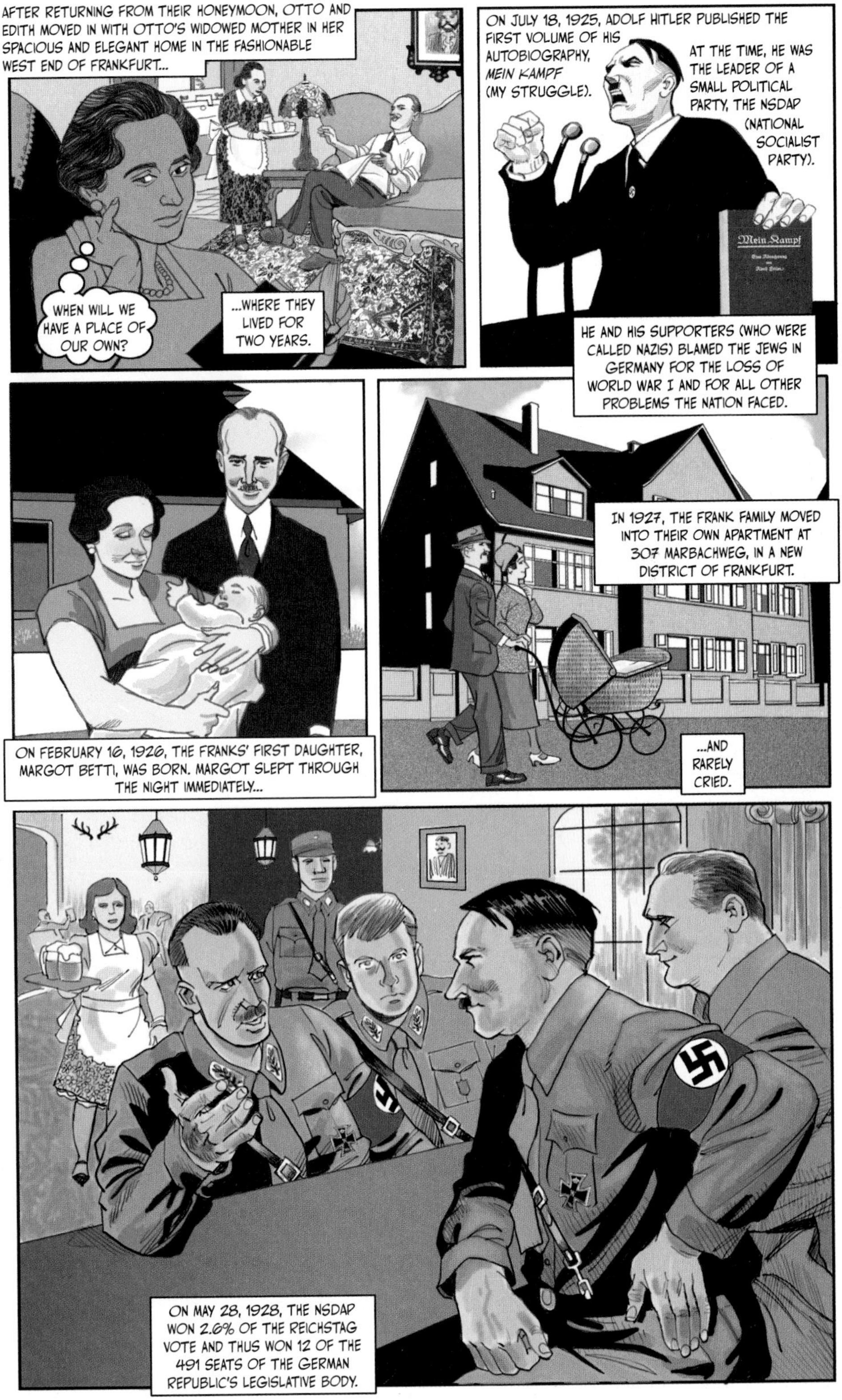
AFTER RETURNING FROM THEIR HONEYMOON, OTTO AND EDITH MOVED IN WITH OTTO'S WIDOWED MOTHER IN HER SPACIOUS AND ELEGANT HOME IN THE FASHIONABLE WEST END OF FRANKFURT...
WHEN WILL WE HAVE A PLACE OF OUR OWN?
...WHERE THEY LIVED FOR TWO YEARS.
ON JULY 18, 1925, ADOLF HITLER PUBLISHED THE FIRST VOLUME OF HIS AUTOBIOGRAPHY, *MEIN KAMPF* (MY STRUGGLE).
AT THE TIME, HE WAS THE LEADER OF A SMALL POLITICAL PARTY, THE NSDAP (NATIONAL SOCIALIST PARTY).
Mein Kampf
HE AND HIS SUPPORTERS (WHO WERE CALLED NAZIS) BLAMED THE JEWS IN GERMANY FOR THE LOSS OF WORLD WAR I AND FOR ALL OTHER PROBLEMS THE NATION FACED.
ON FEBRUARY 16, 1926, THE FRANKS' FIRST DAUGHTER, MARGOT BETTI, WAS BORN. MARGOT SLEPT THROUGH THE NIGHT IMMEDIATELY...
...AND RARELY CRIED.
IN 1927, THE FRANK FAMILY MOVED INTO THEIR OWN APARTMENT AT 307 MARBACHWEG, IN A NEW DISTRICT OF FRANKFURT.
ON MAY 28, 1928, THE NSDAP WON 2.6% OF THE REICHSTAG VOTE AND THUS WON 12 OF THE 491 SEATS OF THE GERMAN REPUBLIC'S LEGISLATIVE BODY.

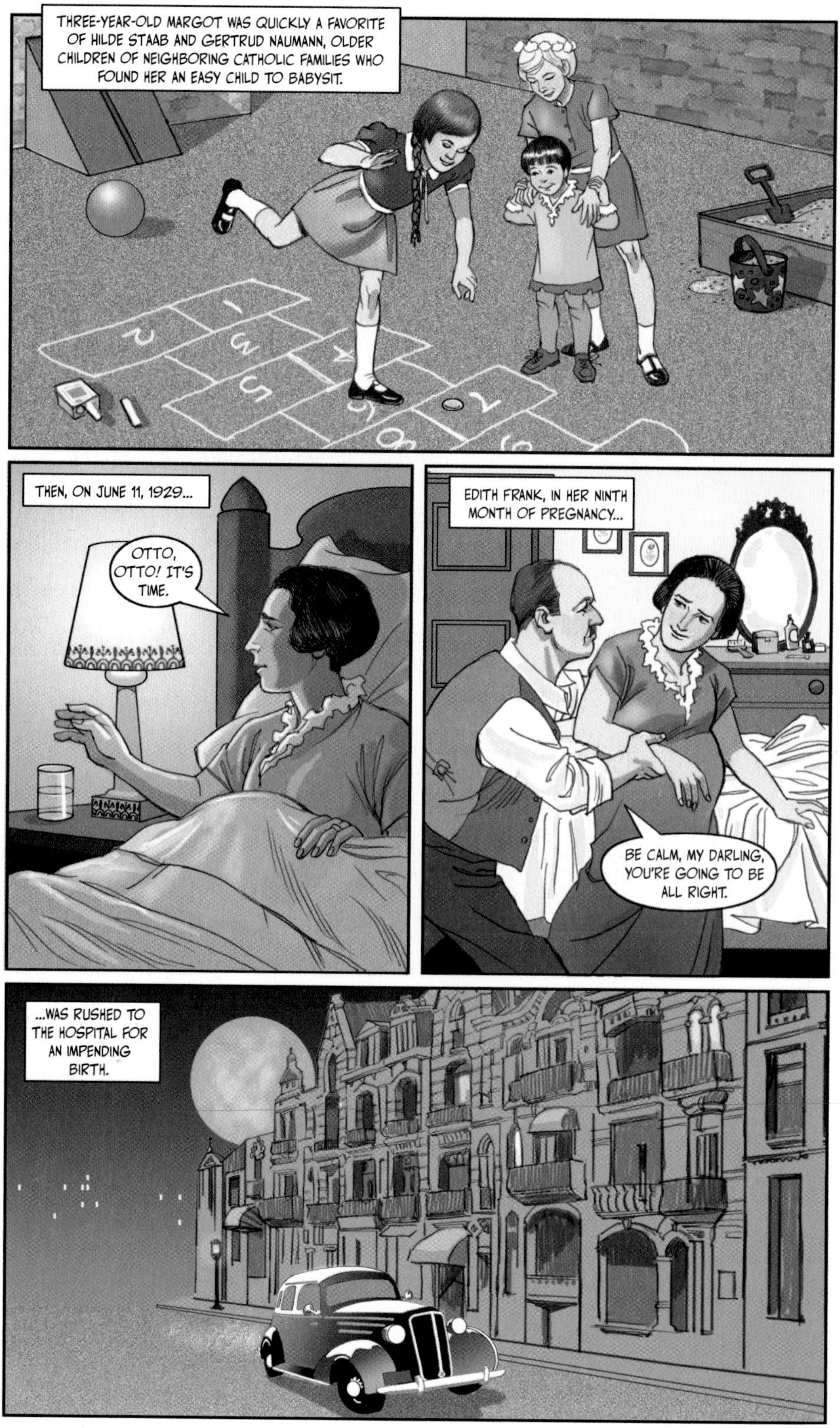
THREE-YEAR-OLD MARGOT WAS QUICKLY A FAVORITE OF HILDE STAAB AND GERTRUD NAUMANN, OLDER CHILDREN OF NEIGHBORING CATHOLIC FAMILIES WHO FOUND HER AN EASY CHILD TO BABYSIT.
THEN, ON JUNE 11, 1929...
OTTO, OTTO! IT'S TIME.
EDITH FRANK, IN HER NINTH MONTH OF PREGNANCY...
BE CALM, MY DARLING, YOU'RE GOING TO BE ALL RIGHT.
...WAS RUSHED TO THE HOSPITAL FOR AN IMPENDING BIRTH.

CHAPTER 2

Annelies Marie Frank

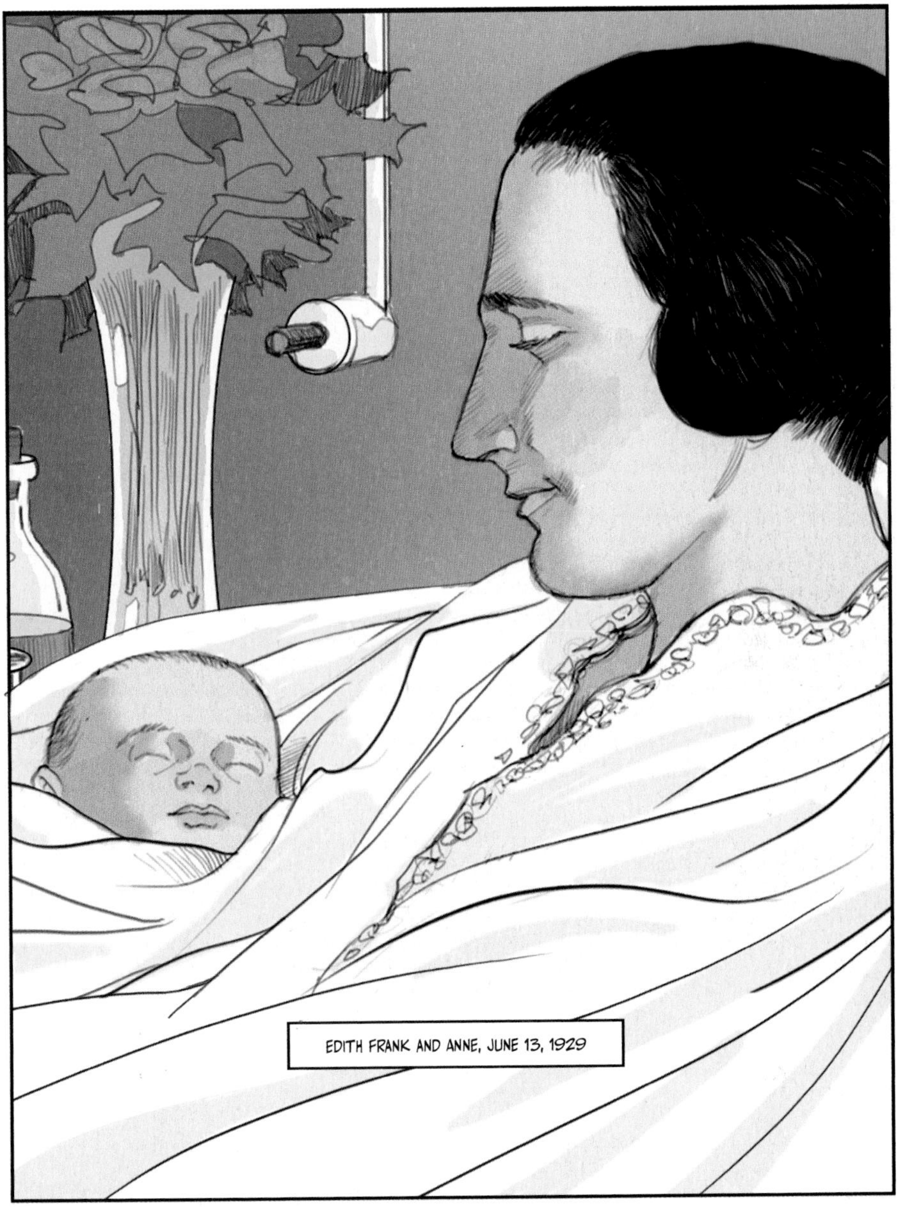
EDITH FRANK AND ANNE, JUNE 13, 1929

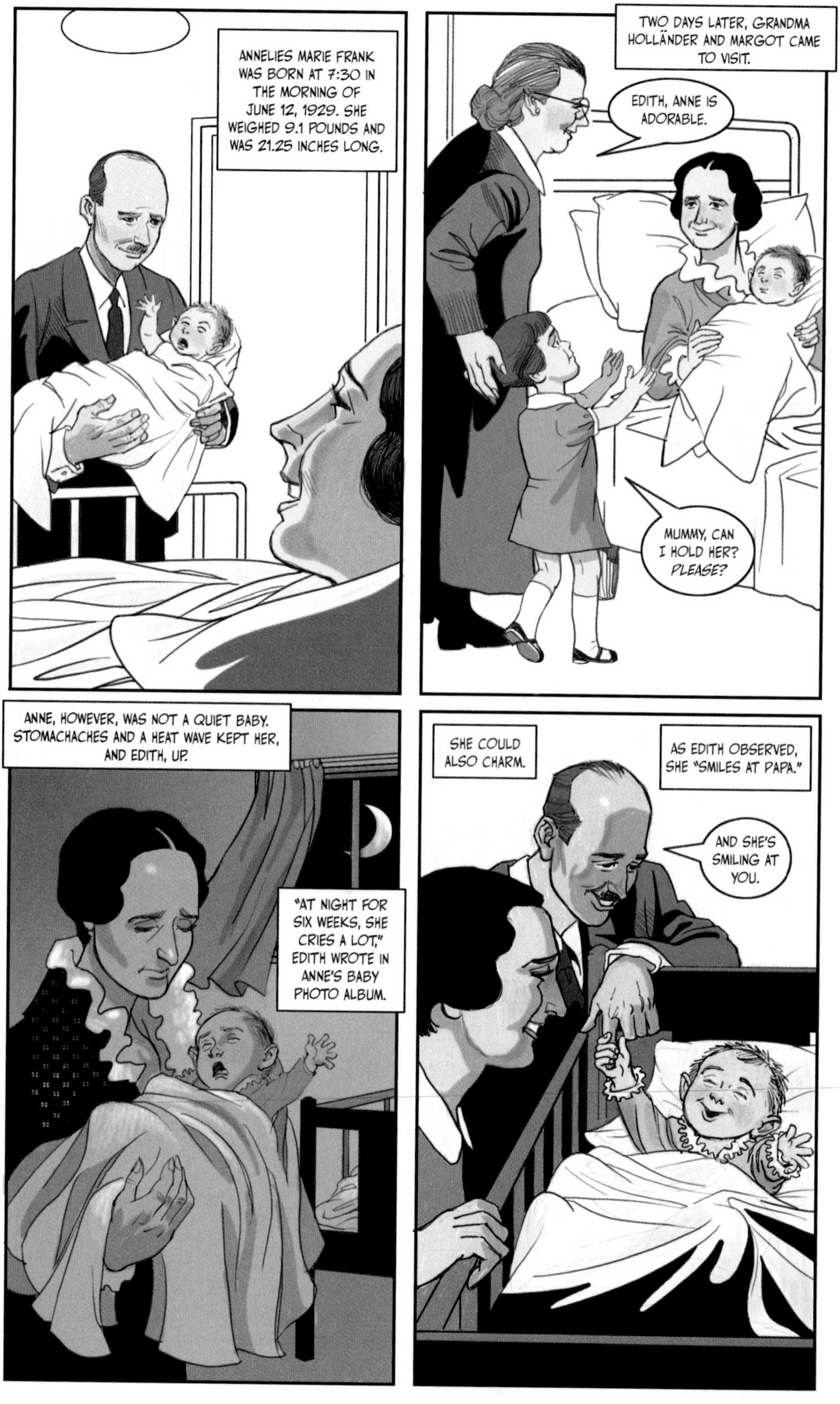
ANNELIES MARIE FRANK WAS BORN AT 7:30 IN THE MORNING OF JUNE 12, 1929. SHE WEIGHED 9.1 POUNDS AND WAS 21.25 INCHES LONG.
TWO DAYS LATER, GRANDMA HOLLÄNDER AND MARGOT CAME TO VISIT.
EDITH, ANNE IS ADORABLE.
MUMMY, CAN I HOLD HER? PLEASE?
ANNE, HOWEVER, WAS NOT A QUIET BABY. STOMACHACHES AND A HEAT WAVE KEPT HER, AND EDITH, UP.
"AT NIGHT FOR SIX WEEKS, SHE CRIES A LOT," EDITH WROTE IN ANNE'S BABY PHOTO ALBUM.
SHE COULD ALSO CHARM.
AS EDITH OBSERVED, SHE "SMILES AT PAPA."
AND SHE'S SMILING AT YOU.

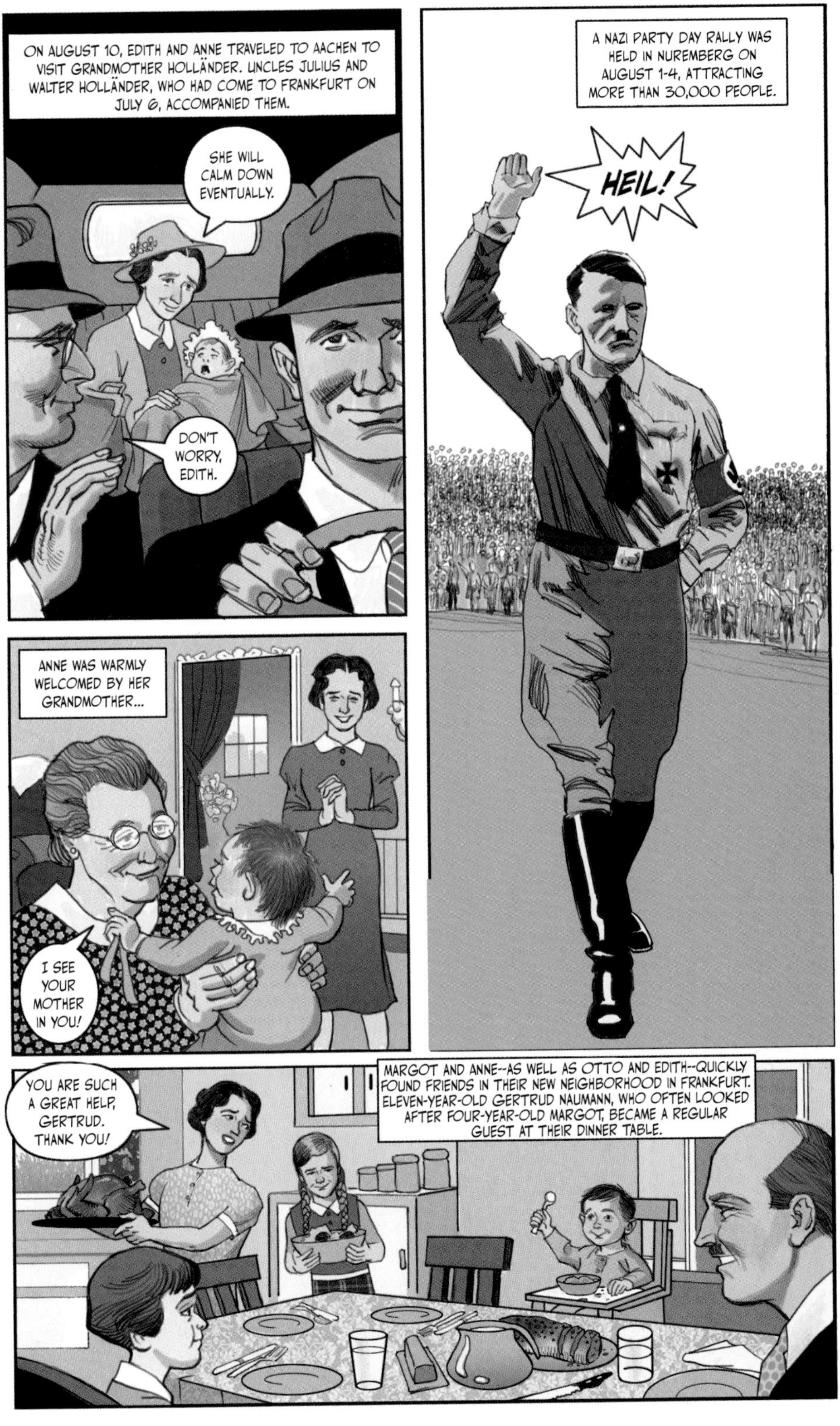
ON AUGUST 10, EDITH AND ANNE TRAVELED TO AACHEN TO VISIT GRANDMOTHER HOLLÄNDER. UNCLES JULIUS AND WALTER HOLLÄNDER, WHO HAD COME TO FRANKFURT ON JULY 6, ACCOMPANIED THEM.
SHE WILL CALM DOWN EVENTUALLY.
DON'T WORRY, EDITH.
A NAZI PARTY DAY RALLY WAS HELD IN NUREMBERG ON AUGUST 1-4, ATTRACTING MORE THAN 30,000 PEOPLE.
HEIL!
ANNE WAS WARMLY WELCOMED BY HER GRANDMOTHER...
I SEE YOUR MOTHER IN YOU!
YOU ARE SUCH A GREAT HELP, GERTRUD. THANK YOU!
MARGOT AND ANNE--AS WELL AS OTTO AND EDITH--QUICKLY FOUND FRIENDS IN THEIR NEW NEIGHBORHOOD IN FRANKFURT. ELEVEN-YEAR-OLD GERTRUD NAUMANN, WHO OFTEN LOOKED AFTER FOUR-YEAR-OLD MARGOT, BECAME A REGULAR GUEST AT THEIR DINNER TABLE.

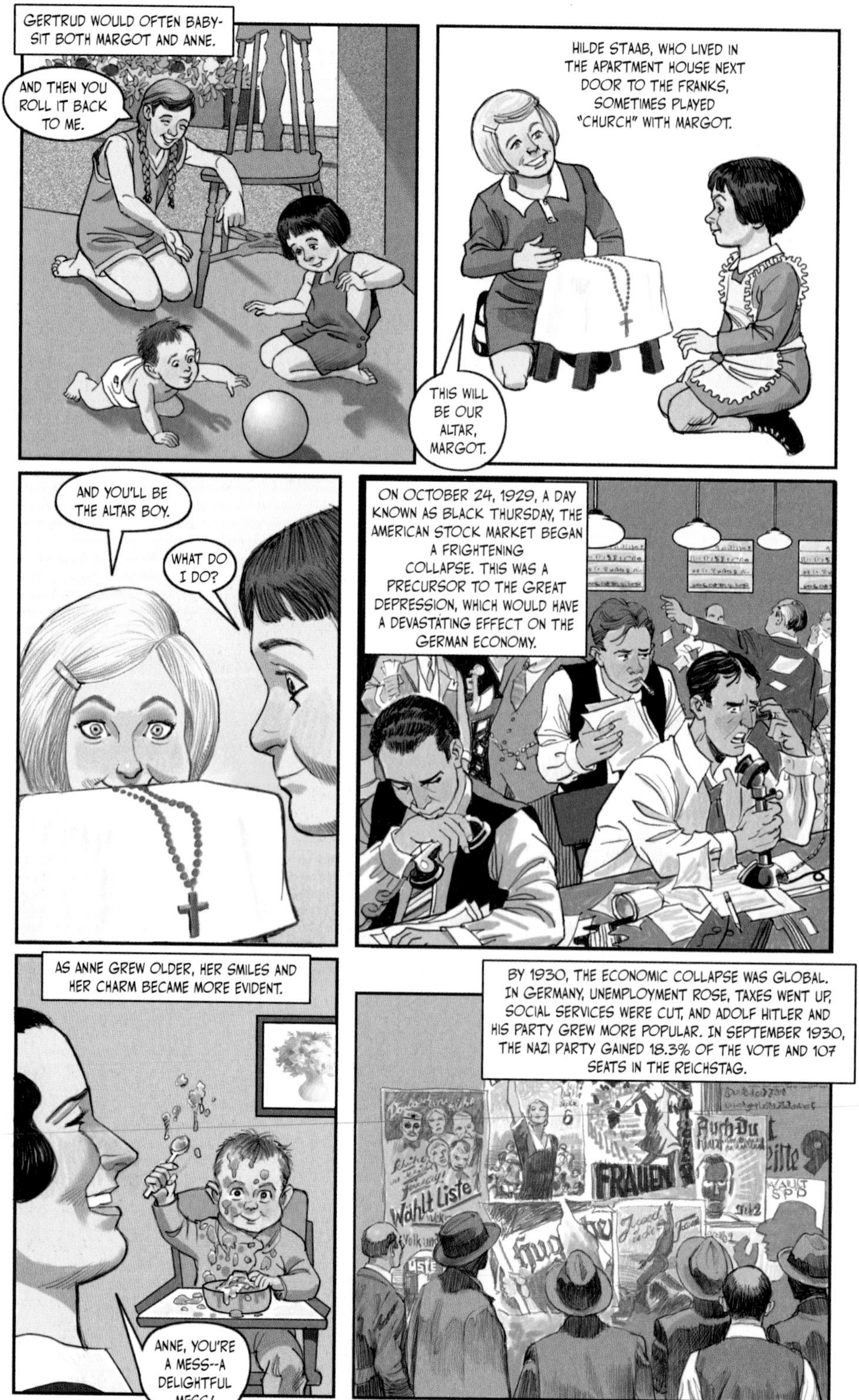
GERTRUD WOULD OFTEN BABY-SIT BOTH MARGOT AND ANNE.
AND THEN YOU ROLL IT BACK TO ME.
HILDE STAAB, WHO LIVED IN THE APARTMENT HOUSE NEXT DOOR TO THE FRANKS, SOMETIMES PLAYED "CHURCH" WITH MARGOT.
THIS WILL BE OUR ALTAR, MARGOT.
AND YOU'LL BE THE ALTAR BOY.
WHAT DO I DO?
ON OCTOBER 24, 1929, A DAY KNOWN AS BLACK THURSDAY, THE AMERICAN STOCK MARKET BEGAN A FRIGHTENING COLLAPSE. THIS WAS A PRECURSOR TO THE GREAT DEPRESSION, WHICH WOULD HAVE A DEVASTATING EFFECT ON THE GERMAN ECONOMY.
AS ANNE GREW OLDER, HER SMILES AND HER CHARM BECAME MORE EVIDENT.
ANNE, YOU'RE A MESS--A DELIGHTFUL MESS!
BY 1930, THE ECONOMIC COLLAPSE WAS GLOBAL. IN GERMANY, UNEMPLOYMENT ROSE, TAXES WENT UP, SOCIAL SERVICES WERE CUT, AND ADOLF HITLER AND HIS PARTY GREW MORE POPULAR. IN SEPTEMBER 1930, THE NAZI PARTY GAINED 18.3% OF THE VOTE AND 107 SEATS IN THE REICHSTAG.
FRAUEN
Auch Du
Wählt Liste
WÄHLT SPD

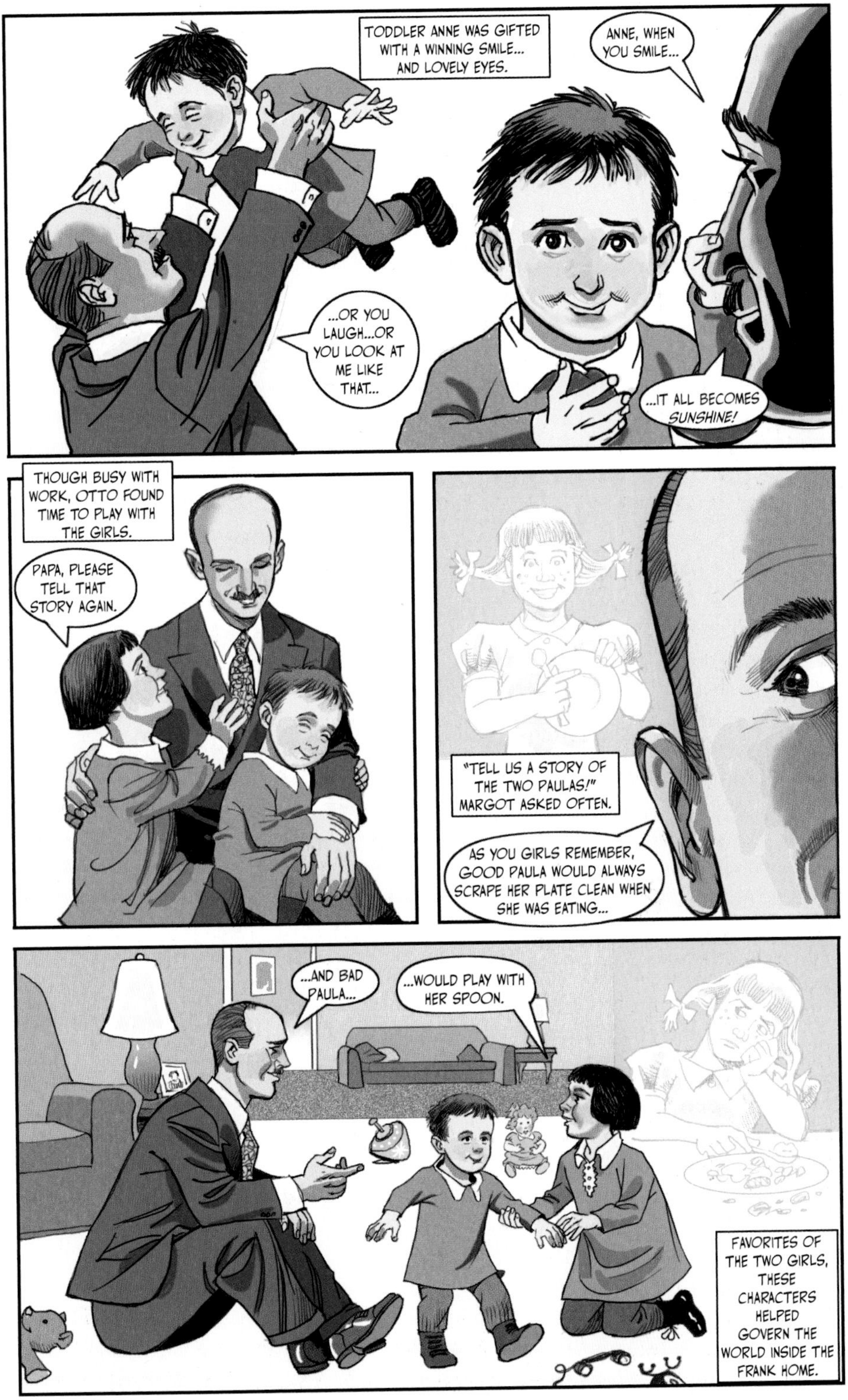
TODDLER ANNE WAS GIFTED WITH A WINNING SMILE... AND LOVELY EYES.
ANNE, WHEN YOU SMILE...
...OR YOU LAUGH...OR YOU LOOK AT ME LIKE THAT...
...IT ALL BECOMES *SUNSHINE!*
THOUGH BUSY WITH WORK, OTTO FOUND TIME TO PLAY WITH THE GIRLS.
PAPA, PLEASE TELL THAT STORY AGAIN.
"TELL US A STORY OF THE TWO PAULAS!" MARGOT ASKED OFTEN.
AS YOU GIRLS REMEMBER, GOOD PAULA WOULD ALWAYS SCRAPE HER PLATE CLEAN WHEN SHE WAS EATING...
...AND BAD PAULA...
...WOULD PLAY WITH HER SPOON.
FAVORITES OF THE TWO GIRLS, THESE CHARACTERS HELPED GOVERN THE WORLD INSIDE THE FRANK HOME.

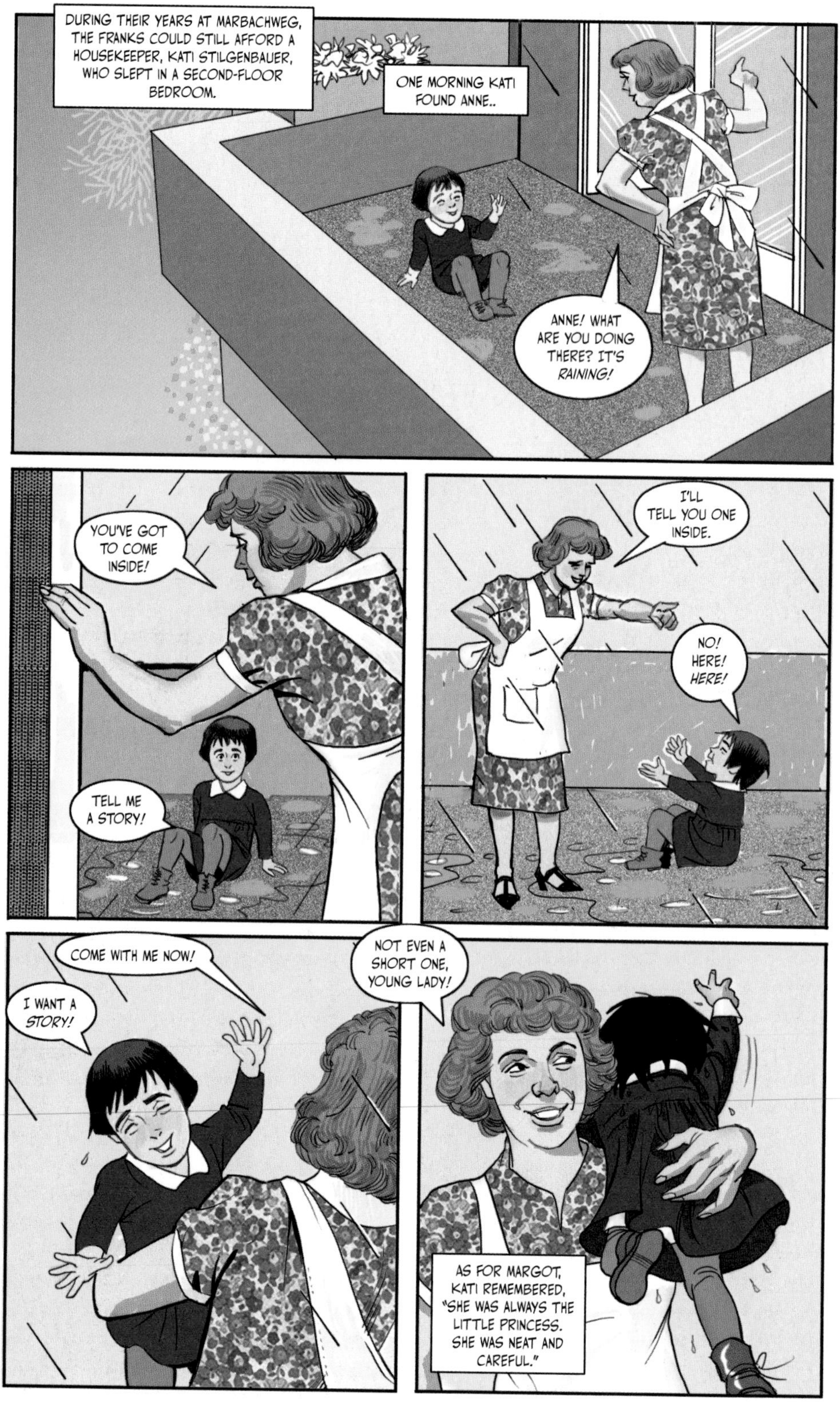
DURING THEIR YEARS AT MARBACHWEG, THE FRANKS COULD STILL AFFORD A HOUSEKEEPER, KATI STILGENBAUER, WHO SLEPT IN A SECOND-FLOOR BEDROOM.
ONE MORNING KATI FOUND ANNE..
ANNE! WHAT ARE YOU DOING THERE? IT'S *RAINING!*
YOU'VE GOT TO COME INSIDE!
TELL ME A STORY!
I'LL TELL YOU ONE INSIDE.
NO! HERE! HERE!
COME WITH ME NOW!
I WANT A *STORY!*
NOT EVEN A SHORT ONE, YOUNG LADY!
AS FOR MARGOT, KATI REMEMBERED, "SHE WAS ALWAYS THE LITTLE PRINCESS. SHE WAS NEAT AND CAREFUL."

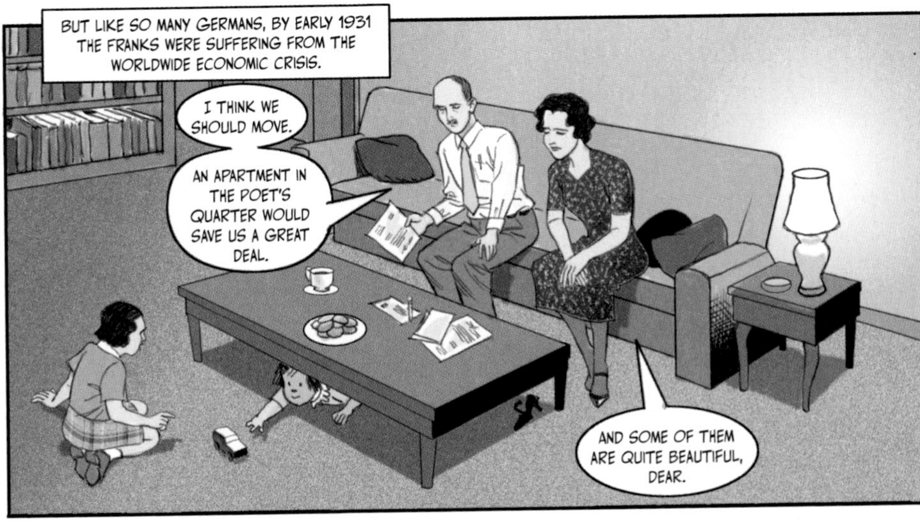
BUT LIKE SO MANY GERMANS, BY EARLY 1931 THE FRANKS WERE SUFFERING FROM THE WORLDWIDE ECONOMIC CRISIS.
I THINK WE SHOULD MOVE.
AN APARTMENT IN THE POET'S QUARTER WOULD SAVE US A GREAT DEAL.
AND SOME OF THEM ARE QUITE BEAUTIFUL, DEAR.

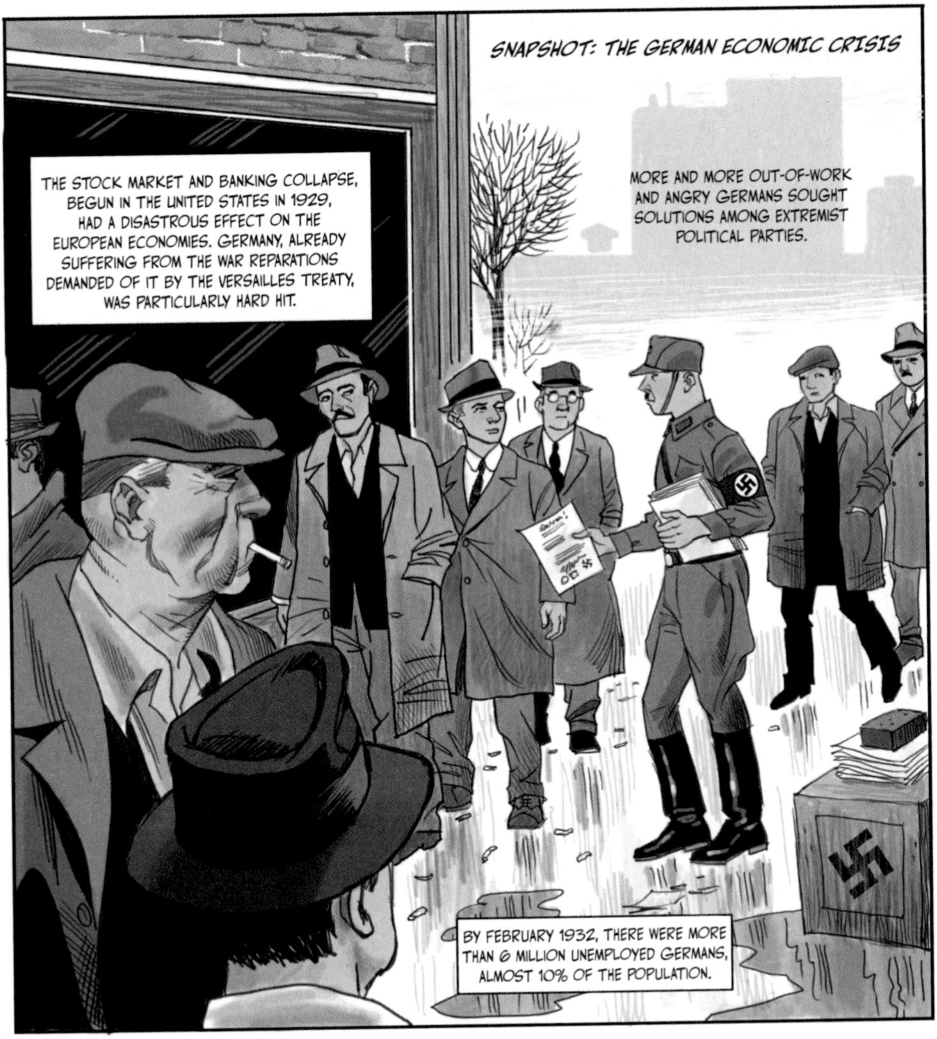
SNAPSHOT: THE GERMAN ECONOMIC CRISIS
THE STOCK MARKET AND BANKING COLLAPSE, BEGUN IN THE UNITED STATES IN 1929, HAD A DISASTROUS EFFECT ON THE EUROPEAN ECONOMIES. GERMANY, ALREADY SUFFERING FROM THE WAR REPARATIONS DEMANDED OF IT BY THE VERSAILLES TREATY, WAS PARTICULARLY HARD HIT.
MORE AND MORE OUT-OF-WORK AND ANGRY GERMANS SOUGHT SOLUTIONS AMONG EXTREMIST POLITICAL PARTIES.
BY FEBRUARY 1932, THERE WERE MORE THAN 6 MILLION UNEMPLOYED GERMANS, ALMOST 10% OF THE POPULATION.

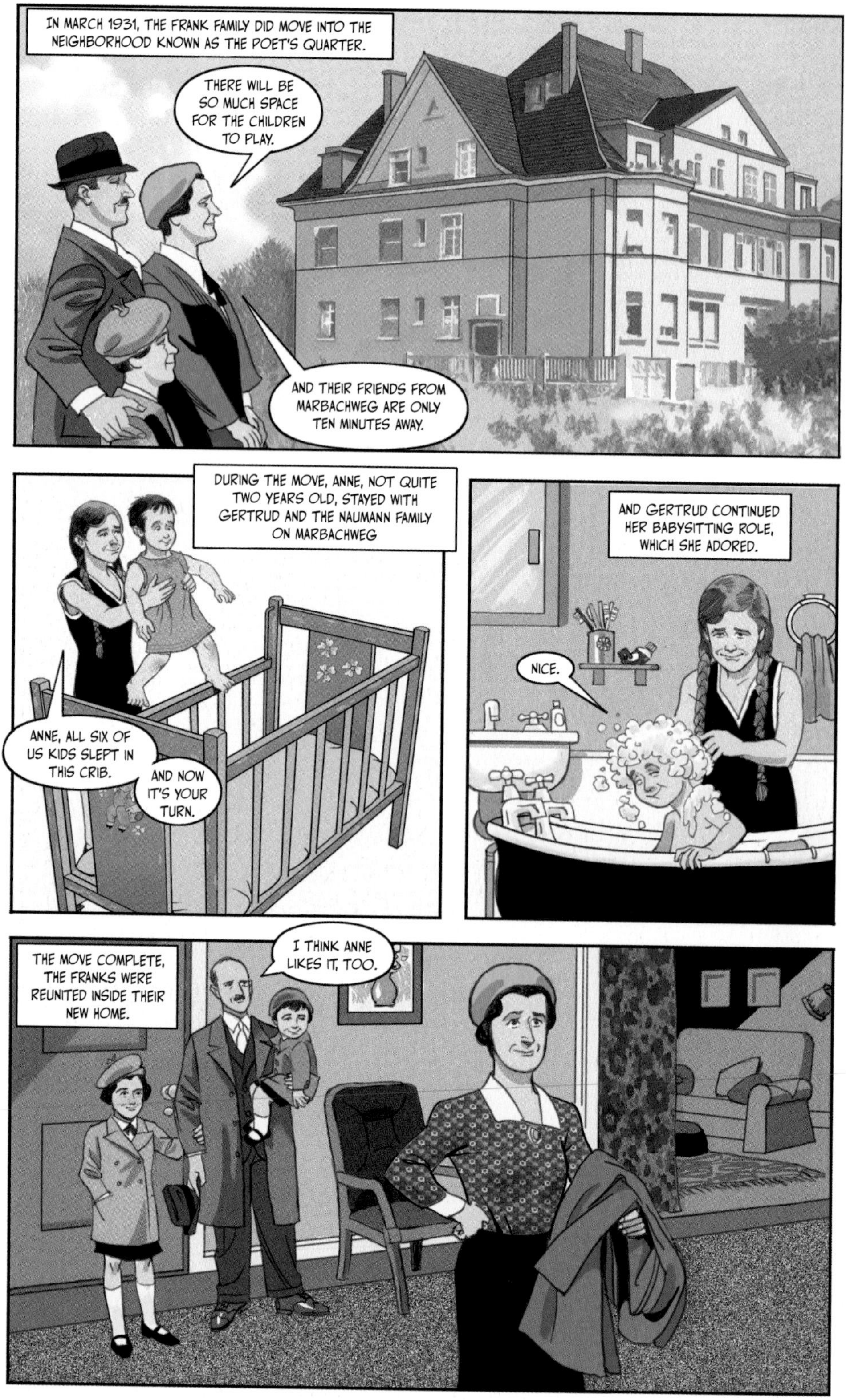
IN MARCH 1931, THE FRANK FAMILY DID MOVE INTO THE NEIGHBORHOOD KNOWN AS THE POET'S QUARTER.
THERE WILL BE SO MUCH SPACE FOR THE CHILDREN TO PLAY.
AND THEIR FRIENDS FROM MARBACHWEG ARE ONLY TEN MINUTES AWAY.
DURING THE MOVE, ANNE, NOT QUITE TWO YEARS OLD, STAYED WITH GERTRUD AND THE NAUMANN FAMILY ON MARBACHWEG
ANNE, ALL SIX OF US KIDS SLEPT IN THIS CRIB.
AND NOW IT'S YOUR TURN.
AND GERTRUD CONTINUED HER BABYSITTING ROLE, WHICH SHE ADORED.
NICE.
THE MOVE COMPLETE, THE FRANKS WERE REUNITED INSIDE THEIR NEW HOME.
I THINK ANNE LIKES IT, TOO.

CHAPTER 3

The Growth of Nazism

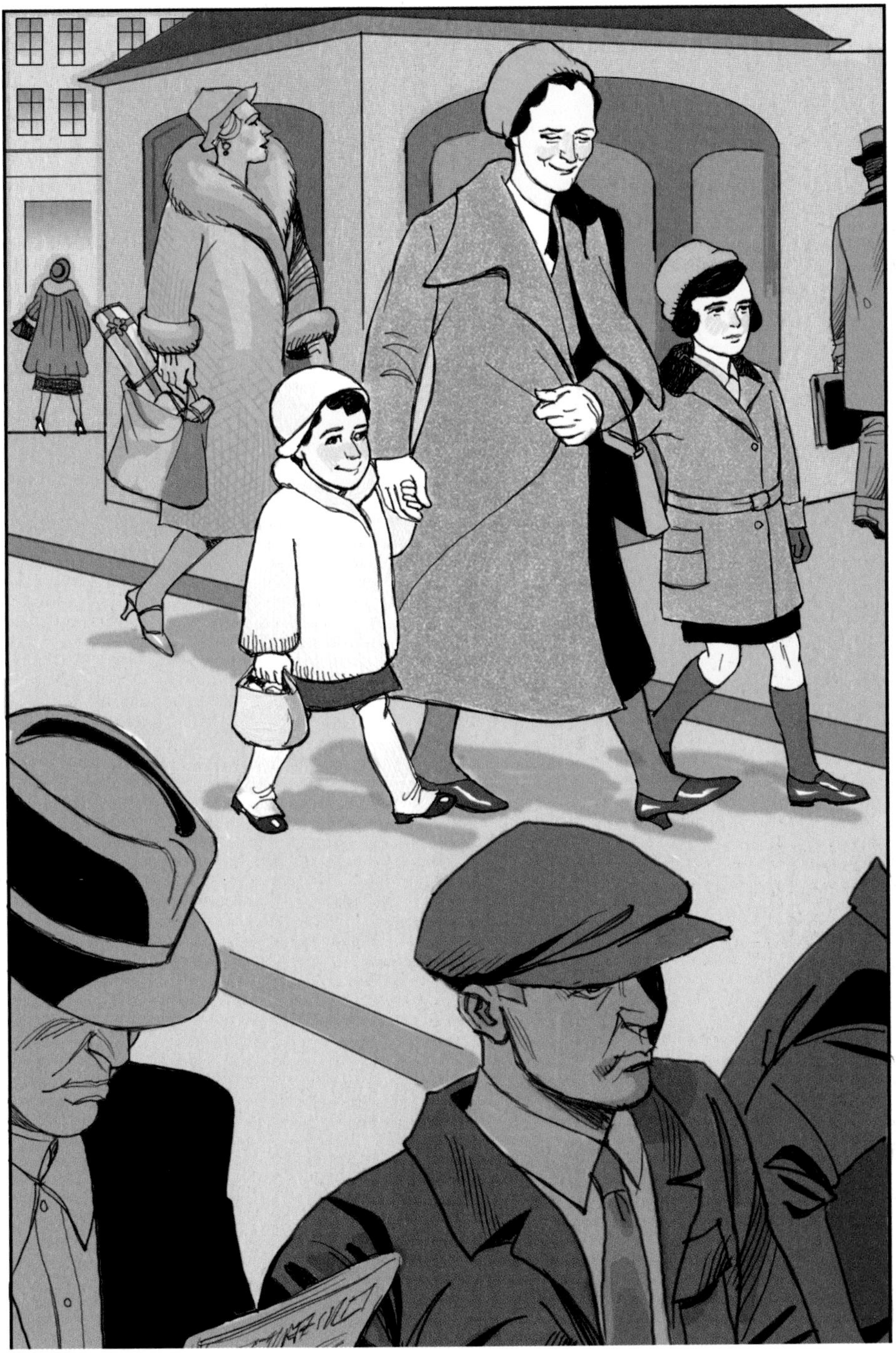

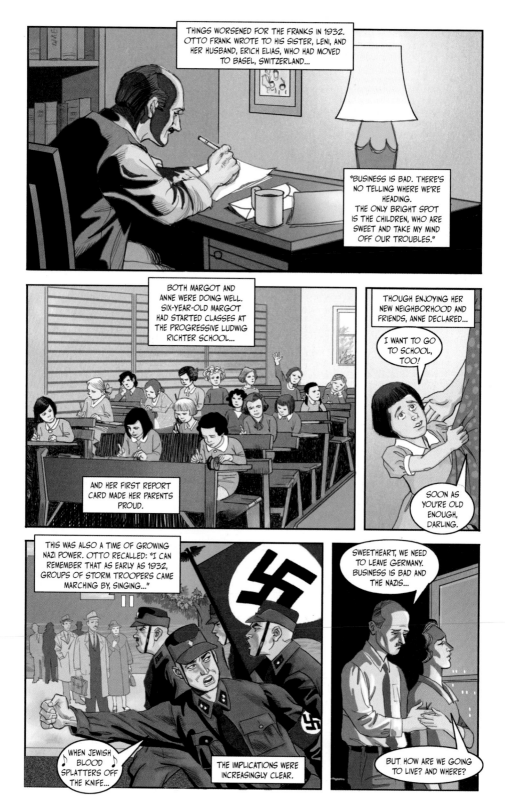

THINGS WORSENED FOR THE FRANKS IN 1932. OTTO FRANK WROTE TO HIS SISTER, LENI, AND HER HUSBAND, ERICH ELIAS, WHO HAD MOVED TO BASEL, SWITZERLAND...

"BUSINESS IS BAD. THERE'S NO TELLING WHERE WE'RE HEADING.
THE ONLY BRIGHT SPOT IS THE CHILDREN, WHO ARE SWEET AND TAKE MY MIND OFF OUR TROUBLES."

BOTH MARGOT AND ANNE WERE DOING WELL. SIX-YEAR-OLD MARGOT HAD STARTED CLASSES AT THE PROGRESSIVE LUDWIG RICHTER SCHOOL...

AND HER FIRST REPORT CARD MADE HER PARENTS PROUD.

THOUGH ENJOYING HER NEW NEIGHBORHOOD AND FRIENDS, ANNE DECLARED...

I WANT TO GO TO SCHOOL, TOO!

SOON AS YOU'RE OLD ENOUGH, DARLING.

THIS WAS ALSO A TIME OF GROWING NAZI POWER. OTTO RECALLED: "I CAN REMEMBER THAT AS EARLY AS 1932, GROUPS OF STORM TROOPERS CAME MARCHING BY, SINGING..."

♪ WHEN JEWISH BLOOD SPLATTERS OFF THE KNIFE... ♪

THE IMPLICATIONS WERE INCREASINGLY CLEAR.

SWEETHEART, WE NEED TO LEAVE GERMANY. BUSINESS IS BAD AND THE NAZIS...

BUT HOW ARE WE GOING TO LIVE? AND WHERE?

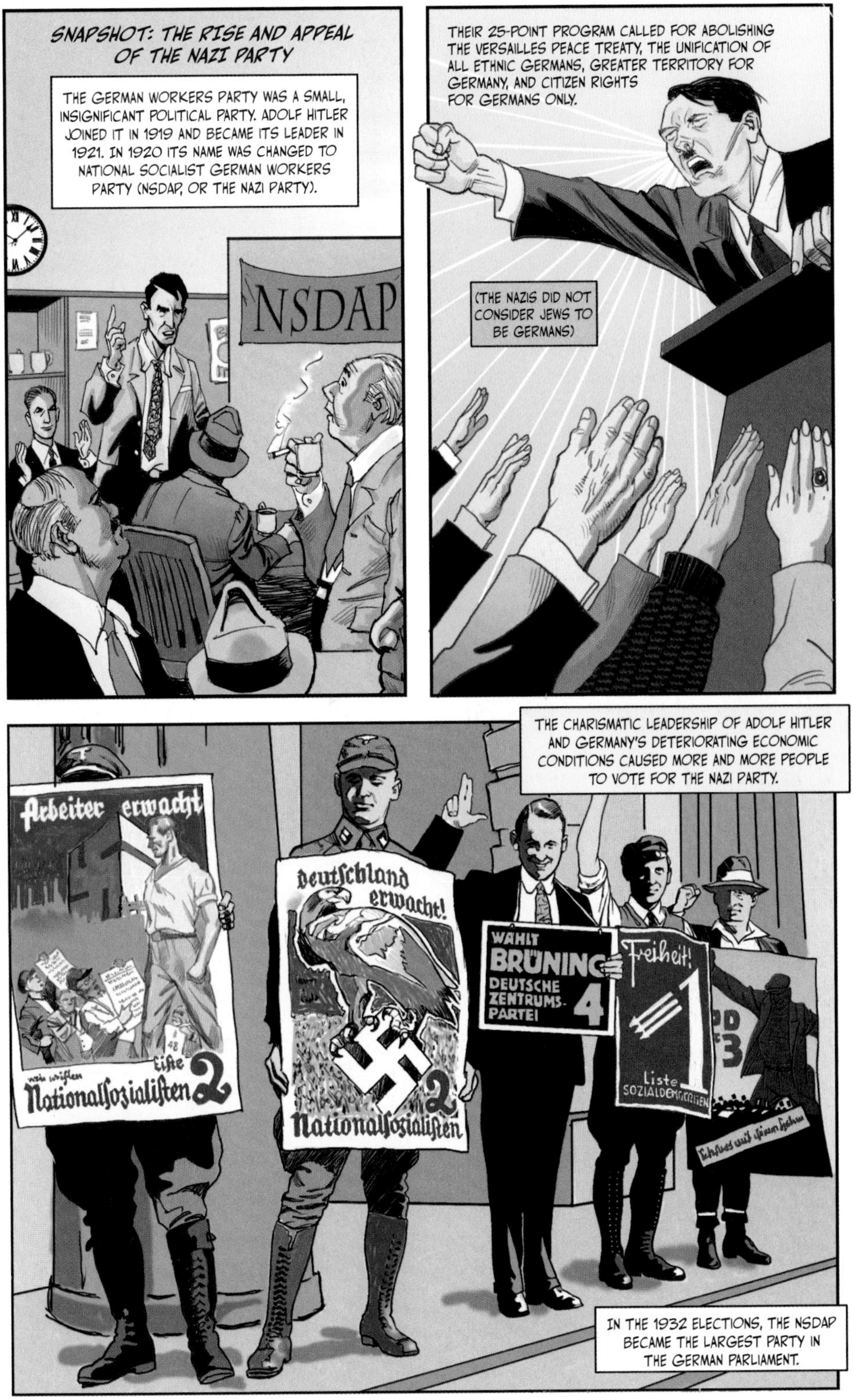
SNAPSHOT: THE RISE AND APPEAL OF THE NAZI PARTY
THE GERMAN WORKERS PARTY WAS A SMALL, INSIGNIFICANT POLITICAL PARTY. ADOLF HITLER JOINED IT IN 1919 AND BECAME ITS LEADER IN 1921. IN 1920 ITS NAME WAS CHANGED TO NATIONAL SOCIALIST GERMAN WORKERS PARTY (NSDAP, OR THE NAZI PARTY).
NSDAP
THEIR 25-POINT PROGRAM CALLED FOR ABOLISHING THE VERSAILLES PEACE TREATY, THE UNIFICATION OF ALL ETHNIC GERMANS, GREATER TERRITORY FOR GERMANY, AND CITIZEN RIGHTS FOR GERMANS ONLY.
(THE NAZIS DID NOT CONSIDER JEWS TO BE GERMANS)
THE CHARISMATIC LEADERSHIP OF ADOLF HITLER AND GERMANY'S DETERIORATING ECONOMIC CONDITIONS CAUSED MORE AND MORE PEOPLE TO VOTE FOR THE NAZI PARTY.
Arbeiter erwacht
Liste
Nationalsozialisten 2
Deutschland erwacht!
2
Nationalsozialisten
WÄHLT
BRÜNING
DEUTSCHE ZENTRUMS-PARTEI
4
Freiheit!
Liste 1
IN THE 1932 ELECTIONS, THE NSDAP BECAME THE LARGEST PARTY IN THE GERMAN PARLIAMENT.

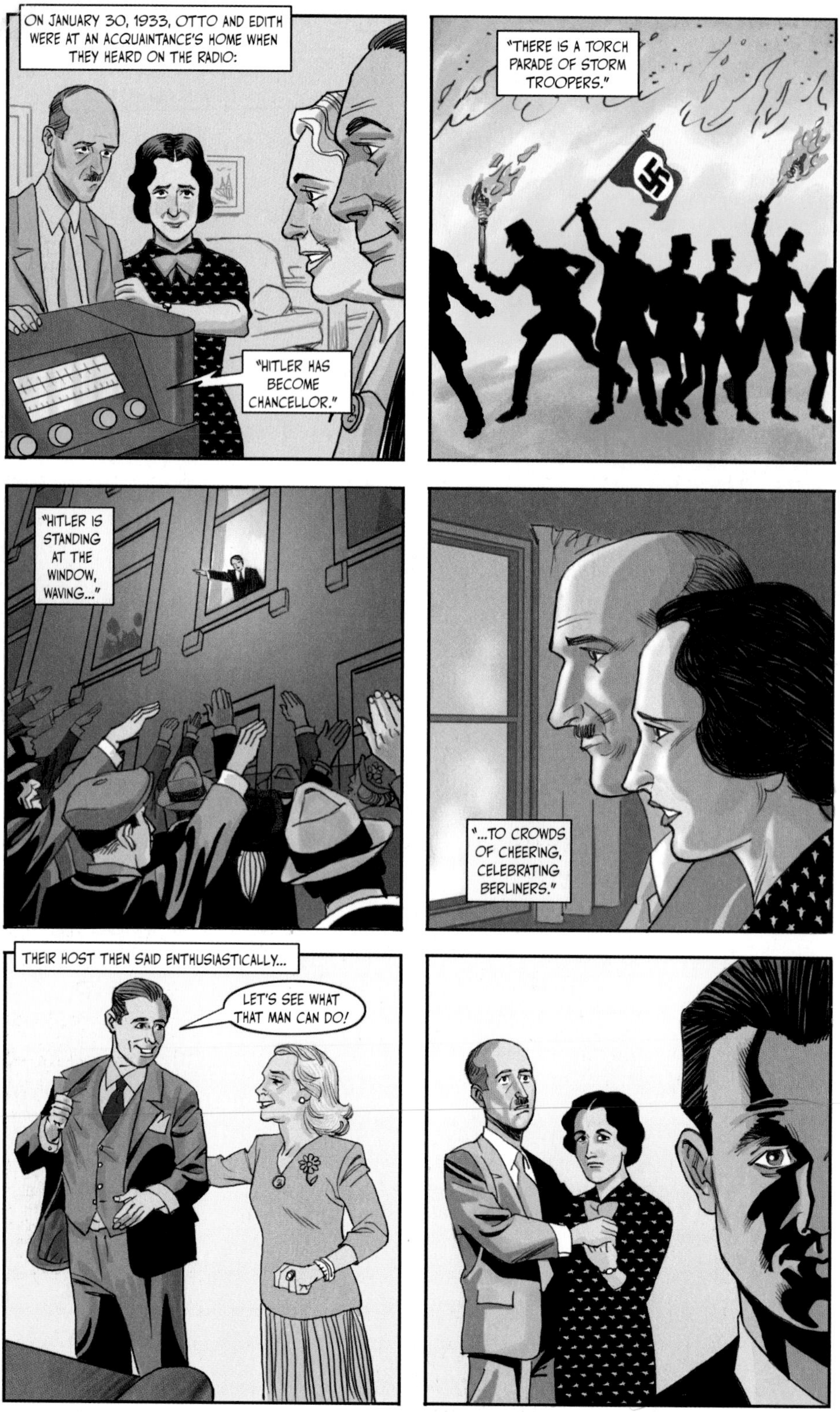
ON JANUARY 30, 1933, OTTO AND EDITH WERE AT AN ACQUAINTANCE'S HOME WHEN THEY HEARD ON THE RADIO:
"HITLER HAS BECOME CHANCELLOR."
"THERE IS A TORCH PARADE OF STORM TROOPERS."
"HITLER IS STANDING AT THE WINDOW, WAVING..."
"...TO CROWDS OF CHEERING, CELEBRATING BERLINERS."
THEIR HOST THEN SAID ENTHUSIASTICALLY...
LET'S SEE WHAT THAT MAN CAN DO!

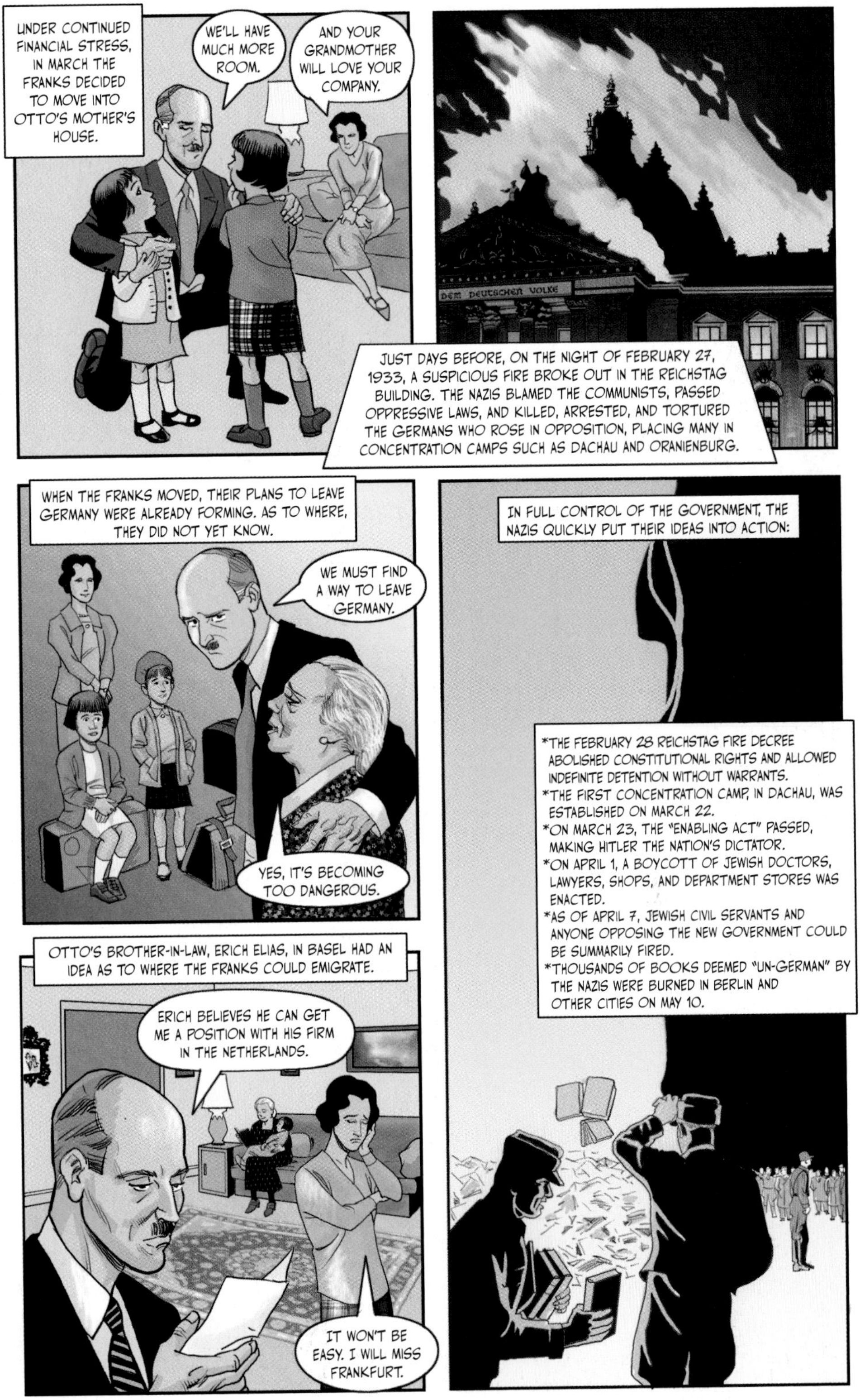

UNDER CONTINUED FINANCIAL STRESS, IN MARCH THE FRANKS DECIDED TO MOVE INTO OTTO'S MOTHER'S HOUSE.
WE'LL HAVE MUCH MORE ROOM.
AND YOUR GRANDMOTHER WILL LOVE YOUR COMPANY.
DEM DEUTSCHEN VOLKE
JUST DAYS BEFORE, ON THE NIGHT OF FEBRUARY 27, 1933, A SUSPICIOUS FIRE BROKE OUT IN THE REICHSTAG BUILDING. THE NAZIS BLAMED THE COMMUNISTS, PASSED OPPRESSIVE LAWS, AND KILLED, ARRESTED, AND TORTURED THE GERMANS WHO ROSE IN OPPOSITION, PLACING MANY IN CONCENTRATION CAMPS SUCH AS DACHAU AND ORANIENBURG.
WHEN THE FRANKS MOVED, THEIR PLANS TO LEAVE GERMANY WERE ALREADY FORMING. AS TO WHERE, THEY DID NOT YET KNOW.
WE MUST FIND A WAY TO LEAVE GERMANY.
YES, IT'S BECOMING TOO DANGEROUS.
OTTO'S BROTHER-IN-LAW, ERICH ELIAS, IN BASEL HAD AN IDEA AS TO WHERE THE FRANKS COULD EMIGRATE.
ERICH BELIEVES HE CAN GET ME A POSITION WITH HIS FIRM IN THE NETHERLANDS.
IT WON'T BE EASY. I WILL MISS FRANKFURT.
IN FULL CONTROL OF THE GOVERNMENT, THE NAZIS QUICKLY PUT THEIR IDEAS INTO ACTION:
*THE FEBRUARY 28 REICHSTAG FIRE DECREE ABOLISHED CONSTITUTIONAL RIGHTS AND ALLOWED INDEFINITE DETENTION WITHOUT WARRANTS.
*THE FIRST CONCENTRATION CAMP, IN DACHAU, WAS ESTABLISHED ON MARCH 22.
*ON MARCH 23, THE "ENABLING ACT" PASSED, MAKING HITLER THE NATION'S DICTATOR.
*ON APRIL 1, A BOYCOTT OF JEWISH DOCTORS, LAWYERS, SHOPS, AND DEPARTMENT STORES WAS ENACTED.
*AS OF APRIL 7, JEWISH CIVIL SERVANTS AND ANYONE OPPOSING THE NEW GOVERNMENT COULD BE SUMMARILY FIRED.
*THOUSANDS OF BOOKS DEEMED "UN-GERMAN" BY THE NAZIS WERE BURNED IN BERLIN AND OTHER CITIES ON MAY 10.

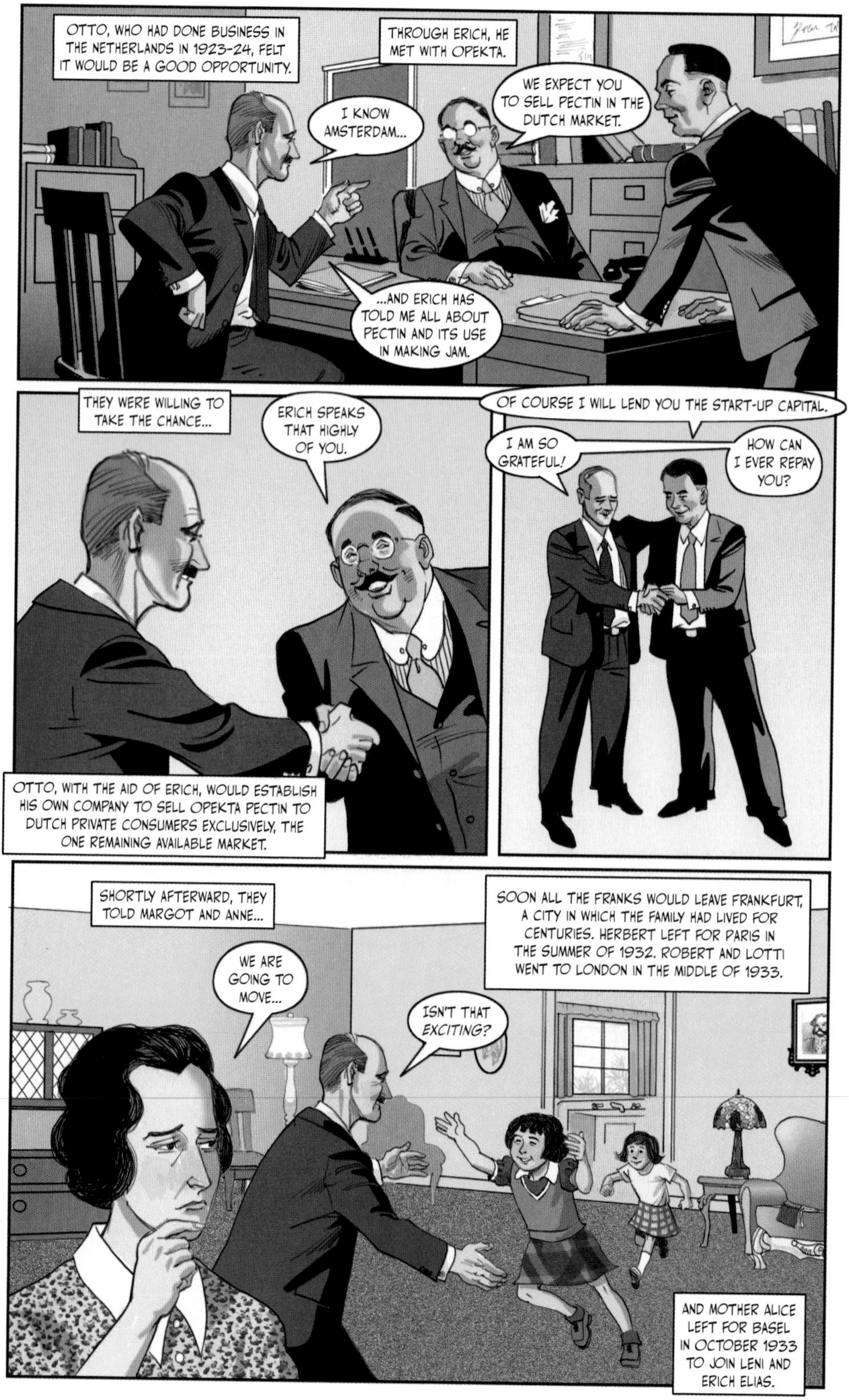
OTTO, WHO HAD DONE BUSINESS IN THE NETHERLANDS IN 1923-24, FELT IT WOULD BE A GOOD OPPORTUNITY.
THROUGH ERICH, HE MET WITH OPEKTA.
I KNOW AMSTERDAM...
WE EXPECT YOU TO SELL PECTIN IN THE DUTCH MARKET.
...AND ERICH HAS TOLD ME ALL ABOUT PECTIN AND ITS USE IN MAKING JAM.
THEY WERE WILLING TO TAKE THE CHANCE...
ERICH SPEAKS THAT HIGHLY OF YOU.
OTTO, WITH THE AID OF ERICH, WOULD ESTABLISH HIS OWN COMPANY TO SELL OPEKTA PECTIN TO DUTCH PRIVATE CONSUMERS EXCLUSIVELY, THE ONE REMAINING AVAILABLE MARKET.
OF COURSE I WILL LEND YOU THE START-UP CAPITAL.
I AM SO GRATEFUL!
HOW CAN I EVER REPAY YOU?
SHORTLY AFTERWARD, THEY TOLD MARGOT AND ANNE...
WE ARE GOING TO MOVE...
ISN'T THAT EXCITING?
SOON ALL THE FRANKS WOULD LEAVE FRANKFURT, A CITY IN WHICH THE FAMILY HAD LIVED FOR CENTURIES. HERBERT LEFT FOR PARIS IN THE SUMMER OF 1932. ROBERT AND LOTTI WENT TO LONDON IN THE MIDDLE OF 1933.
AND MOTHER ALICE LEFT FOR BASEL IN OCTOBER 1933 TO JOIN LENI AND ERICH ELIAS.

CHAPTER 4

Amsterdam

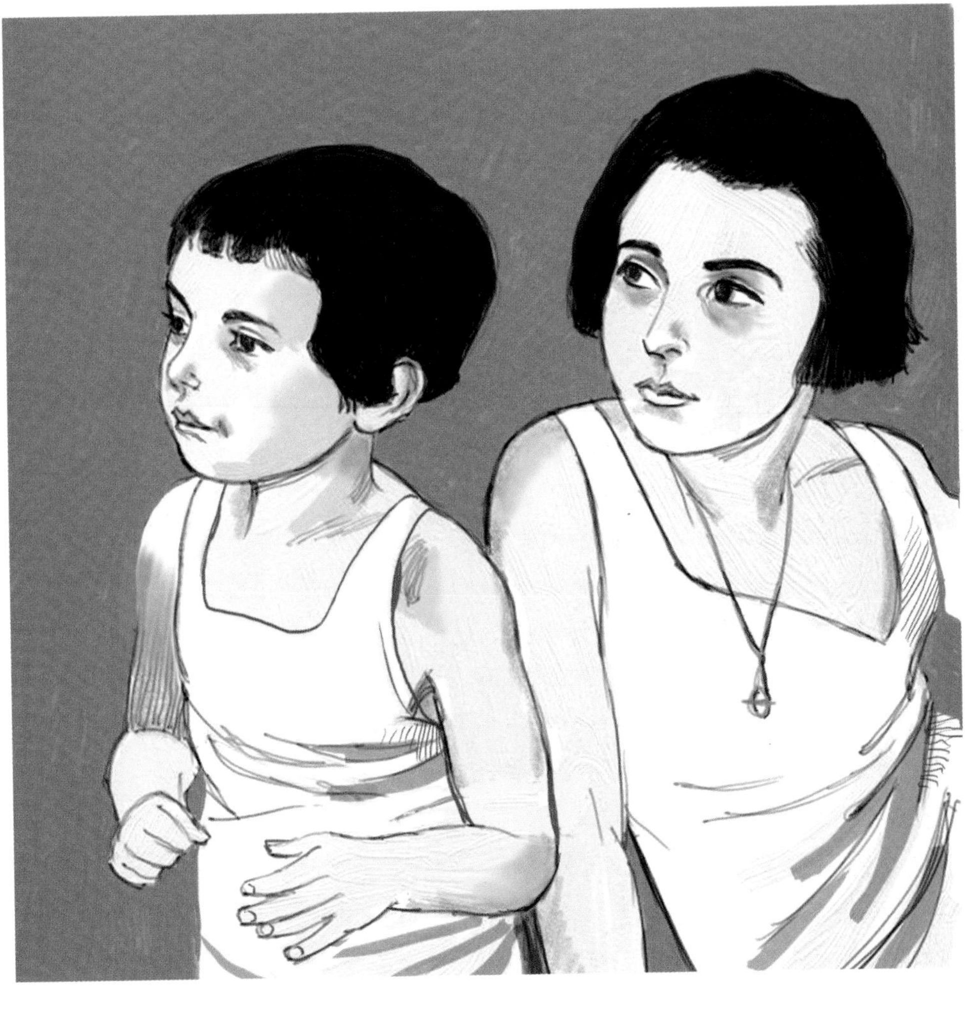

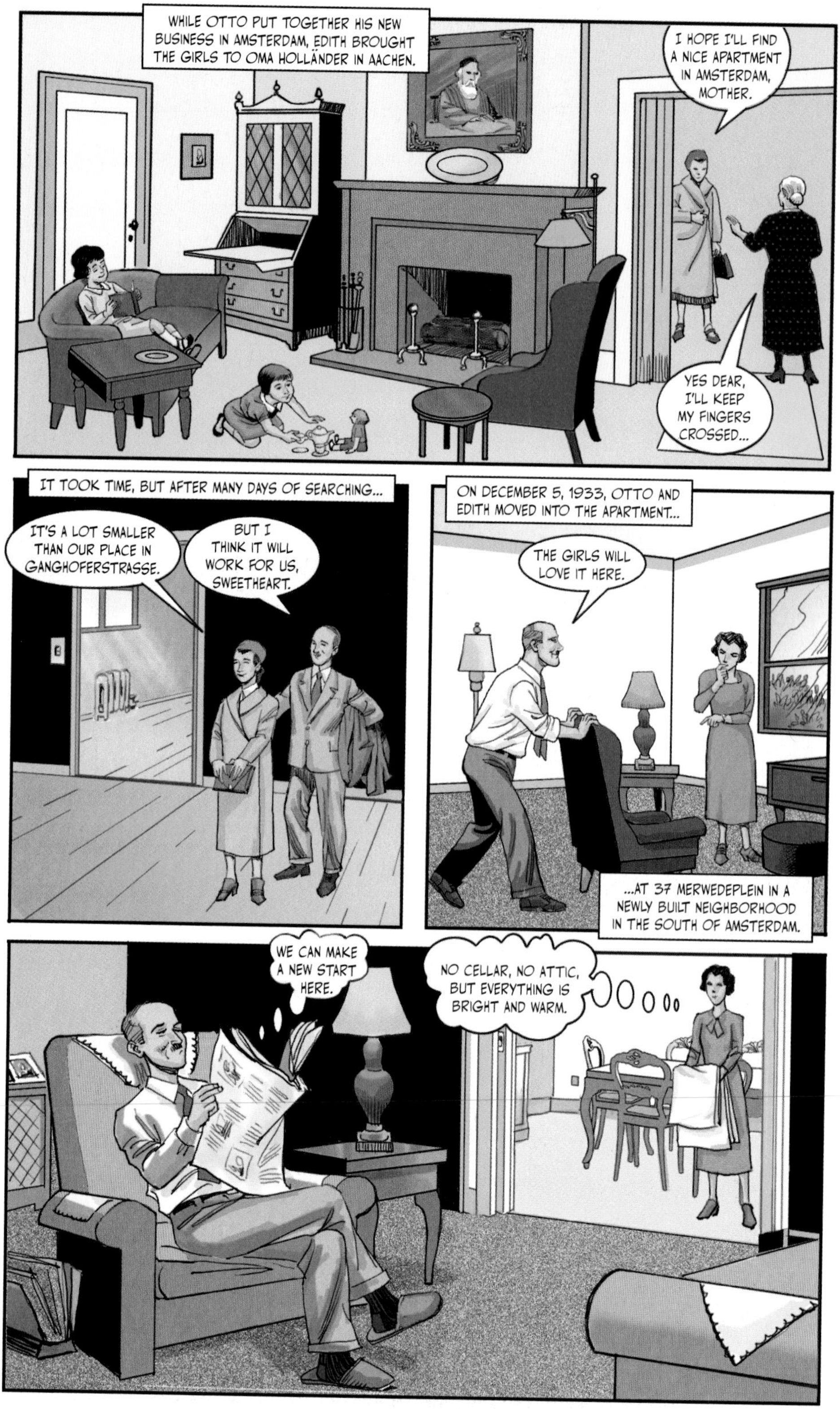
WHILE OTTO PUT TOGETHER HIS NEW BUSINESS IN AMSTERDAM, EDITH BROUGHT THE GIRLS TO OMA HOLLÄNDER IN AACHEN.
I HOPE I'LL FIND A NICE APARTMENT IN AMSTERDAM, MOTHER.
YES DEAR, I'LL KEEP MY FINGERS CROSSED...
IT TOOK TIME, BUT AFTER MANY DAYS OF SEARCHING...
IT'S A LOT SMALLER THAN OUR PLACE IN GANGHOFERSTRASSE.
BUT I THINK IT WILL WORK FOR US, SWEETHEART.
ON DECEMBER 5, 1933, OTTO AND EDITH MOVED INTO THE APARTMENT...
THE GIRLS WILL LOVE IT HERE.
...AT 37 MERWEDEPLEIN IN A NEWLY BUILT NEIGHBORHOOD IN THE SOUTH OF AMSTERDAM.
WE CAN MAKE A NEW START HERE.
NO CELLAR, NO ATTIC, BUT EVERYTHING IS BRIGHT AND WARM.

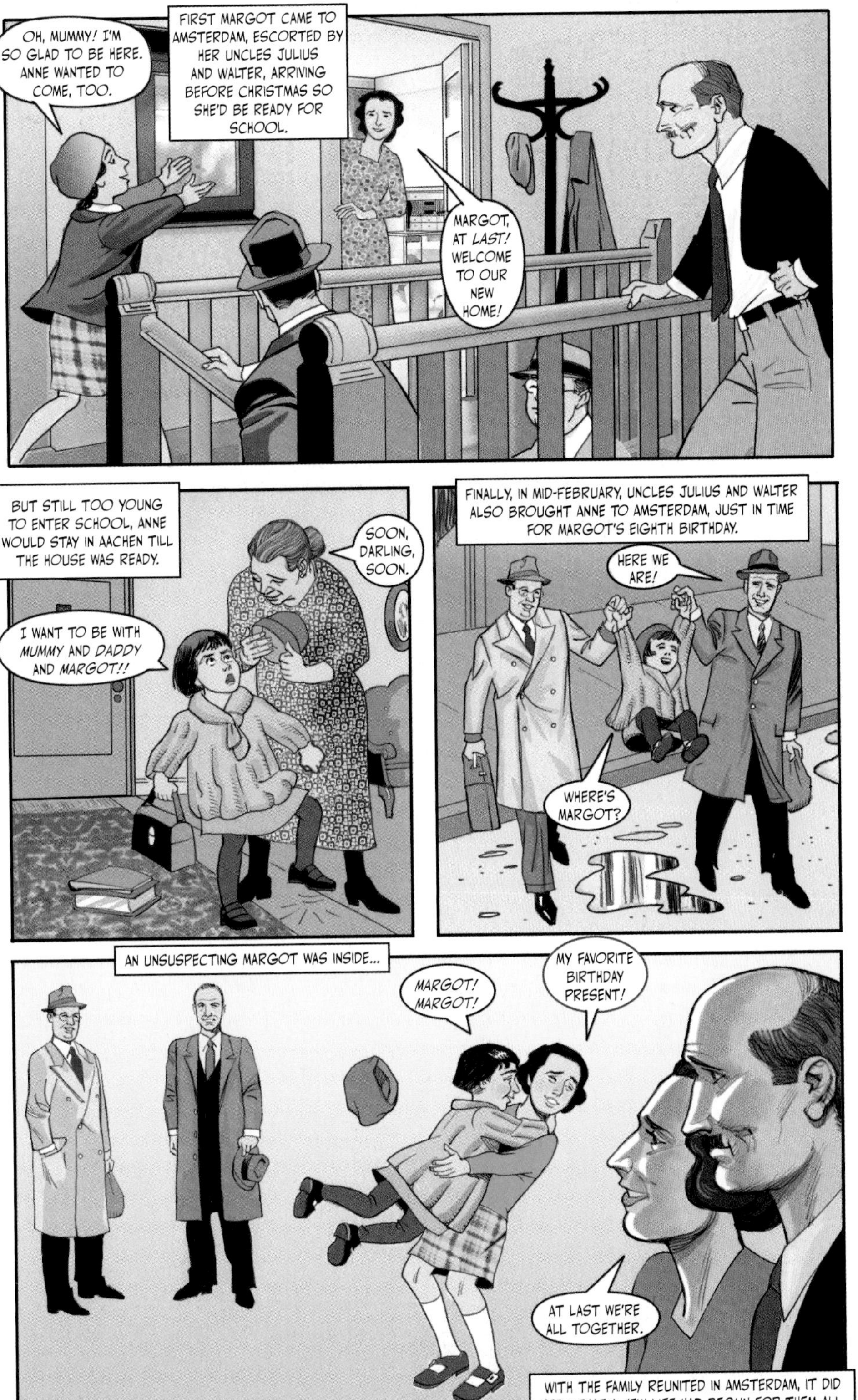
FIRST MARGOT CAME TO AMSTERDAM, ESCORTED BY HER UNCLES JULIUS AND WALTER, ARRIVING BEFORE CHRISTMAS SO SHE'D BE READY FOR SCHOOL.
OH, MUMMY! I'M SO GLAD TO BE HERE. ANNE WANTED TO COME, TOO.
MARGOT, AT LAST! WELCOME TO OUR NEW HOME!
BUT STILL TOO YOUNG TO ENTER SCHOOL, ANNE WOULD STAY IN AACHEN TILL THE HOUSE WAS READY.
SOON, DARLING, SOON.
I WANT TO BE WITH MUMMY AND DADDY AND MARGOT!!
FINALLY, IN MID-FEBRUARY, UNCLES JULIUS AND WALTER ALSO BROUGHT ANNE TO AMSTERDAM, JUST IN TIME FOR MARGOT'S EIGHTH BIRTHDAY.
HERE WE ARE!
WHERE'S MARGOT?
AN UNSUSPECTING MARGOT WAS INSIDE...
MARGOT! MARGOT!
MY FAVORITE BIRTHDAY PRESENT!
AT LAST WE'RE ALL TOGETHER.
WITH THE FAMILY REUNITED IN AMSTERDAM, IT DID SEEM THAT A NEW LIFE HAD BEGUN FOR THEM ALL.

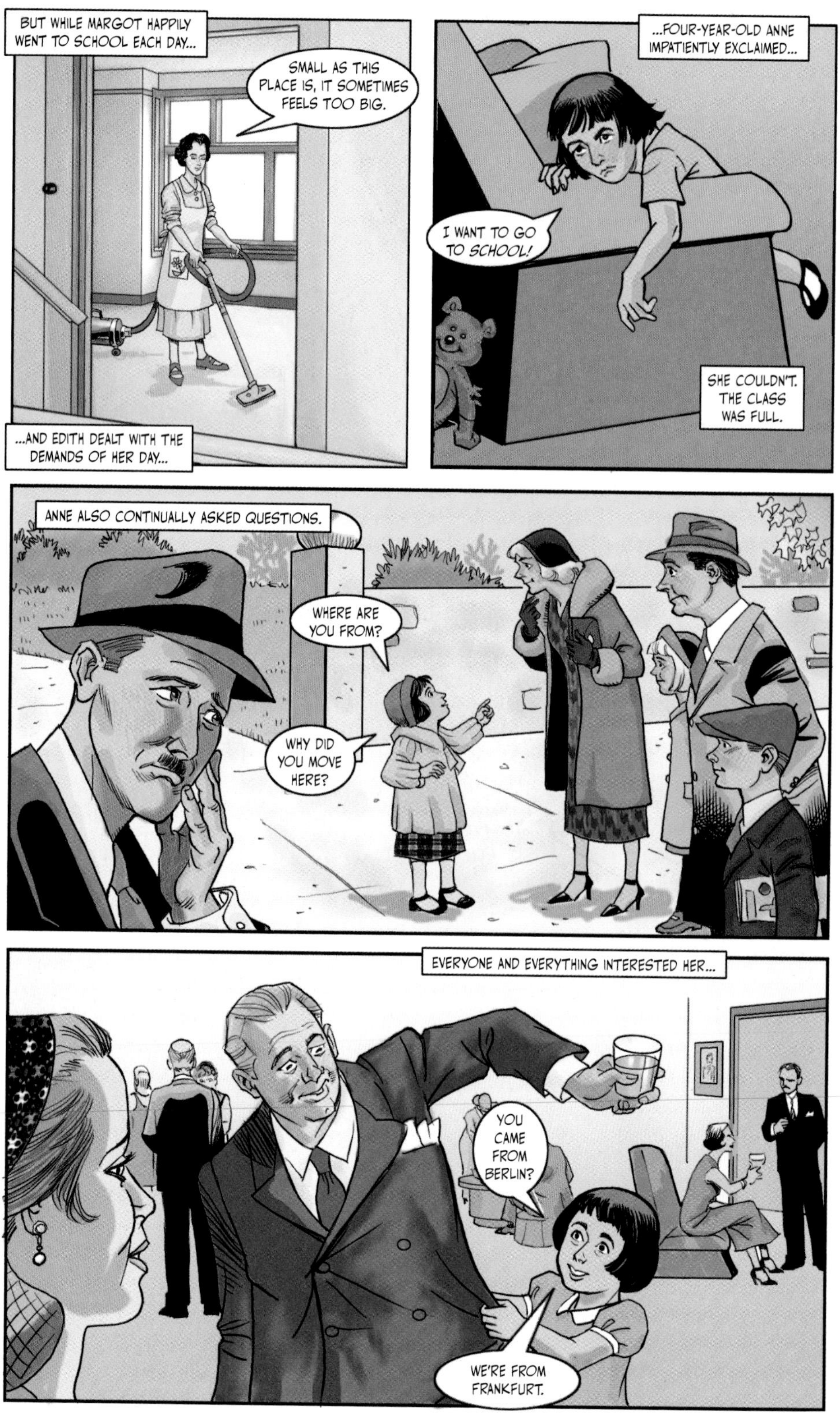
BUT WHILE MARGOT HAPPILY WENT TO SCHOOL EACH DAY...
SMALL AS THIS PLACE IS, IT SOMETIMES FEELS TOO BIG.
...AND EDITH DEALT WITH THE DEMANDS OF HER DAY...
...FOUR-YEAR-OLD ANNE IMPATIENTLY EXCLAIMED...
I WANT TO GO TO SCHOOL!
SHE COULDN'T. THE CLASS WAS FULL.
ANNE ALSO CONTINUALLY ASKED QUESTIONS.
WHERE ARE YOU FROM?
WHY DID YOU MOVE HERE?
EVERYONE AND EVERYTHING INTERESTED HER...
YOU CAME FROM BERLIN?
WE'RE FROM FRANKFURT.

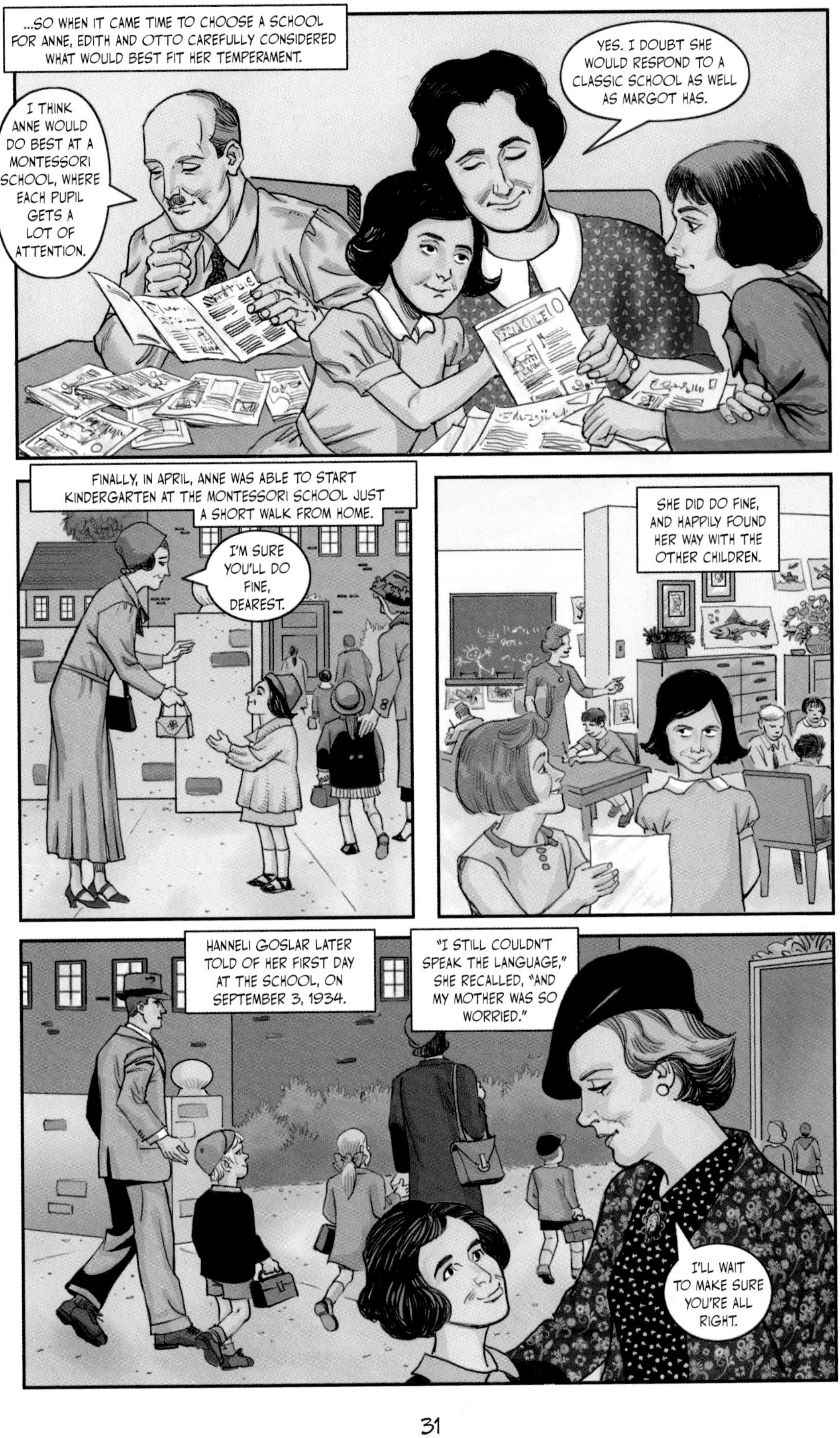
...SO WHEN IT CAME TIME TO CHOOSE A SCHOOL FOR ANNE, EDITH AND OTTO CAREFULLY CONSIDERED WHAT WOULD BEST FIT HER TEMPERAMENT.
I THINK ANNE WOULD DO BEST AT A MONTESSORI SCHOOL, WHERE EACH PUPIL GETS A LOT OF ATTENTION.
YES. I DOUBT SHE WOULD RESPOND TO A CLASSIC SCHOOL AS WELL AS MARGOT HAS.
FINALLY, IN APRIL, ANNE WAS ABLE TO START KINDERGARTEN AT THE MONTESSORI SCHOOL JUST A SHORT WALK FROM HOME.
I'M SURE YOU'LL DO FINE, DEAREST.
SHE DID DO FINE, AND HAPPILY FOUND HER WAY WITH THE OTHER CHILDREN.
HANNELI GOSLAR LATER TOLD OF HER FIRST DAY AT THE SCHOOL, ON SEPTEMBER 3, 1934.
"I STILL COULDN'T SPEAK THE LANGUAGE," SHE RECALLED, "AND MY MOTHER WAS SO WORRIED."
I'LL WAIT TO MAKE SURE YOU'RE ALL RIGHT.

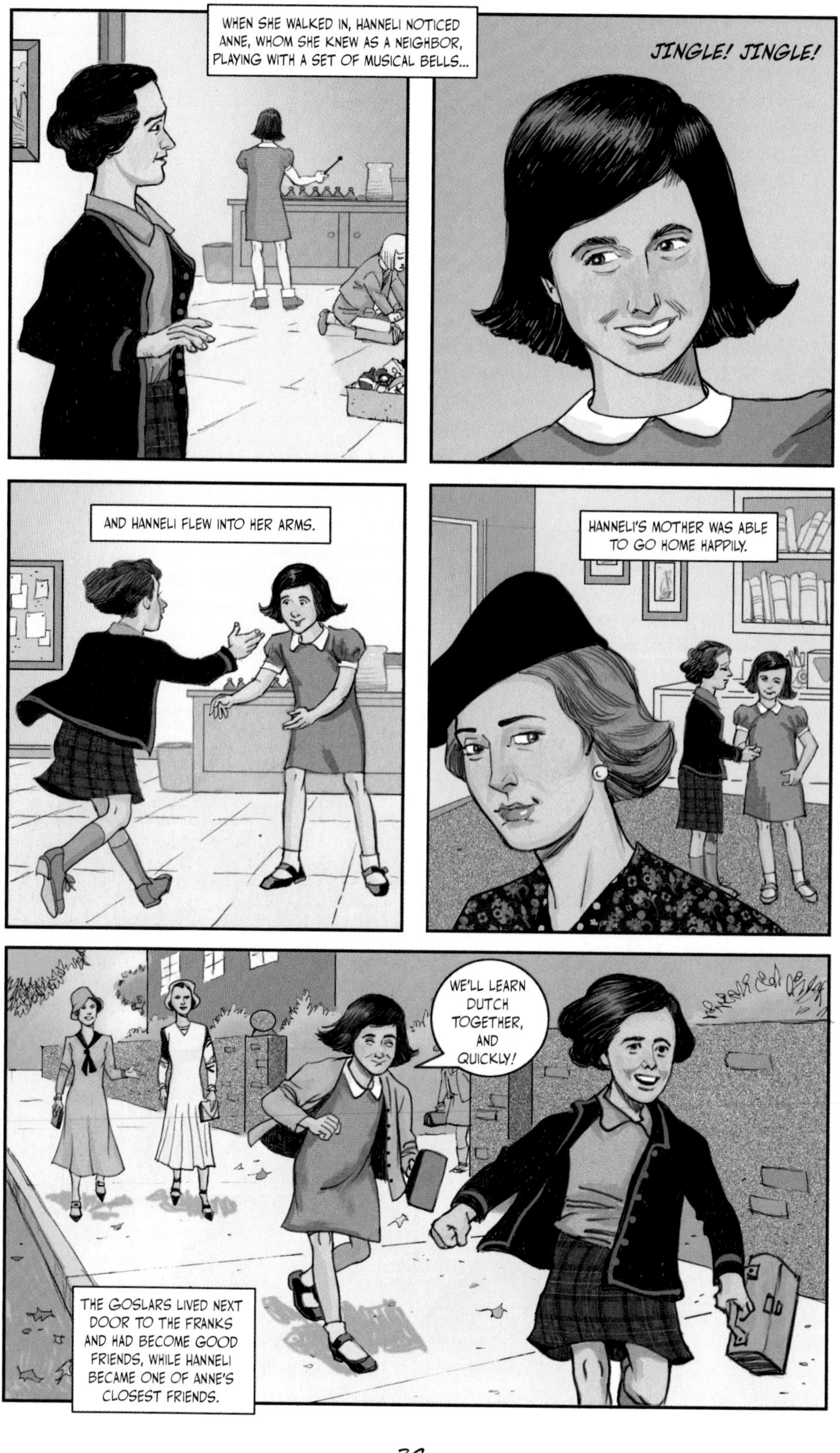
WHEN SHE WALKED IN, HANNELI NOTICED ANNE, WHOM SHE KNEW AS A NEIGHBOR, PLAYING WITH A SET OF MUSICAL BELLS...
JINGLE! JINGLE!
AND HANNELI FLEW INTO HER ARMS.
HANNELI'S MOTHER WAS ABLE TO GO HOME HAPPILY.
WE'LL LEARN DUTCH TOGETHER, AND QUICKLY!
THE GOSLARS LIVED NEXT DOOR TO THE FRANKS AND HAD BECOME GOOD FRIENDS, WHILE HANNELI BECAME ONE OF ANNE'S CLOSEST FRIENDS.

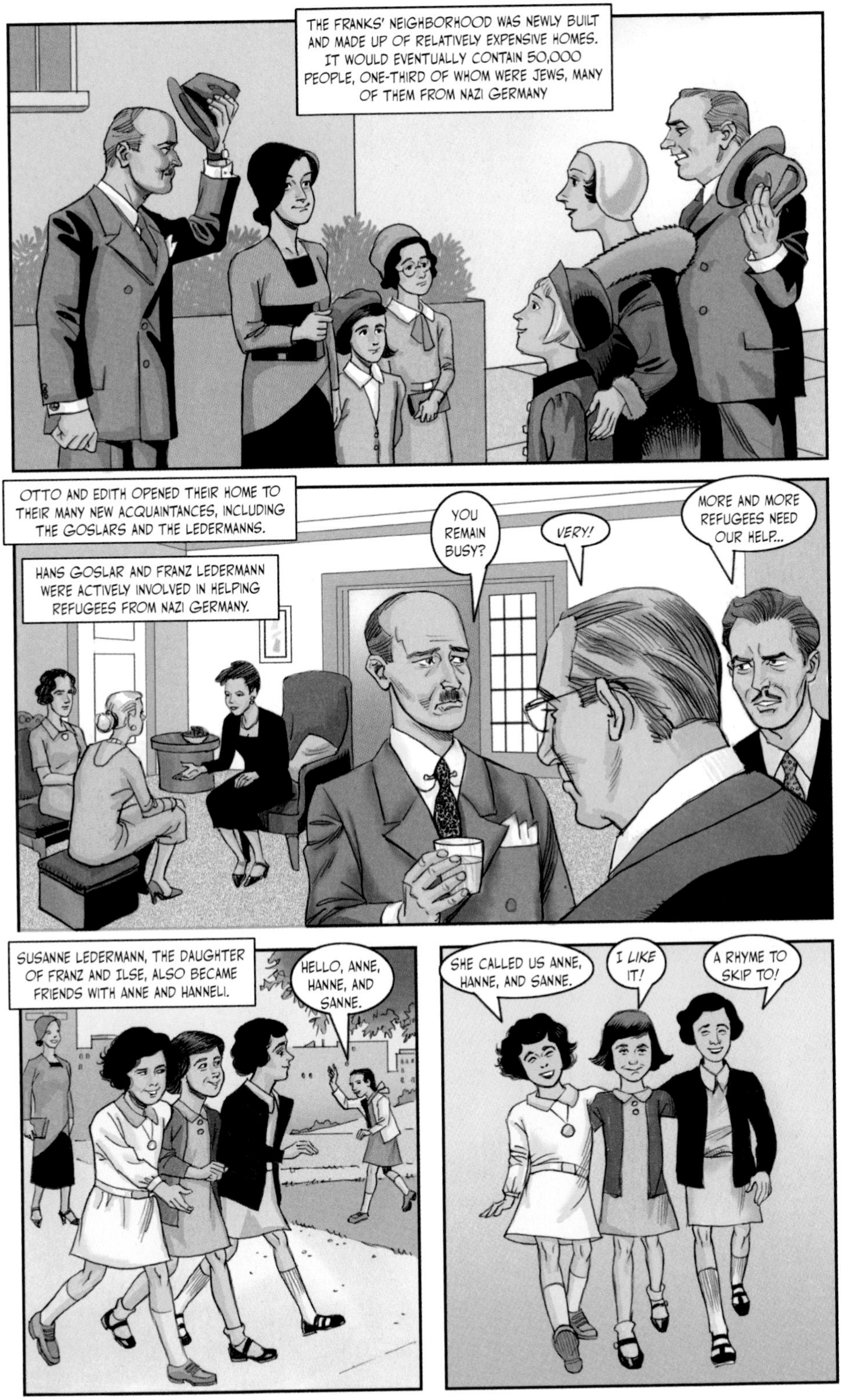
THE FRANKS' NEIGHBORHOOD WAS NEWLY BUILT AND MADE UP OF RELATIVELY EXPENSIVE HOMES. IT WOULD EVENTUALLY CONTAIN 50,000 PEOPLE, ONE-THIRD OF WHOM WERE JEWS, MANY OF THEM FROM NAZI GERMANY
OTTO AND EDITH OPENED THEIR HOME TO THEIR MANY NEW ACQUAINTANCES, INCLUDING THE GOSLARS AND THE LEDERMANNS.
HANS GOSLAR AND FRANZ LEDERMANN WERE ACTIVELY INVOLVED IN HELPING REFUGEES FROM NAZI GERMANY.
YOU REMAIN BUSY?
VERY!
MORE AND MORE REFUGEES NEED OUR HELP...
SUSANNE LEDERMANN, THE DAUGHTER OF FRANZ AND ILSE, ALSO BECAME FRIENDS WITH ANNE AND HANNELI.
HELLO, ANNE, HANNE, AND SANNE.
SHE CALLED US ANNE, HANNE, AND SANNE.
I LIKE IT!
A RHYME TO SKIP TO!

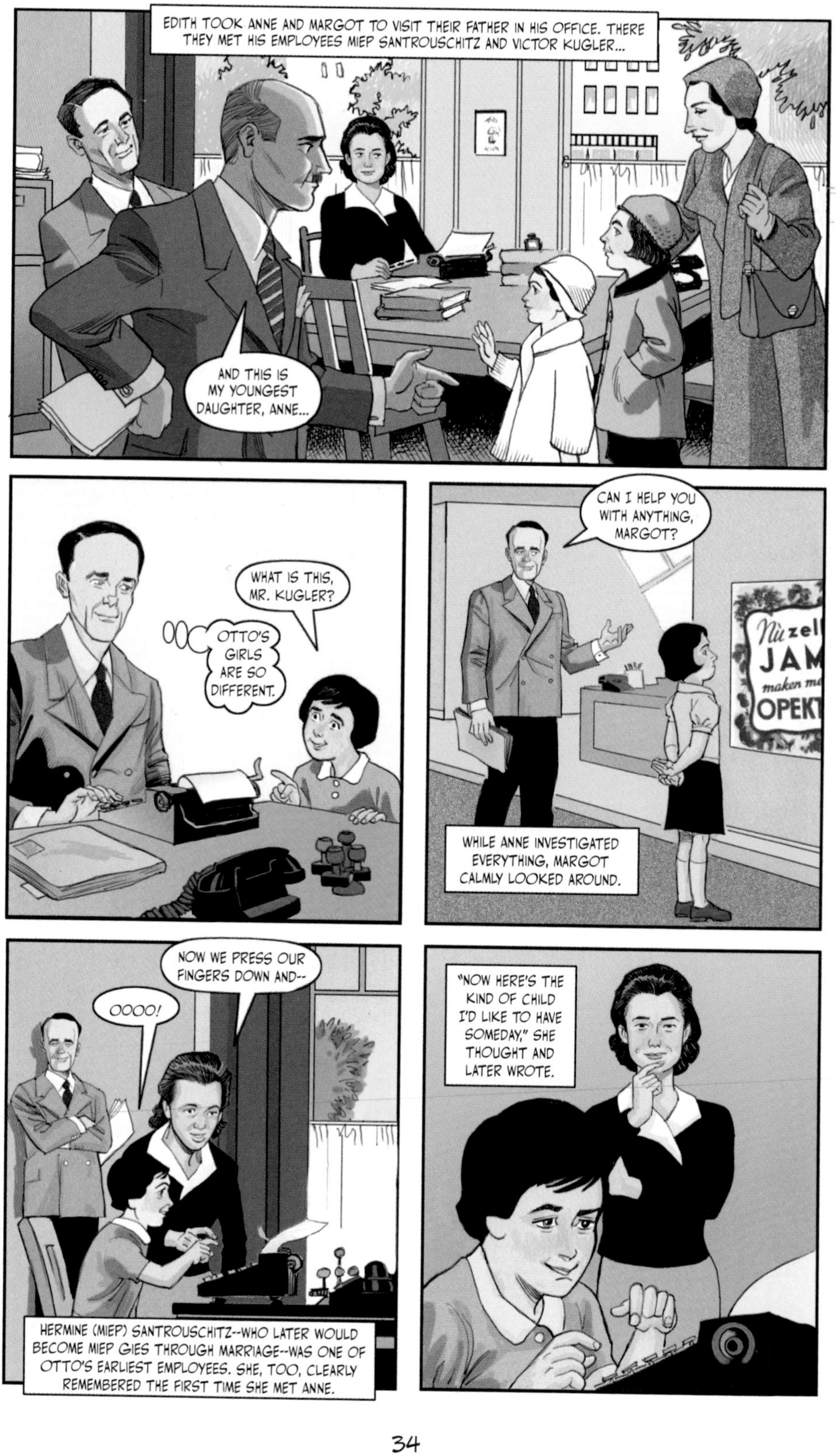
EDITH TOOK ANNE AND MARGOT TO VISIT THEIR FATHER IN HIS OFFICE. THERE THEY MET HIS EMPLOYEES MIEP SANTROUSCHITZ AND VICTOR KUGLER...
AND THIS IS MY YOUNGEST DAUGHTER, ANNE...
WHAT IS THIS, MR. KUGLER?
OTTO'S GIRLS ARE SO DIFFERENT.
CAN I HELP YOU WITH ANYTHING, MARGOT?
WHILE ANNE INVESTIGATED EVERYTHING, MARGOT CALMLY LOOKED AROUND.
NOW WE PRESS OUR FINGERS DOWN AND--
OOOO!
HERMINE (MIEP) SANTROUSCHITZ--WHO LATER WOULD BECOME MIEP GIES THROUGH MARRIAGE--WAS ONE OF OTTO'S EARLIEST EMPLOYEES. SHE, TOO, CLEARLY REMEMBERED THE FIRST TIME SHE MET ANNE.
"NOW HERE'S THE KIND OF CHILD I'D LIKE TO HAVE SOMEDAY," SHE THOUGHT AND LATER WROTE.

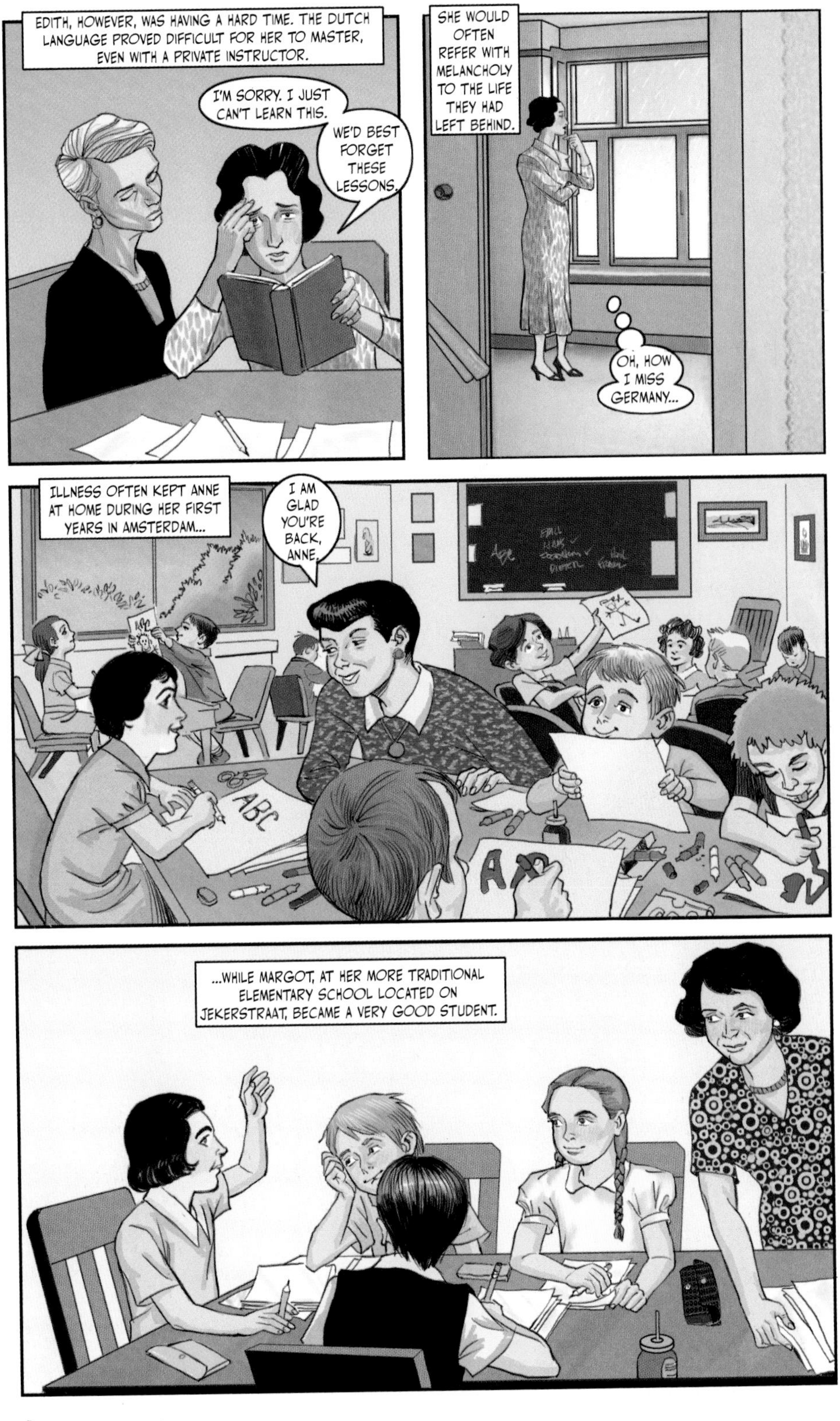
EDITH, HOWEVER, WAS HAVING A HARD TIME. THE DUTCH LANGUAGE PROVED DIFFICULT FOR HER TO MASTER, EVEN WITH A PRIVATE INSTRUCTOR.
I'M SORRY. I JUST CAN'T LEARN THIS.
WE'D BEST FORGET THESE LESSONS.
SHE WOULD OFTEN REFER WITH MELANCHOLY TO THE LIFE THEY HAD LEFT BEHIND.
OH, HOW I MISS GERMANY...
ILLNESS OFTEN KEPT ANNE AT HOME DURING HER FIRST YEARS IN AMSTERDAM...
I AM GLAD YOU'RE BACK, ANNE.
ABC
...WHILE MARGOT, AT HER MORE TRADITIONAL ELEMENTARY SCHOOL LOCATED ON JEKERSTRAAT, BECAME A VERY GOOD STUDENT.

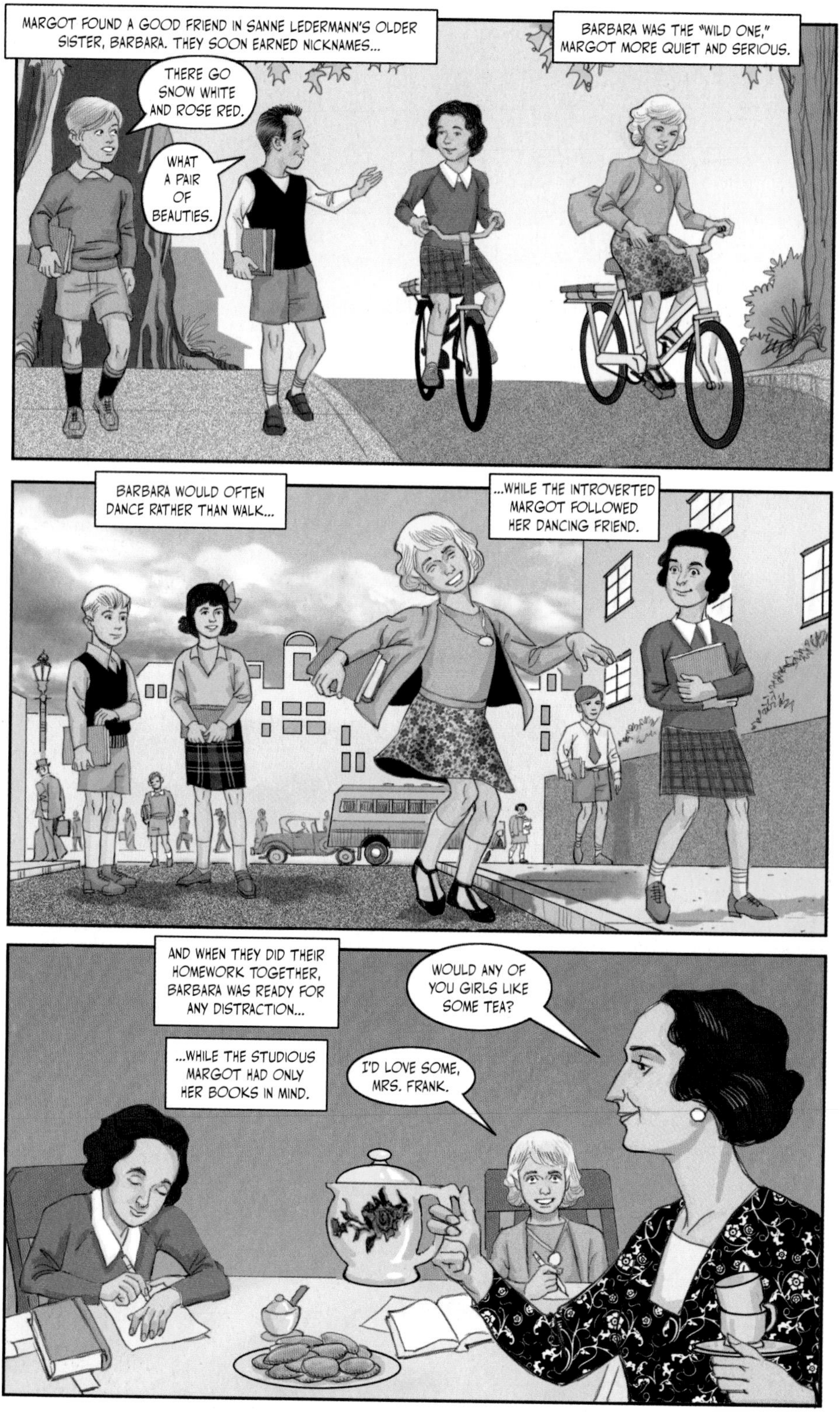
MARGOT FOUND A GOOD FRIEND IN SANNE LEDERMANN'S OLDER SISTER, BARBARA. THEY SOON EARNED NICKNAMES...
THERE GO SNOW WHITE AND ROSE RED.
WHAT A PAIR OF BEAUTIES.
BARBARA WAS THE "WILD ONE," MARGOT MORE QUIET AND SERIOUS.
BARBARA WOULD OFTEN DANCE RATHER THAN WALK...
...WHILE THE INTROVERTED MARGOT FOLLOWED HER DANCING FRIEND.
AND WHEN THEY DID THEIR HOMEWORK TOGETHER, BARBARA WAS READY FOR ANY DISTRACTION...
...WHILE THE STUDIOUS MARGOT HAD ONLY HER BOOKS IN MIND.
WOULD ANY OF YOU GIRLS LIKE SOME TEA?
I'D LOVE SOME, MRS. FRANK.

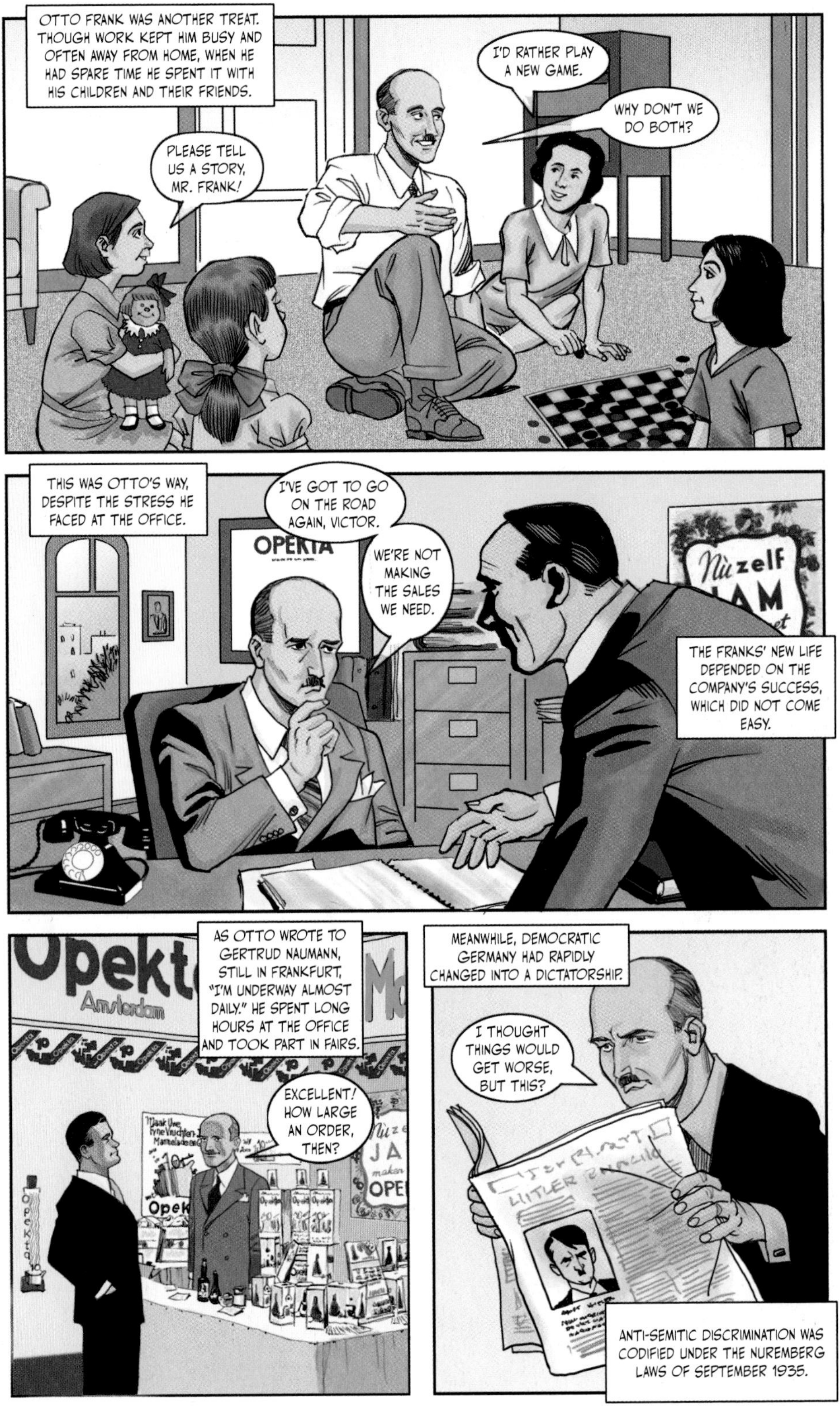
OTTO FRANK WAS ANOTHER TREAT. THOUGH WORK KEPT HIM BUSY AND OFTEN AWAY FROM HOME, WHEN HE HAD SPARE TIME HE SPENT IT WITH HIS CHILDREN AND THEIR FRIENDS.
PLEASE TELL US A STORY, MR. FRANK!
I'D RATHER PLAY A NEW GAME.
WHY DON'T WE DO BOTH?
THIS WAS OTTO'S WAY, DESPITE THE STRESS HE FACED AT THE OFFICE.
I'VE GOT TO GO ON THE ROAD AGAIN, VICTOR.
WE'RE NOT MAKING THE SALES WE NEED.
THE FRANKS' NEW LIFE DEPENDED ON THE COMPANY'S SUCCESS, WHICH DID NOT COME EASY.
AS OTTO WROTE TO GERTRUD NAUMANN, STILL IN FRANKFURT, "I'M UNDERWAY ALMOST DAILY." HE SPENT LONG HOURS AT THE OFFICE AND TOOK PART IN FAIRS.
Opekta
Amsterdam
EXCELLENT! HOW LARGE AN ORDER, THEN?
MEANWHILE, DEMOCRATIC GERMANY HAD RAPIDLY CHANGED INTO A DICTATORSHIP.
I THOUGHT THINGS WOULD GET WORSE, BUT THIS?
HITLER
ANTI-SEMITIC DISCRIMINATION WAS CODIFIED UNDER THE NUREMBERG LAWS OF SEPTEMBER 1935.

SNAPSHOT: NUREMBERG LAWS

ON SEPTEMBER 15, 1935, THE REICHSTAG MET IN NUREMBERG TO COINCIDE WITH A NAZI PARTY RALLY. THAT EVENING, HERMANN GÖRING, AS PRESIDENT OF THE REICHSTAG, PROCLAIMED THE NUREMBERG LAWS, WHICH TOOK AWAY FUNDAMENTAL RIGHTS OF JEWS IN GERMANY.

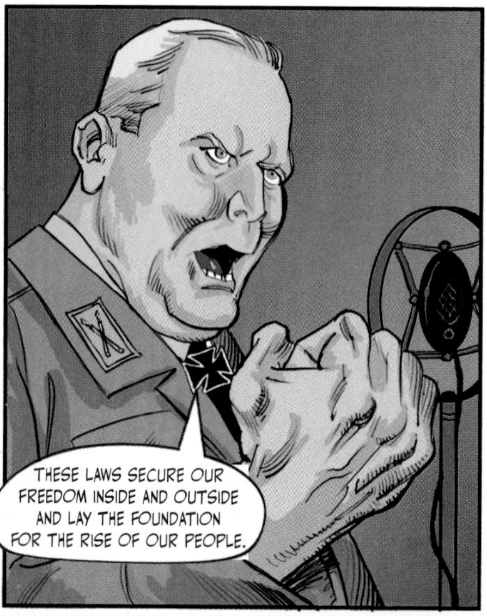
THESE LAWS SECURE OUR FREEDOM INSIDE AND OUTSIDE AND LAY THE FOUNDATION FOR THE RISE OF OUR PEOPLE.

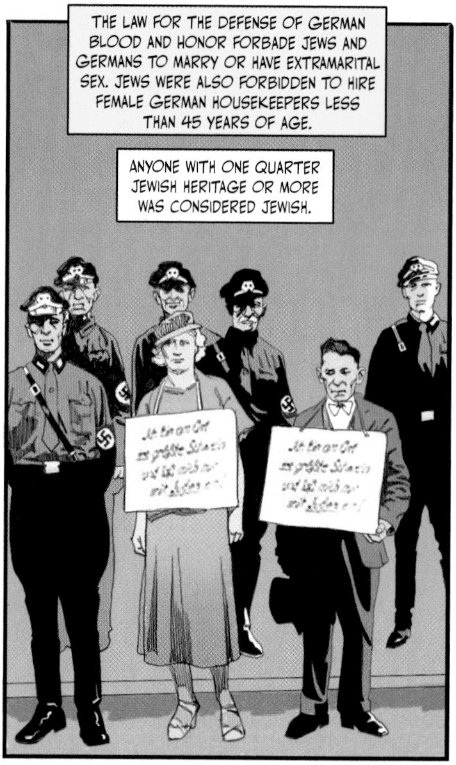
THE LAW FOR THE DEFENSE OF GERMAN BLOOD AND HONOR FORBADE JEWS AND GERMANS TO MARRY OR HAVE EXTRAMARITAL SEX. JEWS WERE ALSO FORBIDDEN TO HIRE FEMALE GERMAN HOUSEKEEPERS LESS THAN 45 YEARS OF AGE.
ANYONE WITH ONE QUARTER JEWISH HERITAGE OR MORE WAS CONSIDERED JEWISH.

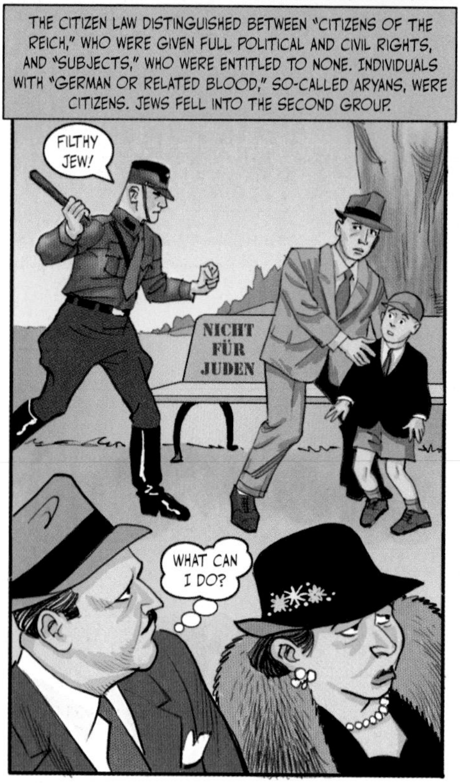
THE CITIZEN LAW DISTINGUISHED BETWEEN "CITIZENS OF THE REICH," WHO WERE GIVEN FULL POLITICAL AND CIVIL RIGHTS, AND "SUBJECTS," WHO WERE ENTITLED TO NONE. INDIVIDUALS WITH "GERMAN OR RELATED BLOOD," SO-CALLED ARYANS, WERE CITIZENS. JEWS FELL INTO THE SECOND GROUP.
FILTHY JEW!
NICHT FÜR JUDEN
WHAT CAN I DO?

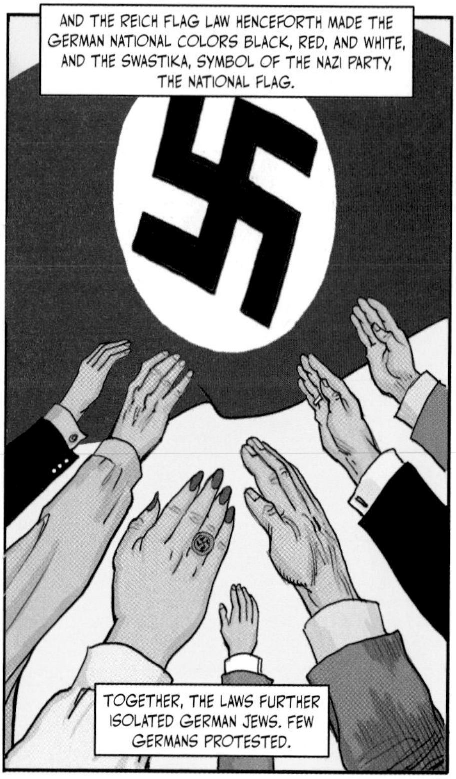
AND THE REICH FLAG LAW HENCEFORTH MADE THE GERMAN NATIONAL COLORS BLACK, RED, AND WHITE, AND THE SWASTIKA, SYMBOL OF THE NAZI PARTY, THE NATIONAL FLAG.
TOGETHER, THE LAWS FURTHER ISOLATED GERMAN JEWS. FEW GERMANS PROTESTED.

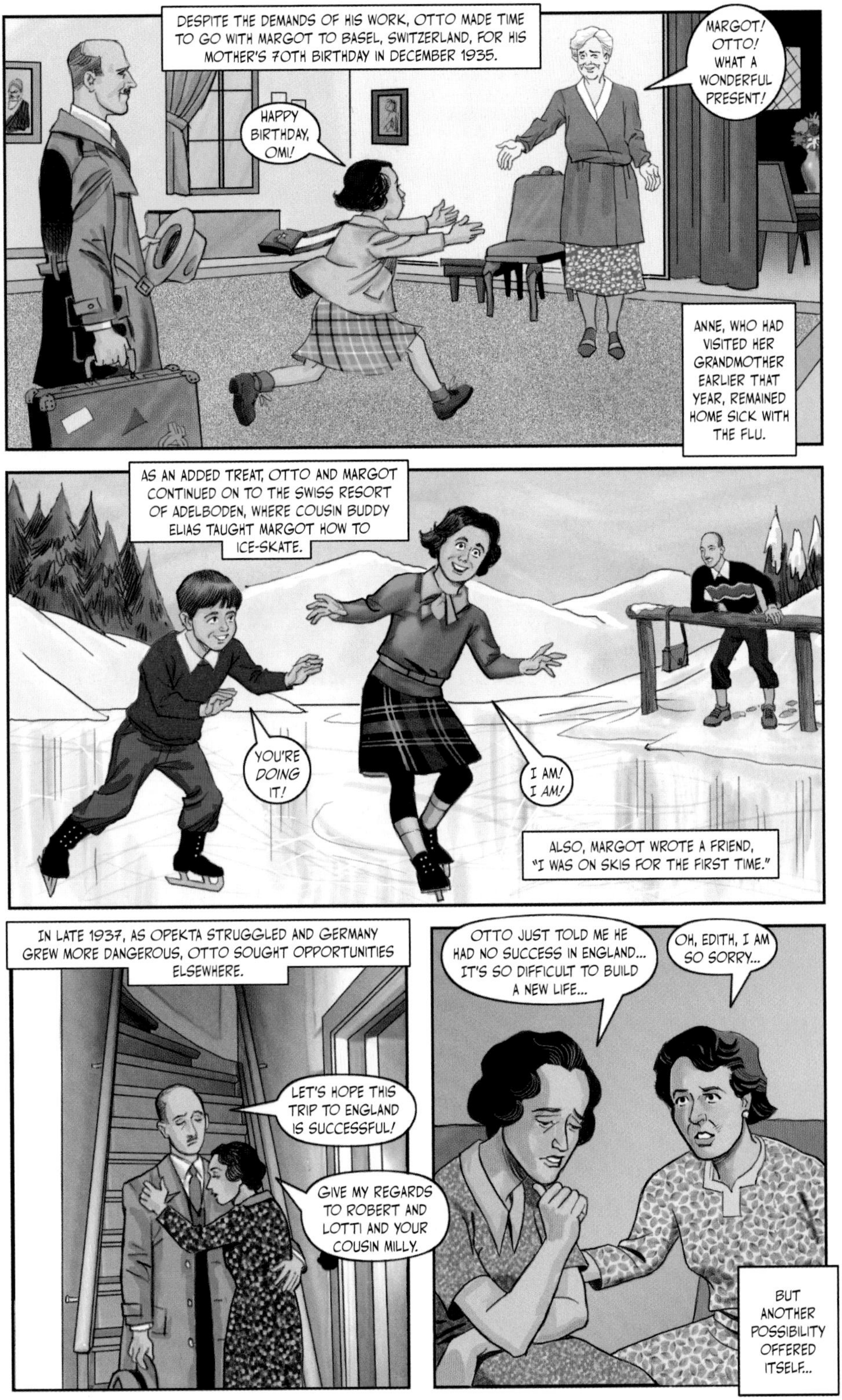
DESPITE THE DEMANDS OF HIS WORK, OTTO MADE TIME TO GO WITH MARGOT TO BASEL, SWITZERLAND, FOR HIS MOTHER'S 70TH BIRTHDAY IN DECEMBER 1935.
HAPPY BIRTHDAY, OMI!
MARGOT! OTTO! WHAT A WONDERFUL PRESENT!
ANNE, WHO HAD VISITED HER GRANDMOTHER EARLIER THAT YEAR, REMAINED HOME SICK WITH THE FLU.
AS AN ADDED TREAT, OTTO AND MARGOT CONTINUED ON TO THE SWISS RESORT OF ADELBODEN, WHERE COUSIN BUDDY ELIAS TAUGHT MARGOT HOW TO ICE-SKATE.
YOU'RE *DOING* IT!
I AM! I AM!
ALSO, MARGOT WROTE A FRIEND, "I WAS ON SKIS FOR THE FIRST TIME."
IN LATE 1937, AS OPEKTA STRUGGLED AND GERMANY GREW MORE DANGEROUS, OTTO SOUGHT OPPORTUNITIES ELSEWHERE.
LET'S HOPE THIS TRIP TO ENGLAND IS SUCCESSFUL!
GIVE MY REGARDS TO ROBERT AND LOTTI AND YOUR COUSIN MILLY.
OTTO JUST TOLD ME HE HAD NO SUCCESS IN ENGLAND... IT'S SO DIFFICULT TO BUILD A NEW LIFE...
OH, EDITH, I AM SO SORRY...
BUT ANOTHER POSSIBILITY OFFERED ITSELF...

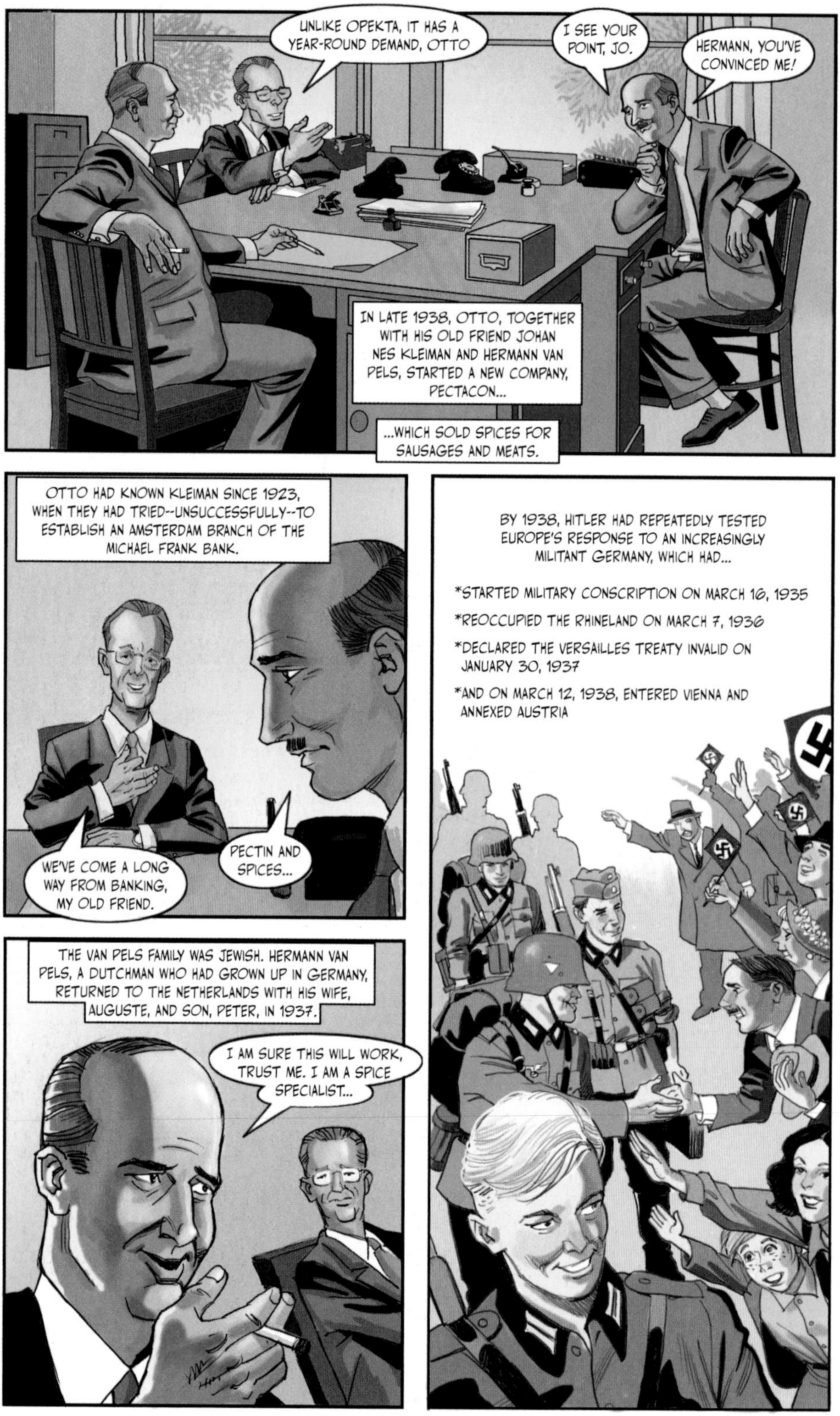
UNLIKE OPEKTA, IT HAS A YEAR-ROUND DEMAND, OTTO
I SEE YOUR POINT, JO.
HERMANN, YOU'VE CONVINCED ME!
IN LATE 1938, OTTO, TOGETHER WITH HIS OLD FRIEND JOHAN NES KLEIMAN AND HERMANN VAN PELS, STARTED A NEW COMPANY, PECTACON...
...WHICH SOLD SPICES FOR SAUSAGES AND MEATS.
OTTO HAD KNOWN KLEIMAN SINCE 1923, WHEN THEY HAD TRIED--UNSUCCESSFULLY--TO ESTABLISH AN AMSTERDAM BRANCH OF THE MICHAEL FRANK BANK.
WE'VE COME A LONG WAY FROM BANKING, MY OLD FRIEND.
PECTIN AND SPICES...
THE VAN PELS FAMILY WAS JEWISH. HERMANN VAN PELS, A DUTCHMAN WHO HAD GROWN UP IN GERMANY, RETURNED TO THE NETHERLANDS WITH HIS WIFE, AUGUSTE, AND SON, PETER, IN 1937.
I AM SURE THIS WILL WORK, TRUST ME. I AM A SPICE SPECIALIST...
BY 1938, HITLER HAD REPEATEDLY TESTED EUROPE'S RESPONSE TO AN INCREASINGLY MILITANT GERMANY, WHICH HAD...
*STARTED MILITARY CONSCRIPTION ON MARCH 16, 1935
*REOCCUPIED THE RHINELAND ON MARCH 7, 1936
*DECLARED THE VERSAILLES TREATY INVALID ON JANUARY 30, 1937
*AND ON MARCH 12, 1938, ENTERED VIENNA AND ANNEXED AUSTRIA

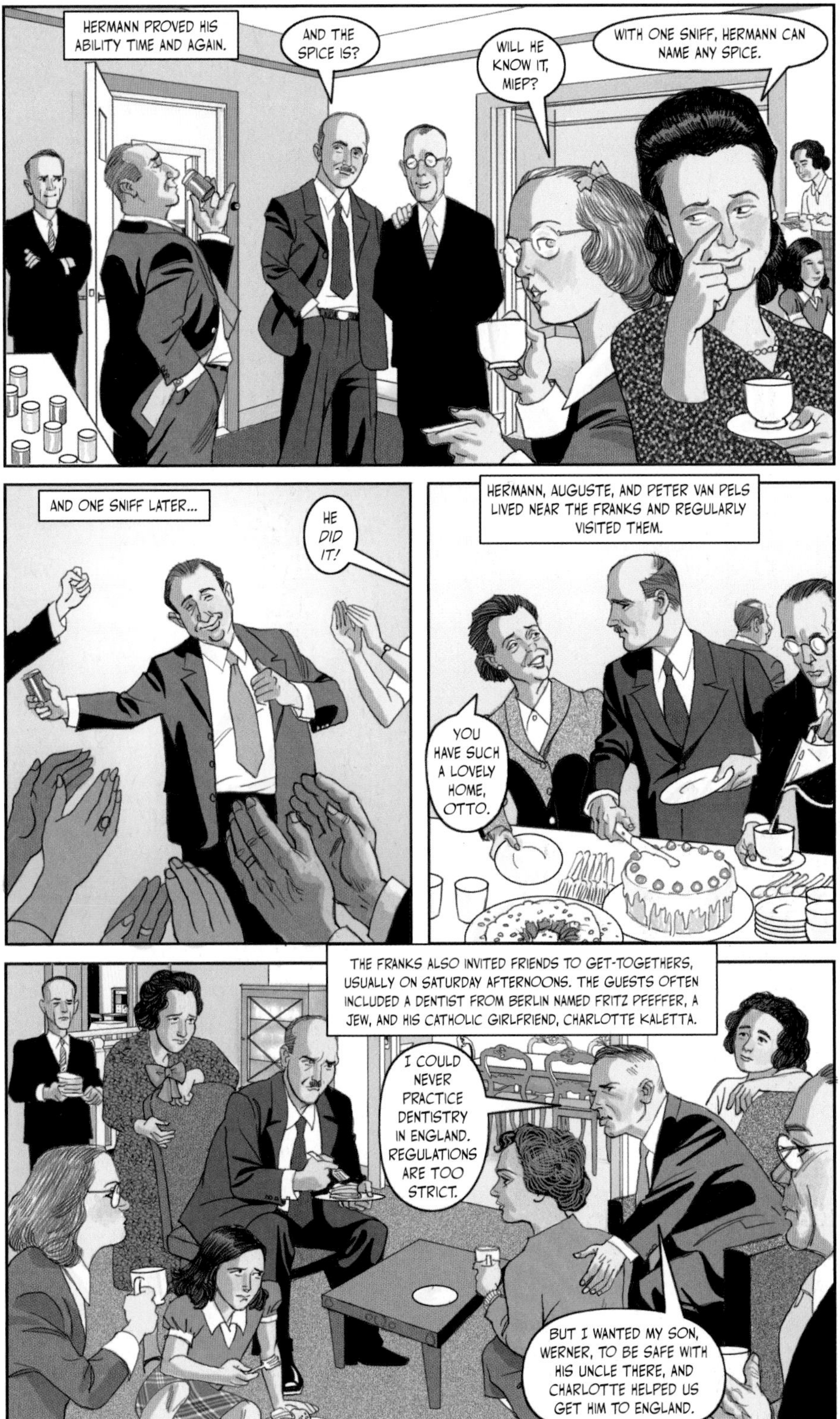
HERMANN PROVED HIS ABILITY TIME AND AGAIN.
AND THE SPICE IS?
WILL HE KNOW IT, MIEP?
WITH ONE SNIFF, HERMANN CAN NAME ANY SPICE.
AND ONE SNIFF LATER...
HE DID IT!
HERMANN, AUGUSTE, AND PETER VAN PELS LIVED NEAR THE FRANKS AND REGULARLY VISITED THEM.
YOU HAVE SUCH A LOVELY HOME, OTTO.
THE FRANKS ALSO INVITED FRIENDS TO GET-TOGETHERS, USUALLY ON SATURDAY AFTERNOONS. THE GUESTS OFTEN INCLUDED A DENTIST FROM BERLIN NAMED FRITZ PFEFFER, A JEW, AND HIS CATHOLIC GIRLFRIEND, CHARLOTTE KALETTA.
I COULD NEVER PRACTICE DENTISTRY IN ENGLAND. REGULATIONS ARE TOO STRICT.
BUT I WANTED MY SON, WERNER, TO BE SAFE WITH HIS UNCLE THERE, AND CHARLOTTE HELPED US GET HIM TO ENGLAND.

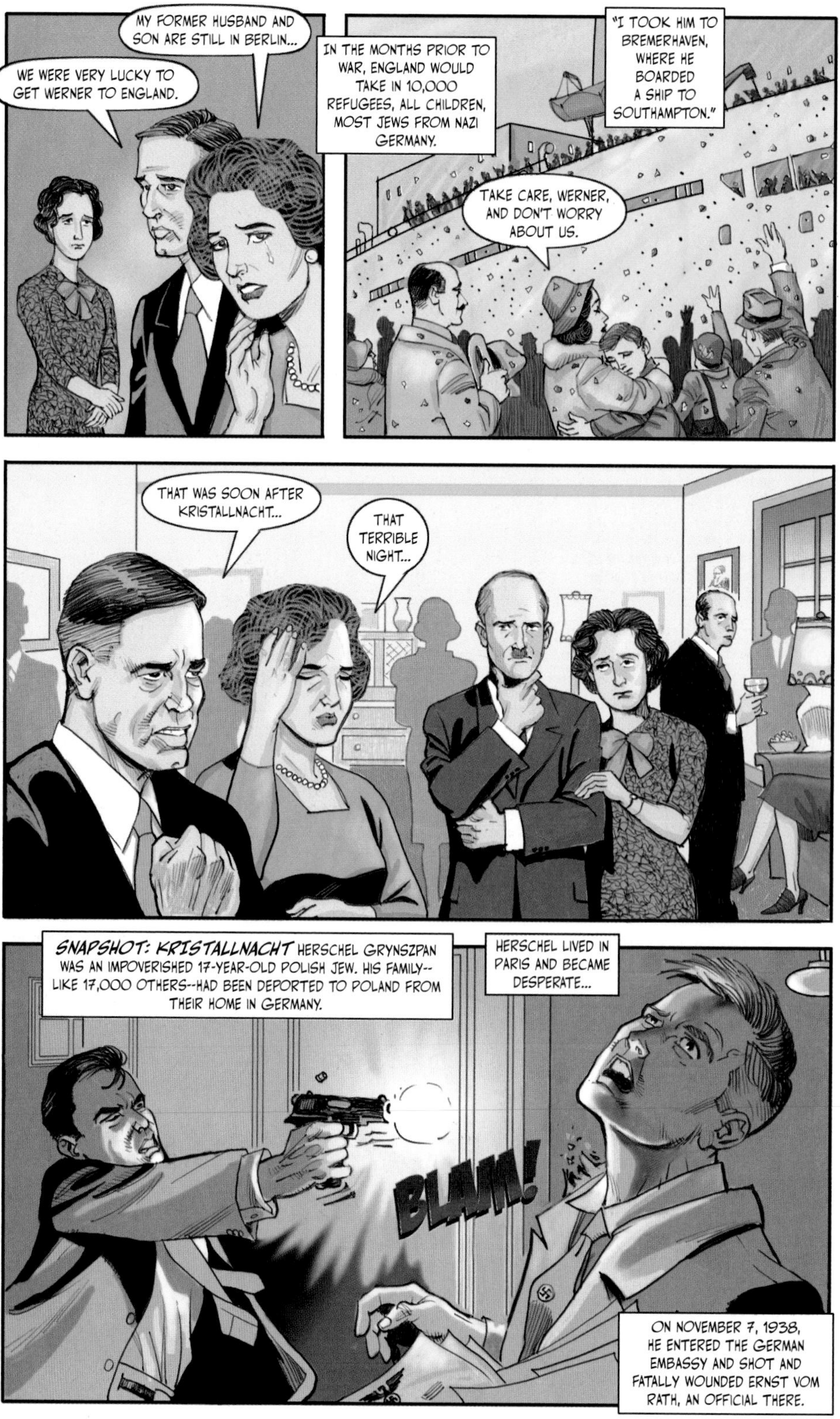
WE WERE VERY LUCKY TO GET WERNER TO ENGLAND.
MY FORMER HUSBAND AND SON ARE STILL IN BERLIN...
IN THE MONTHS PRIOR TO WAR, ENGLAND WOULD TAKE IN 10,000 REFUGEES, ALL CHILDREN, MOST JEWS FROM NAZI GERMANY.
"I TOOK HIM TO BREMERHAVEN, WHERE HE BOARDED A SHIP TO SOUTHAMPTON."
TAKE CARE, WERNER, AND DON'T WORRY ABOUT US.
THAT WAS SOON AFTER KRISTALLNACHT...
THAT TERRIBLE NIGHT...
SNAPSHOT: KRISTALLNACHT HERSCHEL GRYNSZPAN WAS AN IMPOVERISHED 17-YEAR-OLD POLISH JEW. HIS FAMILY--LIKE 17,000 OTHERS--HAD BEEN DEPORTED TO POLAND FROM THEIR HOME IN GERMANY.
HERSCHEL LIVED IN PARIS AND BECAME DESPERATE...
BLAM!
ON NOVEMBER 7, 1938, HE ENTERED THE GERMAN EMBASSY AND SHOT AND FATALLY WOUNDED ERNST VOM RATH, AN OFFICIAL THERE.

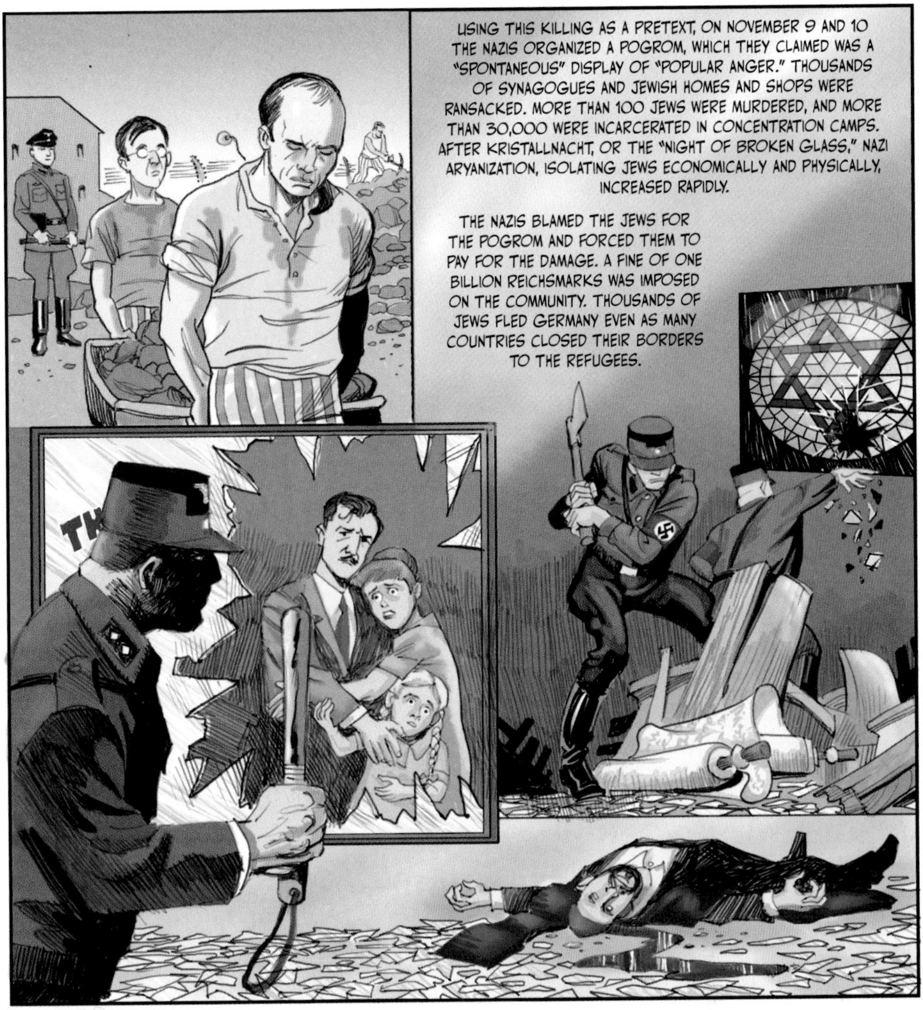
USING THIS KILLING AS A PRETEXT, ON NOVEMBER 9 AND 10 THE NAZIS ORGANIZED A POGROM, WHICH THEY CLAIMED WAS A "SPONTANEOUS" DISPLAY OF "POPULAR ANGER." THOUSANDS OF SYNAGOGUES AND JEWISH HOMES AND SHOPS WERE RANSACKED. MORE THAN 100 JEWS WERE MURDERED, AND MORE THAN 30,000 WERE INCARCERATED IN CONCENTRATION CAMPS. AFTER KRISTALLNACHT, OR THE "NIGHT OF BROKEN GLASS," NAZI ARYANIZATION, ISOLATING JEWS ECONOMICALLY AND PHYSICALLY, INCREASED RAPIDLY.
THE NAZIS BLAMED THE JEWS FOR THE POGROM AND FORCED THEM TO PAY FOR THE DAMAGE. A FINE OF ONE BILLION REICHSMARKS WAS IMPOSED ON THE COMMUNITY. THOUSANDS OF JEWS FLED GERMANY EVEN AS MANY COUNTRIES CLOSED THEIR BORDERS TO THE REFUGEES.

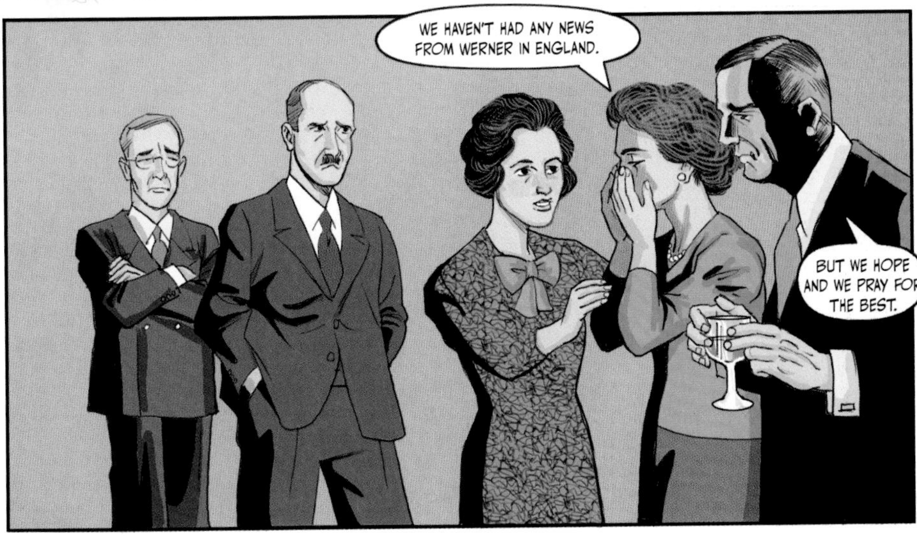
WE HAVEN'T HAD ANY NEWS FROM WERNER IN ENGLAND.
BUT WE HOPE AND WE PRAY FOR THE BEST.

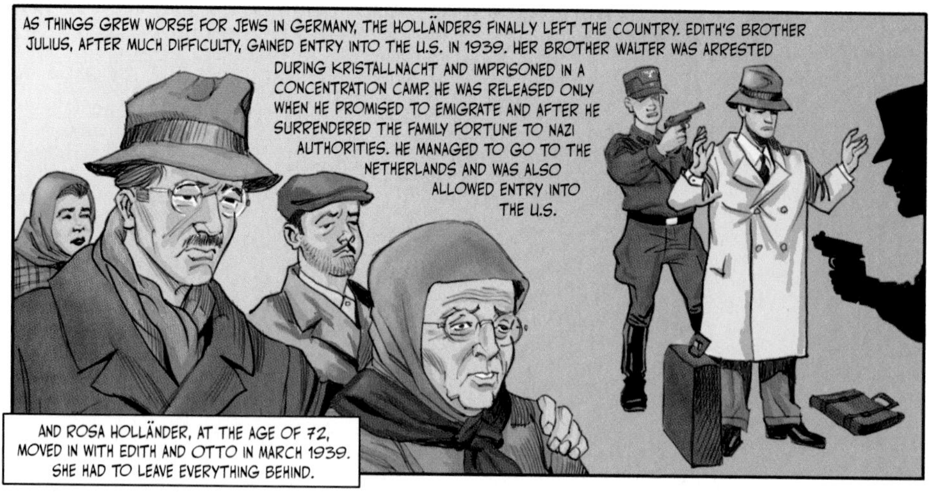
AS THINGS GREW WORSE FOR JEWS IN GERMANY, THE HOLLÄNDERS FINALLY LEFT THE COUNTRY. EDITH'S BROTHER JULIUS, AFTER MUCH DIFFICULTY, GAINED ENTRY INTO THE U.S. IN 1939. HER BROTHER WALTER WAS ARRESTED DURING KRISTALLNACHT AND IMPRISONED IN A CONCENTRATION CAMP. HE WAS RELEASED ONLY WHEN HE PROMISED TO EMIGRATE AND AFTER HE SURRENDERED THE FAMILY FORTUNE TO NAZI AUTHORITIES. HE MANAGED TO GO TO THE NETHERLANDS AND WAS ALSO ALLOWED ENTRY INTO THE U.S.
AND ROSA HOLLÄNDER, AT THE AGE OF 72, MOVED IN WITH EDITH AND OTTO IN MARCH 1939. SHE HAD TO LEAVE EVERYTHING BEHIND.

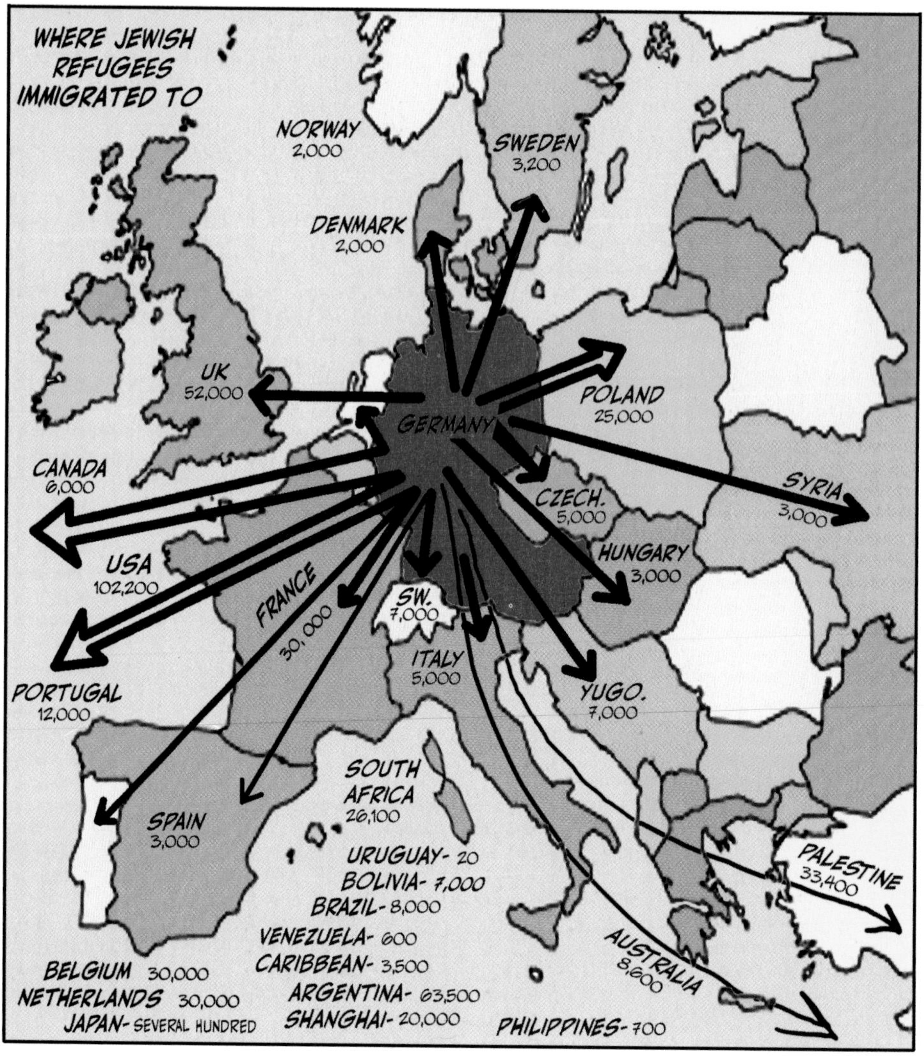
WHERE JEWISH REFUGEES IMMIGRATED TO
NORWAY 2,000
SWEDEN 3,200
DENMARK 2,000
UK 52,000
GERMANY
POLAND 25,000
CANADA 6,000
SYRIA 3,000
CZECH. 5,000
USA 102,200
HUNGARY 3,000
FRANCE 30,000
SW. 7,000
ITALY 5,000
PORTUGAL 12,000
YUGO. 7,000
SOUTH AFRICA 26,100
SPAIN 3,000
URUGUAY- 20
BOLIVIA- 7,000
BRAZIL- 8,000
PALESTINE 33,400
VENEZUELA- 600
CARIBBEAN- 3,500
AUSTRALIA 8,600
BELGIUM 30,000
NETHERLANDS 30,000
JAPAN- SEVERAL HUNDRED
ARGENTINA- 63,500
SHANGHAI- 20,000
PHILIPPINES- 700

CHAPTER 5

Under German Rule

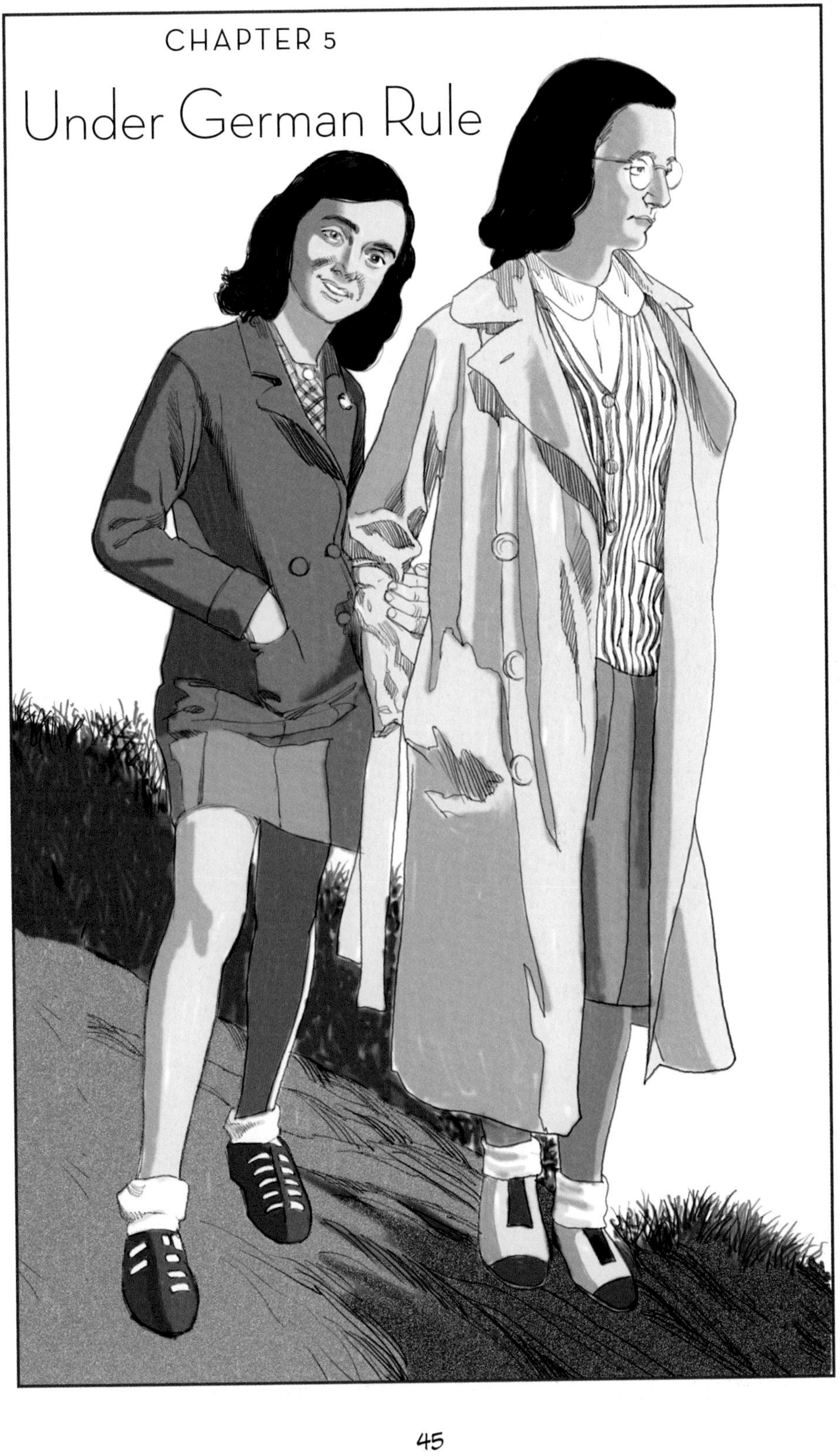

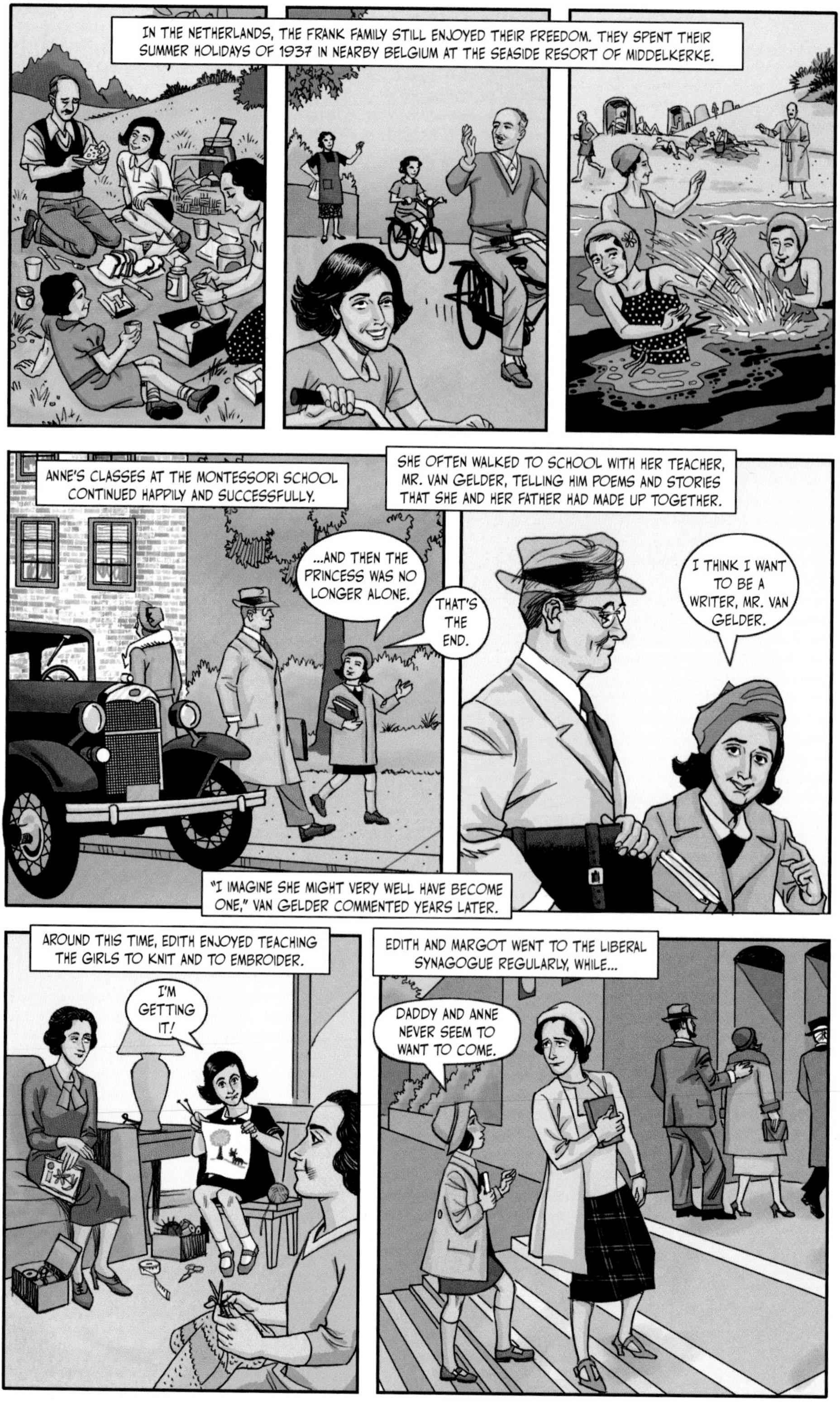
IN THE NETHERLANDS, THE FRANK FAMILY STILL ENJOYED THEIR FREEDOM. THEY SPENT THEIR SUMMER HOLIDAYS OF 1937 IN NEARBY BELGIUM AT THE SEASIDE RESORT OF MIDDELKERKE.
ANNE'S CLASSES AT THE MONTESSORI SCHOOL CONTINUED HAPPILY AND SUCCESSFULLY.
...AND THEN THE PRINCESS WAS NO LONGER ALONE.
THAT'S THE END.
SHE OFTEN WALKED TO SCHOOL WITH HER TEACHER, MR. VAN GELDER, TELLING HIM POEMS AND STORIES THAT SHE AND HER FATHER HAD MADE UP TOGETHER.
I THINK I WANT TO BE A WRITER, MR. VAN GELDER.
"I IMAGINE SHE MIGHT VERY WELL HAVE BECOME ONE," VAN GELDER COMMENTED YEARS LATER.
AROUND THIS TIME, EDITH ENJOYED TEACHING THE GIRLS TO KNIT AND TO EMBROIDER.
I'M GETTING IT!
EDITH AND MARGOT WENT TO THE LIBERAL SYNAGOGUE REGULARLY, WHILE...
DADDY AND ANNE NEVER SEEM TO WANT TO COME.

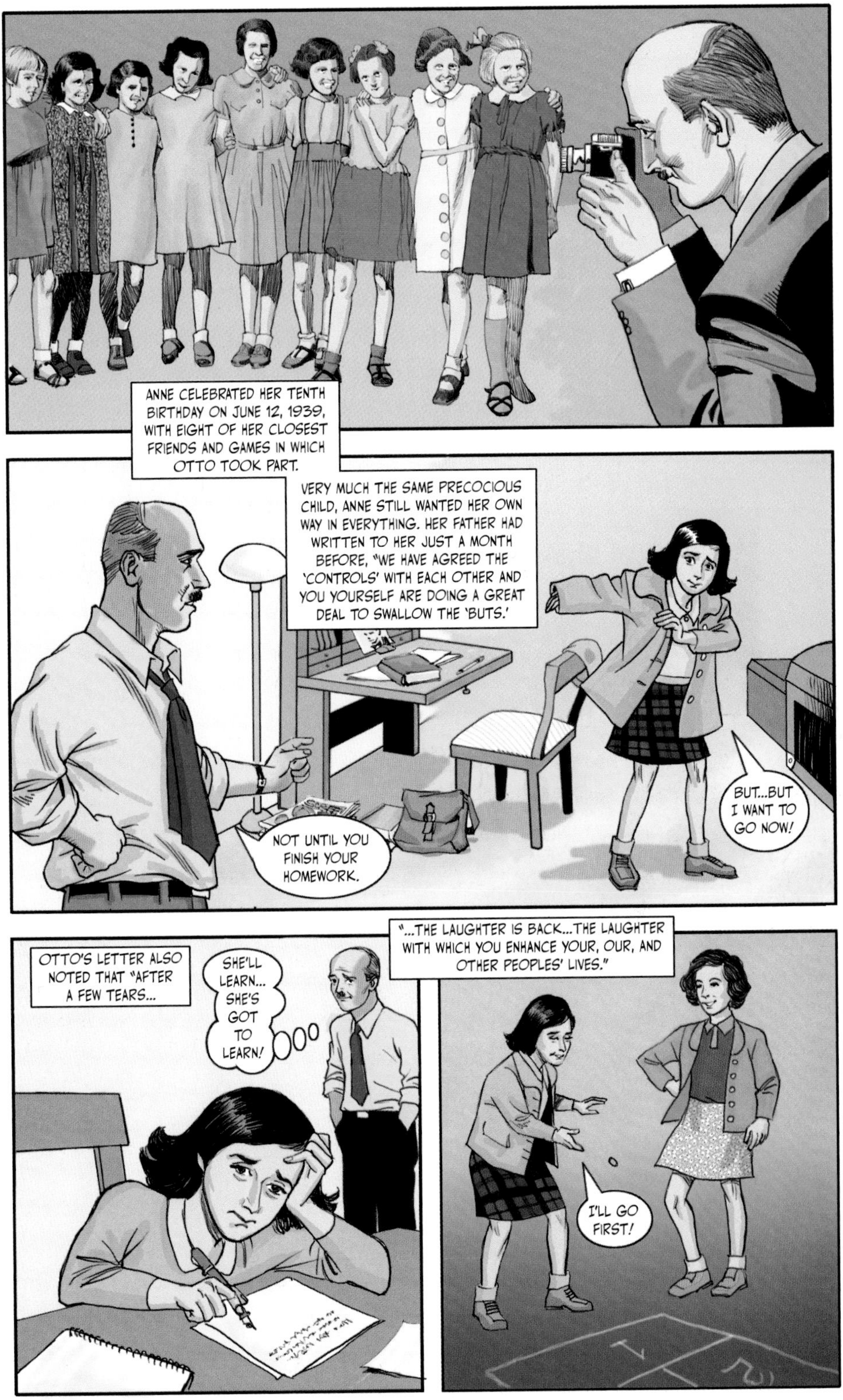
ANNE CELEBRATED HER TENTH BIRTHDAY ON JUNE 12, 1939, WITH EIGHT OF HER CLOSEST FRIENDS AND GAMES IN WHICH OTTO TOOK PART.
VERY MUCH THE SAME PRECOCIOUS CHILD, ANNE STILL WANTED HER OWN WAY IN EVERYTHING. HER FATHER HAD WRITTEN TO HER JUST A MONTH BEFORE, "WE HAVE AGREED THE 'CONTROLS' WITH EACH OTHER AND YOU YOURSELF ARE DOING A GREAT DEAL TO SWALLOW THE 'BUTS.'
NOT UNTIL YOU FINISH YOUR HOMEWORK.
BUT...BUT I WANT TO GO NOW!
OTTO'S LETTER ALSO NOTED THAT "AFTER A FEW TEARS...
SHE'LL LEARN... SHE'S GOT TO LEARN!
"...THE LAUGHTER IS BACK...THE LAUGHTER WITH WHICH YOU ENHANCE YOUR, OUR, AND OTHER PEOPLES' LIVES."
I'LL GO FIRST!

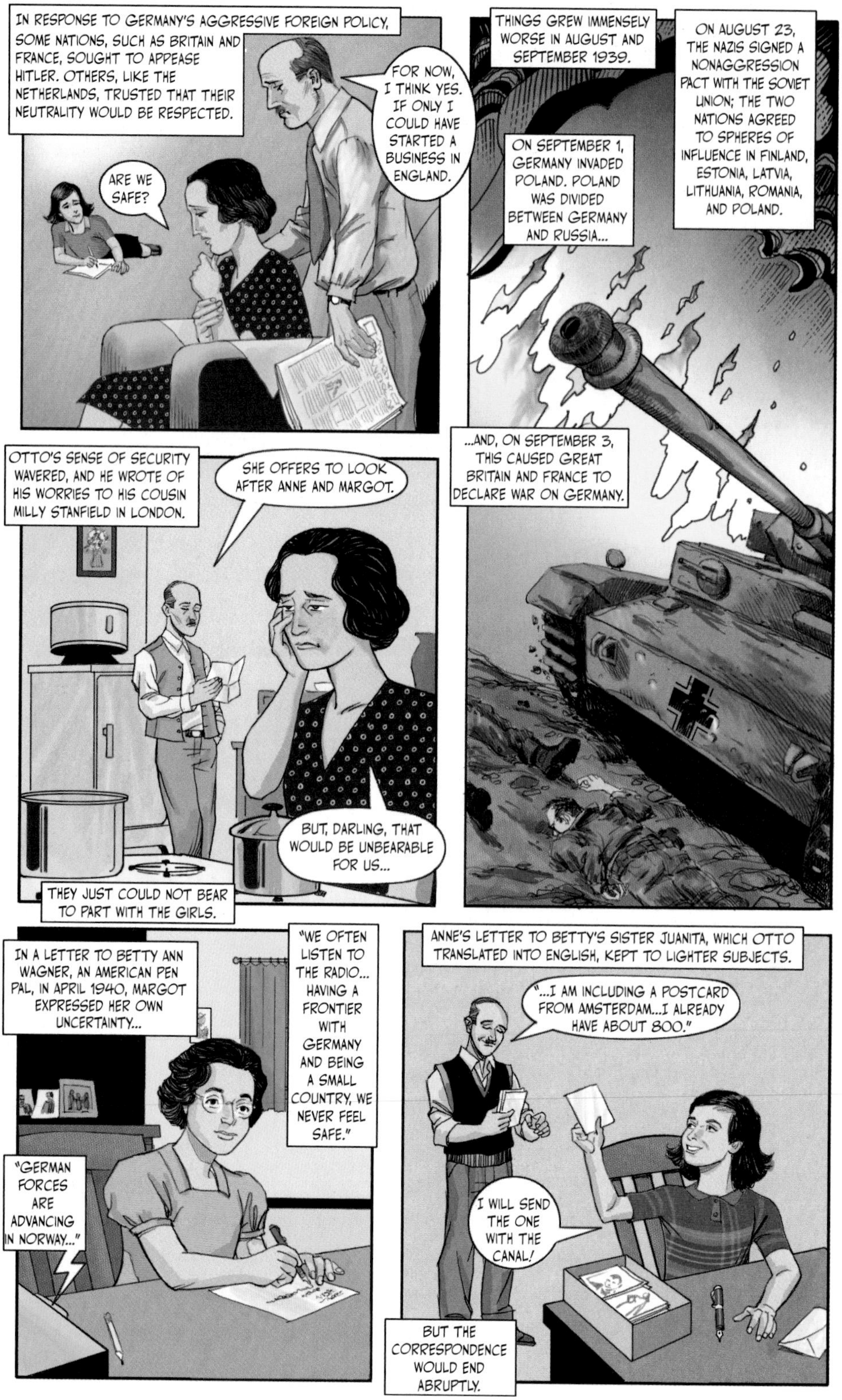
IN RESPONSE TO GERMANY'S AGGRESSIVE FOREIGN POLICY, SOME NATIONS, SUCH AS BRITAIN AND FRANCE, SOUGHT TO APPEASE HITLER. OTHERS, LIKE THE NETHERLANDS, TRUSTED THAT THEIR NEUTRALITY WOULD BE RESPECTED.
ARE WE SAFE?
FOR NOW, I THINK YES. IF ONLY I COULD HAVE STARTED A BUSINESS IN ENGLAND.
THINGS GREW IMMENSELY WORSE IN AUGUST AND SEPTEMBER 1939.
ON AUGUST 23, THE NAZIS SIGNED A NONAGGRESSION PACT WITH THE SOVIET UNION; THE TWO NATIONS AGREED TO SPHERES OF INFLUENCE IN FINLAND, ESTONIA, LATVIA, LITHUANIA, ROMANIA, AND POLAND.
ON SEPTEMBER 1, GERMANY INVADED POLAND. POLAND WAS DIVIDED BETWEEN GERMANY AND RUSSIA...
...AND, ON SEPTEMBER 3, THIS CAUSED GREAT BRITAIN AND FRANCE TO DECLARE WAR ON GERMANY.
OTTO'S SENSE OF SECURITY WAVERED, AND HE WROTE OF HIS WORRIES TO HIS COUSIN MILLY STANFIELD IN LONDON.
SHE OFFERS TO LOOK AFTER ANNE AND MARGOT.
BUT, DARLING, THAT WOULD BE UNBEARABLE FOR US...
THEY JUST COULD NOT BEAR TO PART WITH THE GIRLS.
IN A LETTER TO BETTY ANN WAGNER, AN AMERICAN PEN PAL, IN APRIL 1940, MARGOT EXPRESSED HER OWN UNCERTAINTY...
"WE OFTEN LISTEN TO THE RADIO... HAVING A FRONTIER WITH GERMANY AND BEING A SMALL COUNTRY, WE NEVER FEEL SAFE."
"GERMAN FORCES ARE ADVANCING IN NORWAY..."
ANNE'S LETTER TO BETTY'S SISTER JUANITA, WHICH OTTO TRANSLATED INTO ENGLISH, KEPT TO LIGHTER SUBJECTS.
"...I AM INCLUDING A POSTCARD FROM AMSTERDAM...I ALREADY HAVE ABOUT 800."
I WILL SEND THE ONE WITH THE CANAL!
BUT THE CORRESPONDENCE WOULD END ABRUPTLY.

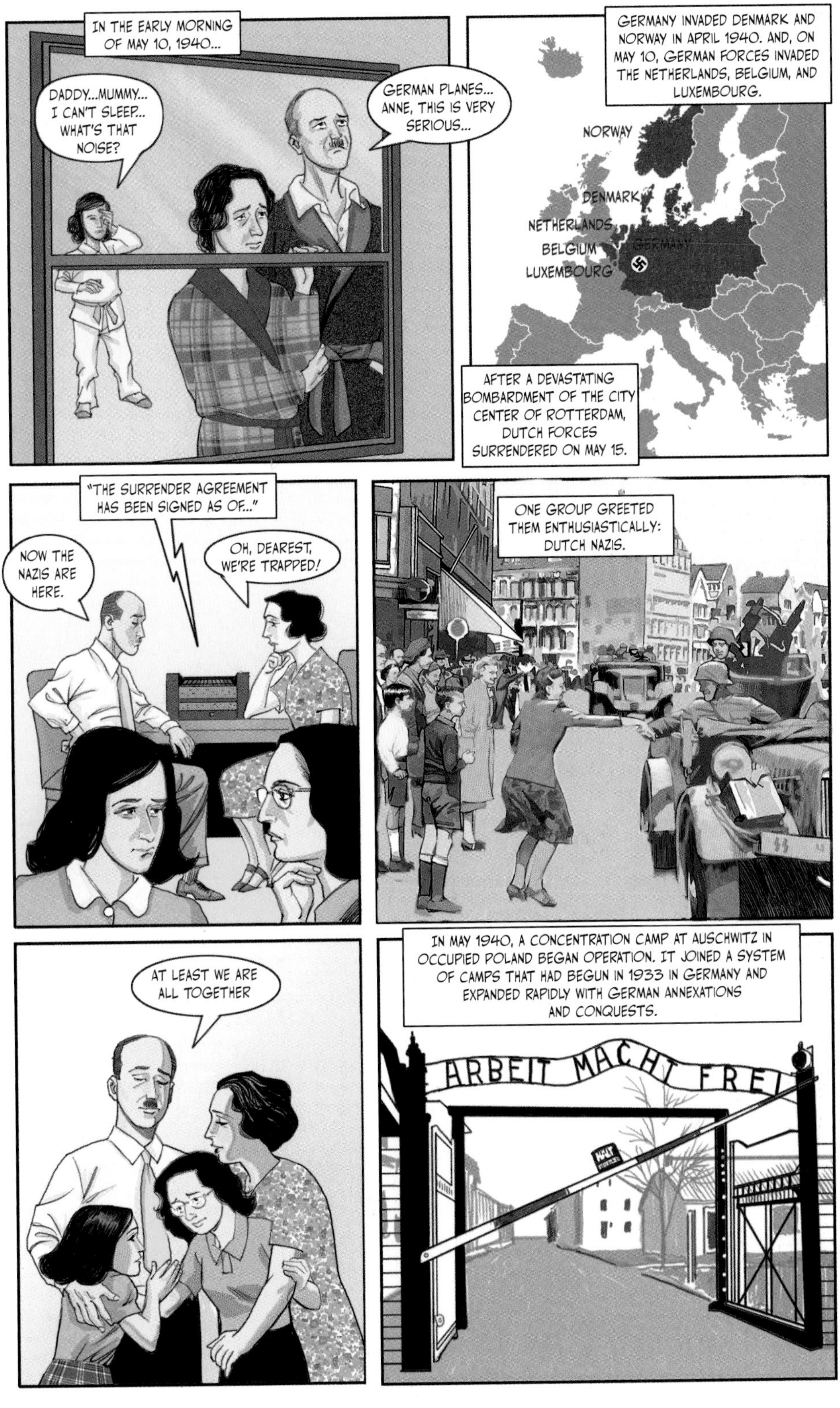
IN THE EARLY MORNING OF MAY 10, 1940...
DADDY...MUMMY... I CAN'T SLEEP... WHAT'S THAT NOISE?
GERMAN PLANES... ANNE, THIS IS VERY SERIOUS...
GERMANY INVADED DENMARK AND NORWAY IN APRIL 1940. AND, ON MAY 10, GERMAN FORCES INVADED THE NETHERLANDS, BELGIUM, AND LUXEMBOURG.
NORWAY
DENMARK
NETHERLANDS
BELGIUM
LUXEMBOURG
GERMANY
AFTER A DEVASTATING BOMBARDMENT OF THE CITY CENTER OF ROTTERDAM, DUTCH FORCES SURRENDERED ON MAY 15.
"THE SURRENDER AGREEMENT HAS BEEN SIGNED AS OF..."
NOW THE NAZIS ARE HERE.
OH, DEAREST, WE'RE TRAPPED!
ONE GROUP GREETED THEM ENTHUSIASTICALLY: DUTCH NAZIS.
AT LEAST WE ARE ALL TOGETHER
IN MAY 1940, A CONCENTRATION CAMP AT AUSCHWITZ IN OCCUPIED POLAND BEGAN OPERATION. IT JOINED A SYSTEM OF CAMPS THAT HAD BEGUN IN 1933 IN GERMANY AND EXPANDED RAPIDLY WITH GERMAN ANNEXATIONS AND CONQUESTS.
ARBEIT MACHT FREI

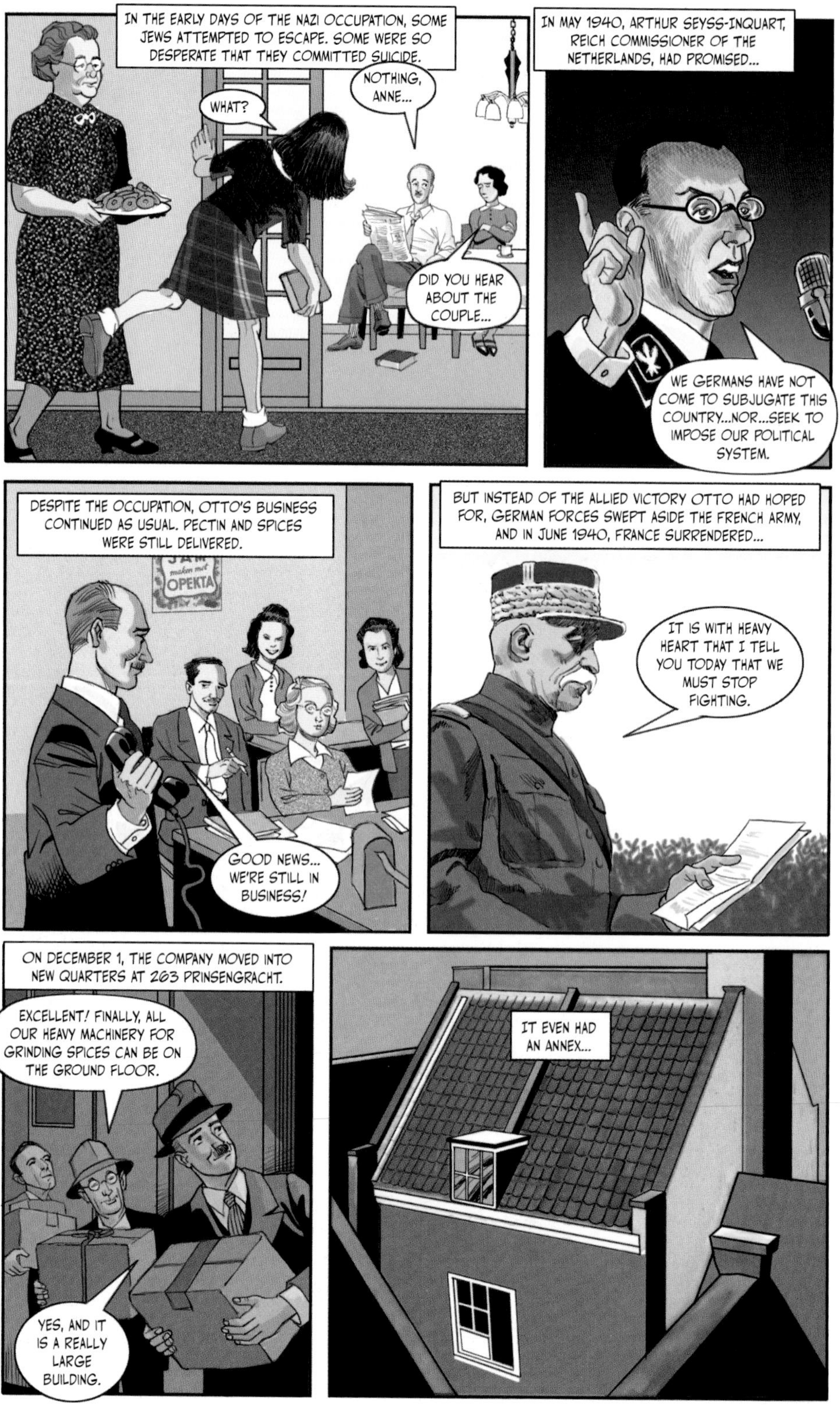
IN THE EARLY DAYS OF THE NAZI OCCUPATION, SOME JEWS ATTEMPTED TO ESCAPE. SOME WERE SO DESPERATE THAT THEY COMMITTED SUICIDE.
WHAT?
NOTHING, ANNE...
DID YOU HEAR ABOUT THE COUPLE...
IN MAY 1940, ARTHUR SEYSS-INQUART, REICH COMMISSIONER OF THE NETHERLANDS, HAD PROMISED...
WE GERMANS HAVE NOT COME TO SUBJUGATE THIS COUNTRY...NOR...SEEK TO IMPOSE OUR POLITICAL SYSTEM.
DESPITE THE OCCUPATION, OTTO'S BUSINESS CONTINUED AS USUAL. PECTIN AND SPICES WERE STILL DELIVERED.
OPEKTA
GOOD NEWS... WE'RE STILL IN BUSINESS!
BUT INSTEAD OF THE ALLIED VICTORY OTTO HAD HOPED FOR, GERMAN FORCES SWEPT ASIDE THE FRENCH ARMY, AND IN JUNE 1940, FRANCE SURRENDERED...
IT IS WITH HEAVY HEART THAT I TELL YOU TODAY THAT WE MUST STOP FIGHTING.
ON DECEMBER 1, THE COMPANY MOVED INTO NEW QUARTERS AT 263 PRINSENGRACHT.
EXCELLENT! FINALLY, ALL OUR HEAVY MACHINERY FOR GRINDING SPICES CAN BE ON THE GROUND FLOOR.
YES, AND IT IS A REALLY LARGE BUILDING.
IT EVEN HAD AN ANNEX...

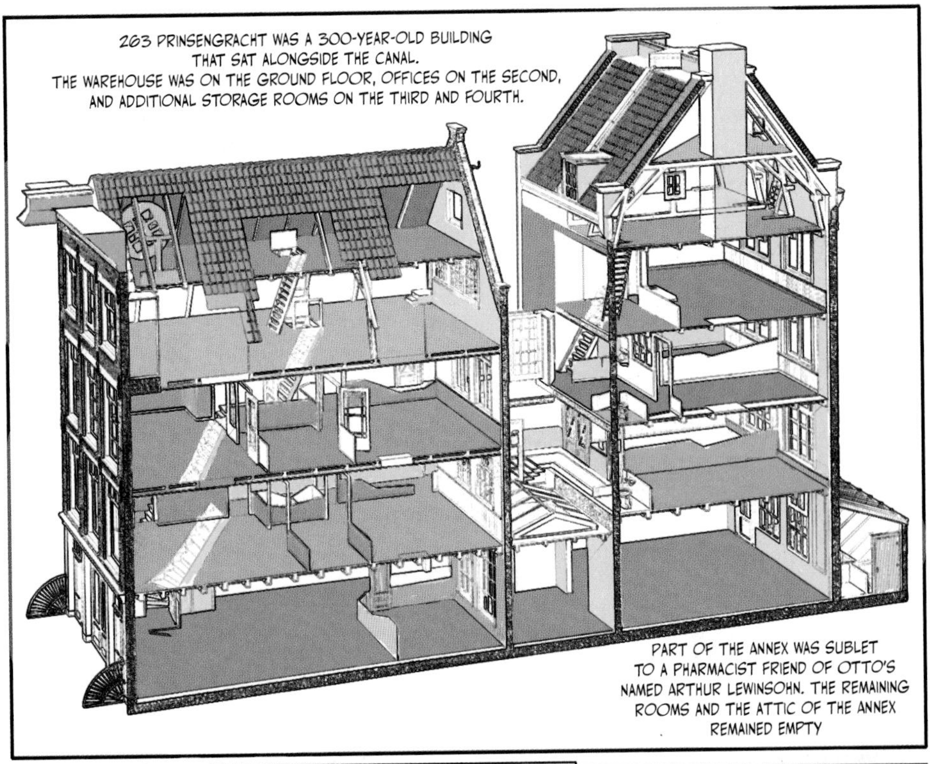
263 PRINSENGRACHT WAS A 300-YEAR-OLD BUILDING THAT SAT ALONGSIDE THE CANAL.
THE WAREHOUSE WAS ON THE GROUND FLOOR, OFFICES ON THE SECOND, AND ADDITIONAL STORAGE ROOMS ON THE THIRD AND FOURTH.
PART OF THE ANNEX WAS SUBLET TO A PHARMACIST FRIEND OF OTTO'S NAMED ARTHUR LEWINSOHN. THE REMAINING ROOMS AND THE ATTIC OF THE ANNEX REMAINED EMPTY

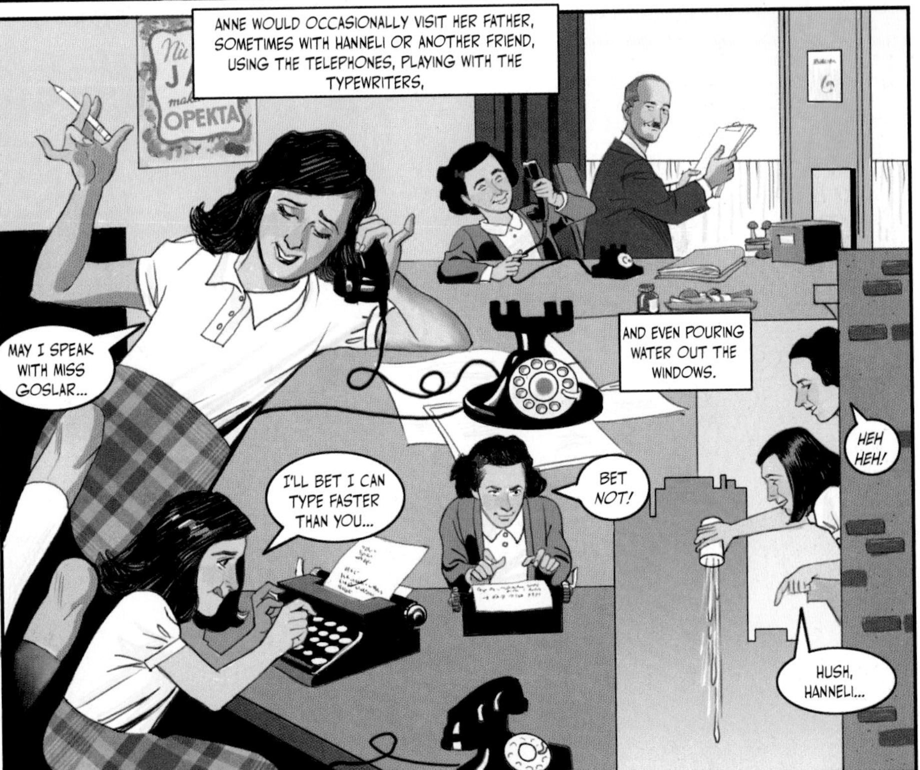
ANNE WOULD OCCASIONALLY VISIT HER FATHER, SOMETIMES WITH HANNELI OR ANOTHER FRIEND, USING THE TELEPHONES, PLAYING WITH THE TYPEWRITERS,
OPEKTA
MAY I SPEAK WITH MISS GOSLAR...
AND EVEN POURING WATER OUT THE WINDOWS.
HEH HEH!
I'LL BET I CAN TYPE FASTER THAN YOU...
BET NOT!
HUSH, HANNELI...

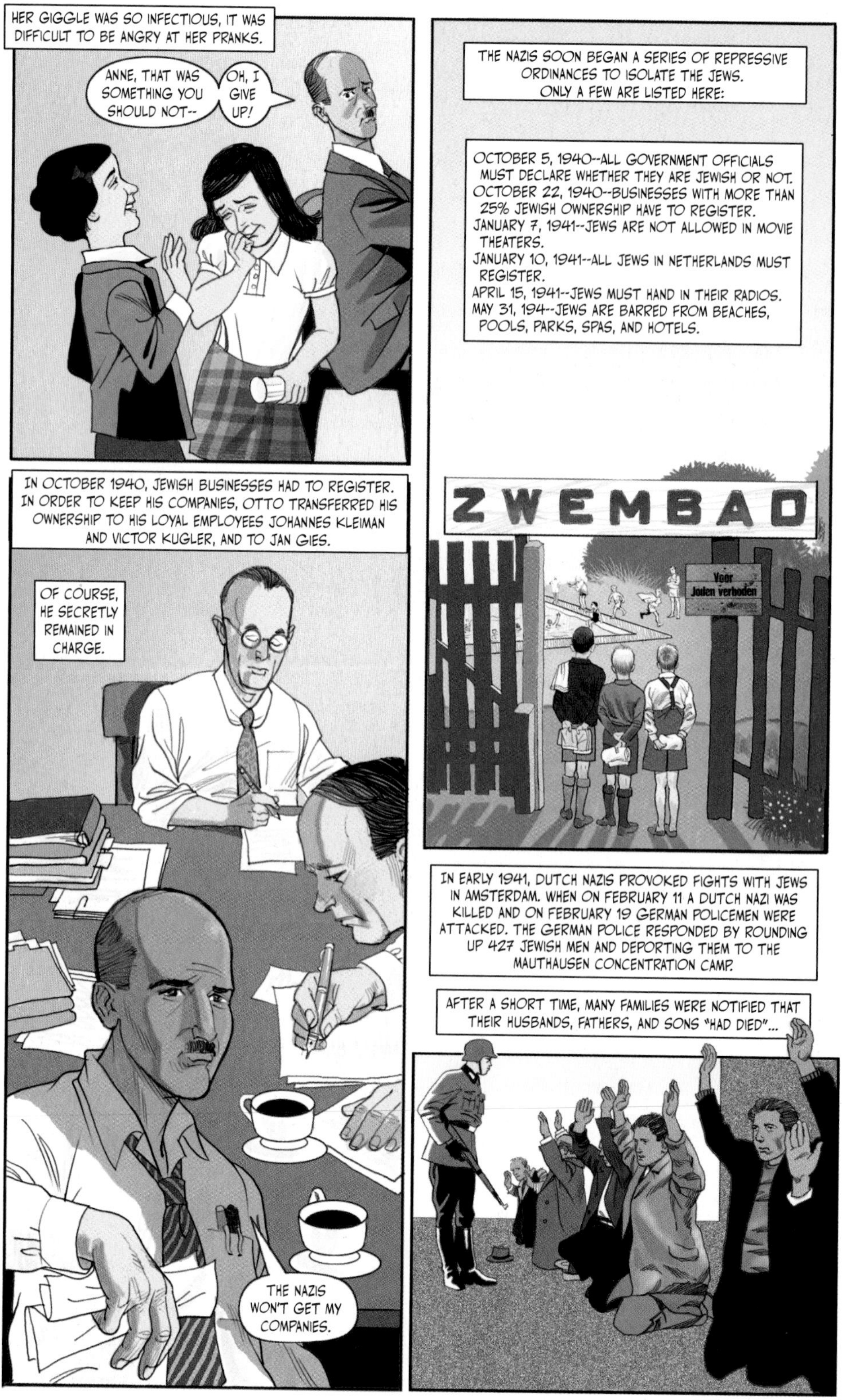
HER GIGGLE WAS SO INFECTIOUS, IT WAS DIFFICULT TO BE ANGRY AT HER PRANKS.
ANNE, THAT WAS SOMETHING YOU SHOULD NOT--
OH, I GIVE UP!
THE NAZIS SOON BEGAN A SERIES OF REPRESSIVE ORDINANCES TO ISOLATE THE JEWS. ONLY A FEW ARE LISTED HERE:
OCTOBER 5, 1940--ALL GOVERNMENT OFFICIALS MUST DECLARE WHETHER THEY ARE JEWISH OR NOT.
OCTOBER 22, 1940--BUSINESSES WITH MORE THAN 25% JEWISH OWNERSHIP HAVE TO REGISTER.
JANUARY 7, 1941--JEWS ARE NOT ALLOWED IN MOVIE THEATERS.
JANUARY 10, 1941--ALL JEWS IN NETHERLANDS MUST REGISTER.
APRIL 15, 1941--JEWS MUST HAND IN THEIR RADIOS.
MAY 31, 194--JEWS ARE BARRED FROM BEACHES, POOLS, PARKS, SPAS, AND HOTELS.
ZWEMBAD
Voor Joden verboden
IN OCTOBER 1940, JEWISH BUSINESSES HAD TO REGISTER. IN ORDER TO KEEP HIS COMPANIES, OTTO TRANSFERRED HIS OWNERSHIP TO HIS LOYAL EMPLOYEES JOHANNES KLEIMAN AND VICTOR KUGLER, AND TO JAN GIES.
OF COURSE, HE SECRETLY REMAINED IN CHARGE.
THE NAZIS WON'T GET MY COMPANIES.
IN EARLY 1941, DUTCH NAZIS PROVOKED FIGHTS WITH JEWS IN AMSTERDAM. WHEN ON FEBRUARY 11 A DUTCH NAZI WAS KILLED AND ON FEBRUARY 19 GERMAN POLICEMEN WERE ATTACKED. THE GERMAN POLICE RESPONDED BY ROUNDING UP 427 JEWISH MEN AND DEPORTING THEM TO THE MAUTHAUSEN CONCENTRATION CAMP.
AFTER A SHORT TIME, MANY FAMILIES WERE NOTIFIED THAT THEIR HUSBANDS, FATHERS, AND SONS "HAD DIED"...

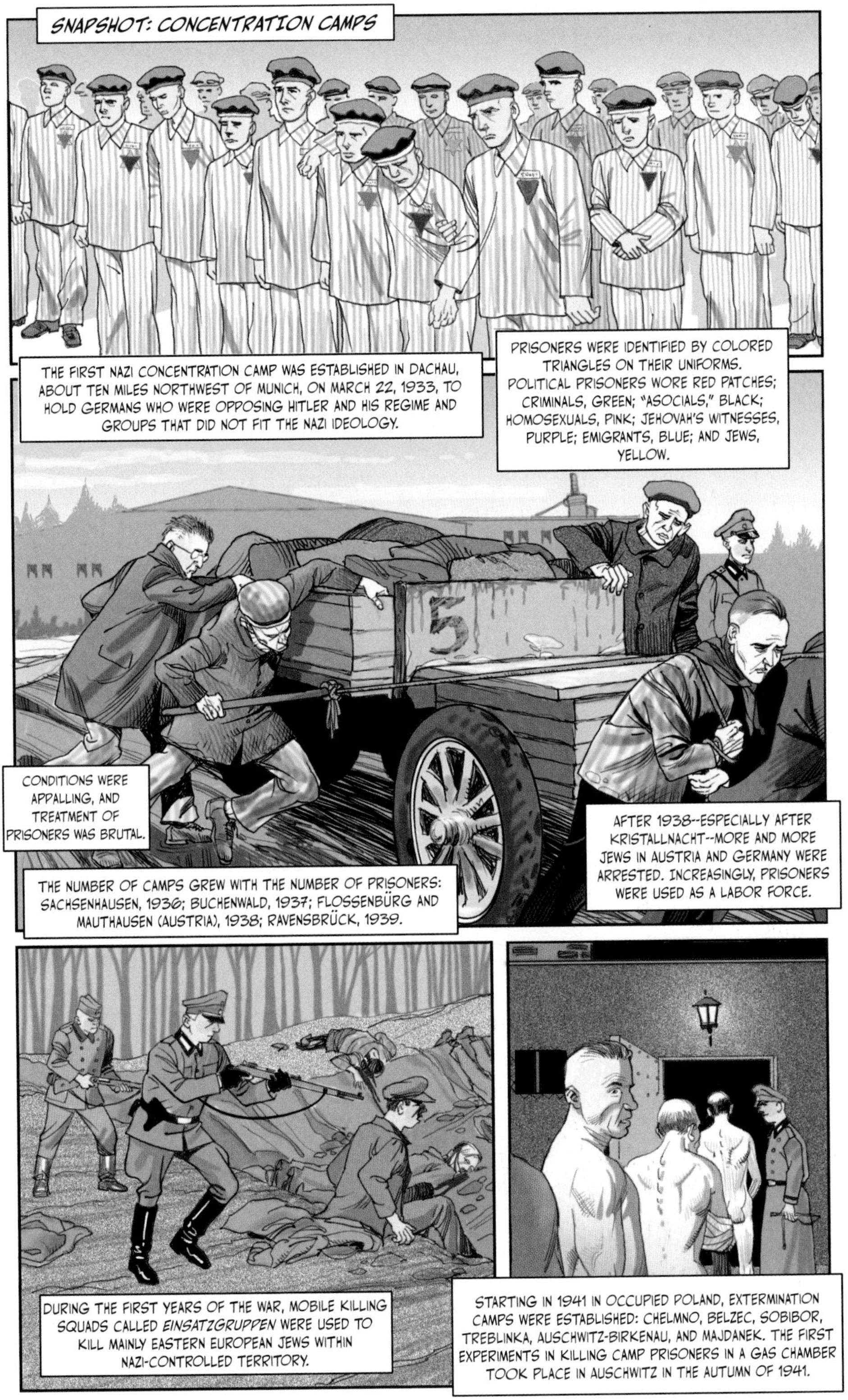
SNAPSHOT: CONCENTRATION CAMPS
THE FIRST NAZI CONCENTRATION CAMP WAS ESTABLISHED IN DACHAU, ABOUT TEN MILES NORTHWEST OF MUNICH, ON MARCH 22, 1933, TO HOLD GERMANS WHO WERE OPPOSING HITLER AND HIS REGIME AND GROUPS THAT DID NOT FIT THE NAZI IDEOLOGY.
PRISONERS WERE IDENTIFIED BY COLORED TRIANGLES ON THEIR UNIFORMS. POLITICAL PRISONERS WORE RED PATCHES; CRIMINALS, GREEN; "ASOCIALS," BLACK; HOMOSEXUALS, PINK; JEHOVAH'S WITNESSES, PURPLE; EMIGRANTS, BLUE; AND JEWS, YELLOW.
5
CONDITIONS WERE APPALLING, AND TREATMENT OF PRISONERS WAS BRUTAL.
AFTER 1938--ESPECIALLY AFTER KRISTALLNACHT--MORE AND MORE JEWS IN AUSTRIA AND GERMANY WERE ARRESTED. INCREASINGLY, PRISONERS WERE USED AS A LABOR FORCE.
THE NUMBER OF CAMPS GREW WITH THE NUMBER OF PRISONERS: SACHSENHAUSEN, 1936; BUCHENWALD, 1937; FLOSSENBÜRG AND MAUTHAUSEN (AUSTRIA), 1938; RAVENSBRÜCK, 1939.
DURING THE FIRST YEARS OF THE WAR, MOBILE KILLING SQUADS CALLED *EINSATZGRUPPEN* WERE USED TO KILL MAINLY EASTERN EUROPEAN JEWS WITHIN NAZI-CONTROLLED TERRITORY.
STARTING IN 1941 IN OCCUPIED POLAND, EXTERMINATION CAMPS WERE ESTABLISHED: CHELMNO, BELZEC, SOBIBOR, TREBLINKA, AUSCHWITZ-BIRKENAU, AND MAJDANEK. THE FIRST EXPERIMENTS IN KILLING CAMP PRISONERS IN A GAS CHAMBER TOOK PLACE IN AUSCHWITZ IN THE AUTUMN OF 1941.

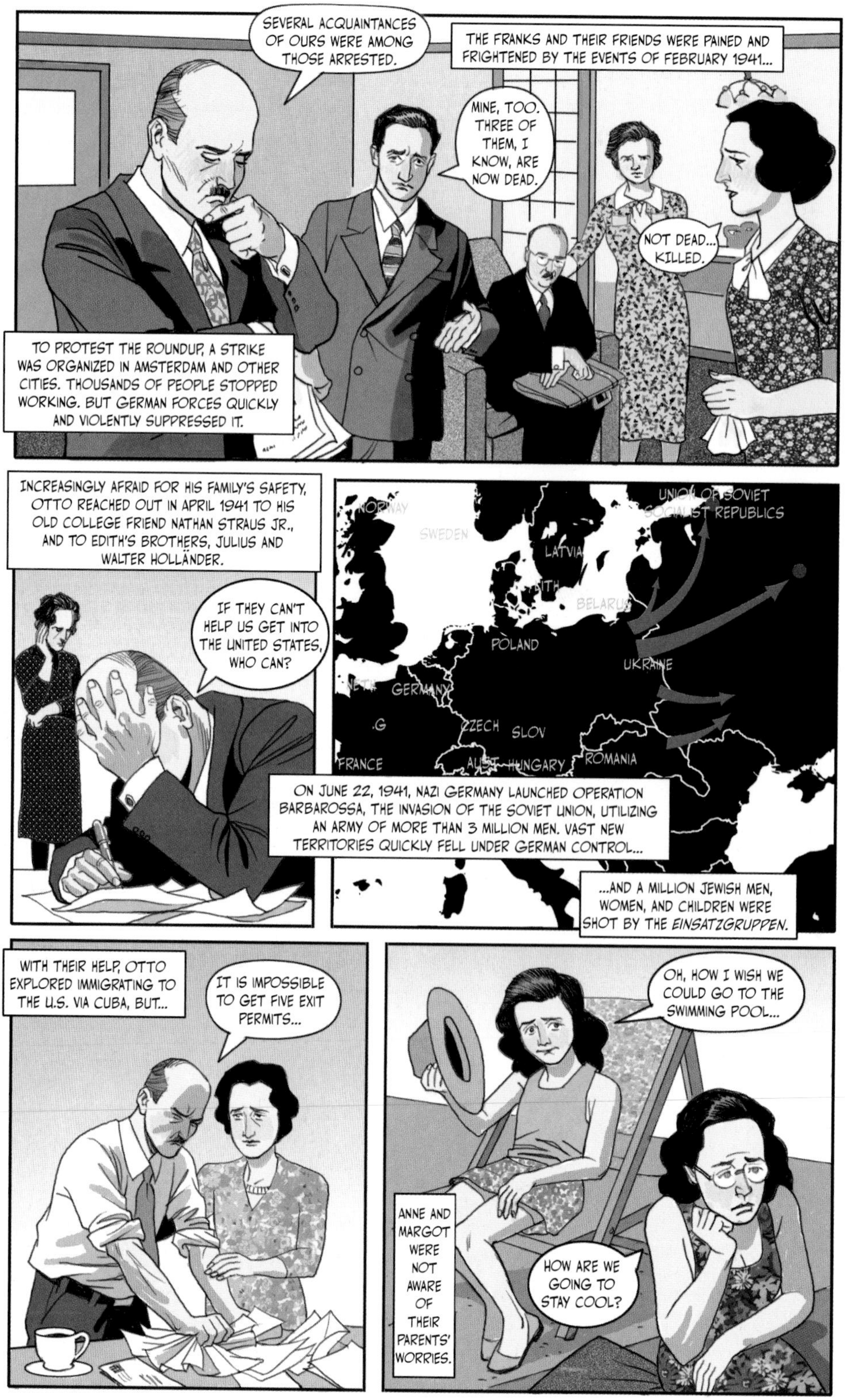
SEVERAL ACQUAINTANCES OF OURS WERE AMONG THOSE ARRESTED.
THE FRANKS AND THEIR FRIENDS WERE PAINED AND FRIGHTENED BY THE EVENTS OF FEBRUARY 1941...
MINE, TOO. THREE OF THEM, I KNOW, ARE NOW DEAD.
NOT DEAD... KILLED.
TO PROTEST THE ROUNDUP, A STRIKE WAS ORGANIZED IN AMSTERDAM AND OTHER CITIES. THOUSANDS OF PEOPLE STOPPED WORKING. BUT GERMAN FORCES QUICKLY AND VIOLENTLY SUPPRESSED IT.
INCREASINGLY AFRAID FOR HIS FAMILY'S SAFETY, OTTO REACHED OUT IN APRIL 1941 TO HIS OLD COLLEGE FRIEND NATHAN STRAUS JR., AND TO EDITH'S BROTHERS, JULIUS AND WALTER HOLLÄNDER.
IF THEY CAN'T HELP US GET INTO THE UNITED STATES, WHO CAN?
NORWAY
SWEDEN
UNION OF SOVIET SOCIALIST REPUBLICS
LATVIA
BELARUS
POLAND
UKRAINE
GERMANY
CZECH
SLOV
FRANCE
HUNGARY
ROMANIA
ON JUNE 22, 1941, NAZI GERMANY LAUNCHED OPERATION BARBAROSSA, THE INVASION OF THE SOVIET UNION, UTILIZING AN ARMY OF MORE THAN 3 MILLION MEN. VAST NEW TERRITORIES QUICKLY FELL UNDER GERMAN CONTROL...
...AND A MILLION JEWISH MEN, WOMEN, AND CHILDREN WERE SHOT BY THE *EINSATZGRUPPEN*.
WITH THEIR HELP, OTTO EXPLORED IMMIGRATING TO THE U.S. VIA CUBA, BUT...
IT IS IMPOSSIBLE TO GET FIVE EXIT PERMITS...
OH, HOW I WISH WE COULD GO TO THE SWIMMING POOL...
ANNE AND MARGOT WERE NOT AWARE OF THEIR PARENTS' WORRIES.
HOW ARE WE GOING TO STAY COOL?

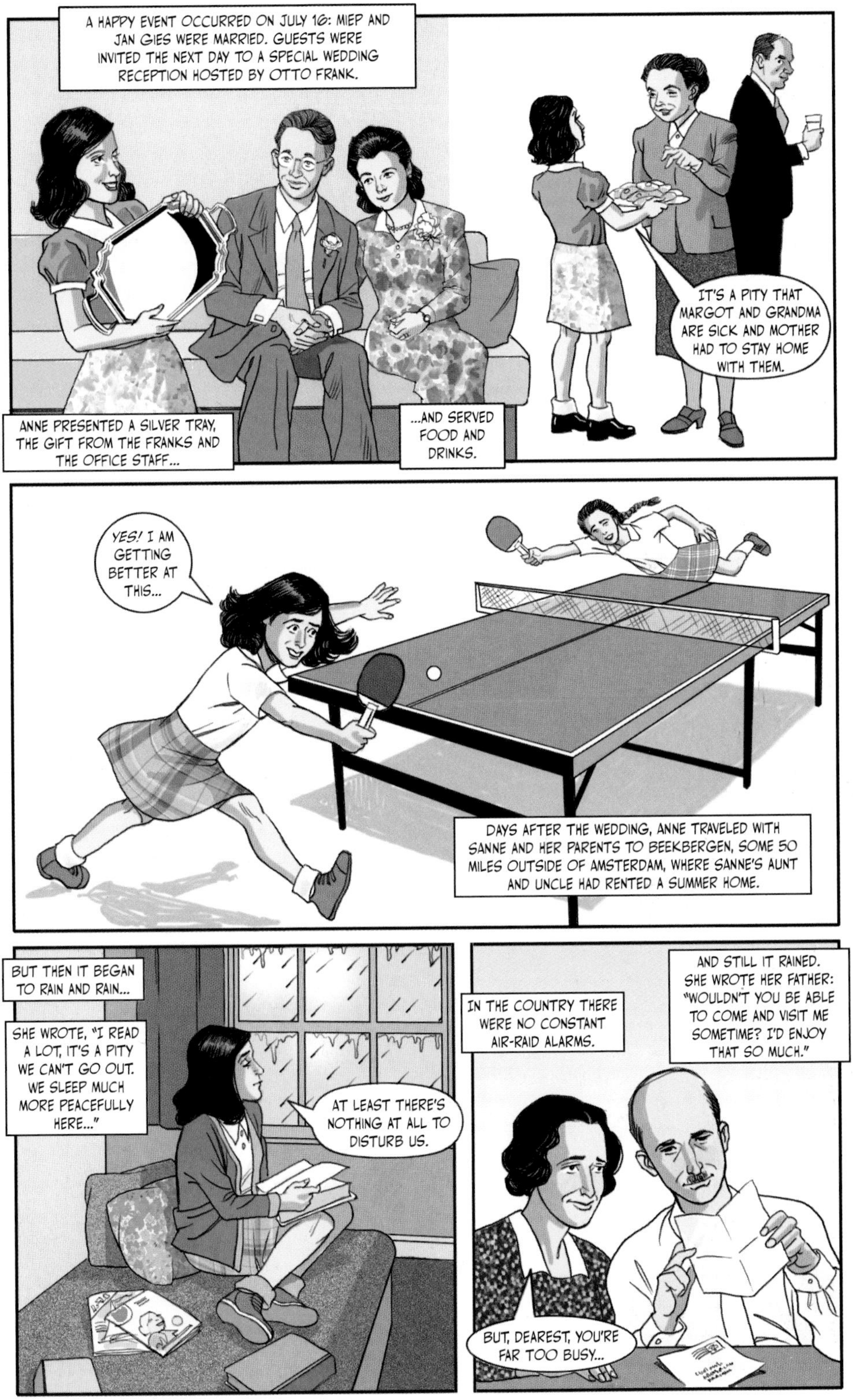
A HAPPY EVENT OCCURRED ON JULY 16: MIEP AND JAN GIES WERE MARRIED. GUESTS WERE INVITED THE NEXT DAY TO A SPECIAL WEDDING RECEPTION HOSTED BY OTTO FRANK.
ANNE PRESENTED A SILVER TRAY, THE GIFT FROM THE FRANKS AND THE OFFICE STAFF...
...AND SERVED FOOD AND DRINKS.
IT'S A PITY THAT MARGOT AND GRANDMA ARE SICK AND MOTHER HAD TO STAY HOME WITH THEM.
YES! I AM GETTING BETTER AT THIS...
DAYS AFTER THE WEDDING, ANNE TRAVELED WITH SANNE AND HER PARENTS TO BEEKBERGEN, SOME 50 MILES OUTSIDE OF AMSTERDAM, WHERE SANNE'S AUNT AND UNCLE HAD RENTED A SUMMER HOME.
BUT THEN IT BEGAN TO RAIN AND RAIN...
SHE WROTE, "I READ A LOT, IT'S A PITY WE CAN'T GO OUT. WE SLEEP MUCH MORE PEACEFULLY HERE..."
AT LEAST THERE'S NOTHING AT ALL TO DISTURB US.
IN THE COUNTRY THERE WERE NO CONSTANT AIR-RAID ALARMS.
AND STILL IT RAINED. SHE WROTE HER FATHER: "WOULDN'T YOU BE ABLE TO COME AND VISIT ME SOMETIME? I'D ENJOY THAT SO MUCH."
BUT, DEAREST, YOU'RE FAR TOO BUSY...

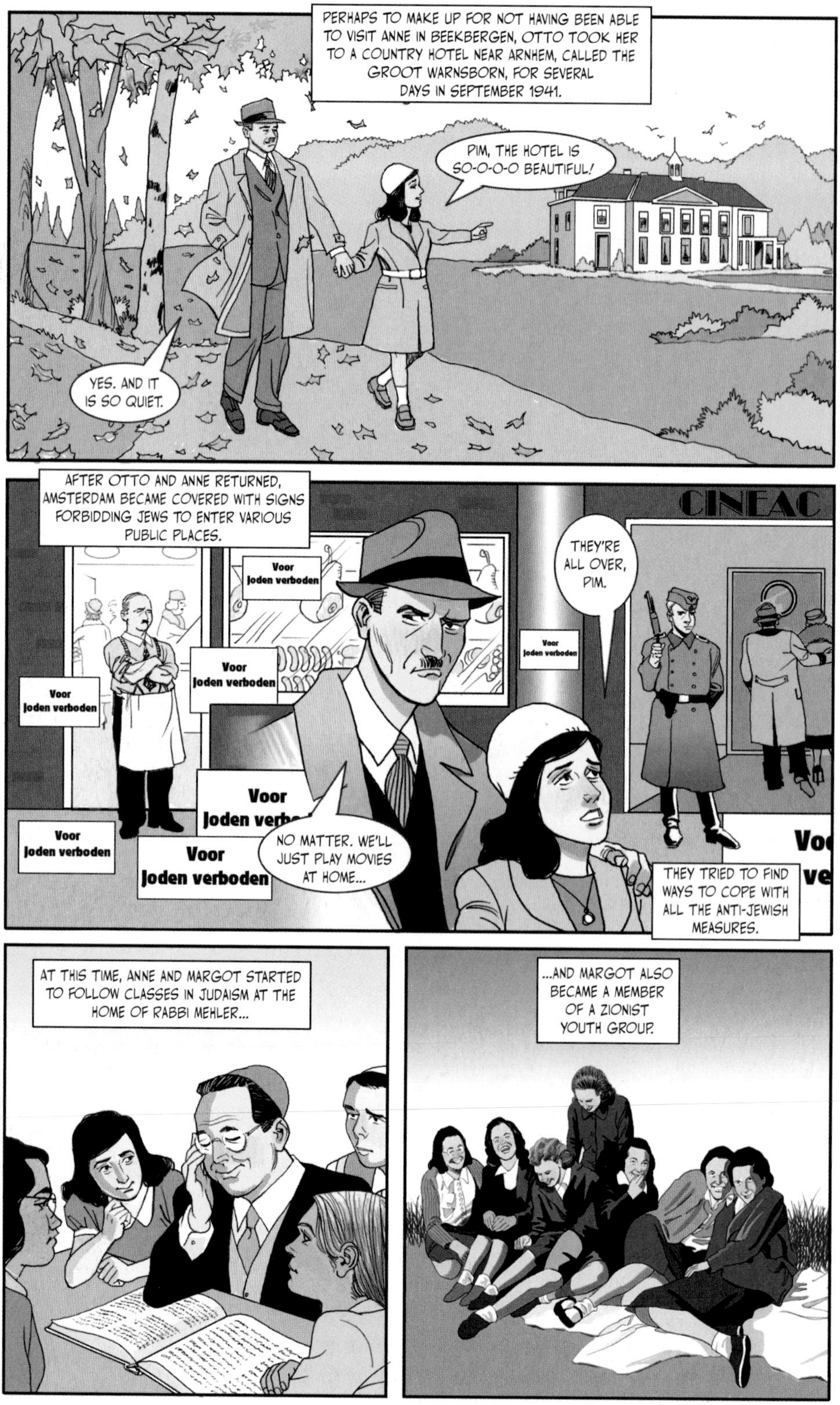
PERHAPS TO MAKE UP FOR NOT HAVING BEEN ABLE TO VISIT ANNE IN BEEKBERGEN, OTTO TOOK HER TO A COUNTRY HOTEL NEAR ARNHEM, CALLED THE GROOT WARNSBORN, FOR SEVERAL DAYS IN SEPTEMBER 1941.
PIM, THE HOTEL IS SO-O-O-O BEAUTIFUL!
YES. AND IT IS SO QUIET.
AFTER OTTO AND ANNE RETURNED, AMSTERDAM BECAME COVERED WITH SIGNS FORBIDDING JEWS TO ENTER VARIOUS PUBLIC PLACES.
CINEAC
Voor Joden verboden
Voor Joden verboden
Voor Joden verboden
Voor Joden verboden
Voor Joden verboden
Voor Joden verboden
THEY'RE ALL OVER, PIM.
NO MATTER. WE'LL JUST PLAY MOVIES AT HOME...
THEY TRIED TO FIND WAYS TO COPE WITH ALL THE ANTI-JEWISH MEASURES.
AT THIS TIME, ANNE AND MARGOT STARTED TO FOLLOW CLASSES IN JUDAISM AT THE HOME OF RABBI MEHLER...
...AND MARGOT ALSO BECAME A MEMBER OF A ZIONIST YOUTH GROUP.

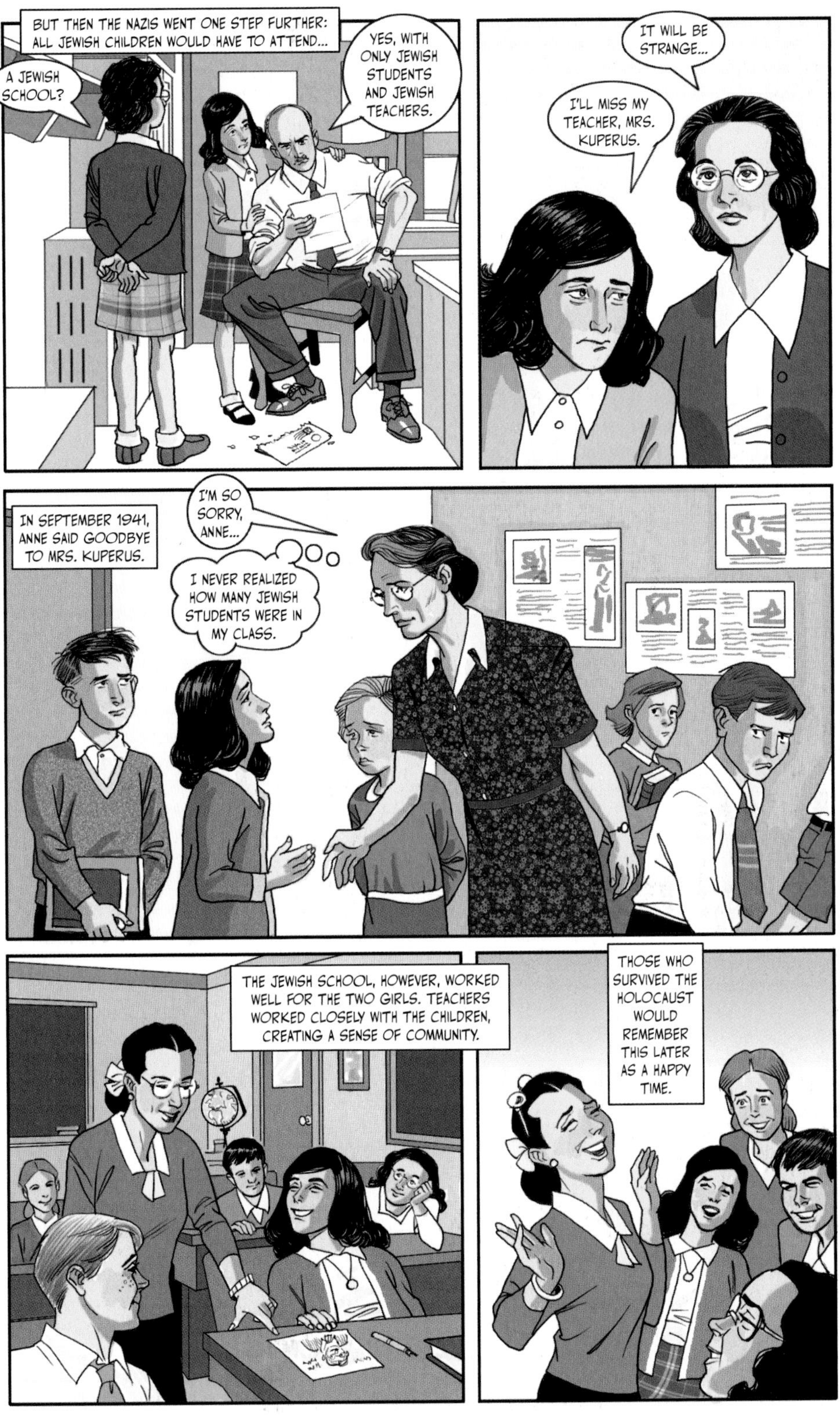
BUT THEN THE NAZIS WENT ONE STEP FURTHER: ALL JEWISH CHILDREN WOULD HAVE TO ATTEND...
A JEWISH SCHOOL?
YES, WITH ONLY JEWISH STUDENTS AND JEWISH TEACHERS.
IT WILL BE STRANGE...
I'LL MISS MY TEACHER, MRS. KUPERUS.
IN SEPTEMBER 1941, ANNE SAID GOODBYE TO MRS. KUPERUS.
I'M SO SORRY, ANNE...
I NEVER REALIZED HOW MANY JEWISH STUDENTS WERE IN MY CLASS.
THE JEWISH SCHOOL, HOWEVER, WORKED WELL FOR THE TWO GIRLS. TEACHERS WORKED CLOSELY WITH THE CHILDREN, CREATING A SENSE OF COMMUNITY.
THOSE WHO SURVIVED THE HOLOCAUST WOULD REMEMBER THIS LATER AS A HAPPY TIME.

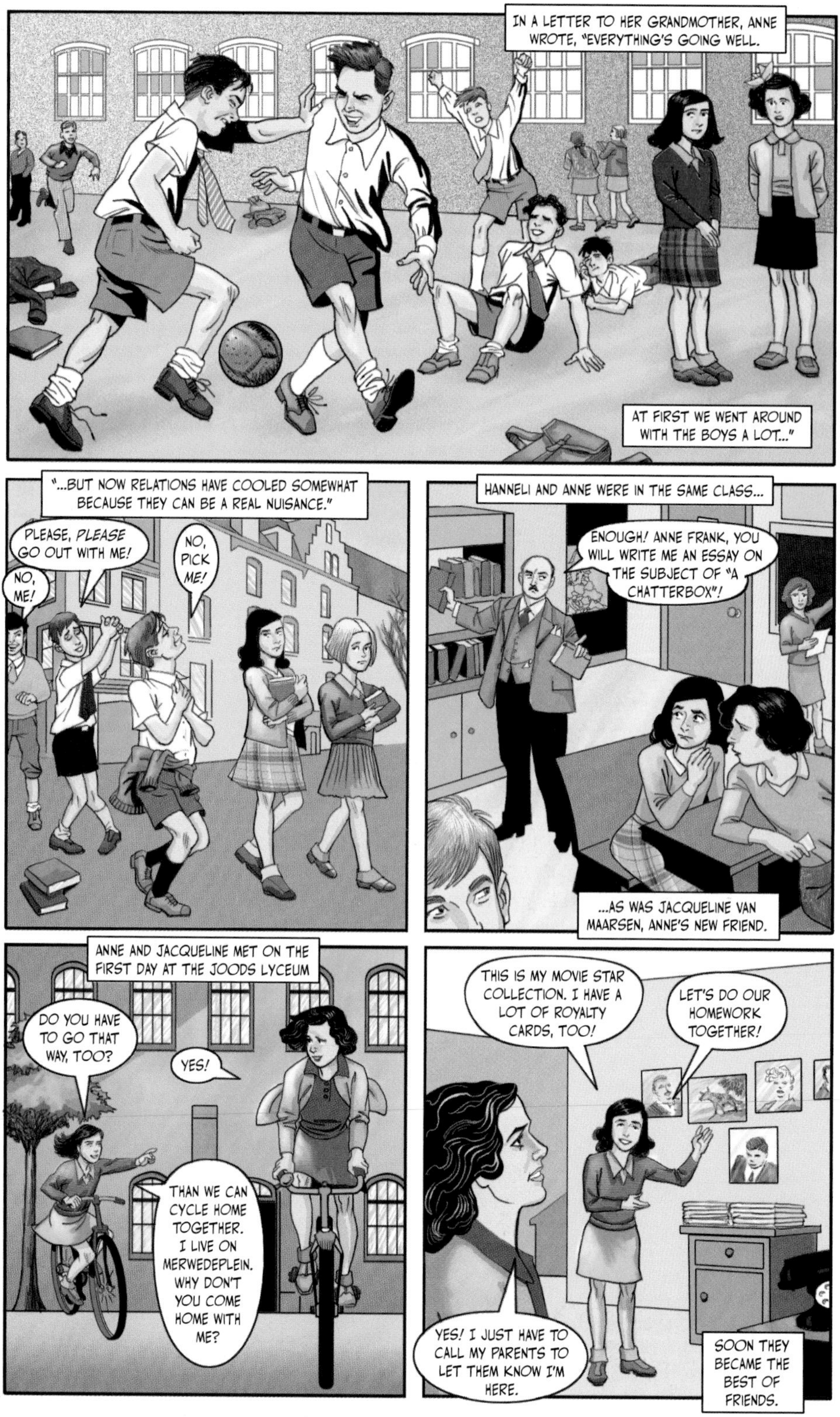
IN A LETTER TO HER GRANDMOTHER, ANNE WROTE, "EVERYTHING'S GOING WELL.
AT FIRST WE WENT AROUND WITH THE BOYS A LOT..."
"...BUT NOW RELATIONS HAVE COOLED SOMEWHAT BECAUSE THEY CAN BE A REAL NUISANCE."
PLEASE, *PLEASE* GO OUT WITH ME!
NO, ME!
NO, PICK ME!
HANNELI AND ANNE WERE IN THE SAME CLASS...
ENOUGH! ANNE FRANK, YOU WILL WRITE ME AN ESSAY ON THE SUBJECT OF "A CHATTERBOX"!
...AS WAS JACQUELINE VAN MAARSEN, ANNE'S NEW FRIEND.
ANNE AND JACQUELINE MET ON THE FIRST DAY AT THE JOODS LYCEUM
DO YOU HAVE TO GO THAT WAY, TOO?
YES!
THAN WE CAN CYCLE HOME TOGETHER. I LIVE ON MERWEDEPLEIN. WHY DON'T YOU COME HOME WITH ME?
THIS IS MY MOVIE STAR COLLECTION. I HAVE A LOT OF ROYALTY CARDS, TOO!
LET'S DO OUR HOMEWORK TOGETHER!
YES! I JUST HAVE TO CALL MY PARENTS TO LET THEM KNOW I'M HERE.
SOON THEY BECAME THE BEST OF FRIENDS.

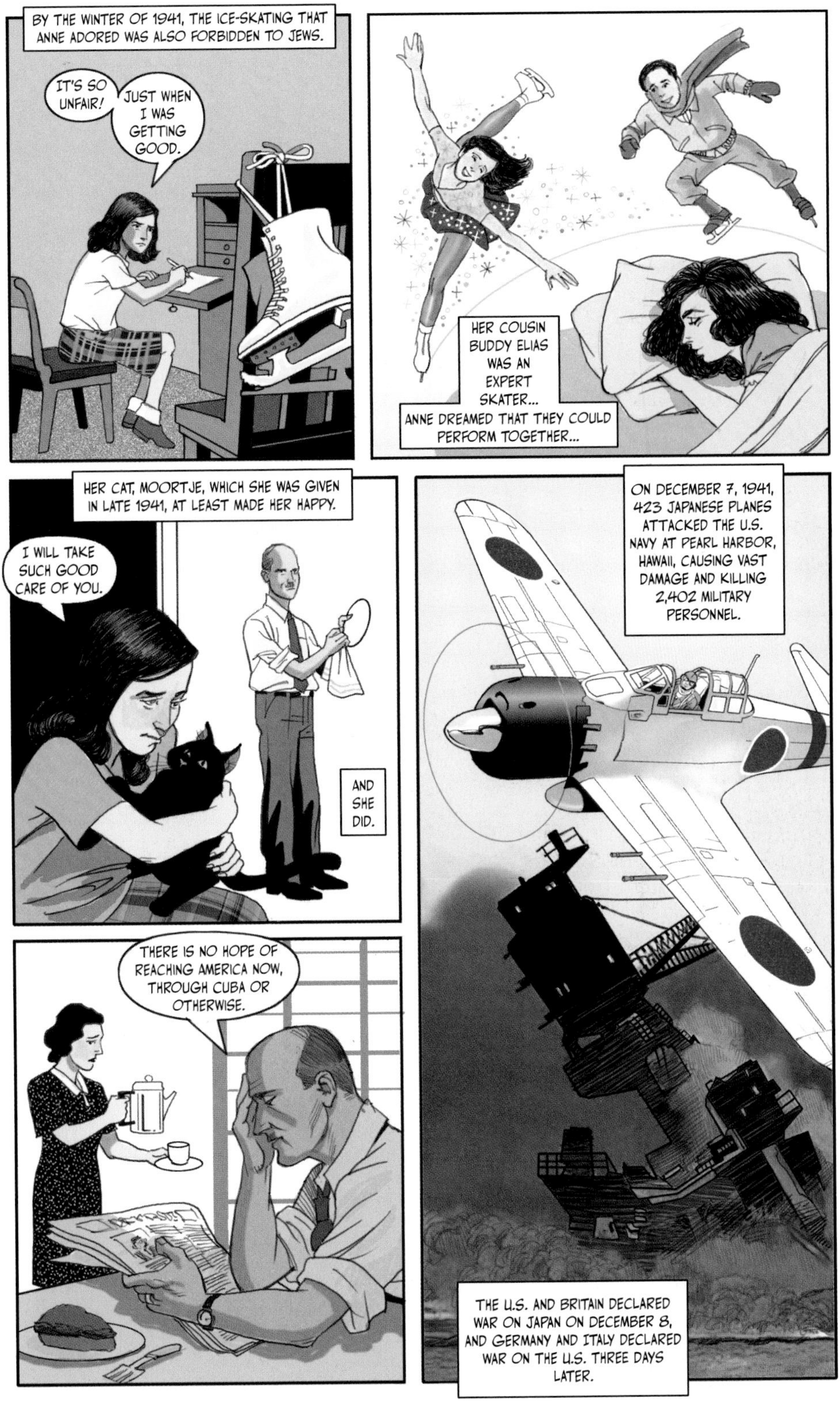

BY THE WINTER OF 1941, THE ICE-SKATING THAT ANNE ADORED WAS ALSO FORBIDDEN TO JEWS.
IT'S SO UNFAIR!
JUST WHEN I WAS GETTING GOOD.
HER COUSIN BUDDY ELIAS WAS AN EXPERT SKATER...
ANNE DREAMED THAT THEY COULD PERFORM TOGETHER...
HER CAT, MOORTJE, WHICH SHE WAS GIVEN IN LATE 1941, AT LEAST MADE HER HAPPY.
I WILL TAKE SUCH GOOD CARE OF YOU.
AND SHE DID.
THERE IS NO HOPE OF REACHING AMERICA NOW, THROUGH CUBA OR OTHERWISE.
ON DECEMBER 7, 1941, 423 JAPANESE PLANES ATTACKED THE U.S. NAVY AT PEARL HARBOR, HAWAII, CAUSING VAST DAMAGE AND KILLING 2,402 MILITARY PERSONNEL.
THE U.S. AND BRITAIN DECLARED WAR ON JAPAN ON DECEMBER 8, AND GERMANY AND ITALY DECLARED WAR ON THE U.S. THREE DAYS LATER.

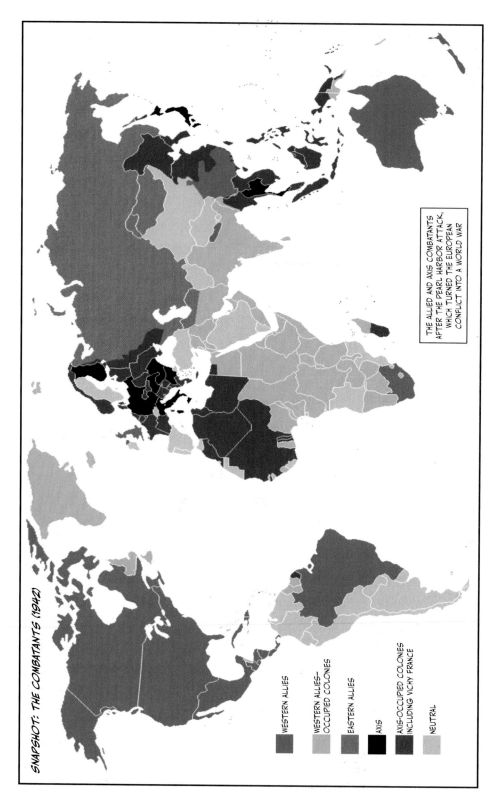

SNAPSHOT: THE COMBATANTS (1942)

THE ALLIED AND AXIS COMBATANTS
AFTER THE PEARL HARBOR ATTACK,
WHICH TURNED THE EUROPEAN
CONFLICT INTO A WORLD WAR

WESTERN ALLIES

WESTERN ALLIES-
OCCUPIED COLONIES

EASTERN ALLIES

AXIS

AXIS-OCCUPIED COLONIES
INCLUDING VICHY FRANCE

NEUTRAL

SNAPSHOT: THE WANNSEE CONFERENCE

HITLER AND THE NAZIS REGARDED THE JEWS AS THEIR GREATEST ENEMY. IN THE SECOND HALF OF 1941, HITLER HAD DECIDED TO KILL ALL THE JEWS OF EUROPE. A SECRET MEETING TO DISCUSS THIS WAS PLANNED, BUT HAD TO BE POSTPONED BECAUSE OF PEARL HARBOR. ON JANUARY 20, 1942, THE MEETING OF 15 HIGH-RANKING CIVIL SERVANTS AND SS OFFICERS WAS HELD IN A VILLA NEAR THE WANNSEE LAKE IN BERLIN. THE MEETING PLANNED THE "FINAL SOLUTION" TO THE SO-CALLED JEWISH QUESTION. THIS "WANNSEE CONFERENCE," CONVENED AND LED BY REINHARD HEYDRICH, THEN CHIEF OF THE NAZI SECURITY POLICE AND SECRET SERVICE, LASTED ABOUT AN HOUR AND A HALF.

ADOLF EICHMANN, A GESTAPO HEAD AND ONE OF THE ATTENDEES, HAD DRAFTED A LIST OF THE NUMBER OF JEWS IN VARIOUS EUROPEAN COUNTRIES THAT THEY EXPECTED TO DEAL WITH. THERE WAS A TOTAL OF 11 MILLION, WITH THE LARGEST NUMBERS IN THE U.S.S.R., POLAND, AND HUNGARY.

	Protektorat Böhmen und Mähren	74.200
	Estland — judenfrei —	
	Lettland	3.500
	Litauen	34.000
	Belgien	43.000
	Dänemark	5.600
	Frankreich / Besetztes Gebiet	165.000
	Unbesetztes Gebiet	700.000
	Griechenland	69.600
	Niederlande	160.800
	Norwegen	1.300
B.	Bulgarien	48.000
	England	330.000
	Finnland	2.300
	Irland	4.000
	Italien einschl. Sardinien	58.000
	Albanien	200
	Kroatien	40.000
	Portugal	3.000
	Rumänien einschl. Bessarabien	342.000
	Schweden	8.000
	Schweiz	18.000
	Serbien	10.000
	Slowakei	88.000
	Spanien	6.000
	Türkei (europ. Teil)	55.500
	Ungarn	742.800
	UdSSR	5.000.000
	Ukraine 2.994.684	
	Weißrußland aus- schl. Bialystok 446.484	
	Zusammen: über	11.000.000

K210405

372829

HEYDRICH OPENED THE MEETING WITH THE ANNOUNCEMENT THAT REICH MARSHAL HERMANN GÖRING HAD PUT HIM IN CHARGE OF PREPARATIONS FOR THE FINAL SOLUTION TO THE JEWISH QUESTION.
HE DECLARED: "UNDER PROPER GUIDANCE, IN THE COURSE OF THE FINAL SOLUTION, THE JEWS ARE TO BE ALLOCATED FOR APPROPRIATE LABOR IN THE EAST..."
"...IN THE COURSE OF WHICH ACTION DOUBTLESS A LARGE PORTION WILL BE ELIMINATED BY NATURAL CAUSES."
HE THEN ADDED: "THE POSSIBLE FINAL REMNANT WILL...HAVE TO BE TREATED ACCORDINGLY BECAUSE IT...WOULD, IF RELEASED, ACT AS THE SEED OF A NEW JEWISH REVIVAL."

SPEAKING ABOUT THE CONFERENCE IN 1960, ADOLF EICHMANN SAID: "I REMEMBER AT THE END OF THIS WANNSEE CONFERENCE, HEYDRICH, MÜLLER, AND MYSELF SETTLED DOWN COMFORTABLY BY THE FIREPLACE..."

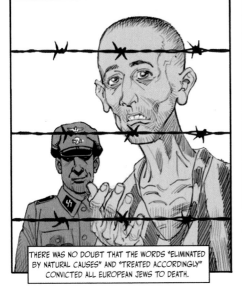

THERE WAS NO DOUBT THAT THE WORDS "ELIMINATED BY NATURAL CAUSES" AND "TREATED ACCORDINGLY" CONVICTED ALL EUROPEAN JEWS TO DEATH.

"...WE WERE SITTING TOGETHER PEACEFULLY, AND NOT IN ORDER TO TALK SHOP BUT IN ORDER TO RELAX AFTER THE LONG HOURS OF STRAIN."

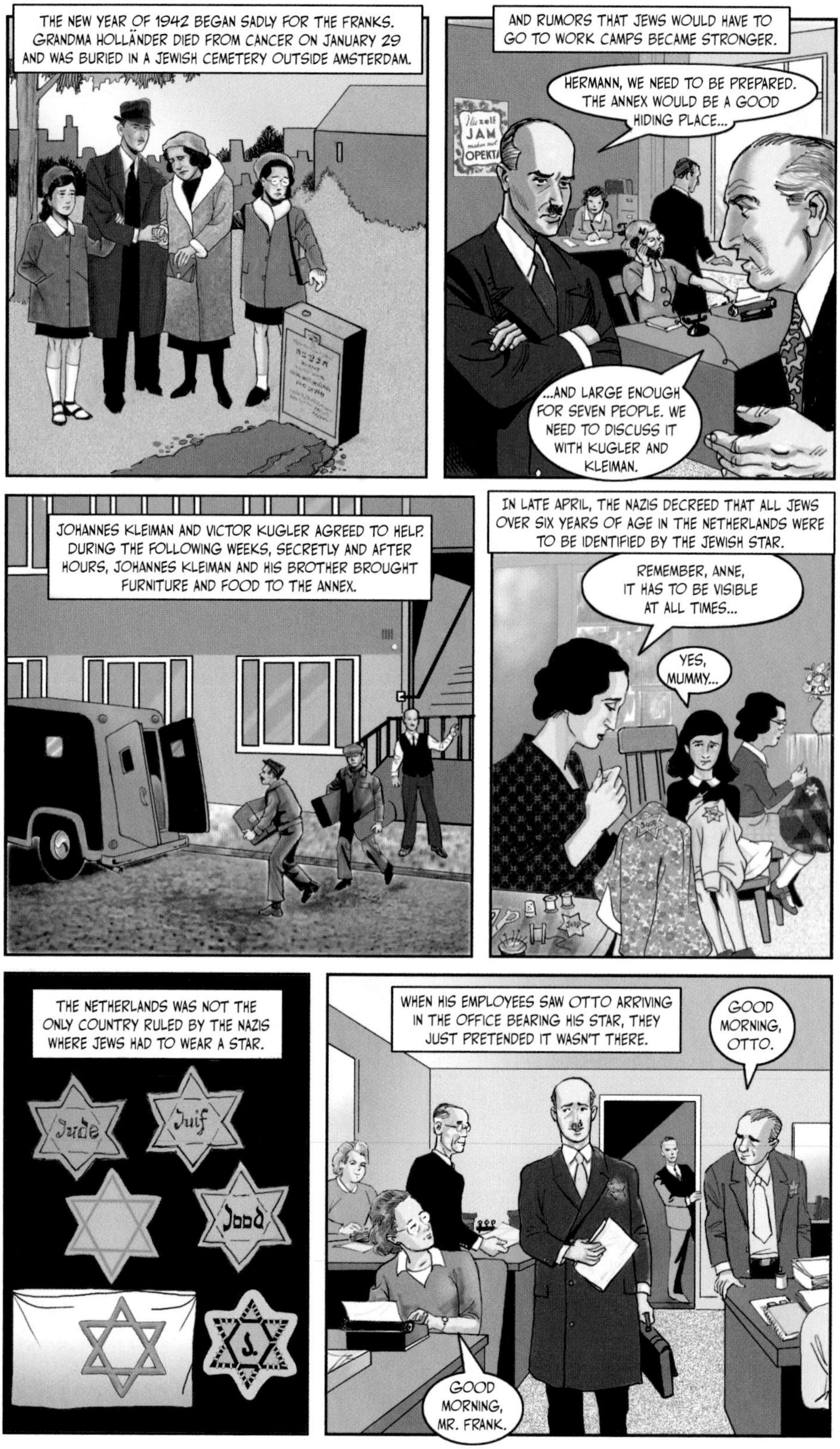
THE NEW YEAR OF 1942 BEGAN SADLY FOR THE FRANKS. GRANDMA HOLLÄNDER DIED FROM CANCER ON JANUARY 29 AND WAS BURIED IN A JEWISH CEMETERY OUTSIDE AMSTERDAM.
AND RUMORS THAT JEWS WOULD HAVE TO GO TO WORK CAMPS BECAME STRONGER.
HERMANN, WE NEED TO BE PREPARED. THE ANNEX WOULD BE A GOOD HIDING PLACE...
...AND LARGE ENOUGH FOR SEVEN PEOPLE. WE NEED TO DISCUSS IT WITH KUGLER AND KLEIMAN.
JAM
OPEKTA
JOHANNES KLEIMAN AND VICTOR KUGLER AGREED TO HELP. DURING THE FOLLOWING WEEKS, SECRETLY AND AFTER HOURS, JOHANNES KLEIMAN AND HIS BROTHER BROUGHT FURNITURE AND FOOD TO THE ANNEX.
IN LATE APRIL, THE NAZIS DECREED THAT ALL JEWS OVER SIX YEARS OF AGE IN THE NETHERLANDS WERE TO BE IDENTIFIED BY THE JEWISH STAR.
REMEMBER, ANNE, IT HAS TO BE VISIBLE AT ALL TIMES...
YES, MUMMY...
THE NETHERLANDS WAS NOT THE ONLY COUNTRY RULED BY THE NAZIS WHERE JEWS HAD TO WEAR A STAR.
Jude
Juif
Jood
J.
WHEN HIS EMPLOYEES SAW OTTO ARRIVING IN THE OFFICE BEARING HIS STAR, THEY JUST PRETENDED IT WASN'T THERE.
GOOD MORNING, OTTO.
GOOD MORNING, MR. FRANK.

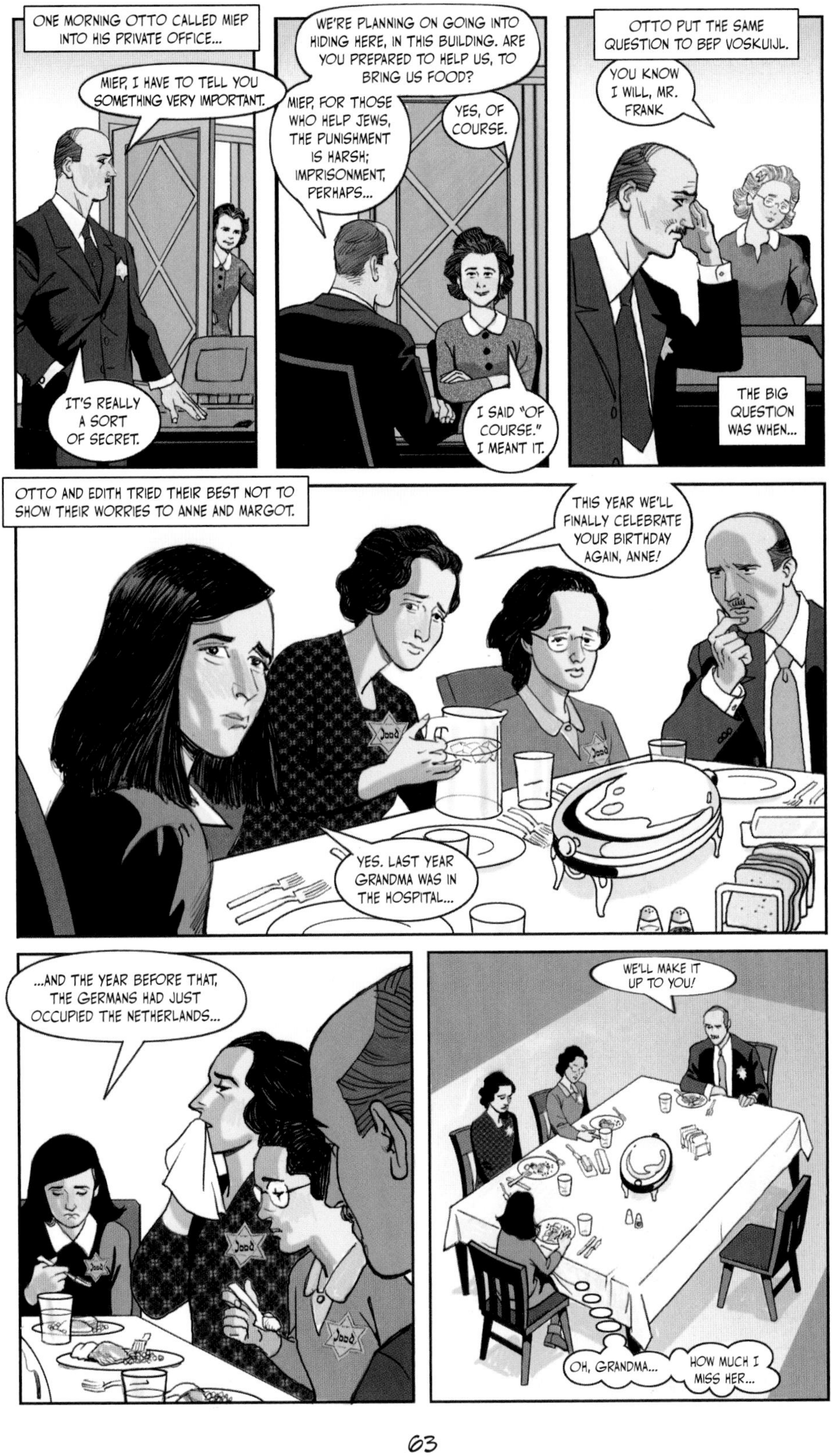
ONE MORNING OTTO CALLED MIEP INTO HIS PRIVATE OFFICE...
MIEP, I HAVE TO TELL YOU SOMETHING VERY IMPORTANT.
IT'S REALLY A SORT OF SECRET.
WE'RE PLANNING ON GOING INTO HIDING HERE, IN THIS BUILDING. ARE YOU PREPARED TO HELP US, TO BRING US FOOD?
MIEP, FOR THOSE WHO HELP JEWS, THE PUNISHMENT IS HARSH; IMPRISONMENT, PERHAPS...
YES, OF COURSE.
I SAID "OF COURSE." I MEANT IT.
OTTO PUT THE SAME QUESTION TO BEP VOSKUIJL.
YOU KNOW I WILL, MR. FRANK
THE BIG QUESTION WAS WHEN...
OTTO AND EDITH TRIED THEIR BEST NOT TO SHOW THEIR WORRIES TO ANNE AND MARGOT.
THIS YEAR WE'LL FINALLY CELEBRATE YOUR BIRTHDAY AGAIN, ANNE!
YES. LAST YEAR GRANDMA WAS IN THE HOSPITAL...
...AND THE YEAR BEFORE THAT, THE GERMANS HAD JUST OCCUPIED THE NETHERLANDS...
WE'LL MAKE IT UP TO YOU!
OH, GRANDMA...
HOW MUCH I MISS HER...

CHAPTER 6

The Diary

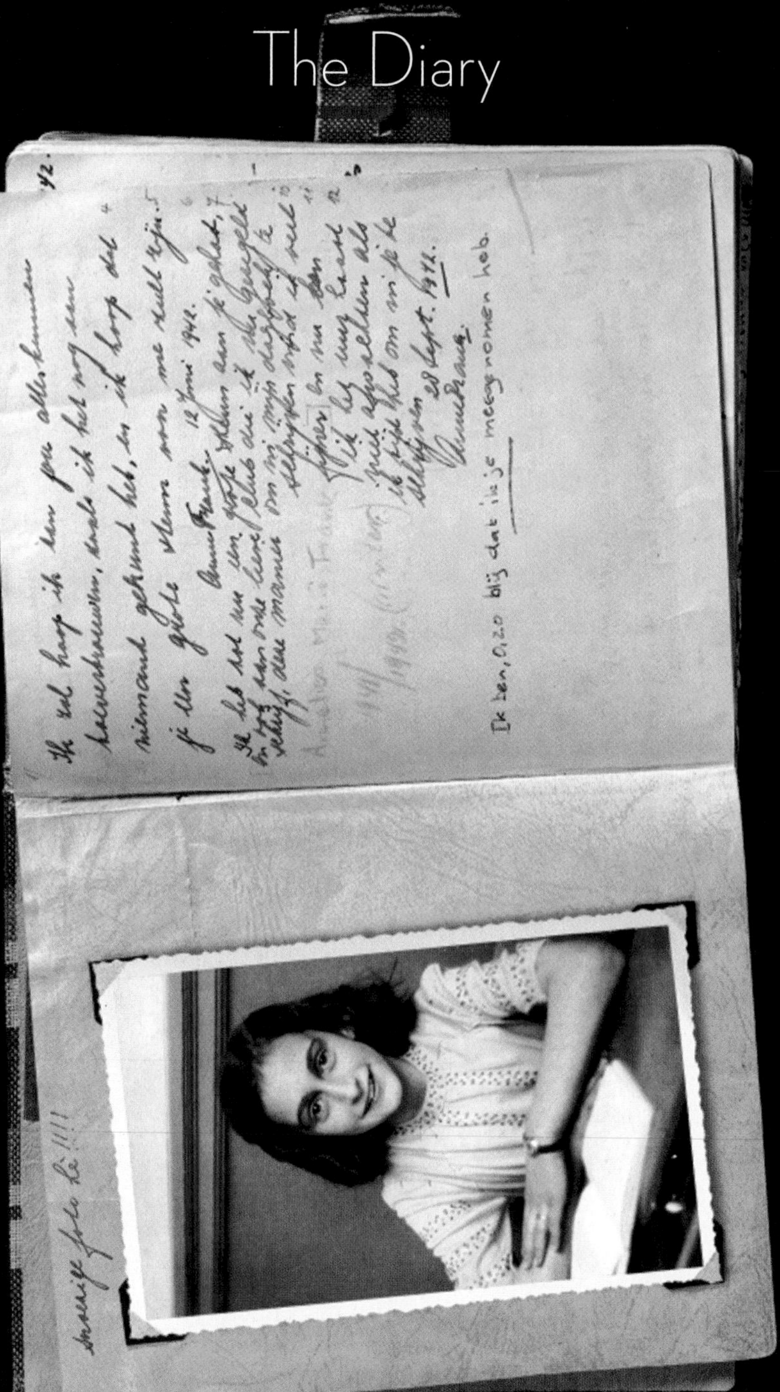

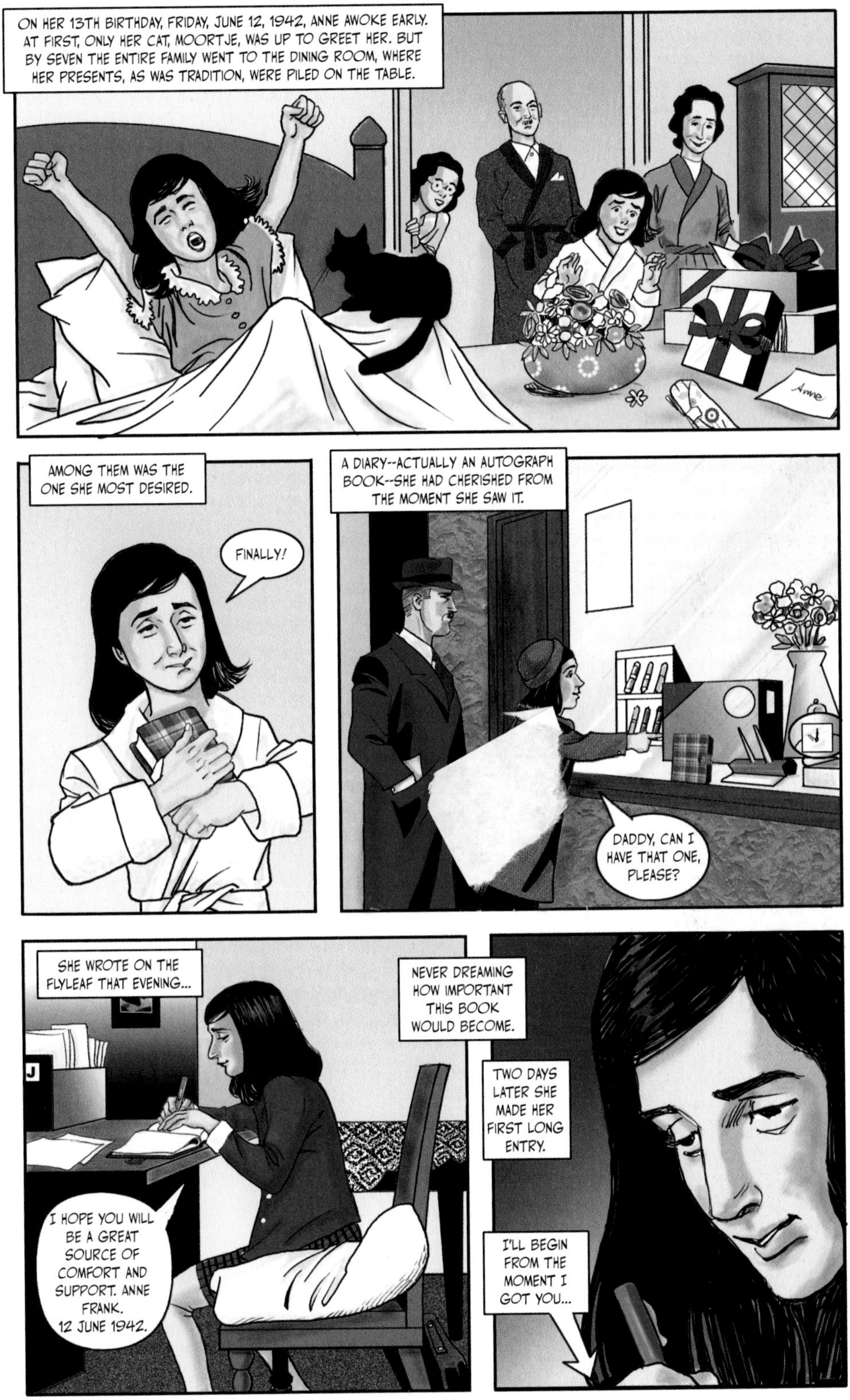
ON HER 13TH BIRTHDAY, FRIDAY, JUNE 12, 1942, ANNE AWOKE EARLY. AT FIRST, ONLY HER CAT, MOORTJE, WAS UP TO GREET HER. BUT BY SEVEN THE ENTIRE FAMILY WENT TO THE DINING ROOM, WHERE HER PRESENTS, AS WAS TRADITION, WERE PILED ON THE TABLE.
Anne
AMONG THEM WAS THE ONE SHE MOST DESIRED.
FINALLY!
A DIARY--ACTUALLY AN AUTOGRAPH BOOK--SHE HAD CHERISHED FROM THE MOMENT SHE SAW IT.
DADDY, CAN I HAVE THAT ONE, PLEASE?
SHE WROTE ON THE FLYLEAF THAT EVENING...
J
I HOPE YOU WILL BE A GREAT SOURCE OF COMFORT AND SUPPORT. ANNE FRANK. 12 JUNE 1942.
NEVER DREAMING HOW IMPORTANT THIS BOOK WOULD BECOME.
TWO DAYS LATER SHE MADE HER FIRST LONG ENTRY.
I'LL BEGIN FROM THE MOMENT I GOT YOU...

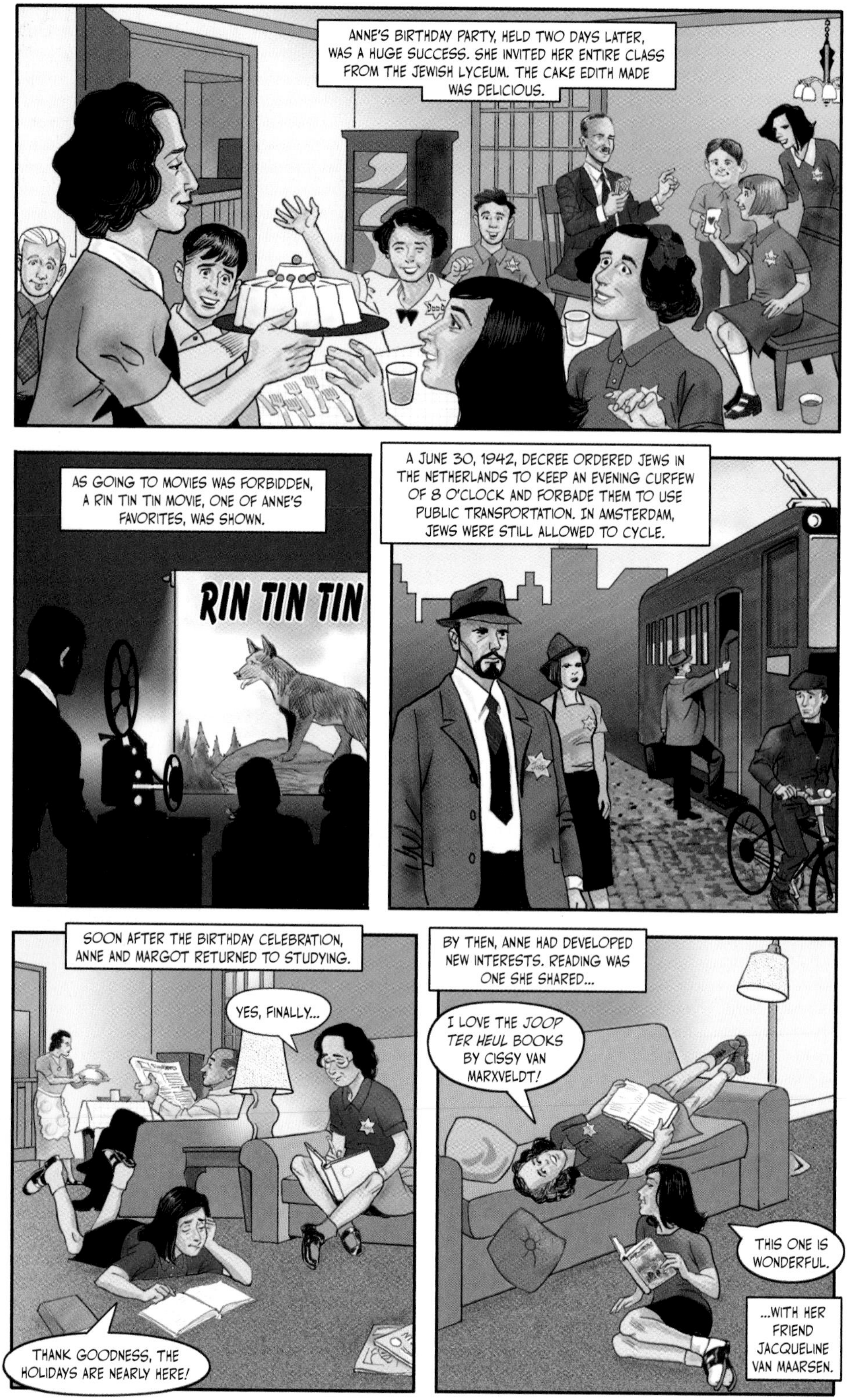
ANNE'S BIRTHDAY PARTY, HELD TWO DAYS LATER, WAS A HUGE SUCCESS. SHE INVITED HER ENTIRE CLASS FROM THE JEWISH LYCEUM. THE CAKE EDITH MADE WAS DELICIOUS.
AS GOING TO MOVIES WAS FORBIDDEN, A RIN TIN TIN MOVIE, ONE OF ANNE'S FAVORITES, WAS SHOWN.
RIN TIN TIN
A JUNE 30, 1942, DECREE ORDERED JEWS IN THE NETHERLANDS TO KEEP AN EVENING CURFEW OF 8 O'CLOCK AND FORBADE THEM TO USE PUBLIC TRANSPORTATION. IN AMSTERDAM, JEWS WERE STILL ALLOWED TO CYCLE.
SOON AFTER THE BIRTHDAY CELEBRATION, ANNE AND MARGOT RETURNED TO STUDYING.
YES, FINALLY...
THANK GOODNESS, THE HOLIDAYS ARE NEARLY HERE!
BY THEN, ANNE HAD DEVELOPED NEW INTERESTS. READING WAS ONE SHE SHARED...
I LOVE THE *JOOP TER HEUL* BOOKS BY CISSY VAN MARXVELDT!
THIS ONE IS WONDERFUL.
...WITH HER FRIEND JACQUELINE VAN MAARSEN.

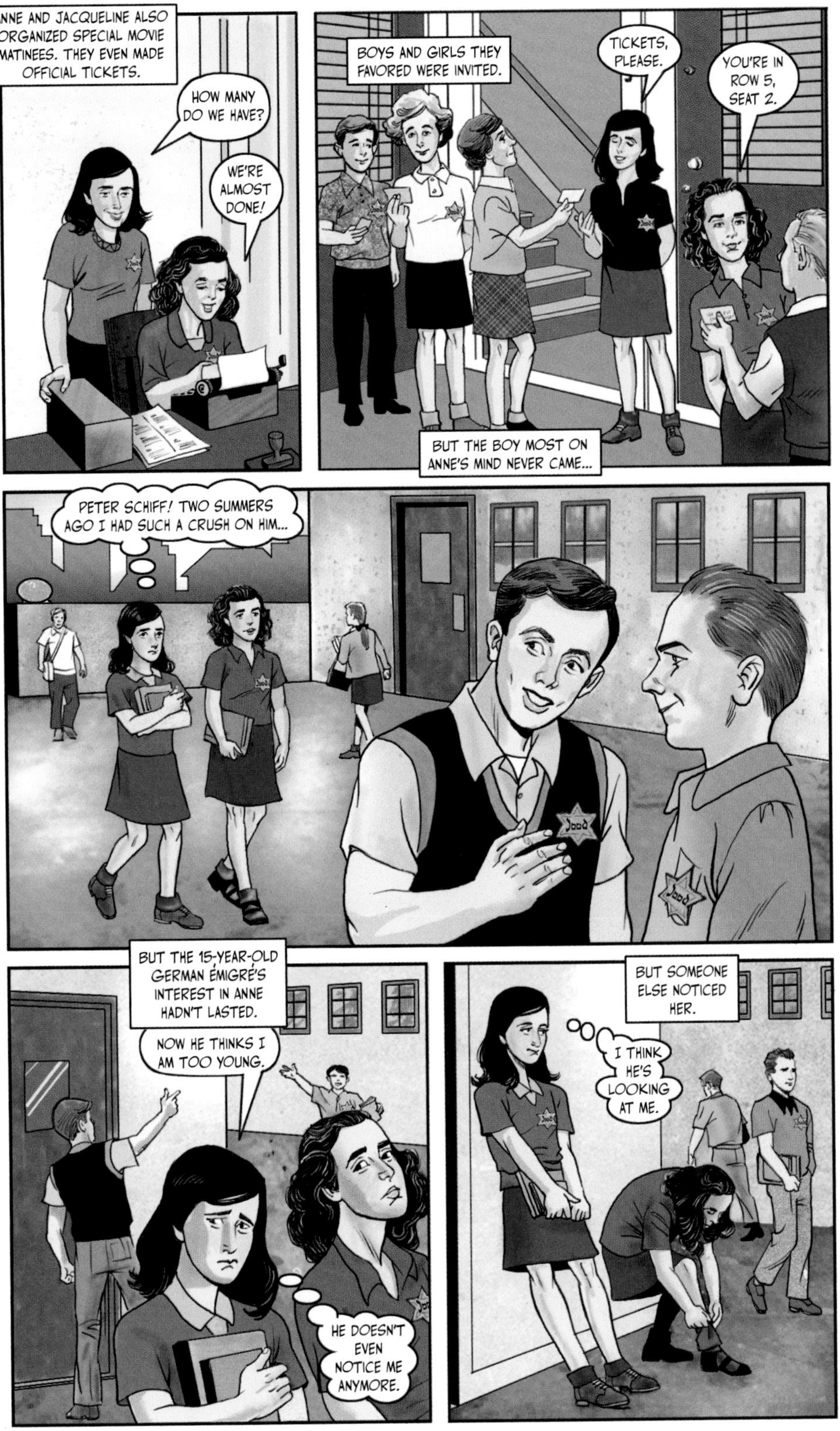
ANNE AND JACQUELINE ALSO ORGANIZED SPECIAL MOVIE MATINEES. THEY EVEN MADE OFFICIAL TICKETS.
HOW MANY DO WE HAVE?
WE'RE ALMOST DONE!
BOYS AND GIRLS THEY FAVORED WERE INVITED.
TICKETS, PLEASE.
YOU'RE IN ROW 5, SEAT 2.
BUT THE BOY MOST ON ANNE'S MIND NEVER CAME...
PETER SCHIFF! TWO SUMMERS AGO I HAD SUCH A CRUSH ON HIM...
BUT THE 15-YEAR-OLD GERMAN ÉMIGRÉ'S INTEREST IN ANNE HADN'T LASTED.
NOW HE THINKS I AM TOO YOUNG.
HE DOESN'T EVEN NOTICE ME ANYMORE.
BUT SOMEONE ELSE NOTICED HER.
I THINK HE'S LOOKING AT ME.

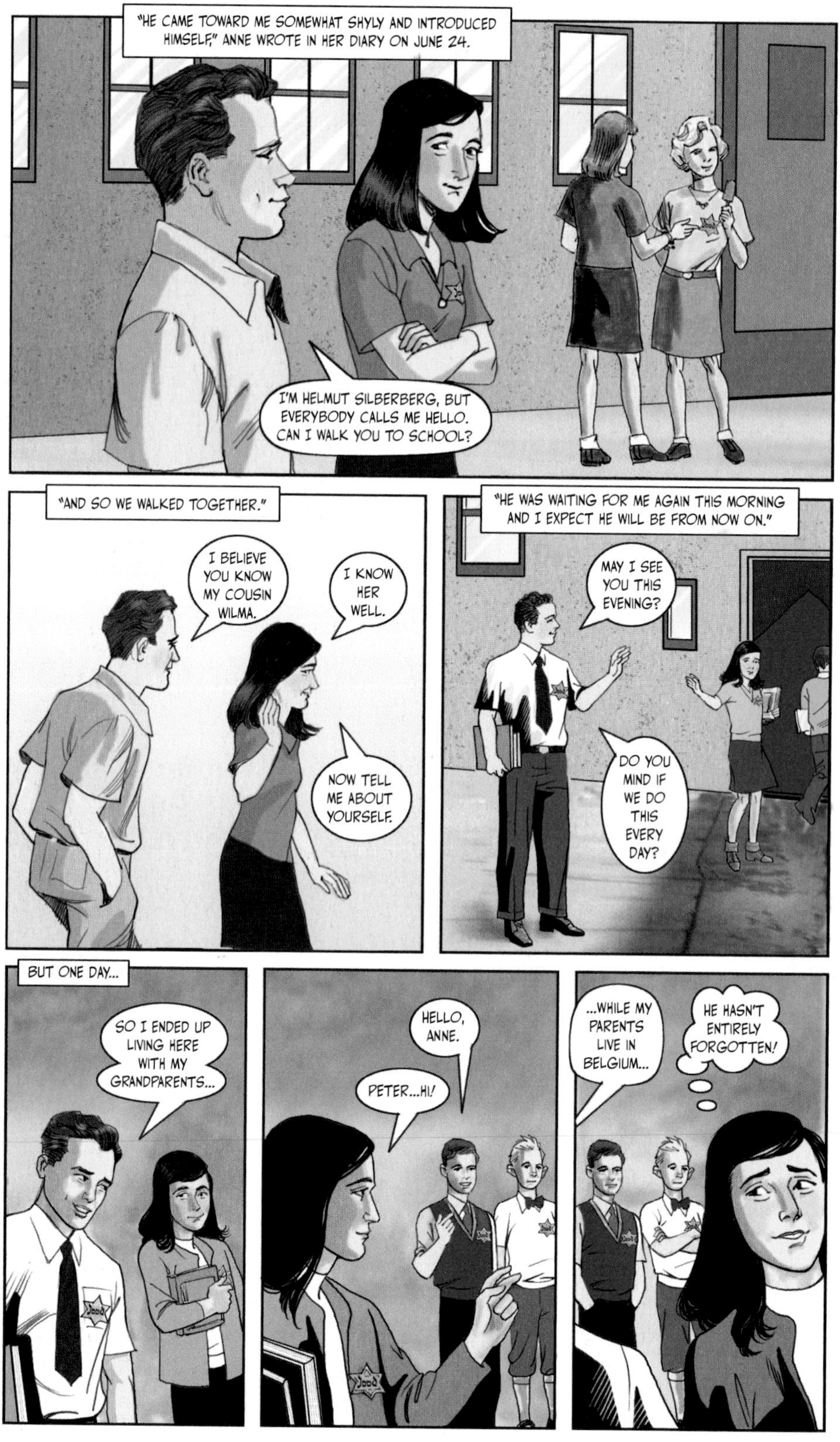

"HE CAME TOWARD ME SOMEWHAT SHYLY AND INTRODUCED HIMSELF," ANNE WROTE IN HER DIARY ON JUNE 24.
I'M HELMUT SILBERBERG, BUT EVERYBODY CALLS ME HELLO. CAN I WALK YOU TO SCHOOL?
"AND SO WE WALKED TOGETHER."
I BELIEVE YOU KNOW MY COUSIN WILMA.
I KNOW HER WELL.
NOW TELL ME ABOUT YOURSELF.
"HE WAS WAITING FOR ME AGAIN THIS MORNING AND I EXPECT HE WILL BE FROM NOW ON."
MAY I SEE YOU THIS EVENING?
DO YOU MIND IF WE DO THIS EVERY DAY?
BUT ONE DAY...
SO I ENDED UP LIVING HERE WITH MY GRANDPARENTS...
HELLO, ANNE.
PETER...HI!
...WHILE MY PARENTS LIVE IN BELGIUM...
HE HASN'T ENTIRELY FORGOTTEN!

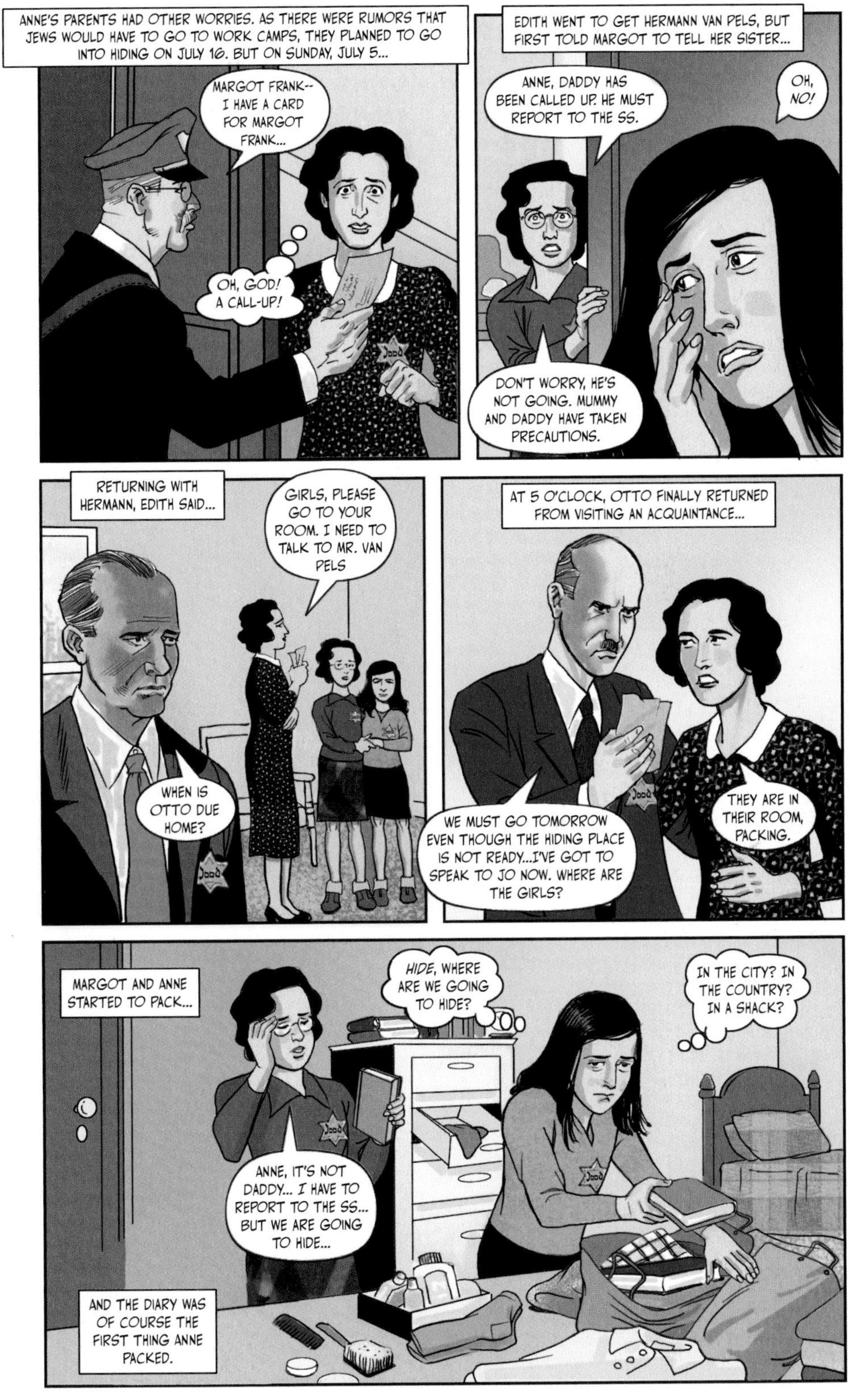
ANNE'S PARENTS HAD OTHER WORRIES. AS THERE WERE RUMORS THAT JEWS WOULD HAVE TO GO TO WORK CAMPS, THEY PLANNED TO GO INTO HIDING ON JULY 16. BUT ON SUNDAY, JULY 5...
MARGOT FRANK-- I HAVE A CARD FOR MARGOT FRANK...
OH, GOD! A CALL-UP!
EDITH WENT TO GET HERMANN VAN PELS, BUT FIRST TOLD MARGOT TO TELL HER SISTER...
ANNE, DADDY HAS BEEN CALLED UP. HE MUST REPORT TO THE SS.
OH, NO!
DON'T WORRY, HE'S NOT GOING. MUMMY AND DADDY HAVE TAKEN PRECAUTIONS.
RETURNING WITH HERMANN, EDITH SAID...
GIRLS, PLEASE GO TO YOUR ROOM. I NEED TO TALK TO MR. VAN PELS
WHEN IS OTTO DUE HOME?
AT 5 O'CLOCK, OTTO FINALLY RETURNED FROM VISITING AN ACQUAINTANCE...
WE MUST GO TOMORROW EVEN THOUGH THE HIDING PLACE IS NOT READY...I'VE GOT TO SPEAK TO JO NOW. WHERE ARE THE GIRLS?
THEY ARE IN THEIR ROOM, PACKING.
MARGOT AND ANNE STARTED TO PACK...
HIDE, WHERE ARE WE GOING TO HIDE?
IN THE CITY? IN THE COUNTRY? IN A SHACK?
ANNE, IT'S NOT DADDY... I HAVE TO REPORT TO THE SS... BUT WE ARE GOING TO HIDE...
AND THE DIARY WAS OF COURSE THE FIRST THING ANNE PACKED.

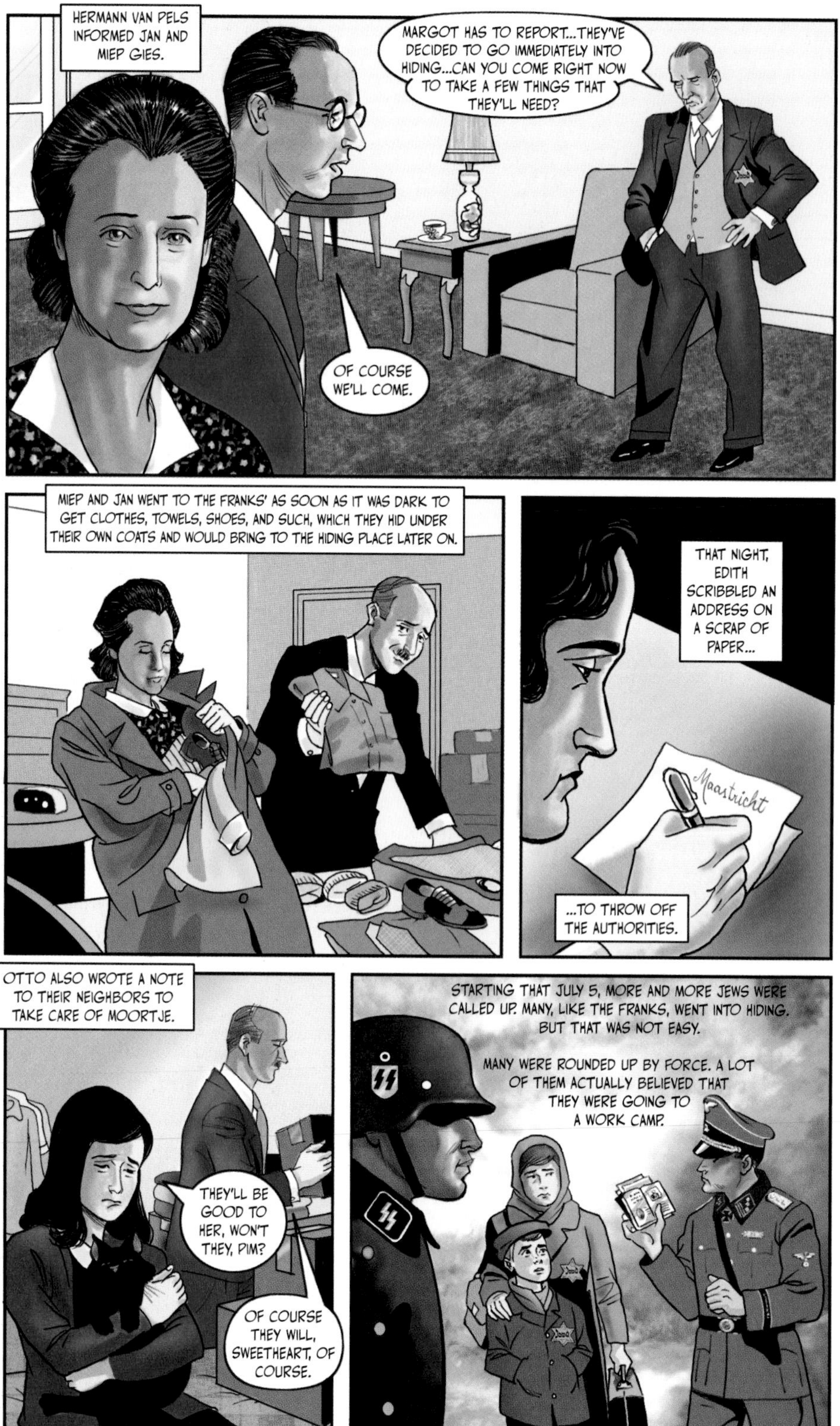
HERMANN VAN PELS INFORMED JAN AND MIEP GIES.
MARGOT HAS TO REPORT...THEY'VE DECIDED TO GO IMMEDIATELY INTO HIDING...CAN YOU COME RIGHT NOW TO TAKE A FEW THINGS THAT THEY'LL NEED?
OF COURSE WE'LL COME.
MIEP AND JAN WENT TO THE FRANKS' AS SOON AS IT WAS DARK TO GET CLOTHES, TOWELS, SHOES, AND SUCH, WHICH THEY HID UNDER THEIR OWN COATS AND WOULD BRING TO THE HIDING PLACE LATER ON.
THAT NIGHT, EDITH SCRIBBLED AN ADDRESS ON A SCRAP OF PAPER...
Maastricht
...TO THROW OFF THE AUTHORITIES.
OTTO ALSO WROTE A NOTE TO THEIR NEIGHBORS TO TAKE CARE OF MOORTJE.
THEY'LL BE GOOD TO HER, WON'T THEY, PIM?
OF COURSE THEY WILL, SWEETHEART, OF COURSE.
STARTING THAT JULY 5, MORE AND MORE JEWS WERE CALLED UP. MANY, LIKE THE FRANKS, WENT INTO HIDING. BUT THAT WAS NOT EASY.
MANY WERE ROUNDED UP BY FORCE. A LOT OF THEM ACTUALLY BELIEVED THAT THEY WERE GOING TO A WORK CAMP.

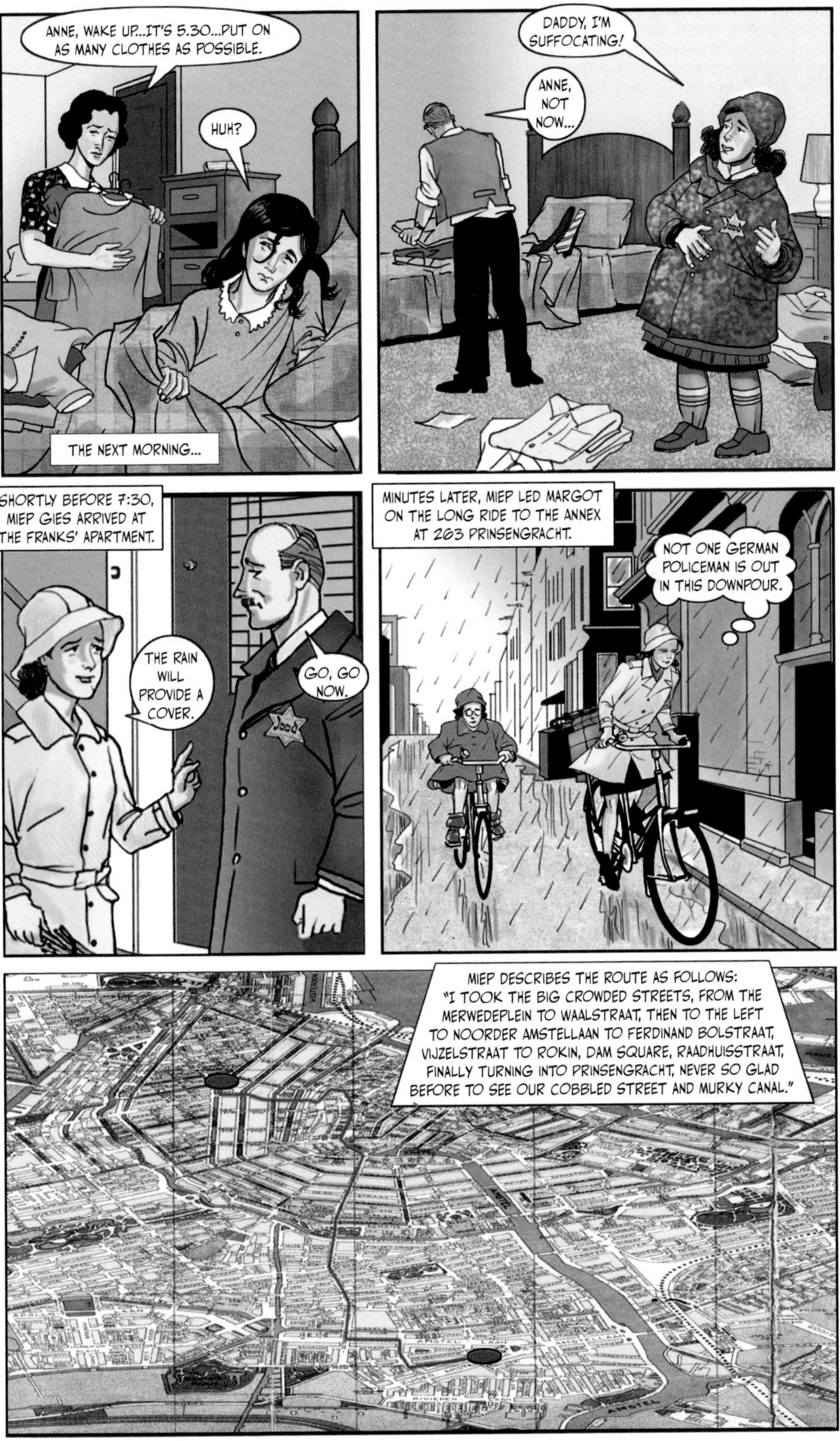
ANNE, WAKE UP...IT'S 5.30...PUT ON AS MANY CLOTHES AS POSSIBLE.
HUH?
THE NEXT MORNING...
DADDY, I'M SUFFOCATING!
ANNE, NOT NOW...
SHORTLY BEFORE 7:30, MIEP GIES ARRIVED AT THE FRANKS' APARTMENT.
THE RAIN WILL PROVIDE A COVER.
GO, GO NOW.
MINUTES LATER, MIEP LED MARGOT ON THE LONG RIDE TO THE ANNEX AT 263 PRINSENGRACHT.
NOT ONE GERMAN POLICEMAN IS OUT IN THIS DOWNPOUR.
MIEP DESCRIBES THE ROUTE AS FOLLOWS: "I TOOK THE BIG CROWDED STREETS, FROM THE MERWEDEPLEIN TO WAALSTRAAT, THEN TO THE LEFT TO NOORDER AMSTELLAAN TO FERDINAND BOLSTRAAT, VIJZELSTRAAT TO ROKIN, DAM SQUARE, RAADHUISSTRAAT, FINALLY TURNING INTO PRINSENGRACHT, NEVER SO GLAD BEFORE TO SEE OUR COBBLED STREET AND MURKY CANAL."
AMSTEL

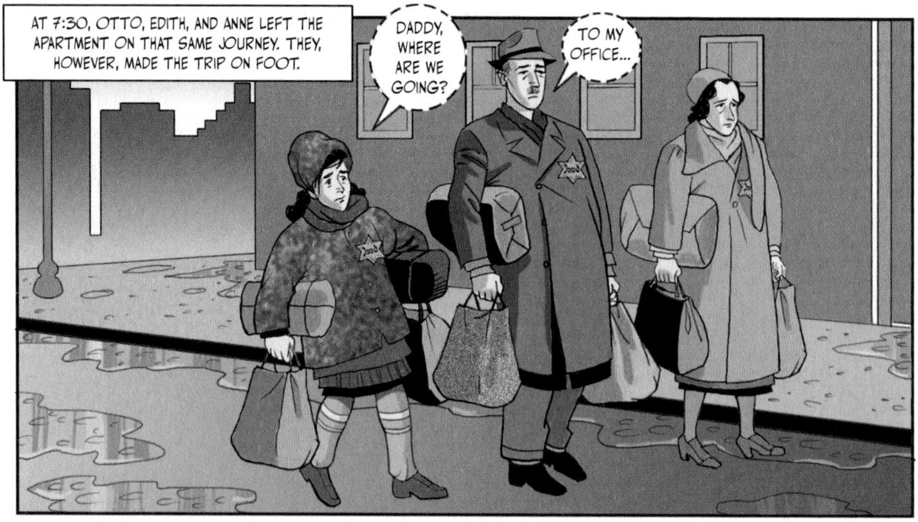
AT 7:30, OTTO, EDITH, AND ANNE LEFT THE APARTMENT ON THAT SAME JOURNEY. THEY, HOWEVER, MADE THE TRIP ON FOOT.
DADDY, WHERE ARE WE GOING?
TO MY OFFICE...

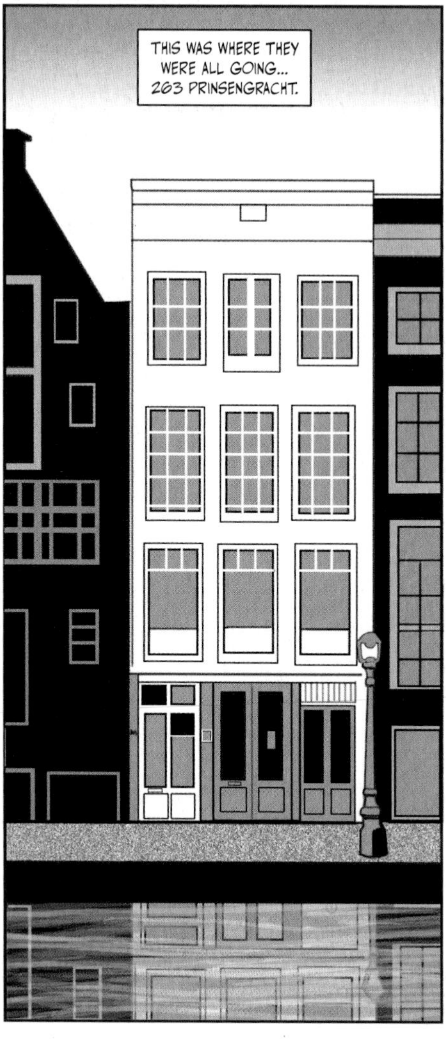
THIS WAS WHERE THEY WERE ALL GOING... 263 PRINSENGRACHT.

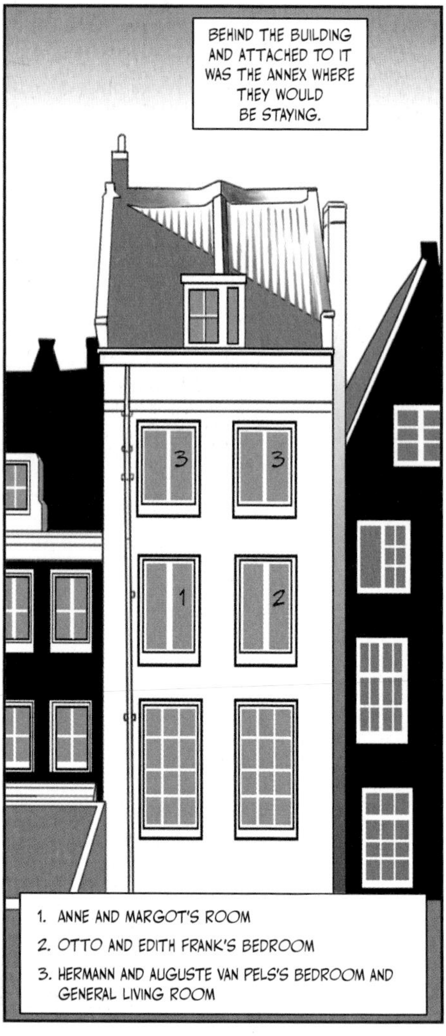
BEHIND THE BUILDING AND ATTACHED TO IT WAS THE ANNEX WHERE THEY WOULD BE STAYING.
3
3
1
2
1. ANNE AND MARGOT'S ROOM
2. OTTO AND EDITH FRANK'S BEDROOM
3. HERMANN AND AUGUSTE VAN PELS'S BEDROOM AND GENERAL LIVING ROOM

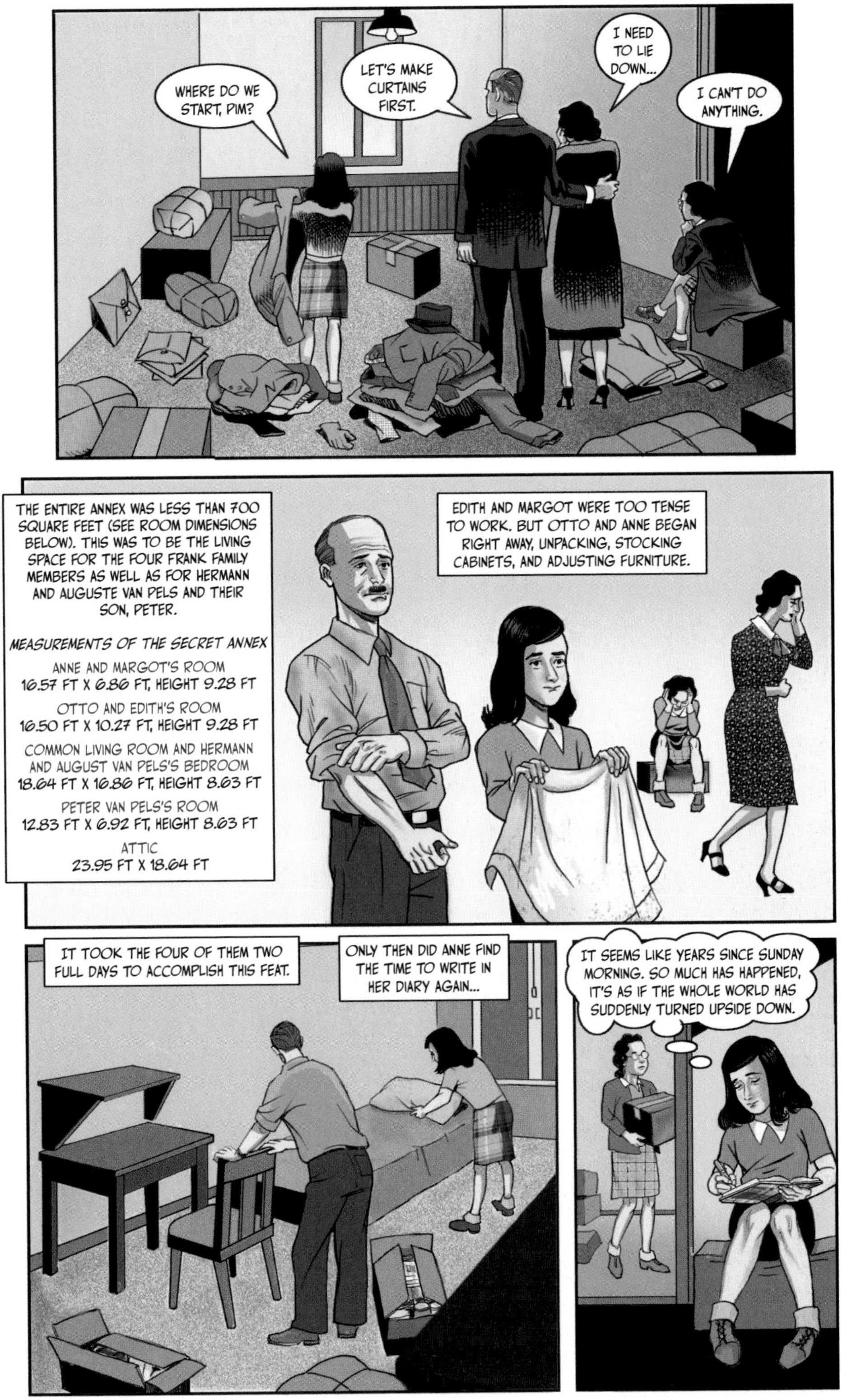
WHERE DO WE START, PIM?
LET'S MAKE CURTAINS FIRST.
I NEED TO LIE DOWN...
I CAN'T DO ANYTHING.
THE ENTIRE ANNEX WAS LESS THAN 700 SQUARE FEET (SEE ROOM DIMENSIONS BELOW). THIS WAS TO BE THE LIVING SPACE FOR THE FOUR FRANK FAMILY MEMBERS AS WELL AS FOR HERMANN AND AUGUSTE VAN PELS AND THEIR SON, PETER.
MEASUREMENTS OF THE SECRET ANNEX
ANNE AND MARGOT'S ROOM
16.57 FT X 6.86 FT, HEIGHT 9.28 FT
OTTO AND EDITH'S ROOM
16.50 FT X 10.27 FT, HEIGHT 9.28 FT
COMMON LIVING ROOM AND HERMANN AND AUGUST VAN PELS'S BEDROOM
18.64 FT X 16.86 FT, HEIGHT 8.63 FT
PETER VAN PELS'S ROOM
12.83 FT X 6.92 FT, HEIGHT 8.63 FT
ATTIC
23.95 FT X 18.64 FT
EDITH AND MARGOT WERE TOO TENSE TO WORK. BUT OTTO AND ANNE BEGAN RIGHT AWAY, UNPACKING, STOCKING CABINETS, AND ADJUSTING FURNITURE.
IT TOOK THE FOUR OF THEM TWO FULL DAYS TO ACCOMPLISH THIS FEAT.
ONLY THEN DID ANNE FIND THE TIME TO WRITE IN HER DIARY AGAIN...
IT SEEMS LIKE YEARS SINCE SUNDAY MORNING. SO MUCH HAS HAPPENED, IT'S AS IF THE WHOLE WORLD HAS SUDDENLY TURNED UPSIDE DOWN.

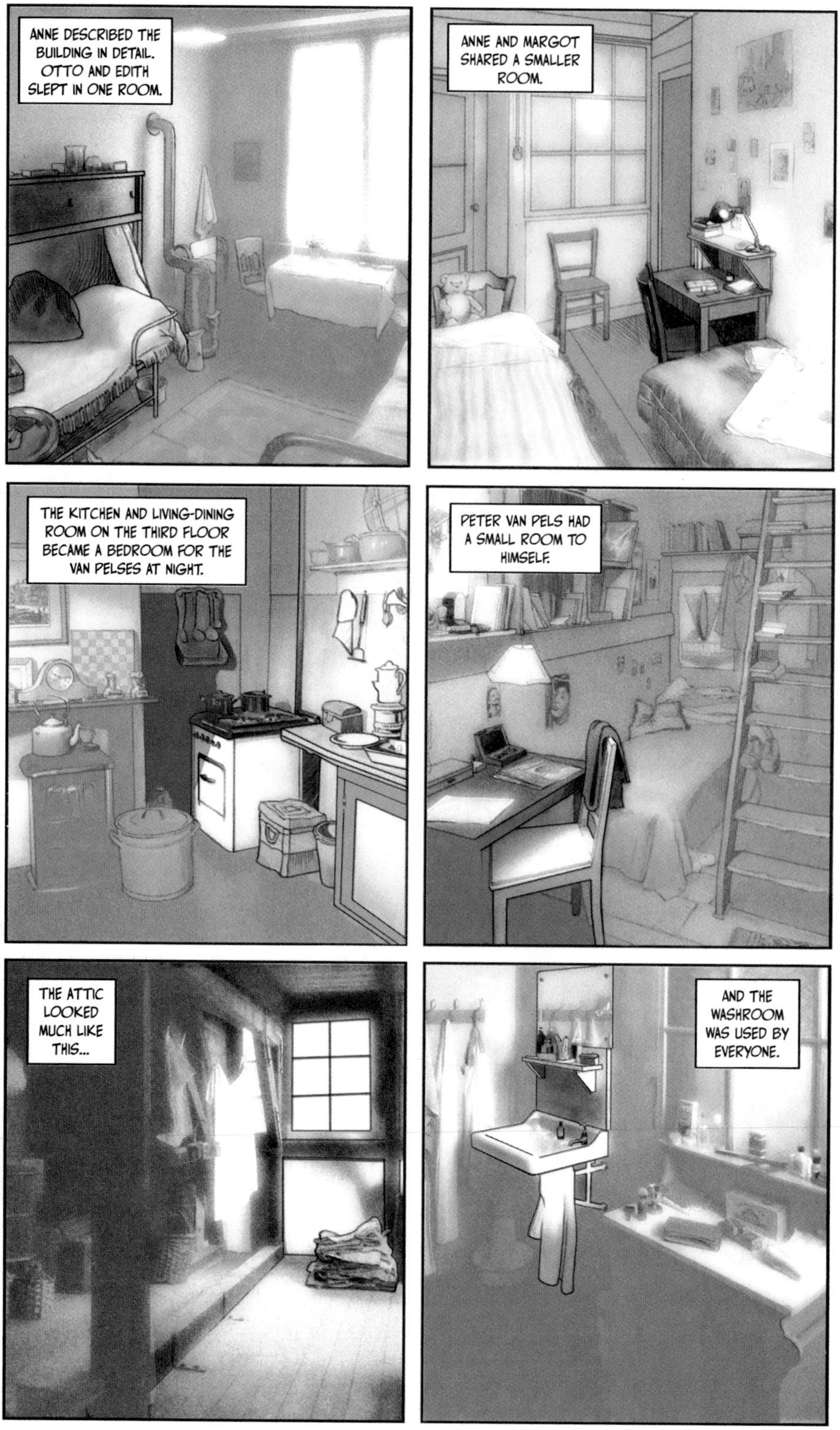
ANNE DESCRIBED THE BUILDING IN DETAIL. OTTO AND EDITH SLEPT IN ONE ROOM.
ANNE AND MARGOT SHARED A SMALLER ROOM.
THE KITCHEN AND LIVING-DINING ROOM ON THE THIRD FLOOR BECAME A BEDROOM FOR THE VAN PELSES AT NIGHT.
PETER VAN PELS HAD A SMALL ROOM TO HIMSELF.
THE ATTIC LOOKED MUCH LIKE THIS...
AND THE WASHROOM WAS USED BY EVERYONE.

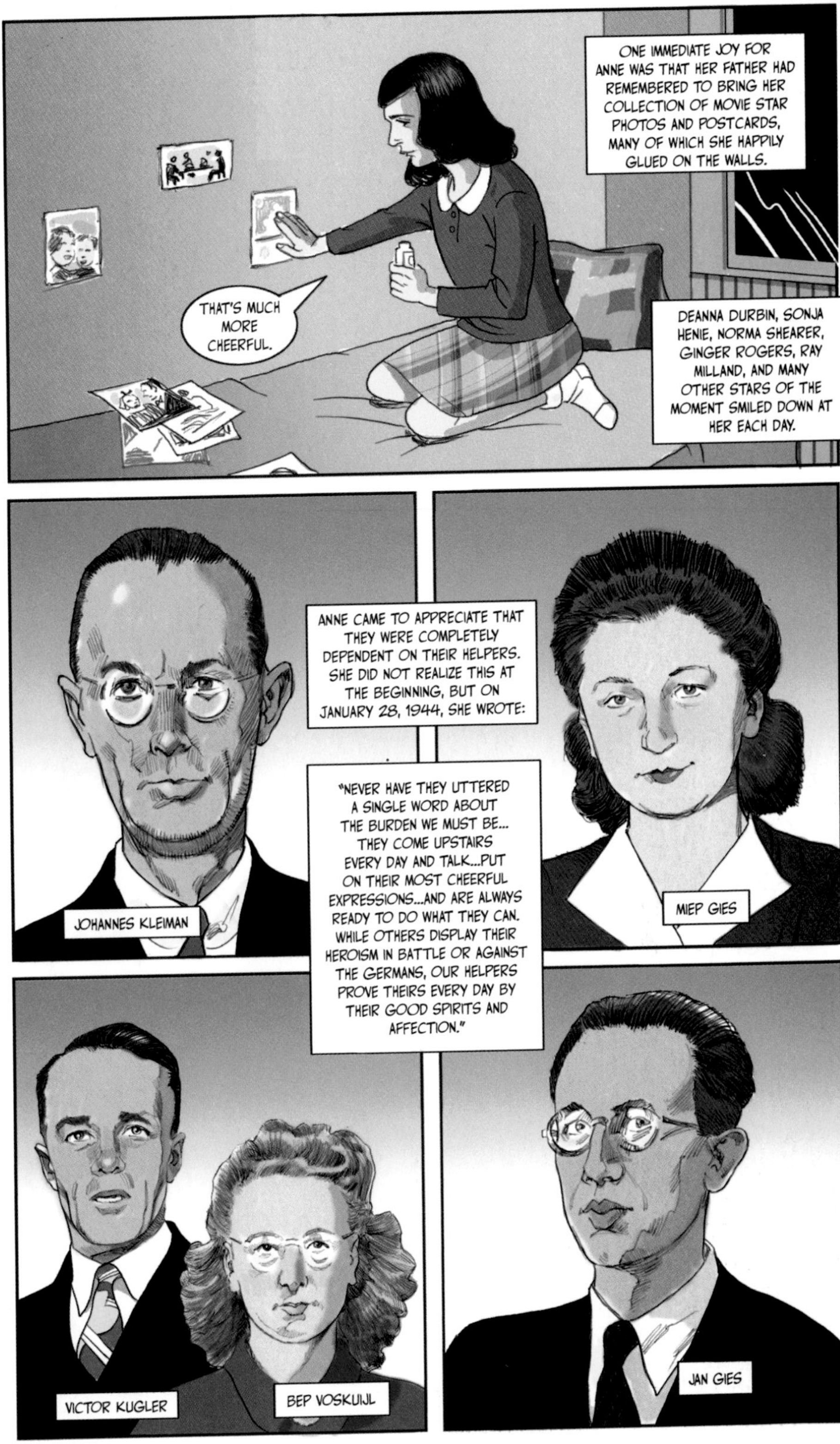
ONE IMMEDIATE JOY FOR ANNE WAS THAT HER FATHER HAD REMEMBERED TO BRING HER COLLECTION OF MOVIE STAR PHOTOS AND POSTCARDS, MANY OF WHICH SHE HAPPILY GLUED ON THE WALLS.
THAT'S MUCH MORE CHEERFUL.
DEANNA DURBIN, SONJA HENIE, NORMA SHEARER, GINGER ROGERS, RAY MILLAND, AND MANY OTHER STARS OF THE MOMENT SMILED DOWN AT HER EACH DAY.
ANNE CAME TO APPRECIATE THAT THEY WERE COMPLETELY DEPENDENT ON THEIR HELPERS. SHE DID NOT REALIZE THIS AT THE BEGINNING, BUT ON JANUARY 28, 1944, SHE WROTE:
"NEVER HAVE THEY UTTERED A SINGLE WORD ABOUT THE BURDEN WE MUST BE... THEY COME UPSTAIRS EVERY DAY AND TALK...PUT ON THEIR MOST CHEERFUL EXPRESSIONS...AND ARE ALWAYS READY TO DO WHAT THEY CAN. WHILE OTHERS DISPLAY THEIR HEROISM IN BATTLE OR AGAINST THE GERMANS, OUR HELPERS PROVE THEIRS EVERY DAY BY THEIR GOOD SPIRITS AND AFFECTION."
JOHANNES KLEIMAN
MIEP GIES
VICTOR KUGLER
BEP VOSKUIJL
JAN GIES

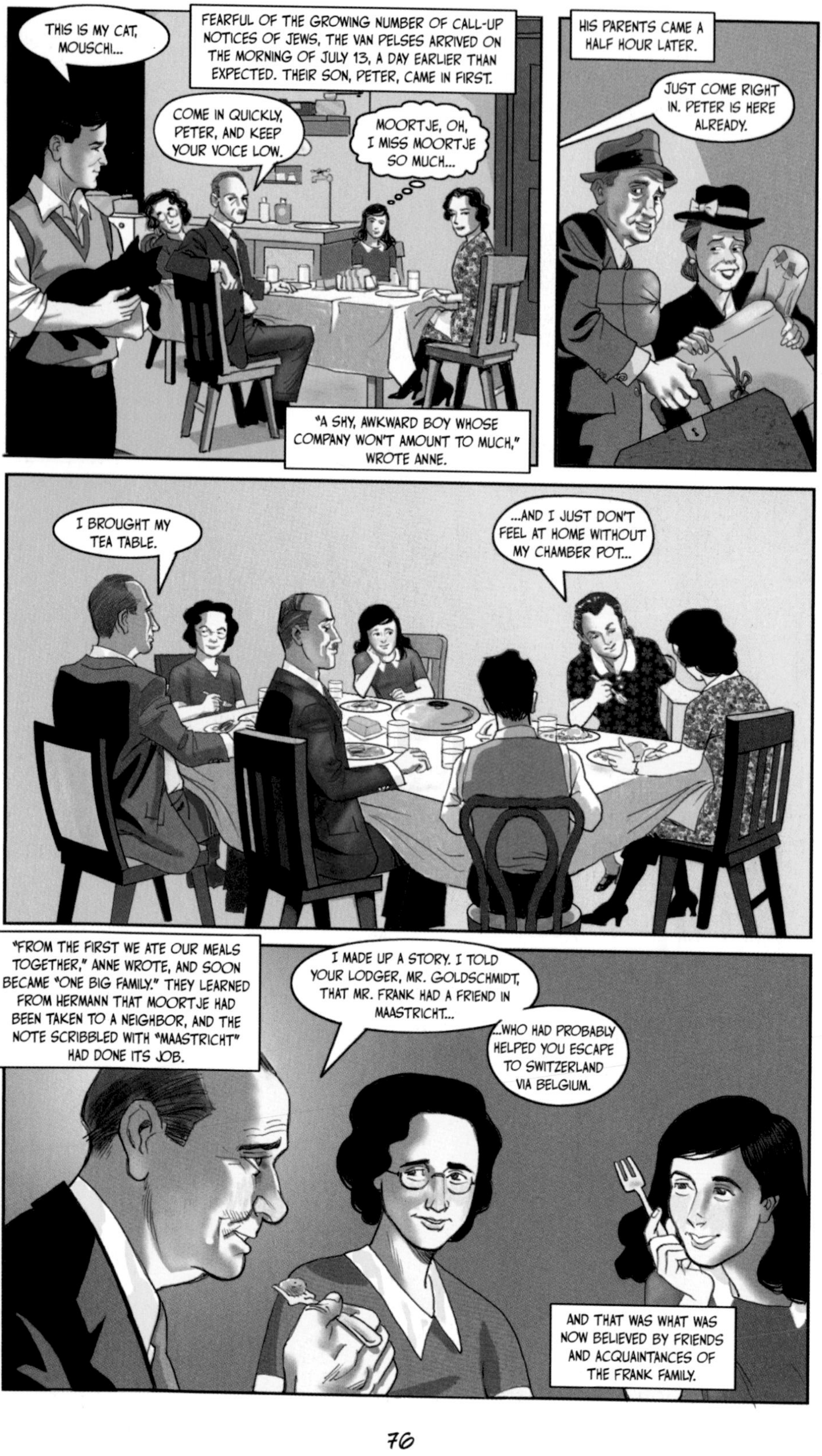
FEARFUL OF THE GROWING NUMBER OF CALL-UP NOTICES OF JEWS, THE VAN PELSES ARRIVED ON THE MORNING OF JULY 13, A DAY EARLIER THAN EXPECTED. THEIR SON, PETER, CAME IN FIRST.
THIS IS MY CAT, MOUSCHI...
COME IN QUICKLY, PETER, AND KEEP YOUR VOICE LOW.
MOORTJE, OH, I MISS MOORTJE SO MUCH...
"A SHY, AWKWARD BOY WHOSE COMPANY WON'T AMOUNT TO MUCH," WROTE ANNE.
HIS PARENTS CAME A HALF HOUR LATER.
JUST COME RIGHT IN. PETER IS HERE ALREADY.
I BROUGHT MY TEA TABLE.
...AND I JUST DON'T FEEL AT HOME WITHOUT MY CHAMBER POT...
"FROM THE FIRST WE ATE OUR MEALS TOGETHER," ANNE WROTE, AND SOON BECAME "ONE BIG FAMILY." THEY LEARNED FROM HERMANN THAT MOORTJE HAD BEEN TAKEN TO A NEIGHBOR, AND THE NOTE SCRIBBLED WITH "MAASTRICHT" HAD DONE ITS JOB.
I MADE UP A STORY. I TOLD YOUR LODGER, MR. GOLDSCHMIDT, THAT MR. FRANK HAD A FRIEND IN MAASTRICHT...
...WHO HAD PROBABLY HELPED YOU ESCAPE TO SWITZERLAND VIA BELGIUM.
AND THAT WAS WHAT WAS NOW BELIEVED BY FRIENDS AND ACQUAINTANCES OF THE FRANK FAMILY.

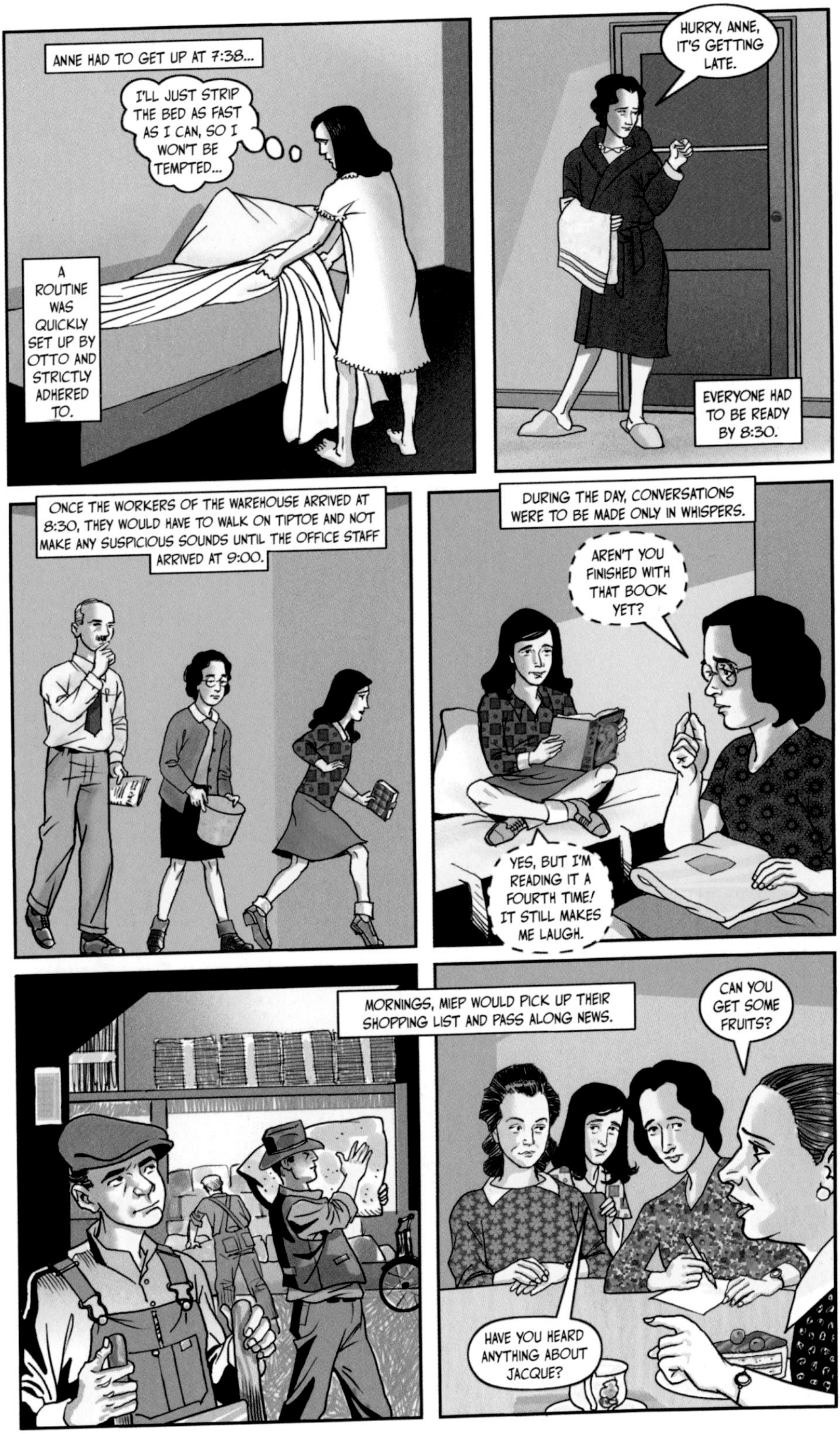
ANNE HAD TO GET UP AT 7:38...
I'LL JUST STRIP THE BED AS FAST AS I CAN, SO I WON'T BE TEMPTED...
A ROUTINE WAS QUICKLY SET UP BY OTTO AND STRICTLY ADHERED TO.
HURRY, ANNE, IT'S GETTING LATE.
EVERYONE HAD TO BE READY BY 8:30.
ONCE THE WORKERS OF THE WAREHOUSE ARRIVED AT 8:30, THEY WOULD HAVE TO WALK ON TIPTOE AND NOT MAKE ANY SUSPICIOUS SOUNDS UNTIL THE OFFICE STAFF ARRIVED AT 9:00.
DURING THE DAY, CONVERSATIONS WERE TO BE MADE ONLY IN WHISPERS.
AREN'T YOU FINISHED WITH THAT BOOK YET?
YES, BUT I'M READING IT A FOURTH TIME! IT STILL MAKES ME LAUGH.
MORNINGS, MIEP WOULD PICK UP THEIR SHOPPING LIST AND PASS ALONG NEWS.
CAN YOU GET SOME FRUITS?
HAVE YOU HEARD ANYTHING ABOUT JACQUE?

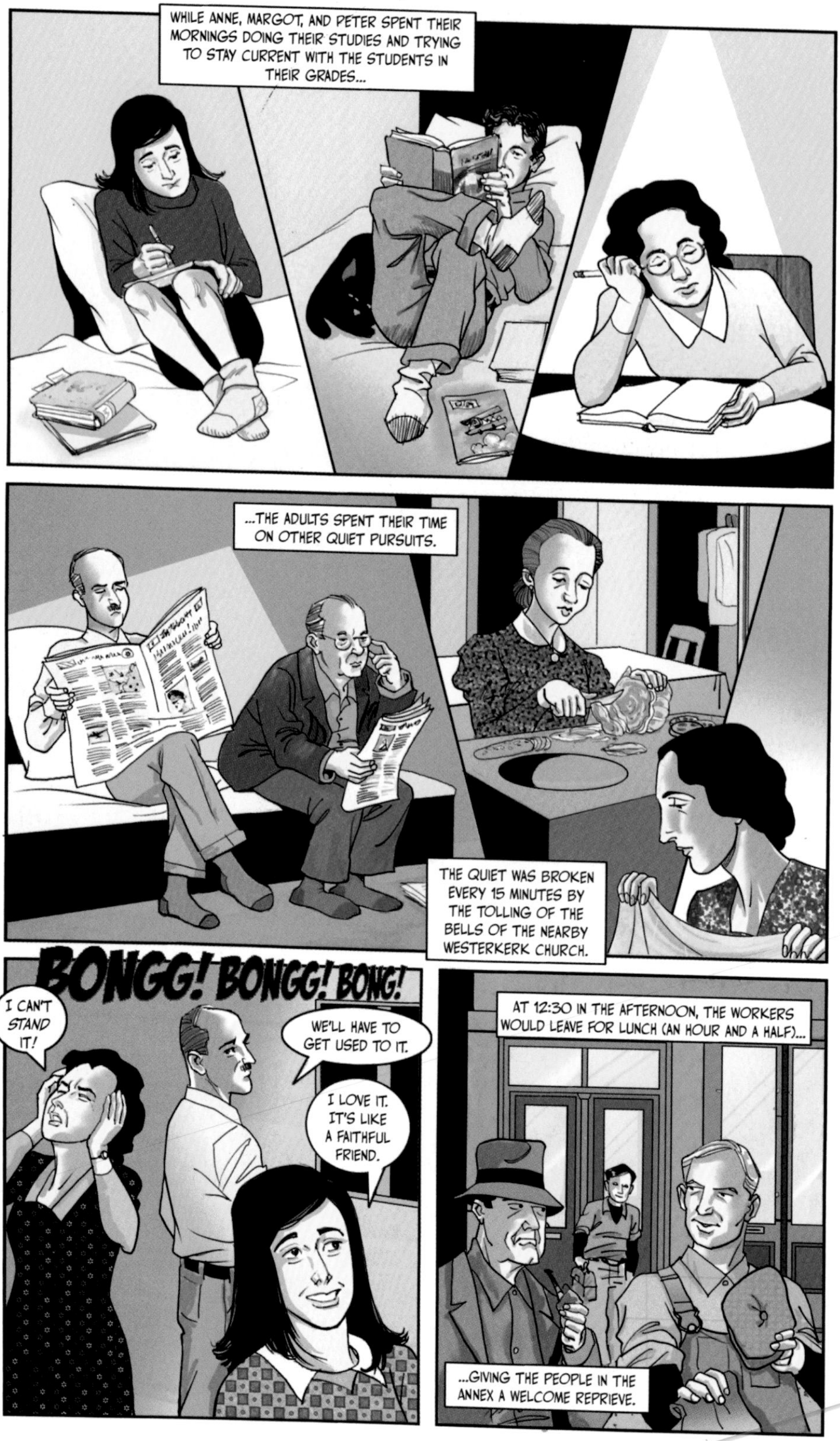
WHILE ANNE, MARGOT, AND PETER SPENT THEIR MORNINGS DOING THEIR STUDIES AND TRYING TO STAY CURRENT WITH THE STUDENTS IN THEIR GRADES...
...THE ADULTS SPENT THEIR TIME ON OTHER QUIET PURSUITS.
THE QUIET WAS BROKEN EVERY 15 MINUTES BY THE TOLLING OF THE BELLS OF THE NEARBY WESTERKERK CHURCH.
BONGG! BONGG! BONG!
I CAN'T STAND IT!
WE'LL HAVE TO GET USED TO IT.
I LOVE IT. IT'S LIKE A FAITHFUL FRIEND.
AT 12:30 IN THE AFTERNOON, THE WORKERS WOULD LEAVE FOR LUNCH (AN HOUR AND A HALF)...
...GIVING THE PEOPLE IN THE ANNEX A WELCOME REPRIEVE.

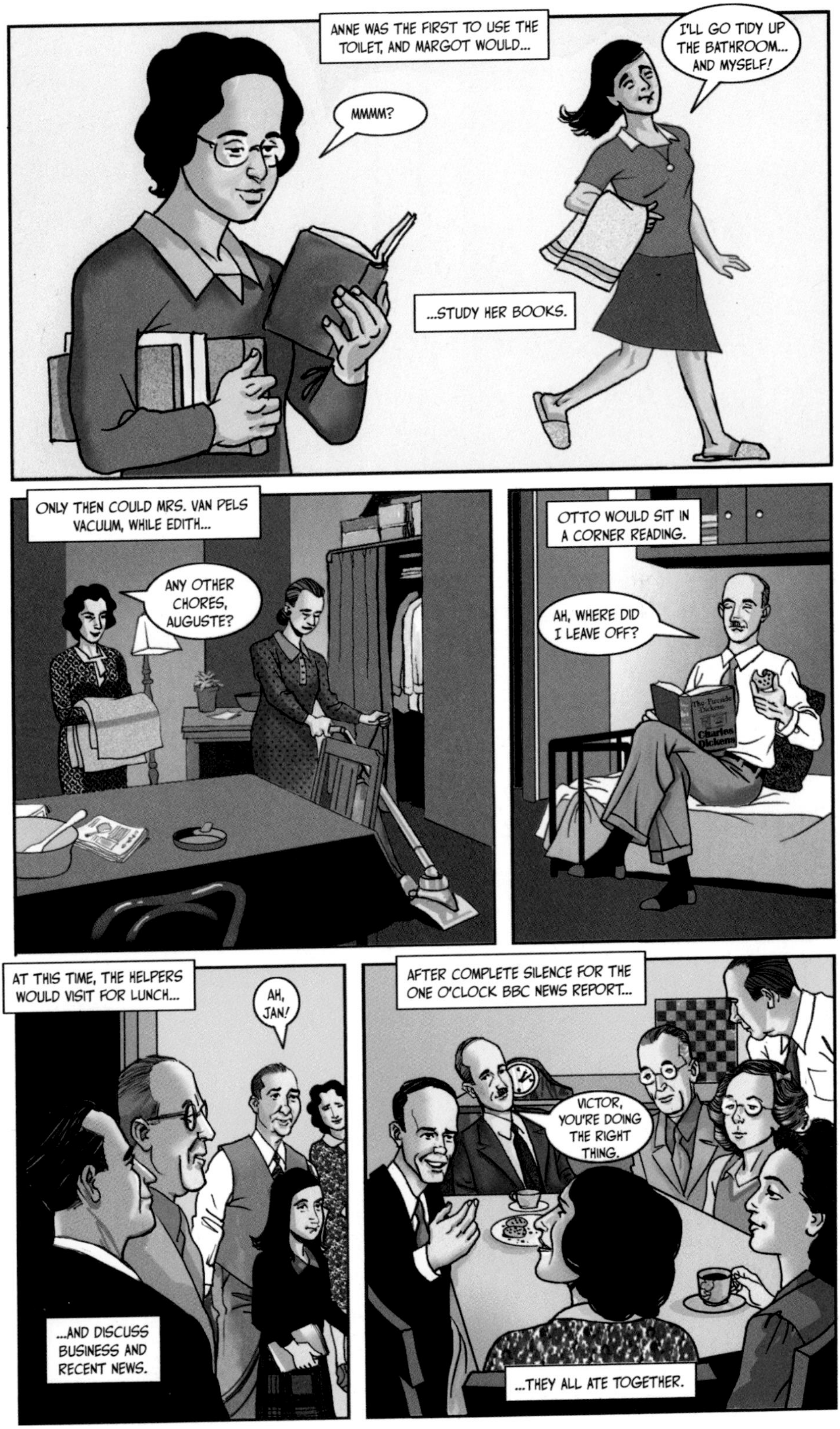
ANNE WAS THE FIRST TO USE THE TOILET, AND MARGOT WOULD...
MMMM?
I'LL GO TIDY UP THE BATHROOM... AND MYSELF!
...STUDY HER BOOKS.
ONLY THEN COULD MRS. VAN PELS VACUUM, WHILE EDITH...
ANY OTHER CHORES, AUGUSTE?
OTTO WOULD SIT IN A CORNER READING.
AH, WHERE DID I LEAVE OFF?
AT THIS TIME, THE HELPERS WOULD VISIT FOR LUNCH...
AH, JAN!
...AND DISCUSS BUSINESS AND RECENT NEWS.
AFTER COMPLETE SILENCE FOR THE ONE O'CLOCK BBC NEWS REPORT...
VICTOR, YOU'RE DOING THE RIGHT THING.
...THEY ALL ATE TOGETHER.

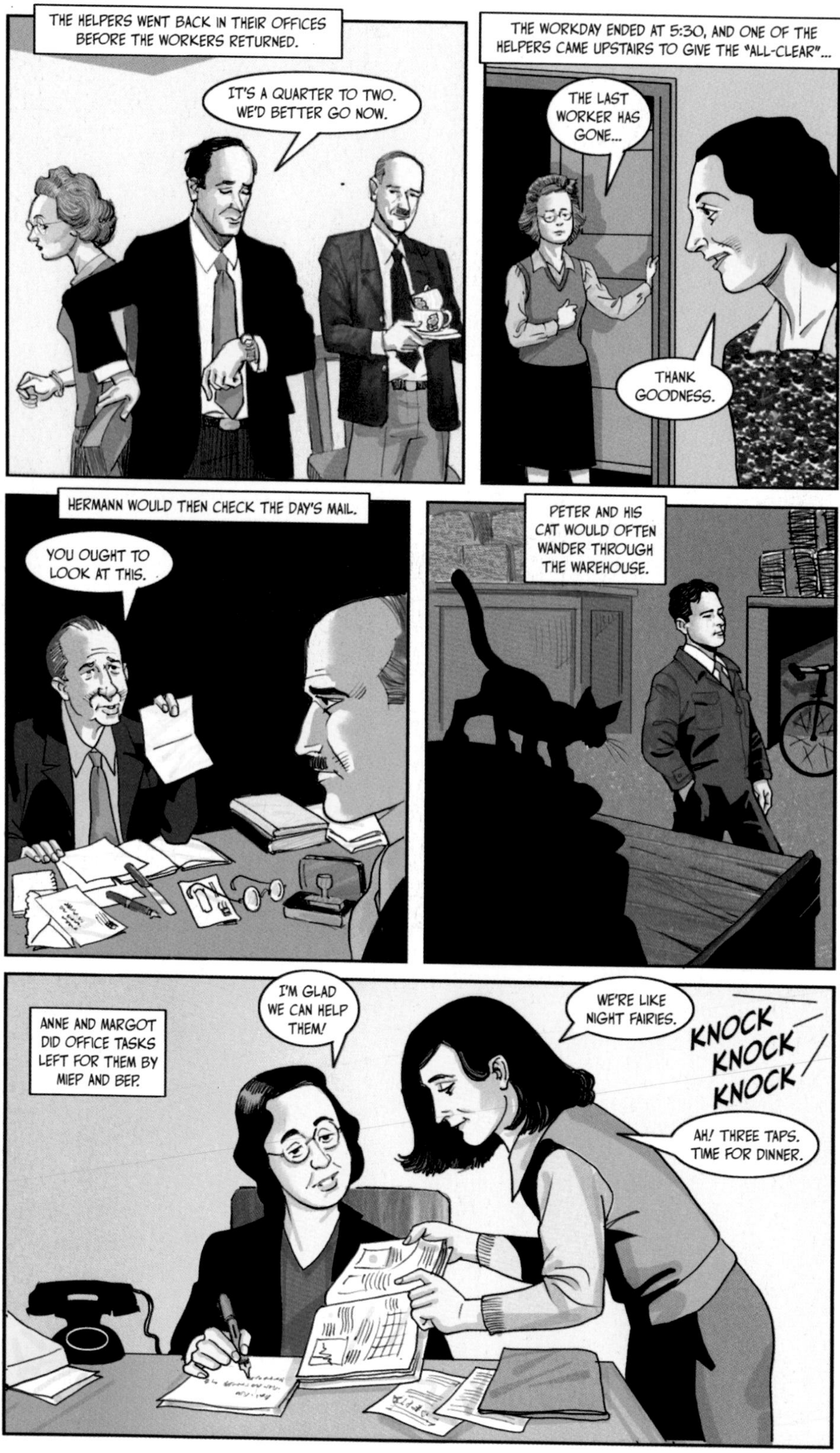
THE HELPERS WENT BACK IN THEIR OFFICES BEFORE THE WORKERS RETURNED.
IT'S A QUARTER TO TWO. WE'D BETTER GO NOW.
THE WORKDAY ENDED AT 5:30, AND ONE OF THE HELPERS CAME UPSTAIRS TO GIVE THE "ALL-CLEAR"...
THE LAST WORKER HAS GONE...
THANK GOODNESS.
HERMANN WOULD THEN CHECK THE DAY'S MAIL.
YOU OUGHT TO LOOK AT THIS.
PETER AND HIS CAT WOULD OFTEN WANDER THROUGH THE WAREHOUSE.
ANNE AND MARGOT DID OFFICE TASKS LEFT FOR THEM BY MIEP AND BEP.
I'M GLAD WE CAN HELP THEM!
WE'RE LIKE NIGHT FAIRIES.
KNOCK KNOCK KNOCK
AH! THREE TAPS. TIME FOR DINNER.

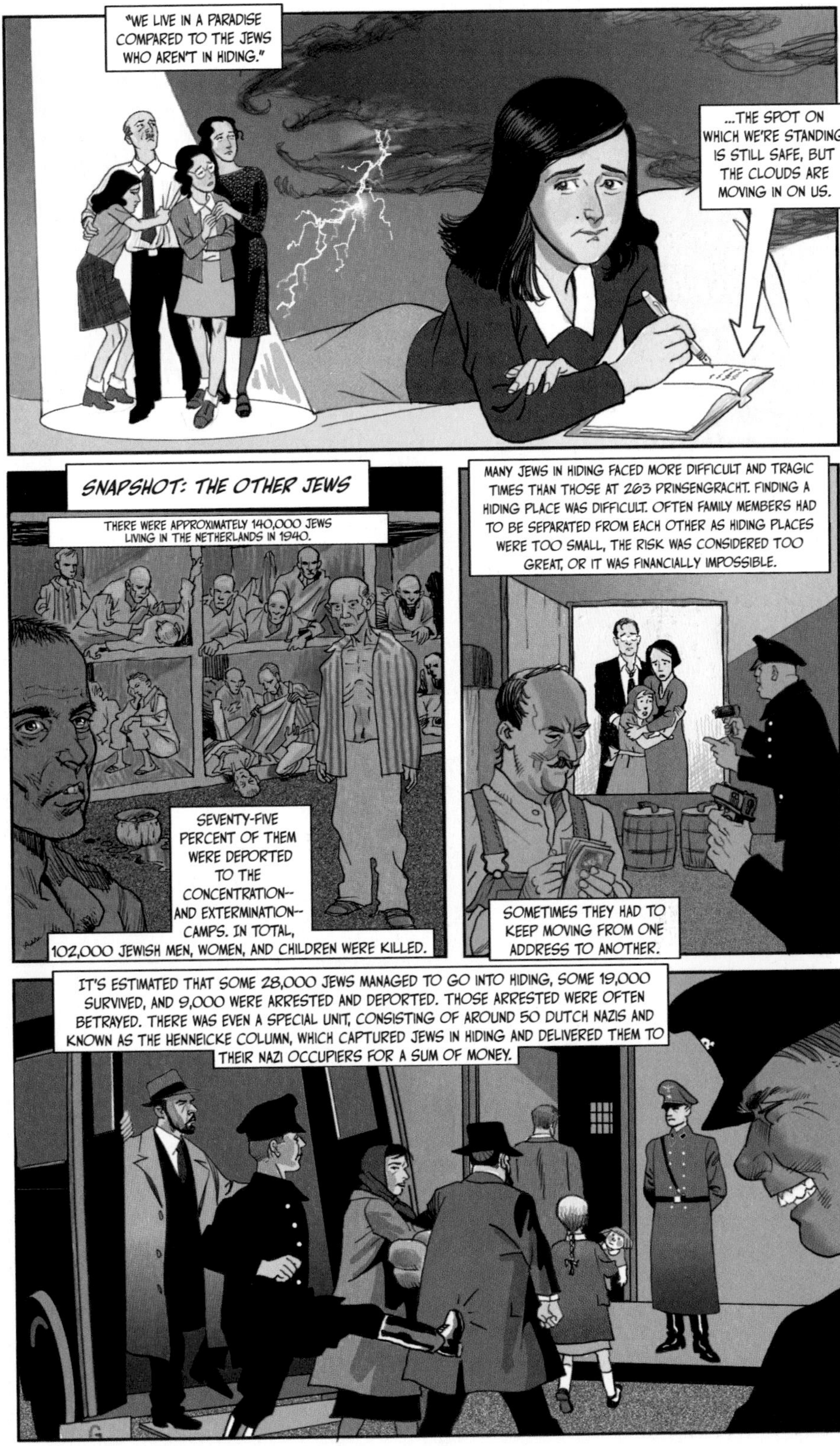
"WE LIVE IN A PARADISE COMPARED TO THE JEWS WHO AREN'T IN HIDING."
...THE SPOT ON WHICH WE'RE STANDING IS STILL SAFE, BUT THE CLOUDS ARE MOVING IN ON US.
SNAPSHOT: THE OTHER JEWS
THERE WERE APPROXIMATELY 140,000 JEWS LIVING IN THE NETHERLANDS IN 1940.
SEVENTY-FIVE PERCENT OF THEM WERE DEPORTED TO THE CONCENTRATION-- AND EXTERMINATION-- CAMPS. IN TOTAL, 102,000 JEWISH MEN, WOMEN, AND CHILDREN WERE KILLED.
MANY JEWS IN HIDING FACED MORE DIFFICULT AND TRAGIC TIMES THAN THOSE AT 263 PRINSENGRACHT. FINDING A HIDING PLACE WAS DIFFICULT. OFTEN FAMILY MEMBERS HAD TO BE SEPARATED FROM EACH OTHER AS HIDING PLACES WERE TOO SMALL, THE RISK WAS CONSIDERED TOO GREAT, OR IT WAS FINANCIALLY IMPOSSIBLE.
SOMETIMES THEY HAD TO KEEP MOVING FROM ONE ADDRESS TO ANOTHER.
IT'S ESTIMATED THAT SOME 28,000 JEWS MANAGED TO GO INTO HIDING, SOME 19,000 SURVIVED, AND 9,000 WERE ARRESTED AND DEPORTED. THOSE ARRESTED WERE OFTEN BETRAYED. THERE WAS EVEN A SPECIAL UNIT, CONSISTING OF AROUND 50 DUTCH NAZIS AND KNOWN AS THE HENNEICKE COLUMN, WHICH CAPTURED JEWS IN HIDING AND DELIVERED THEM TO THEIR NAZI OCCUPIERS FOR A SUM OF MONEY.

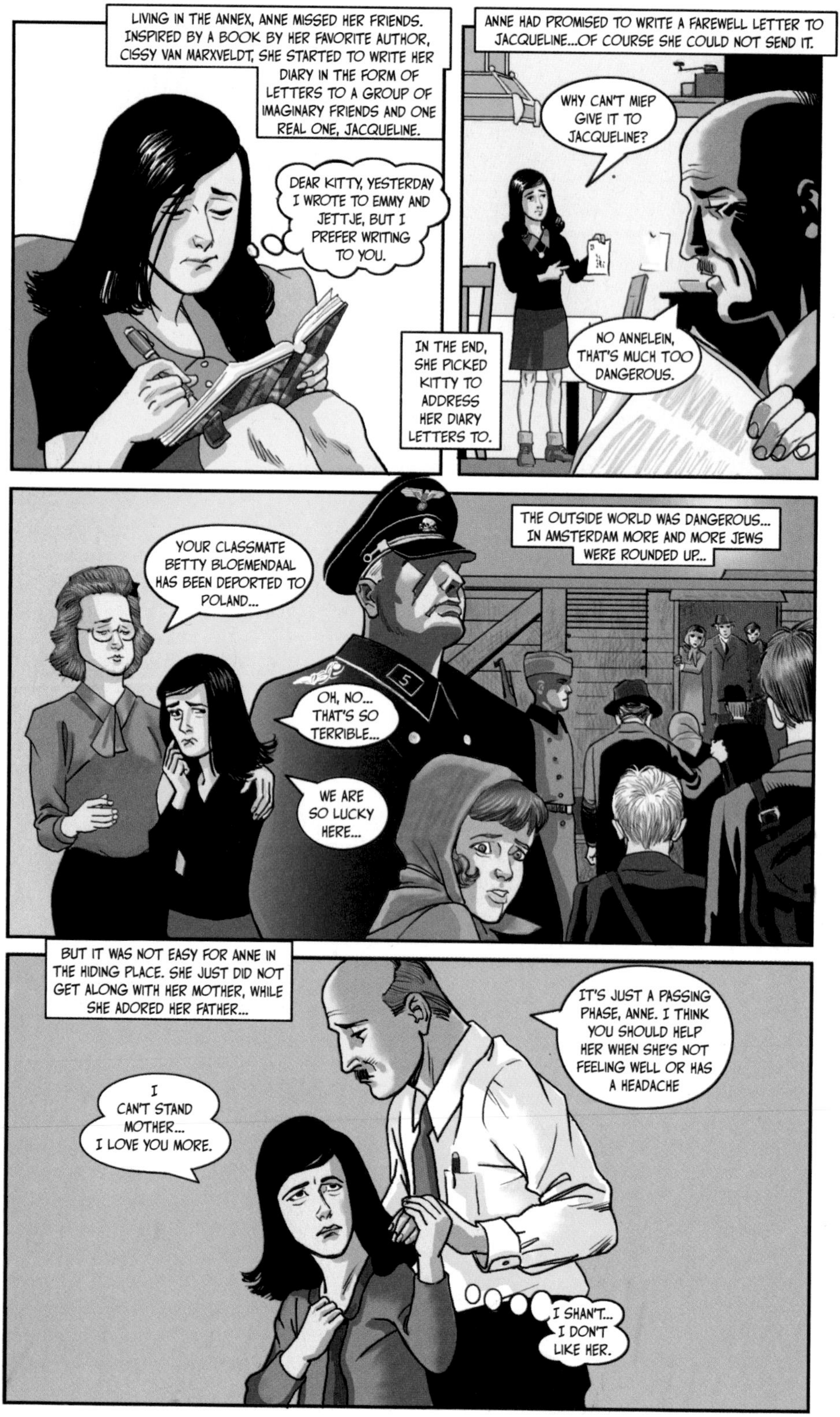
LIVING IN THE ANNEX, ANNE MISSED HER FRIENDS. INSPIRED BY A BOOK BY HER FAVORITE AUTHOR, CISSY VAN MARXVELDT, SHE STARTED TO WRITE HER DIARY IN THE FORM OF LETTERS TO A GROUP OF IMAGINARY FRIENDS AND ONE REAL ONE, JACQUELINE.
DEAR KITTY, YESTERDAY I WROTE TO EMMY AND JETTJE, BUT I PREFER WRITING TO YOU.
ANNE HAD PROMISED TO WRITE A FAREWELL LETTER TO JACQUELINE...OF COURSE SHE COULD NOT SEND IT.
WHY CAN'T MIEP GIVE IT TO JACQUELINE?
NO ANNELEIN, THAT'S MUCH TOO DANGEROUS.
IN THE END, SHE PICKED KITTY TO ADDRESS HER DIARY LETTERS TO.
YOUR CLASSMATE BETTY BLOEMENDAAL HAS BEEN DEPORTED TO POLAND...
OH, NO... THAT'S SO TERRIBLE...
WE ARE SO LUCKY HERE...
THE OUTSIDE WORLD WAS DANGEROUS... IN AMSTERDAM MORE AND MORE JEWS WERE ROUNDED UP...
BUT IT WAS NOT EASY FOR ANNE IN THE HIDING PLACE. SHE JUST DID NOT GET ALONG WITH HER MOTHER, WHILE SHE ADORED HER FATHER...
I CAN'T STAND MOTHER... I LOVE YOU MORE.
IT'S JUST A PASSING PHASE, ANNE. I THINK YOU SHOULD HELP HER WHEN SHE'S NOT FEELING WELL OR HAS A HEADACHE
I SHAN'T... I DON'T LIKE HER.

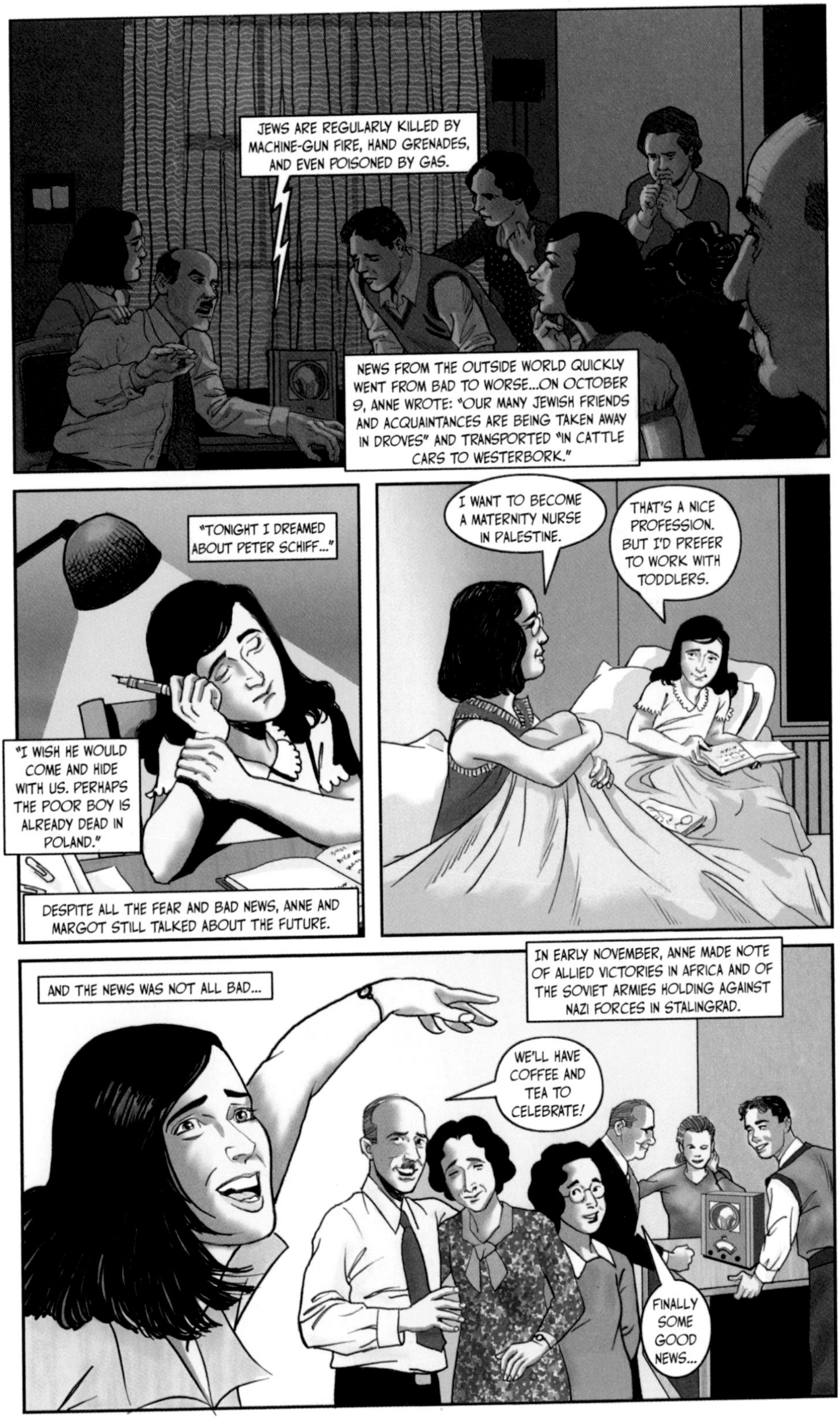
JEWS ARE REGULARLY KILLED BY MACHINE-GUN FIRE, HAND GRENADES, AND EVEN POISONED BY GAS.
NEWS FROM THE OUTSIDE WORLD QUICKLY WENT FROM BAD TO WORSE...ON OCTOBER 9, ANNE WROTE: "OUR MANY JEWISH FRIENDS AND ACQUAINTANCES ARE BEING TAKEN AWAY IN DROVES" AND TRANSPORTED "IN CATTLE CARS TO WESTERBORK."
"TONIGHT I DREAMED ABOUT PETER SCHIFF..."
"I WISH HE WOULD COME AND HIDE WITH US. PERHAPS THE POOR BOY IS ALREADY DEAD IN POLAND."
DESPITE ALL THE FEAR AND BAD NEWS, ANNE AND MARGOT STILL TALKED ABOUT THE FUTURE.
I WANT TO BECOME A MATERNITY NURSE IN PALESTINE.
THAT'S A NICE PROFESSION. BUT I'D PREFER TO WORK WITH TODDLERS.
AND THE NEWS WAS NOT ALL BAD...
IN EARLY NOVEMBER, ANNE MADE NOTE OF ALLIED VICTORIES IN AFRICA AND OF THE SOVIET ARMIES HOLDING AGAINST NAZI FORCES IN STALINGRAD.
WE'LL HAVE COFFEE AND TEA TO CELEBRATE!
FINALLY SOME GOOD NEWS...

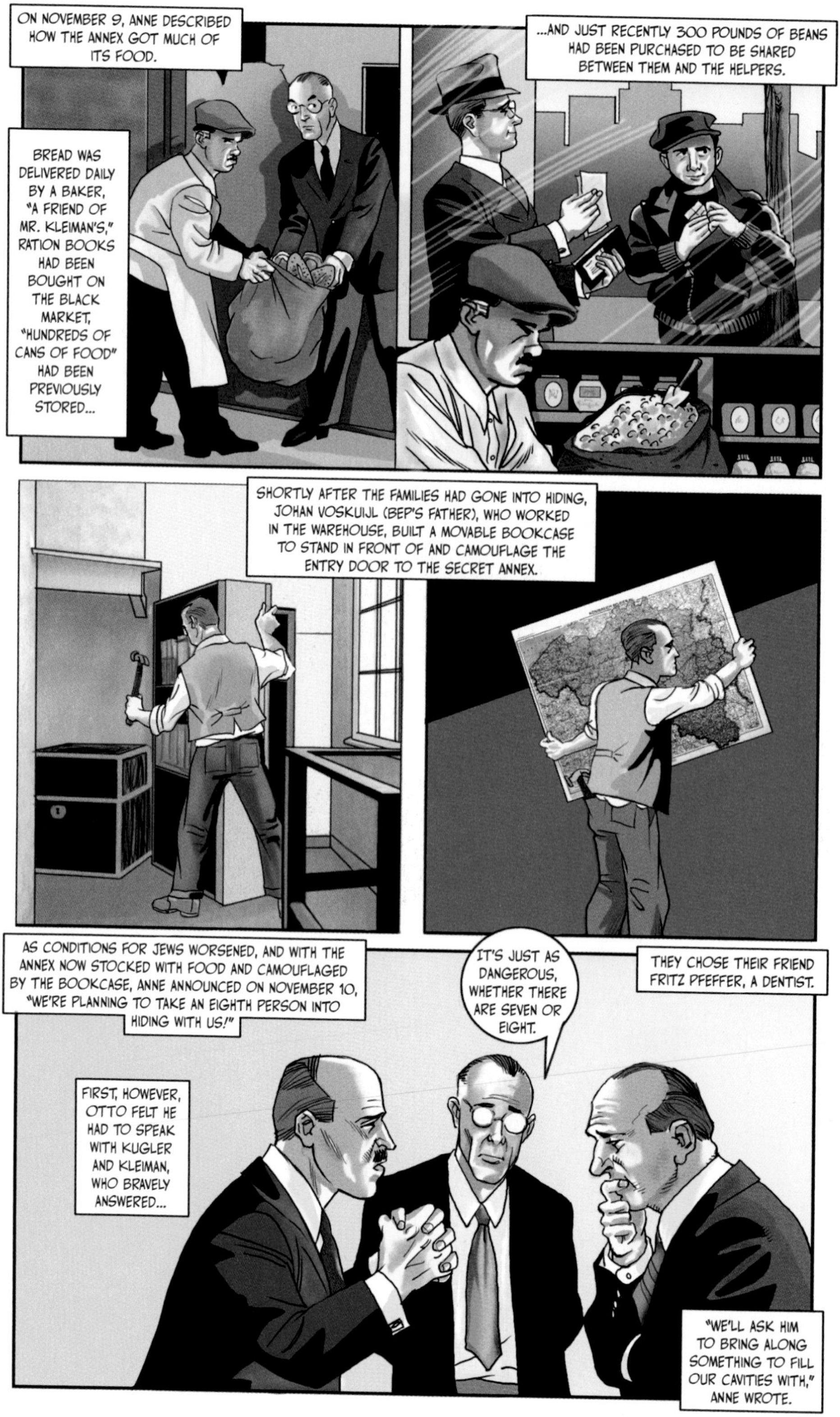

ON NOVEMBER 9, ANNE DESCRIBED HOW THE ANNEX GOT MUCH OF ITS FOOD.
BREAD WAS DELIVERED DAILY BY A BAKER, "A FRIEND OF MR. KLEIMAN'S," RATION BOOKS HAD BEEN BOUGHT ON THE BLACK MARKET, "HUNDREDS OF CANS OF FOOD" HAD BEEN PREVIOUSLY STORED...
...AND JUST RECENTLY 300 POUNDS OF BEANS HAD BEEN PURCHASED TO BE SHARED BETWEEN THEM AND THE HELPERS.
SHORTLY AFTER THE FAMILIES HAD GONE INTO HIDING, JOHAN VOSKUIJL (BEP'S FATHER), WHO WORKED IN THE WAREHOUSE, BUILT A MOVABLE BOOKCASE TO STAND IN FRONT OF AND CAMOUFLAGE THE ENTRY DOOR TO THE SECRET ANNEX.
AS CONDITIONS FOR JEWS WORSENED, AND WITH THE ANNEX NOW STOCKED WITH FOOD AND CAMOUFLAGED BY THE BOOKCASE, ANNE ANNOUNCED ON NOVEMBER 10, "WE'RE PLANNING TO TAKE AN EIGHTH PERSON INTO HIDING WITH US!"
FIRST, HOWEVER, OTTO FELT HE HAD TO SPEAK WITH KUGLER AND KLEIMAN, WHO BRAVELY ANSWERED...
IT'S JUST AS DANGEROUS, WHETHER THERE ARE SEVEN OR EIGHT.
THEY CHOSE THEIR FRIEND FRITZ PFEFFER, A DENTIST.
"WE'LL ASK HIM TO BRING ALONG SOMETHING TO FILL OUR CAVITIES WITH," ANNE WROTE.

CHAPTER 7

The Eight Hiders

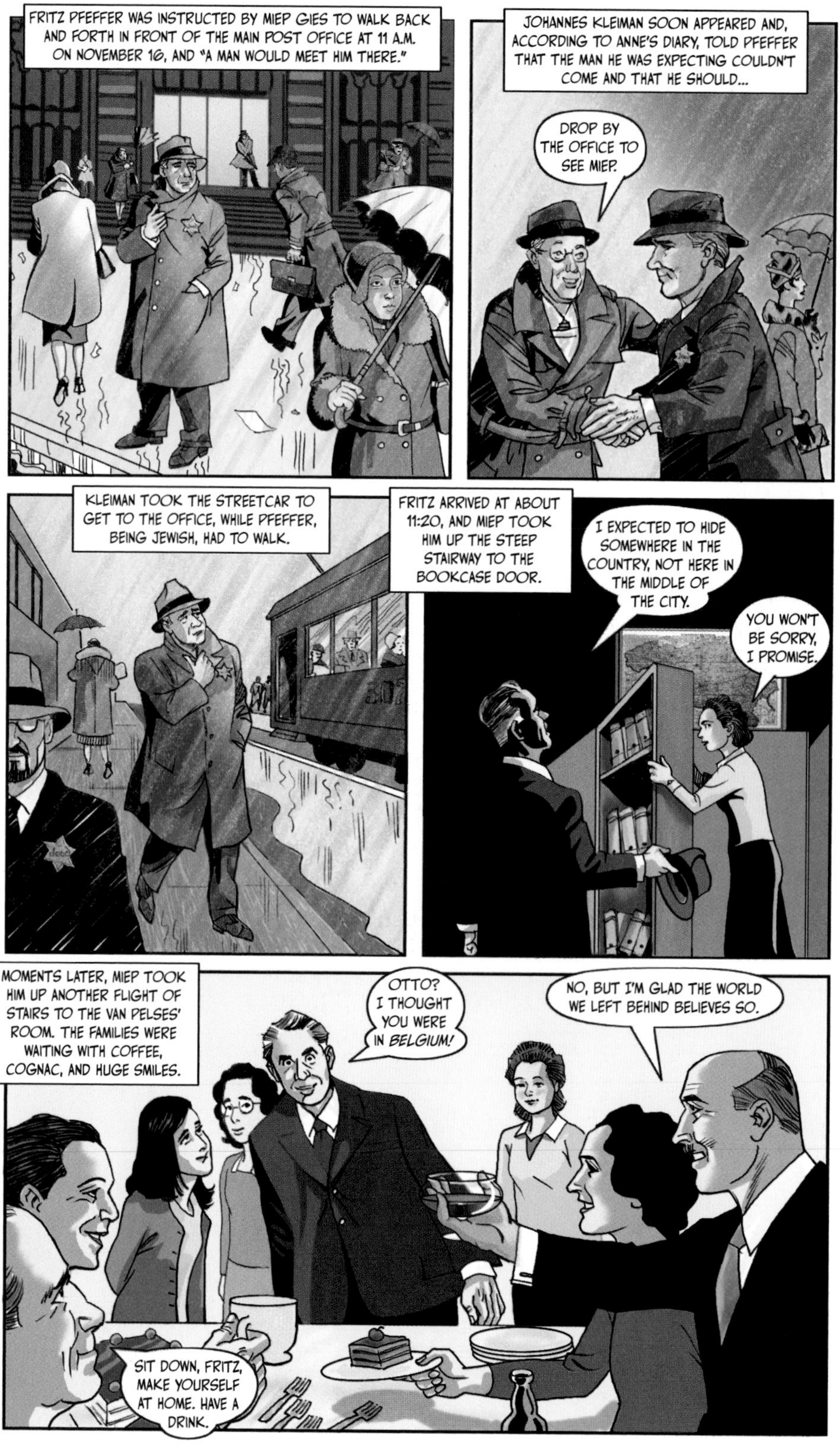
FRITZ PFEFFER WAS INSTRUCTED BY MIEP GIES TO WALK BACK AND FORTH IN FRONT OF THE MAIN POST OFFICE AT 11 A.M. ON NOVEMBER 16, AND "A MAN WOULD MEET HIM THERE."
JOHANNES KLEIMAN SOON APPEARED AND, ACCORDING TO ANNE'S DIARY, TOLD PFEFFER THAT THE MAN HE WAS EXPECTING COULDN'T COME AND THAT HE SHOULD...
DROP BY THE OFFICE TO SEE MIEP.
KLEIMAN TOOK THE STREETCAR TO GET TO THE OFFICE, WHILE PFEFFER, BEING JEWISH, HAD TO WALK.
FRITZ ARRIVED AT ABOUT 11:20, AND MIEP TOOK HIM UP THE STEEP STAIRWAY TO THE BOOKCASE DOOR.
I EXPECTED TO HIDE SOMEWHERE IN THE COUNTRY, NOT HERE IN THE MIDDLE OF THE CITY.
YOU WON'T BE SORRY, I PROMISE.
MOMENTS LATER, MIEP TOOK HIM UP ANOTHER FLIGHT OF STAIRS TO THE VAN PELSES' ROOM. THE FAMILIES WERE WAITING WITH COFFEE, COGNAC, AND HUGE SMILES.
OTTO? I THOUGHT YOU WERE IN *BELGIUM!*
NO, BUT I'M GLAD THE WORLD WE LEFT BEHIND BELIEVES SO.
SIT DOWN, FRITZ, MAKE YOURSELF AT HOME. HAVE A DRINK.

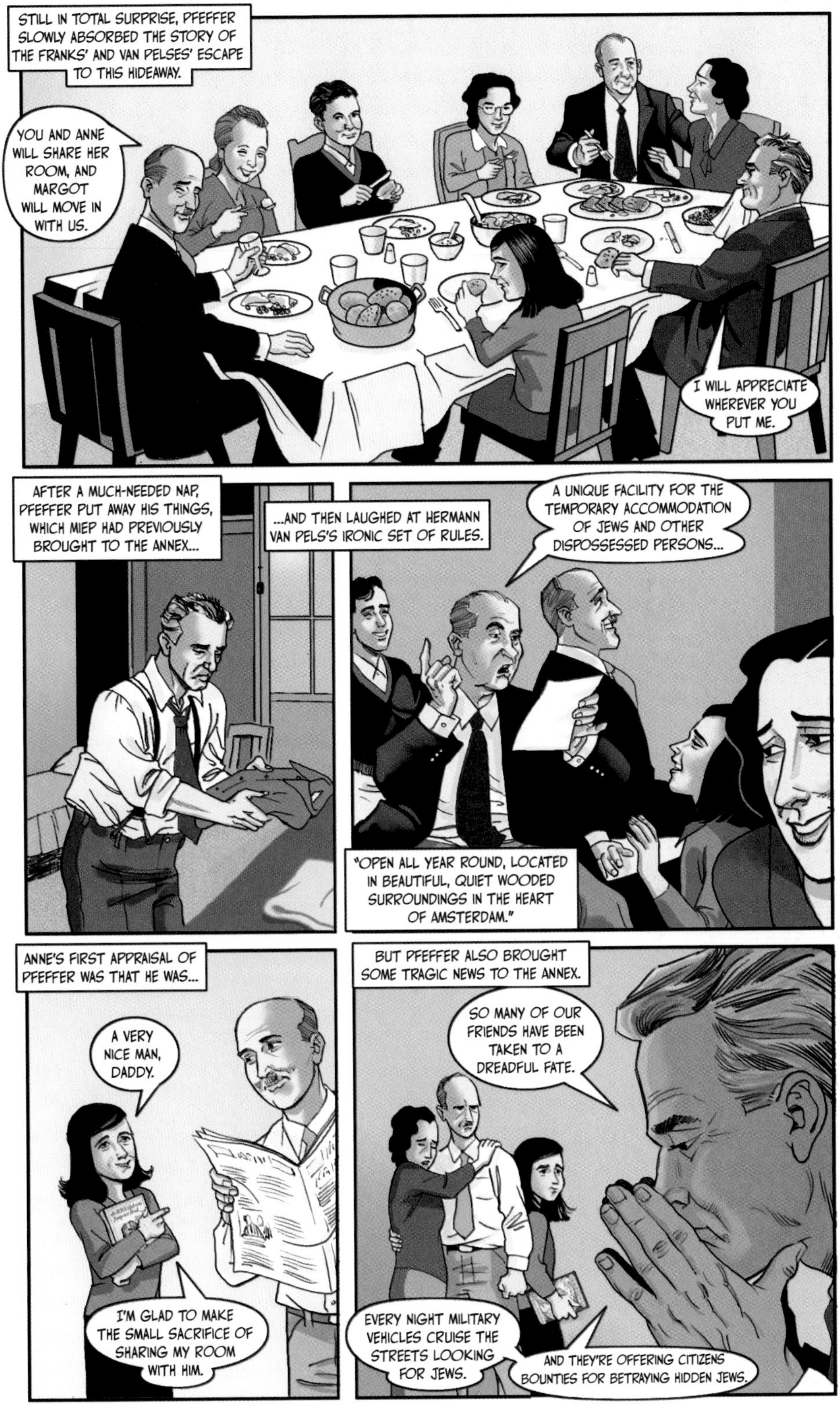
STILL IN TOTAL SURPRISE, PFEFFER SLOWLY ABSORBED THE STORY OF THE FRANKS' AND VAN PELSES' ESCAPE TO THIS HIDEAWAY.
YOU AND ANNE WILL SHARE HER ROOM, AND MARGOT WILL MOVE IN WITH US.
I WILL APPRECIATE WHEREVER YOU PUT ME.
AFTER A MUCH-NEEDED NAP, PFEFFER PUT AWAY HIS THINGS, WHICH MIEP HAD PREVIOUSLY BROUGHT TO THE ANNEX...
...AND THEN LAUGHED AT HERMANN VAN PELS'S IRONIC SET OF RULES.
A UNIQUE FACILITY FOR THE TEMPORARY ACCOMMODATION OF JEWS AND OTHER DISPOSSESSED PERSONS...
"OPEN ALL YEAR ROUND, LOCATED IN BEAUTIFUL, QUIET WOODED SURROUNDINGS IN THE HEART OF AMSTERDAM."
ANNE'S FIRST APPRAISAL OF PFEFFER WAS THAT HE WAS...
A VERY NICE MAN, DADDY.
I'M GLAD TO MAKE THE SMALL SACRIFICE OF SHARING MY ROOM WITH HIM.
BUT PFEFFER ALSO BROUGHT SOME TRAGIC NEWS TO THE ANNEX.
SO MANY OF OUR FRIENDS HAVE BEEN TAKEN TO A DREADFUL FATE.
EVERY NIGHT MILITARY VEHICLES CRUISE THE STREETS LOOKING FOR JEWS.
AND THEY'RE OFFERING CITIZENS BOUNTIES FOR BETRAYING HIDDEN JEWS.

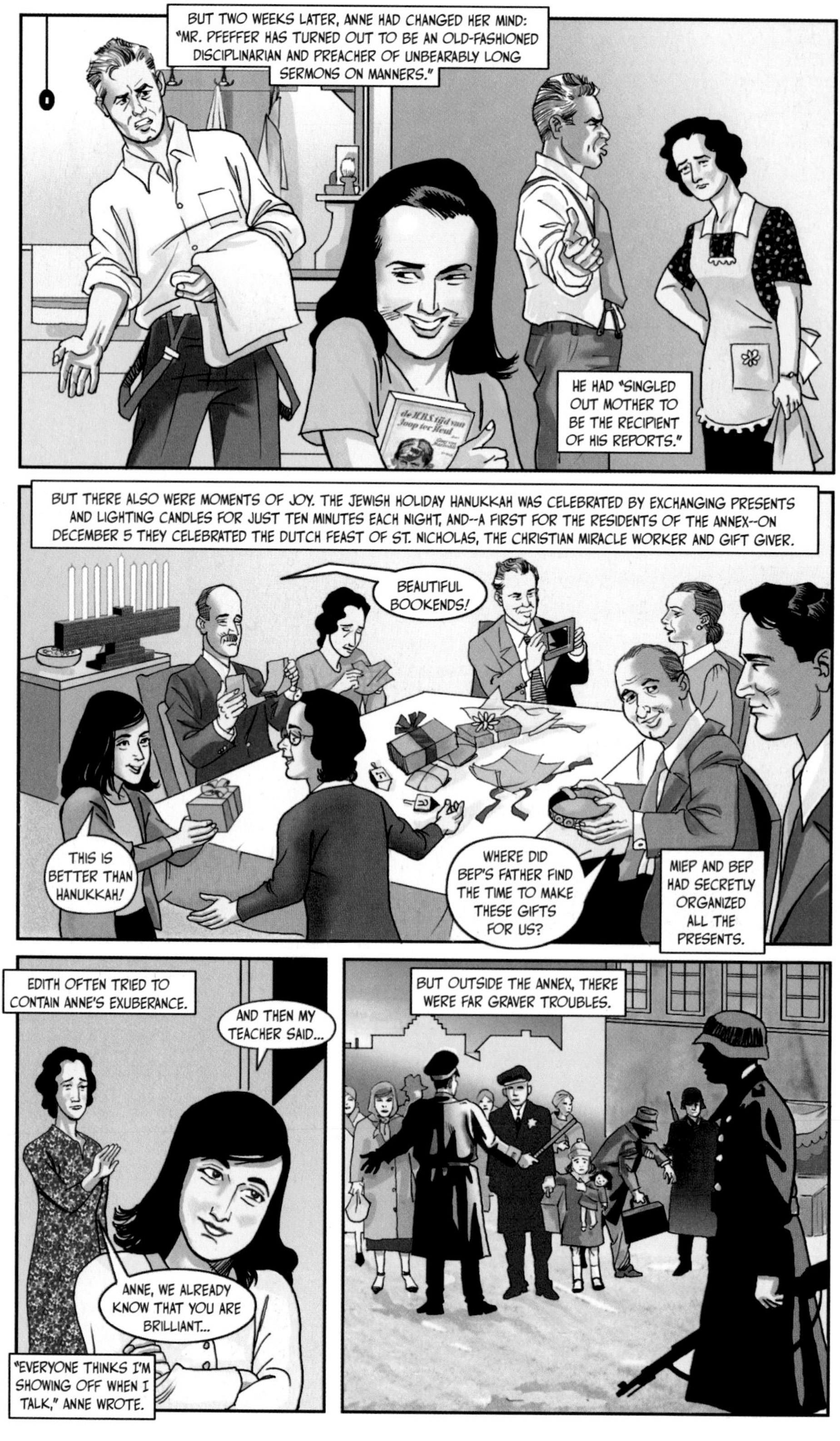

BUT TWO WEEKS LATER, ANNE HAD CHANGED HER MIND: "MR. PFEFFER HAS TURNED OUT TO BE AN OLD-FASHIONED DISCIPLINARIAN AND PREACHER OF UNBEARABLY LONG SERMONS ON MANNERS."
HE HAD "SINGLED OUT MOTHER TO BE THE RECIPIENT OF HIS REPORTS."
BUT THERE ALSO WERE MOMENTS OF JOY. THE JEWISH HOLIDAY HANUKKAH WAS CELEBRATED BY EXCHANGING PRESENTS AND LIGHTING CANDLES FOR JUST TEN MINUTES EACH NIGHT, AND--A FIRST FOR THE RESIDENTS OF THE ANNEX--ON DECEMBER 5 THEY CELEBRATED THE DUTCH FEAST OF ST. NICHOLAS, THE CHRISTIAN MIRACLE WORKER AND GIFT GIVER.
BEAUTIFUL BOOKENDS!
THIS IS BETTER THAN HANUKKAH!
WHERE DID BEP'S FATHER FIND THE TIME TO MAKE THESE GIFTS FOR US?
MIEP AND BEP HAD SECRETLY ORGANIZED ALL THE PRESENTS.
EDITH OFTEN TRIED TO CONTAIN ANNE'S EXUBERANCE.
AND THEN MY TEACHER SAID...
ANNE, WE ALREADY KNOW THAT YOU ARE BRILLIANT...
"EVERYONE THINKS I'M SHOWING OFF WHEN I TALK," ANNE WROTE.
BUT OUTSIDE THE ANNEX, THERE WERE FAR GRAVER TROUBLES.

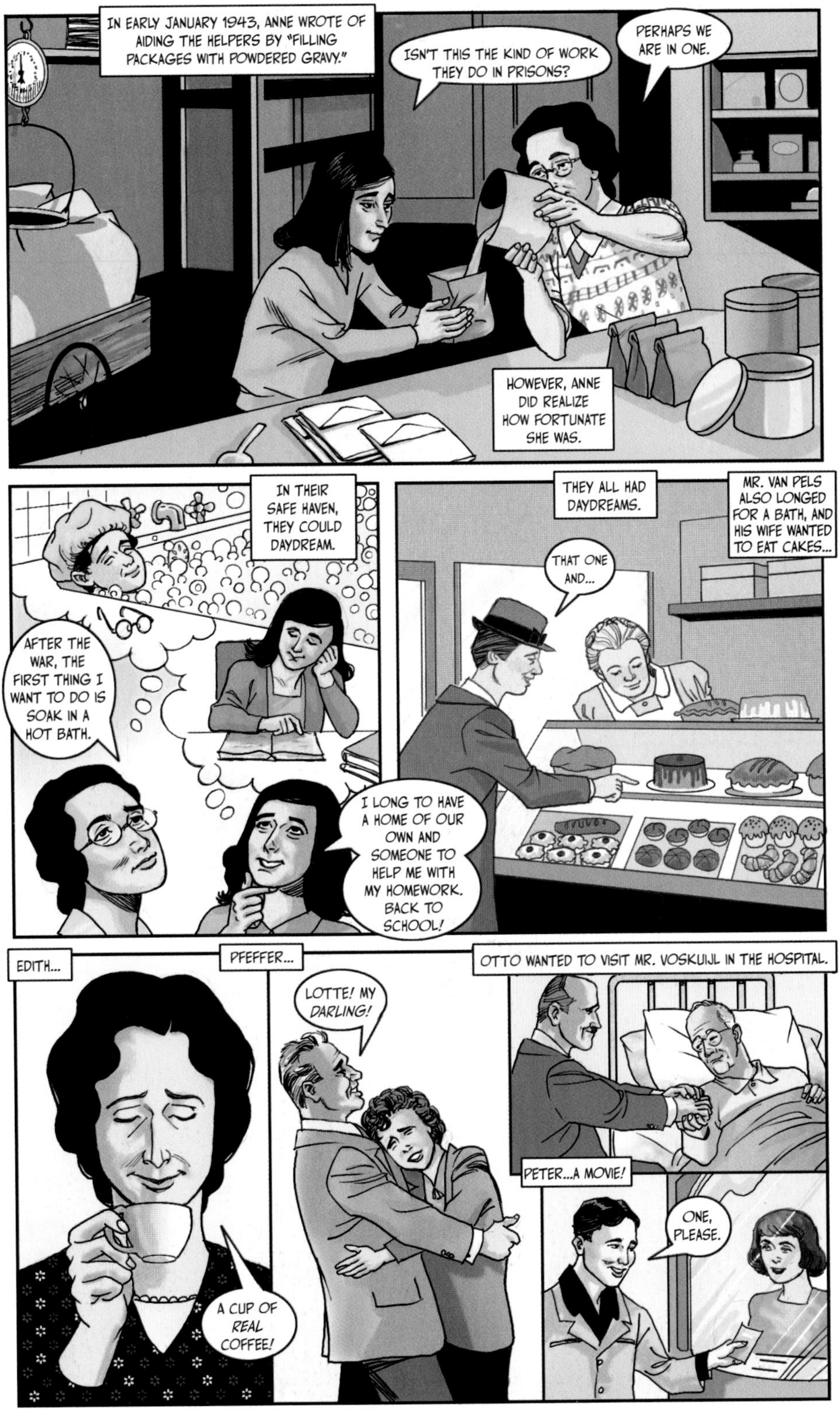
IN EARLY JANUARY 1943, ANNE WROTE OF AIDING THE HELPERS BY "FILLING PACKAGES WITH POWDERED GRAVY."
ISN'T THIS THE KIND OF WORK THEY DO IN PRISONS?
PERHAPS WE ARE IN ONE.
HOWEVER, ANNE DID REALIZE HOW FORTUNATE SHE WAS.
IN THEIR SAFE HAVEN, THEY COULD DAYDREAM.
AFTER THE WAR, THE FIRST THING I WANT TO DO IS SOAK IN A HOT BATH.
I LONG TO HAVE A HOME OF OUR OWN AND SOMEONE TO HELP ME WITH MY HOMEWORK. BACK TO SCHOOL!
THEY ALL HAD DAYDREAMS.
MR. VAN PELS ALSO LONGED FOR A BATH, AND HIS WIFE WANTED TO EAT CAKES...
THAT ONE AND...
EDITH...
A CUP OF REAL COFFEE!
PFEFFER...
LOTTE! MY DARLING!
OTTO WANTED TO VISIT MR. VOSKUIJL IN THE HOSPITAL.
PETER...A MOVIE!
ONE, PLEASE.

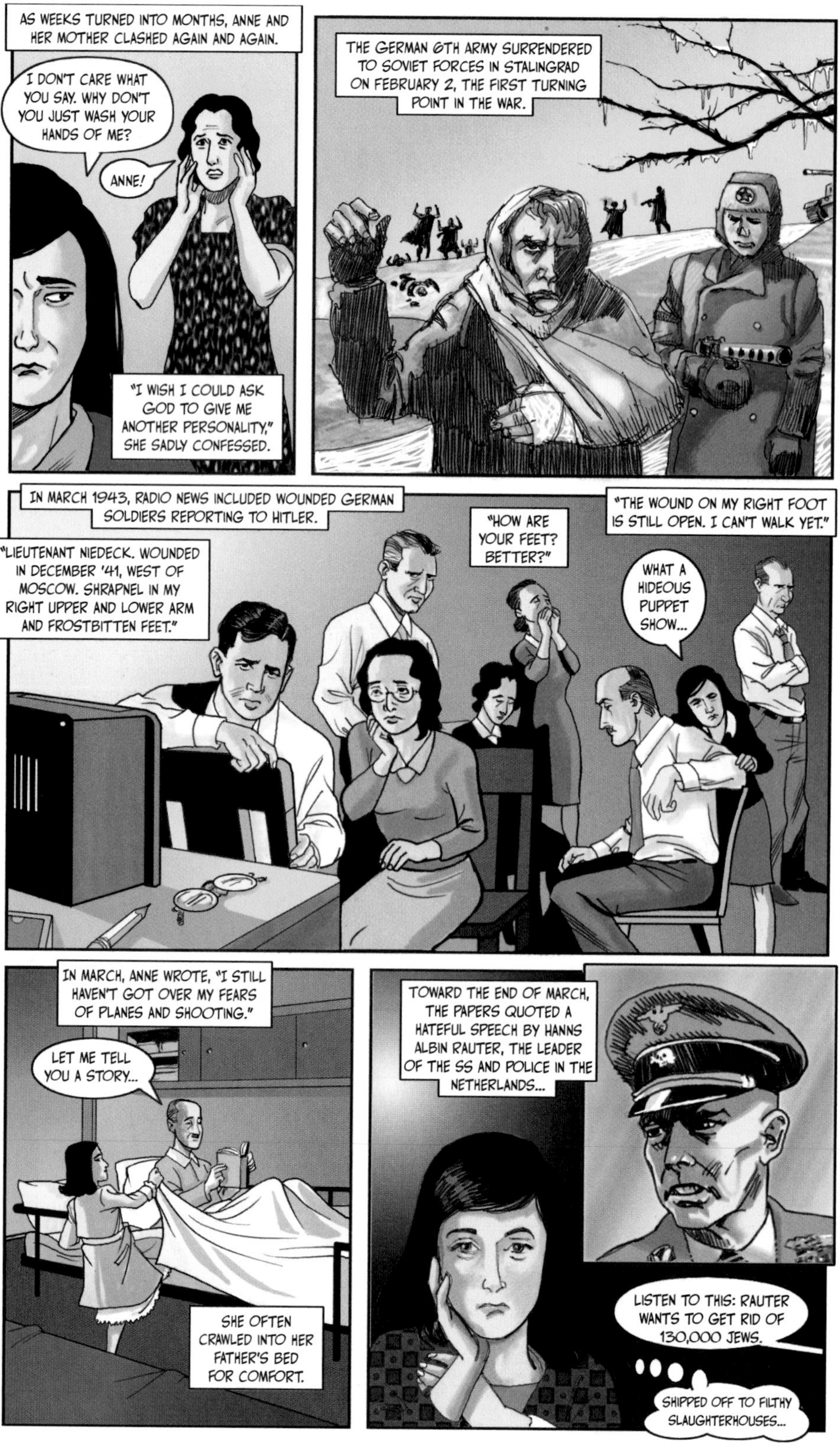
AS WEEKS TURNED INTO MONTHS, ANNE AND HER MOTHER CLASHED AGAIN AND AGAIN.
I DON'T CARE WHAT YOU SAY. WHY DON'T YOU JUST WASH YOUR HANDS OF ME?
ANNE!
"I WISH I COULD ASK GOD TO GIVE ME ANOTHER PERSONALITY," SHE SADLY CONFESSED.
THE GERMAN 6TH ARMY SURRENDERED TO SOVIET FORCES IN STALINGRAD ON FEBRUARY 2, THE FIRST TURNING POINT IN THE WAR.
IN MARCH 1943, RADIO NEWS INCLUDED WOUNDED GERMAN SOLDIERS REPORTING TO HITLER.
"LIEUTENANT NIEDECK. WOUNDED IN DECEMBER '41, WEST OF MOSCOW. SHRAPNEL IN MY RIGHT UPPER AND LOWER ARM AND FROSTBITTEN FEET."
"HOW ARE YOUR FEET? BETTER?"
"THE WOUND ON MY RIGHT FOOT IS STILL OPEN. I CAN'T WALK YET."
WHAT A HIDEOUS PUPPET SHOW...
IN MARCH, ANNE WROTE, "I STILL HAVEN'T GOT OVER MY FEARS OF PLANES AND SHOOTING."
LET ME TELL YOU A STORY...
SHE OFTEN CRAWLED INTO HER FATHER'S BED FOR COMFORT.
TOWARD THE END OF MARCH, THE PAPERS QUOTED A HATEFUL SPEECH BY HANNS ALBIN RAUTER, THE LEADER OF THE SS AND POLICE IN THE NETHERLANDS...
LISTEN TO THIS: RAUTER WANTS TO GET RID OF 130,000 JEWS.
SHIPPED OFF TO FILTHY SLAUGHTERHOUSES...

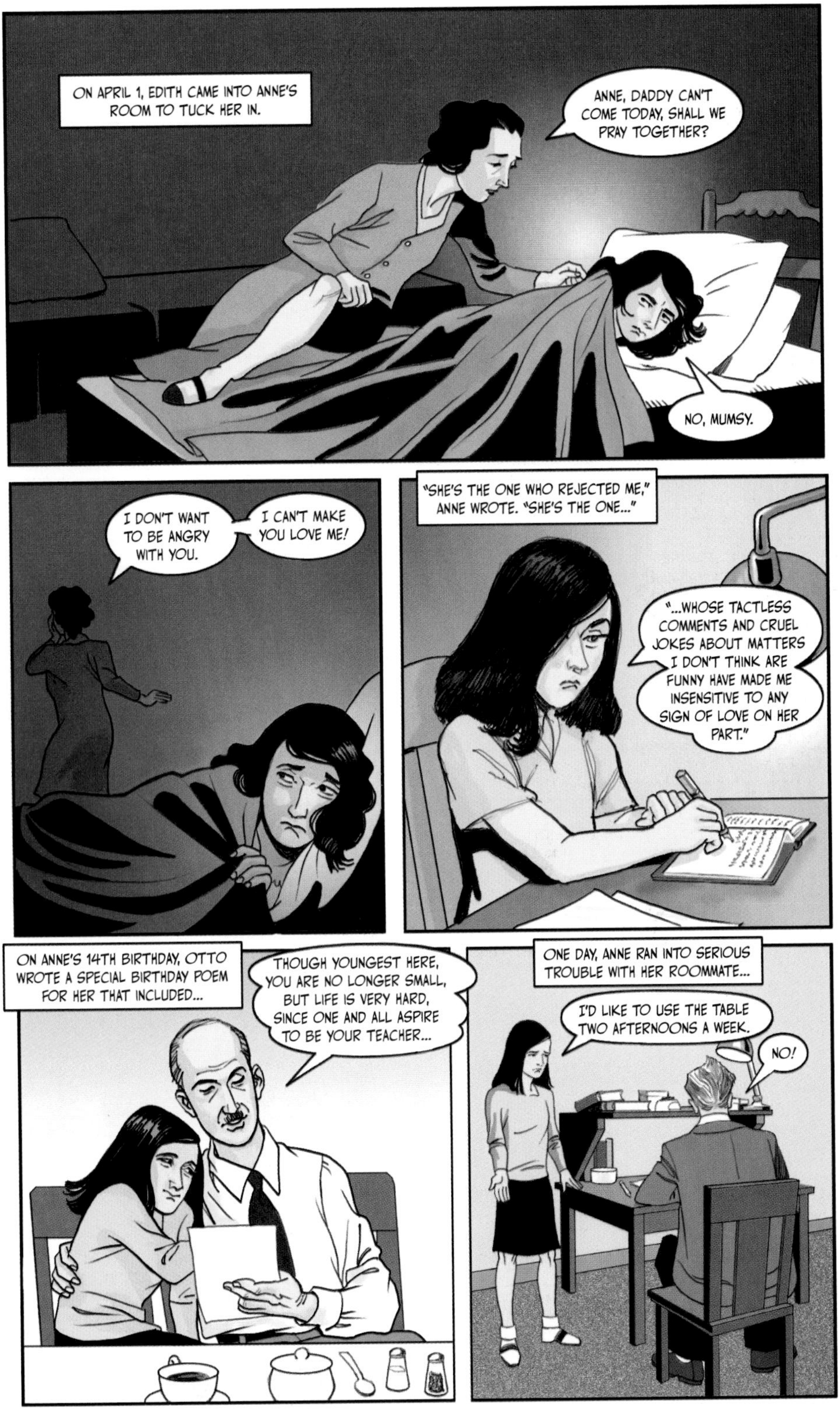
ON APRIL 1, EDITH CAME INTO ANNE'S ROOM TO TUCK HER IN.
ANNE, DADDY CAN'T COME TODAY, SHALL WE PRAY TOGETHER?
NO, MUMSY.
I DON'T WANT TO BE ANGRY WITH YOU.
I CAN'T MAKE YOU LOVE ME!
"SHE'S THE ONE WHO REJECTED ME," ANNE WROTE. "SHE'S THE ONE..."
"...WHOSE TACTLESS COMMENTS AND CRUEL JOKES ABOUT MATTERS I DON'T THINK ARE FUNNY HAVE MADE ME INSENSITIVE TO ANY SIGN OF LOVE ON HER PART."
ON ANNE'S 14TH BIRTHDAY, OTTO WROTE A SPECIAL BIRTHDAY POEM FOR HER THAT INCLUDED...
THOUGH YOUNGEST HERE, YOU ARE NO LONGER SMALL, BUT LIFE IS VERY HARD, SINCE ONE AND ALL ASPIRE TO BE YOUR TEACHER...
ONE DAY, ANNE RAN INTO SERIOUS TROUBLE WITH HER ROOMMATE...
I'D LIKE TO USE THE TABLE TWO AFTERNOONS A WEEK.
NO!

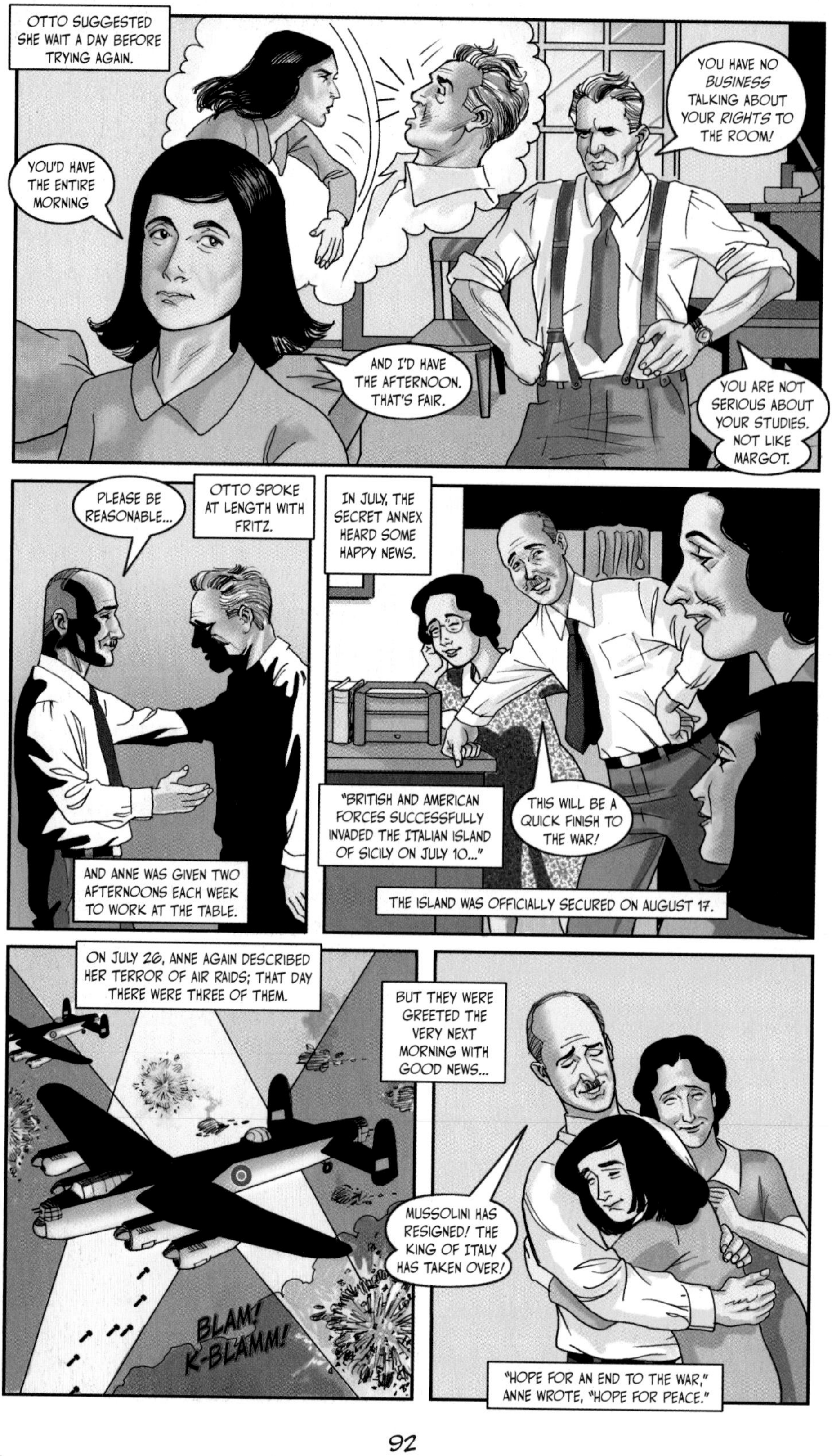

OTTO SUGGESTED SHE WAIT A DAY BEFORE TRYING AGAIN.
YOU'D HAVE THE ENTIRE MORNING
AND I'D HAVE THE AFTERNOON. THAT'S FAIR.
YOU HAVE NO *BUSINESS* TALKING ABOUT YOUR *RIGHTS* TO THE ROOM!
YOU ARE NOT SERIOUS ABOUT YOUR STUDIES. NOT LIKE MARGOT.
PLEASE BE REASONABLE...
OTTO SPOKE AT LENGTH WITH FRITZ.
AND ANNE WAS GIVEN TWO AFTERNOONS EACH WEEK TO WORK AT THE TABLE.
IN JULY, THE SECRET ANNEX HEARD SOME HAPPY NEWS.
"BRITISH AND AMERICAN FORCES SUCCESSFULLY INVADED THE ITALIAN ISLAND OF SICILY ON JULY 10..."
THIS WILL BE A QUICK FINISH TO THE WAR!
THE ISLAND WAS OFFICIALLY SECURED ON AUGUST 17.
ON JULY 26, ANNE AGAIN DESCRIBED HER TERROR OF AIR RAIDS; THAT DAY THERE WERE THREE OF THEM.
BLAM! K-BLAMM!
BUT THEY WERE GREETED THE VERY NEXT MORNING WITH GOOD NEWS...
MUSSOLINI HAS RESIGNED! THE KING OF ITALY HAS TAKEN OVER!
"HOPE FOR AN END TO THE WAR," ANNE WROTE, "HOPE FOR PEACE."

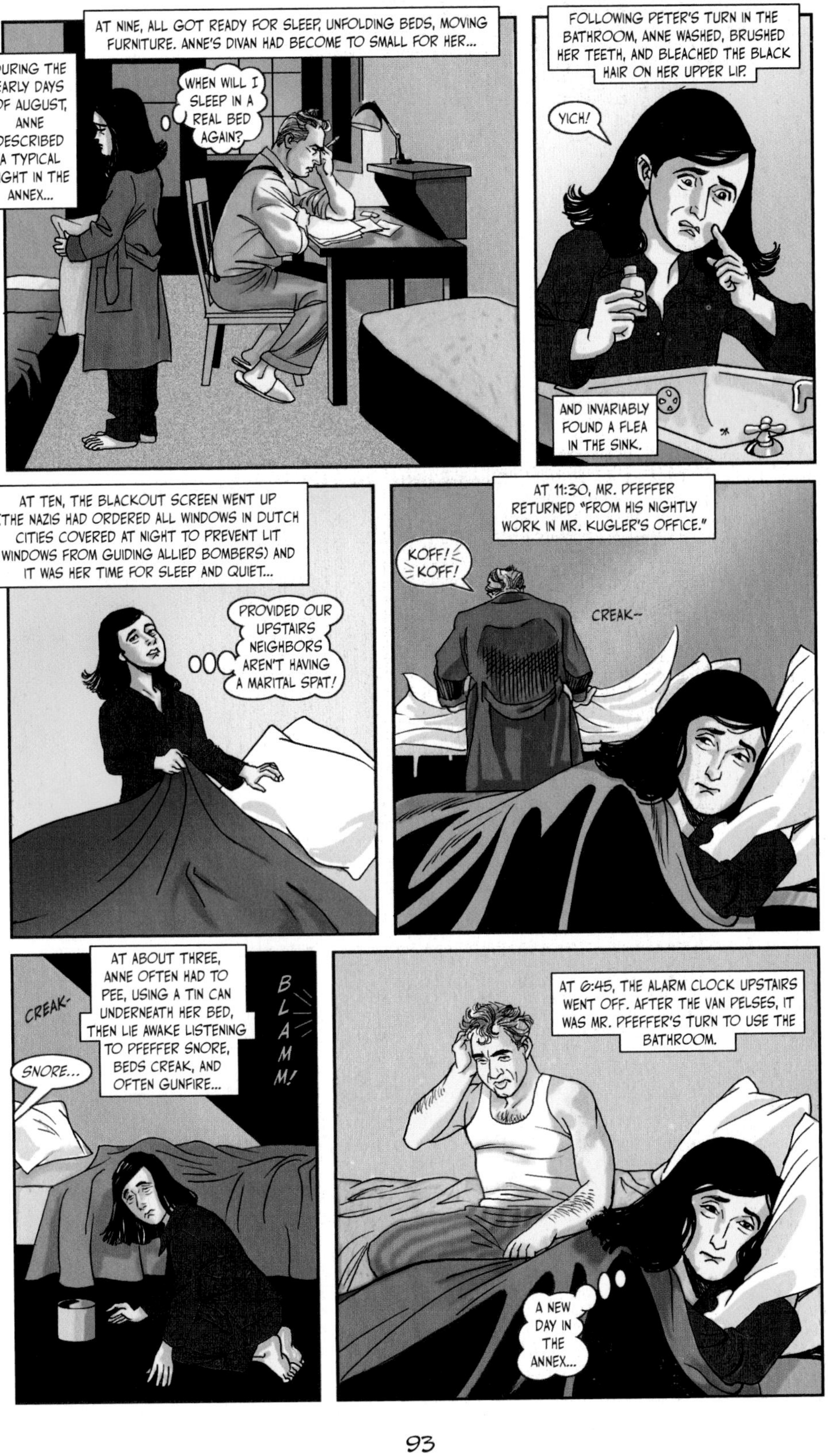
AT NINE, ALL GOT READY FOR SLEEP, UNFOLDING BEDS, MOVING FURNITURE. ANNE'S DIVAN HAD BECOME TO SMALL FOR HER...
DURING THE EARLY DAYS OF AUGUST, ANNE DESCRIBED A TYPICAL NIGHT IN THE ANNEX...
WHEN WILL I SLEEP IN A REAL BED AGAIN?
FOLLOWING PETER'S TURN IN THE BATHROOM, ANNE WASHED, BRUSHED HER TEETH, AND BLEACHED THE BLACK HAIR ON HER UPPER LIP.
YICH!
AND INVARIABLY FOUND A FLEA IN THE SINK.
AT TEN, THE BLACKOUT SCREEN WENT UP (THE NAZIS HAD ORDERED ALL WINDOWS IN DUTCH CITIES COVERED AT NIGHT TO PREVENT LIT WINDOWS FROM GUIDING ALLIED BOMBERS) AND IT WAS HER TIME FOR SLEEP AND QUIET...
PROVIDED OUR UPSTAIRS NEIGHBORS AREN'T HAVING A MARITAL SPAT!
AT 11:30, MR. PFEFFER RETURNED "FROM HIS NIGHTLY WORK IN MR. KUGLER'S OFFICE."
KOFF! KOFF!
CREAK~
AT ABOUT THREE, ANNE OFTEN HAD TO PEE, USING A TIN CAN UNDERNEATH HER BED, THEN LIE AWAKE LISTENING TO PFEFFER SNORE, BEDS CREAK, AND OFTEN GUNFIRE...
CREAK-
SNORE...
BLAMM!
AT 6:45, THE ALARM CLOCK UPSTAIRS WENT OFF. AFTER THE VAN PELSES, IT WAS MR. PFEFFER'S TURN TO USE THE BATHROOM.
A NEW DAY IN THE ANNEX...

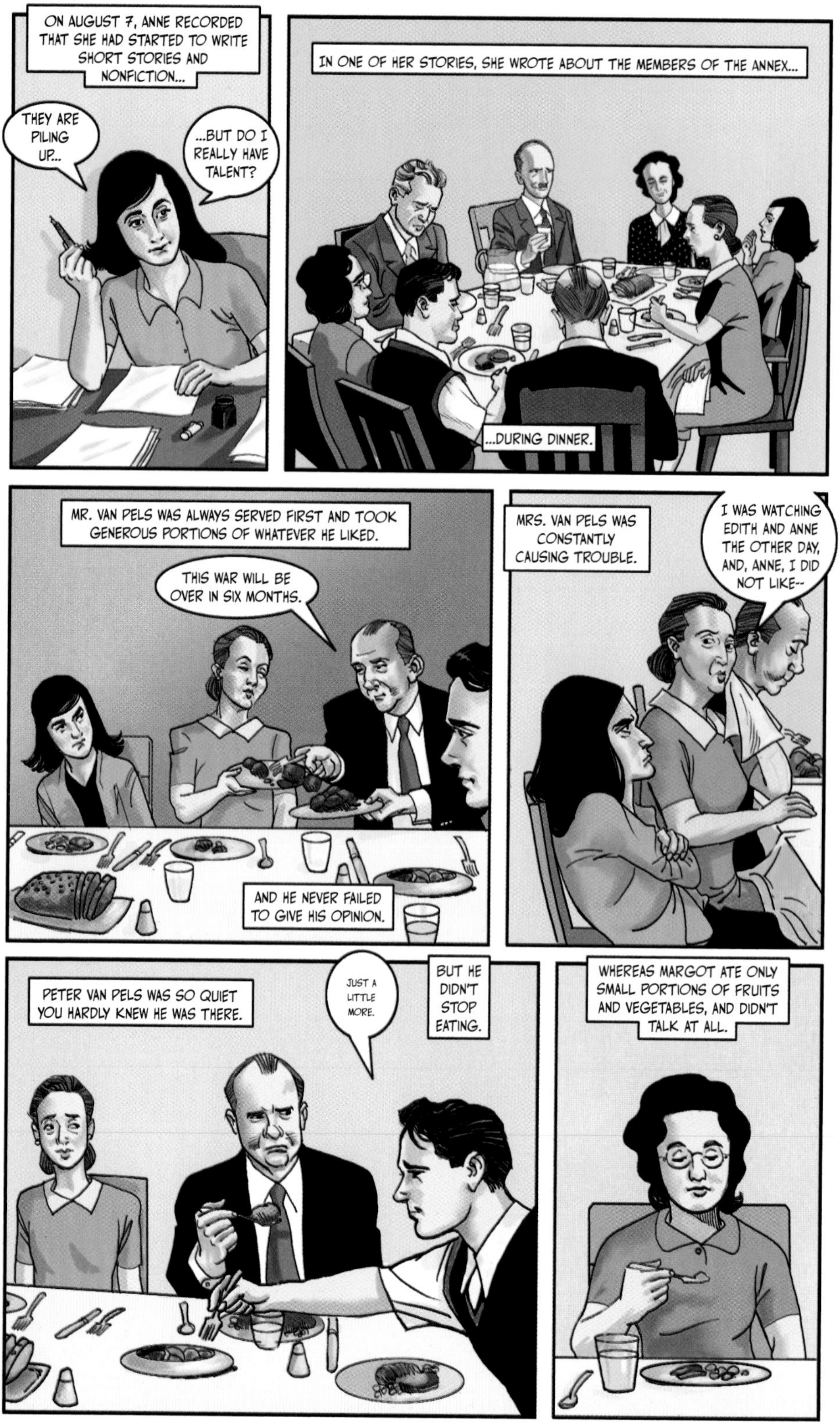
ON AUGUST 7, ANNE RECORDED THAT SHE HAD STARTED TO WRITE SHORT STORIES AND NONFICTION...
THEY ARE PILING UP...
...BUT DO I REALLY HAVE TALENT?
IN ONE OF HER STORIES, SHE WROTE ABOUT THE MEMBERS OF THE ANNEX...
...DURING DINNER.
MR. VAN PELS WAS ALWAYS SERVED FIRST AND TOOK GENEROUS PORTIONS OF WHATEVER HE LIKED.
THIS WAR WILL BE OVER IN SIX MONTHS.
AND HE NEVER FAILED TO GIVE HIS OPINION.
MRS. VAN PELS WAS CONSTANTLY CAUSING TROUBLE.
I WAS WATCHING EDITH AND ANNE THE OTHER DAY, AND, ANNE, I DID NOT LIKE--
PETER VAN PELS WAS SO QUIET YOU HARDLY KNEW HE WAS THERE.
JUST A LITTLE MORE.
BUT HE DIDN'T STOP EATING.
WHEREAS MARGOT ATE ONLY SMALL PORTIONS OF FRUITS AND VEGETABLES, AND DIDN'T TALK AT ALL.

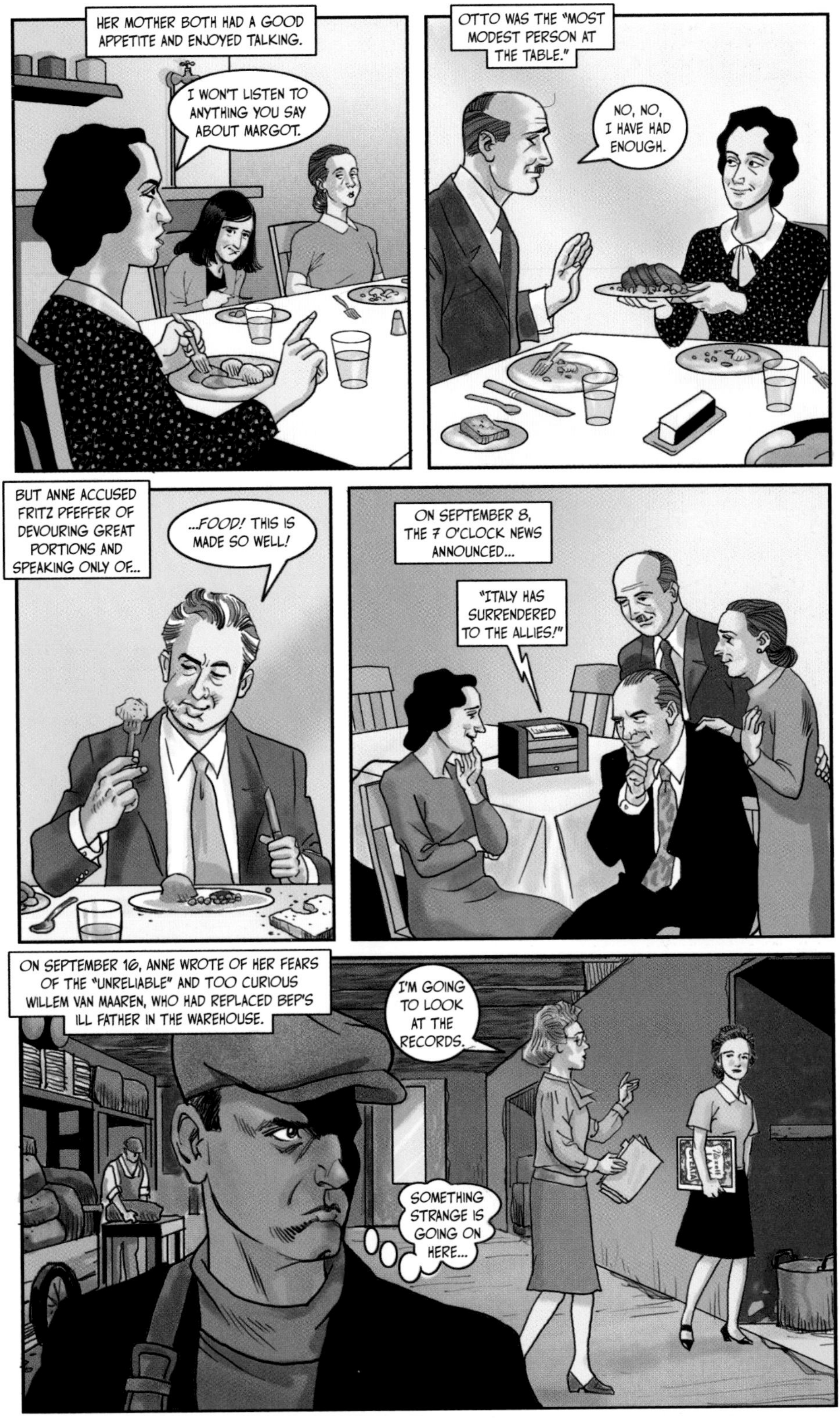
HER MOTHER BOTH HAD A GOOD APPETITE AND ENJOYED TALKING.
I WON'T LISTEN TO ANYTHING YOU SAY ABOUT MARGOT.
OTTO WAS THE "MOST MODEST PERSON AT THE TABLE."
NO, NO, I HAVE HAD ENOUGH.
BUT ANNE ACCUSED FRITZ PFEFFER OF DEVOURING GREAT PORTIONS AND SPEAKING ONLY OF...
...FOOD! THIS IS MADE SO WELL!
ON SEPTEMBER 8, THE 7 O'CLOCK NEWS ANNOUNCED...
"ITALY HAS SURRENDERED TO THE ALLIES!"
ON SEPTEMBER 16, ANNE WROTE OF HER FEARS OF THE "UNRELIABLE" AND TOO CURIOUS WILLEM VAN MAAREN, WHO HAD REPLACED BEP'S ILL FATHER IN THE WAREHOUSE.
I'M GOING TO LOOK AT THE RECORDS.
SOMETHING STRANGE IS GOING ON HERE...

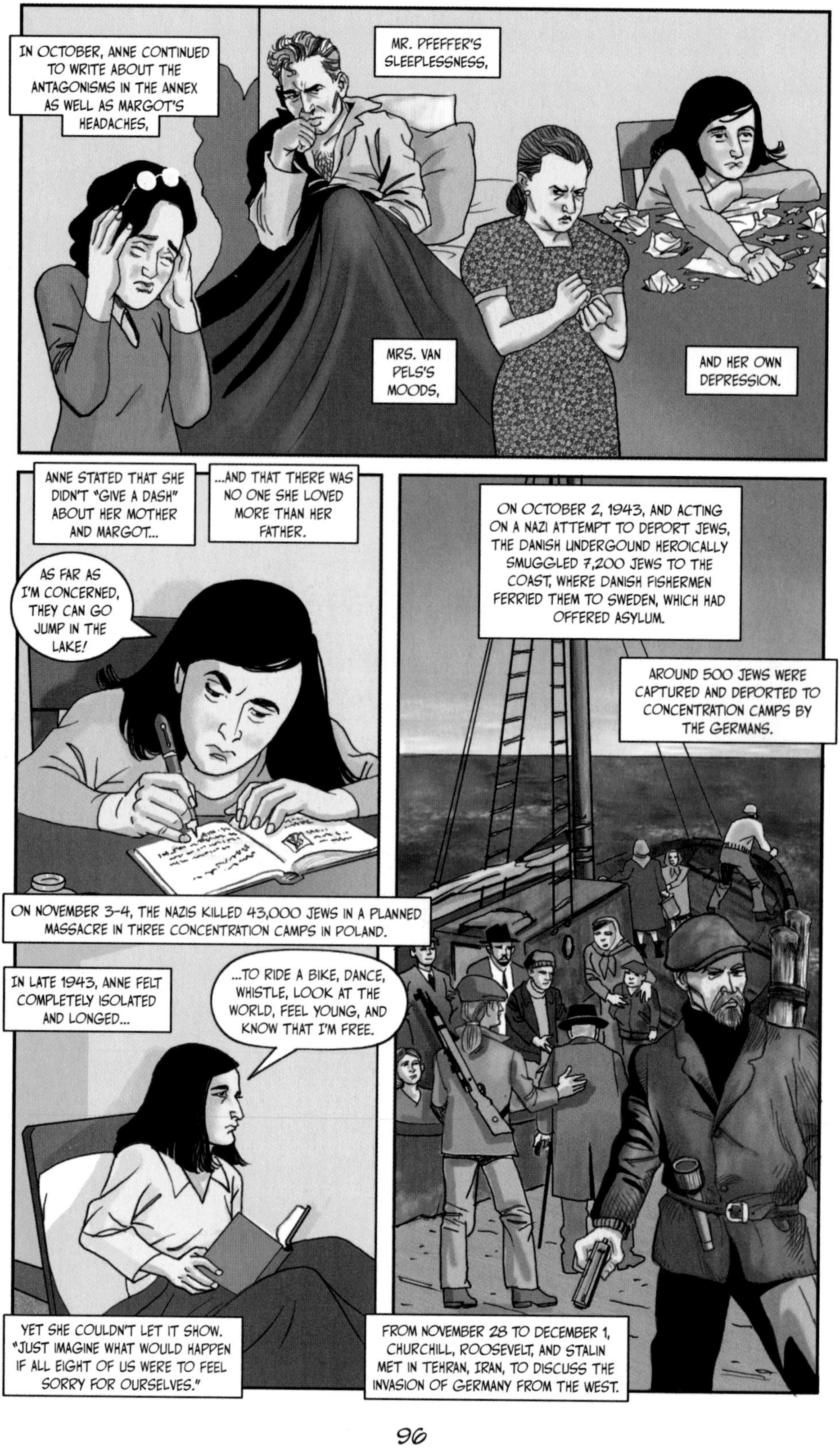
IN OCTOBER, ANNE CONTINUED TO WRITE ABOUT THE ANTAGONISMS IN THE ANNEX AS WELL AS MARGOT'S HEADACHES,
MR. PFEFFER'S SLEEPLESSNESS,
MRS. VAN PELS'S MOODS,
AND HER OWN DEPRESSION.
ANNE STATED THAT SHE DIDN'T "GIVE A DASH" ABOUT HER MOTHER AND MARGOT...
...AND THAT THERE WAS NO ONE SHE LOVED MORE THAN HER FATHER.
AS FAR AS I'M CONCERNED, THEY CAN GO JUMP IN THE LAKE!
ON OCTOBER 2, 1943, AND ACTING ON A NAZI ATTEMPT TO DEPORT JEWS, THE DANISH UNDERGOUND HEROICALLY SMUGGLED 7,200 JEWS TO THE COAST, WHERE DANISH FISHERMEN FERRIED THEM TO SWEDEN, WHICH HAD OFFERED ASYLUM.
AROUND 500 JEWS WERE CAPTURED AND DEPORTED TO CONCENTRATION CAMPS BY THE GERMANS.
ON NOVEMBER 3-4, THE NAZIS KILLED 43,000 JEWS IN A PLANNED MASSACRE IN THREE CONCENTRATION CAMPS IN POLAND.
IN LATE 1943, ANNE FELT COMPLETELY ISOLATED AND LONGED...
...TO RIDE A BIKE, DANCE, WHISTLE, LOOK AT THE WORLD, FEEL YOUNG, AND KNOW THAT I'M FREE.
YET SHE COULDN'T LET IT SHOW. "JUST IMAGINE WHAT WOULD HAPPEN IF ALL EIGHT OF US WERE TO FEEL SORRY FOR OURSELVES."
FROM NOVEMBER 28 TO DECEMBER 1, CHURCHILL, ROOSEVELT, AND STALIN MET IN TEHRAN, IRAN, TO DISCUSS THE INVASION OF GERMANY FROM THE WEST.

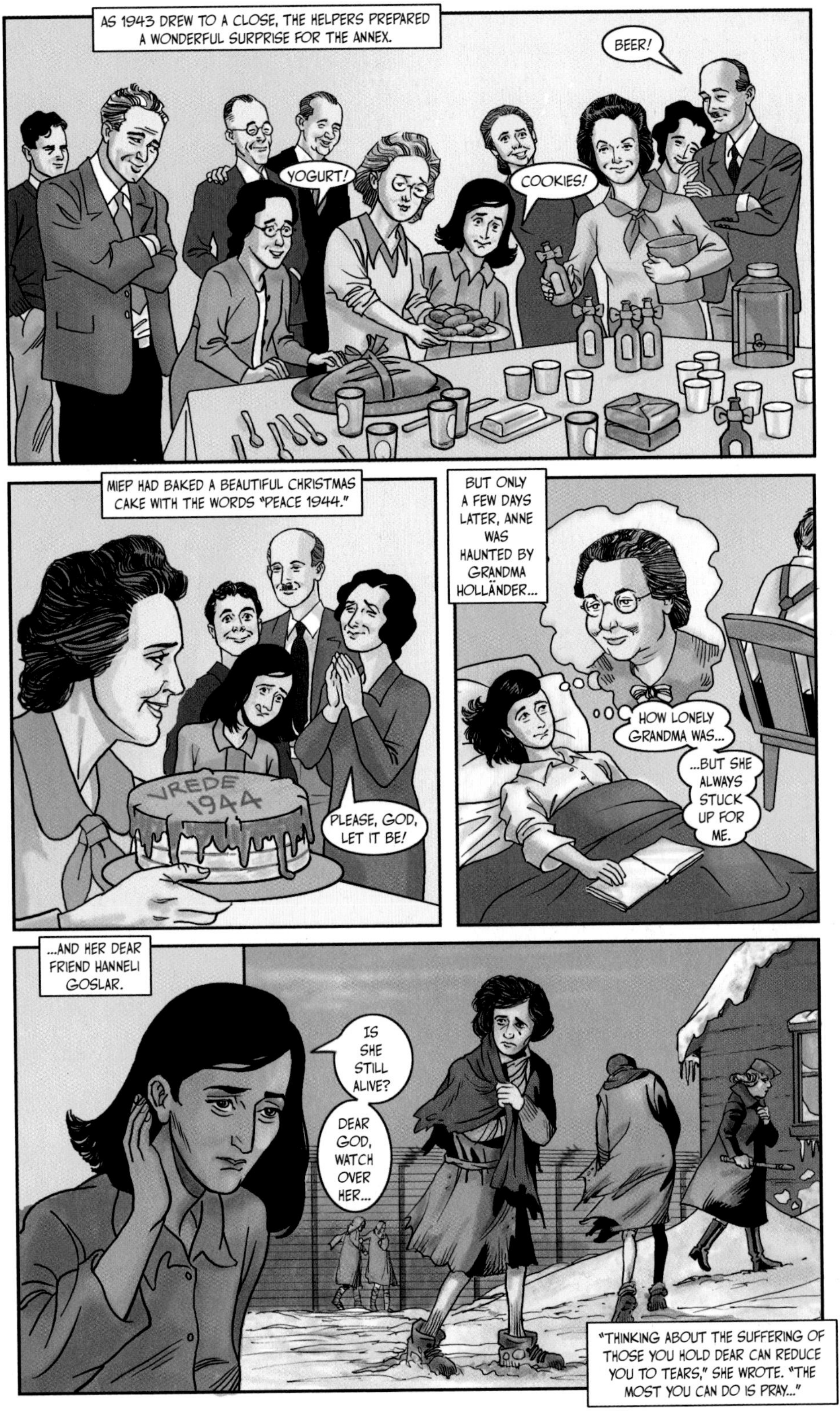
AS 1943 DREW TO A CLOSE, THE HELPERS PREPARED A WONDERFUL SURPRISE FOR THE ANNEX.
YOGURT!
COOKIES!
BEER!
MIEP HAD BAKED A BEAUTIFUL CHRISTMAS CAKE WITH THE WORDS "PEACE 1944."
VREDE 1944
PLEASE, GOD, LET IT BE!
BUT ONLY A FEW DAYS LATER, ANNE WAS HAUNTED BY GRANDMA HOLLÄNDER...
HOW LONELY GRANDMA WAS...
...BUT SHE ALWAYS STUCK UP FOR ME.
...AND HER DEAR FRIEND HANNELI GOSLAR.
IS SHE STILL ALIVE?
DEAR GOD, WATCH OVER HER...
"THINKING ABOUT THE SUFFERING OF THOSE YOU HOLD DEAR CAN REDUCE YOU TO TEARS," SHE WROTE. "THE MOST YOU CAN DO IS PRAY..."

CHAPTER 8

The New Year

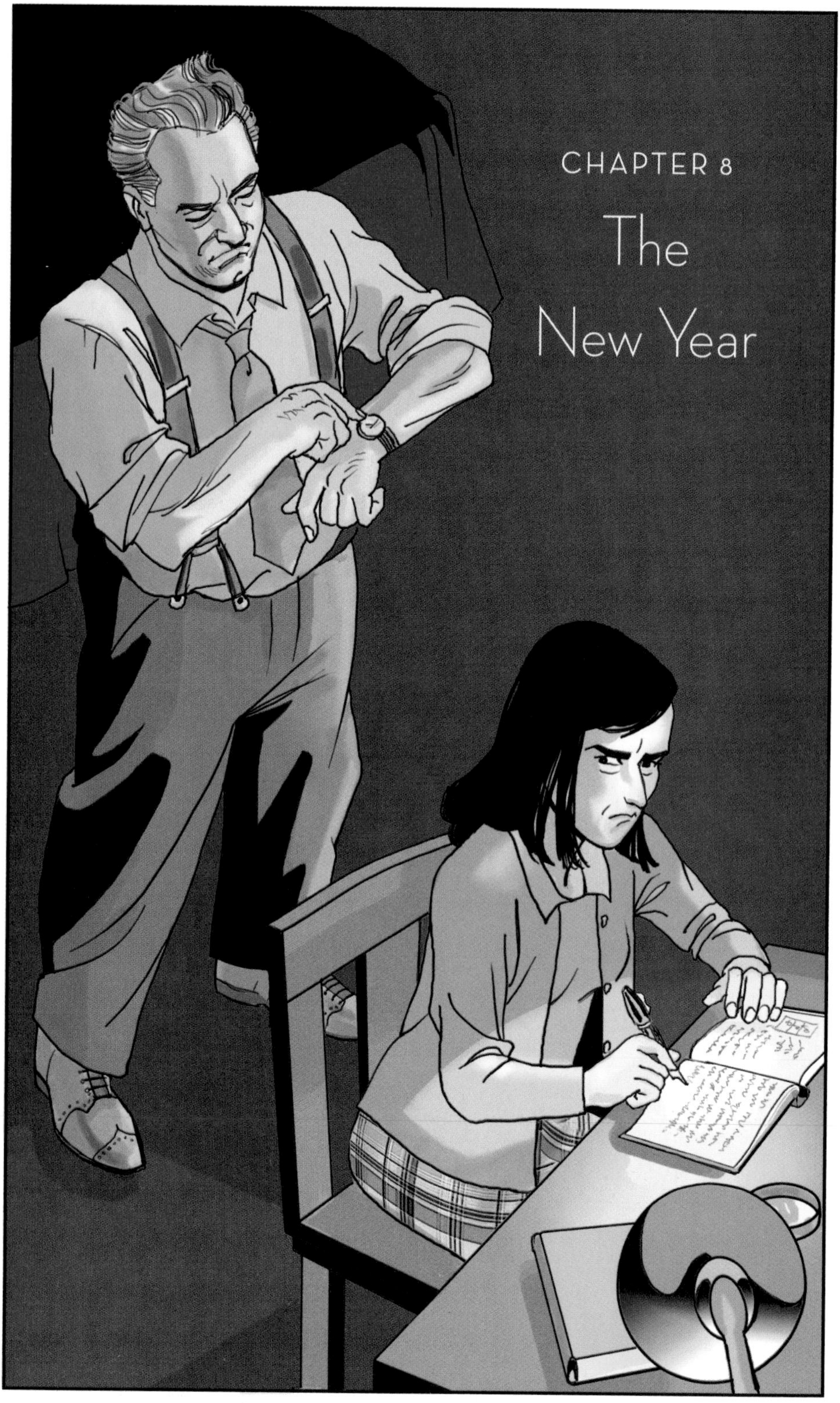

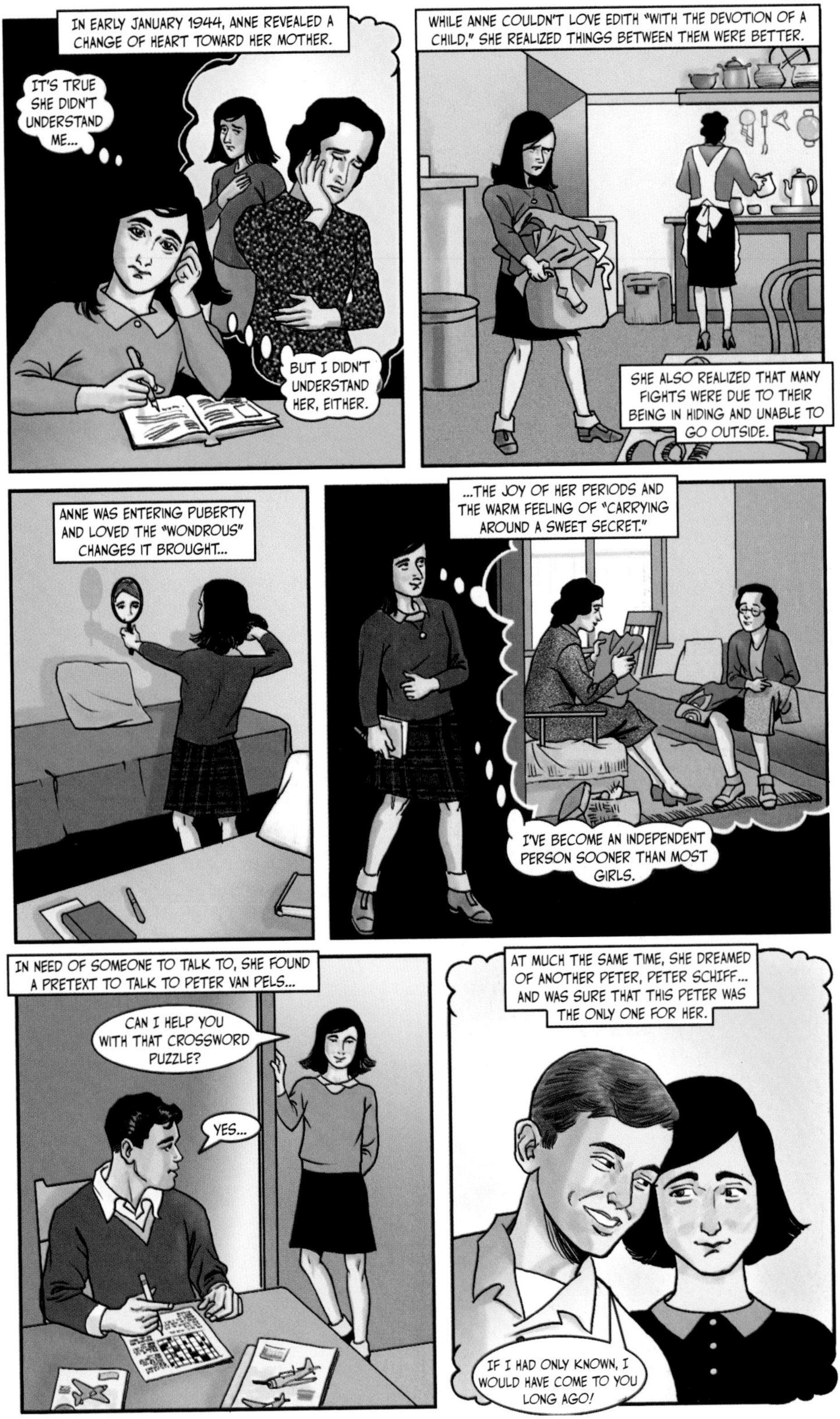
IN EARLY JANUARY 1944, ANNE REVEALED A CHANGE OF HEART TOWARD HER MOTHER.
IT'S TRUE SHE DIDN'T UNDERSTAND ME...
BUT I DIDN'T UNDERSTAND HER, EITHER.
WHILE ANNE COULDN'T LOVE EDITH "WITH THE DEVOTION OF A CHILD," SHE REALIZED THINGS BETWEEN THEM WERE BETTER.
SHE ALSO REALIZED THAT MANY FIGHTS WERE DUE TO THEIR BEING IN HIDING AND UNABLE TO GO OUTSIDE.
ANNE WAS ENTERING PUBERTY AND LOVED THE "WONDROUS" CHANGES IT BROUGHT...
...THE JOY OF HER PERIODS AND THE WARM FEELING OF "CARRYING AROUND A SWEET SECRET."
I'VE BECOME AN INDEPENDENT PERSON SOONER THAN MOST GIRLS.
IN NEED OF SOMEONE TO TALK TO, SHE FOUND A PRETEXT TO TALK TO PETER VAN PELS...
CAN I HELP YOU WITH THAT CROSSWORD PUZZLE?
YES...
AT MUCH THE SAME TIME, SHE DREAMED OF ANOTHER PETER, PETER SCHIFF... AND WAS SURE THAT THIS PETER WAS THE ONLY ONE FOR HER.
IF I HAD ONLY KNOWN, I WOULD HAVE COME TO YOU LONG AGO!

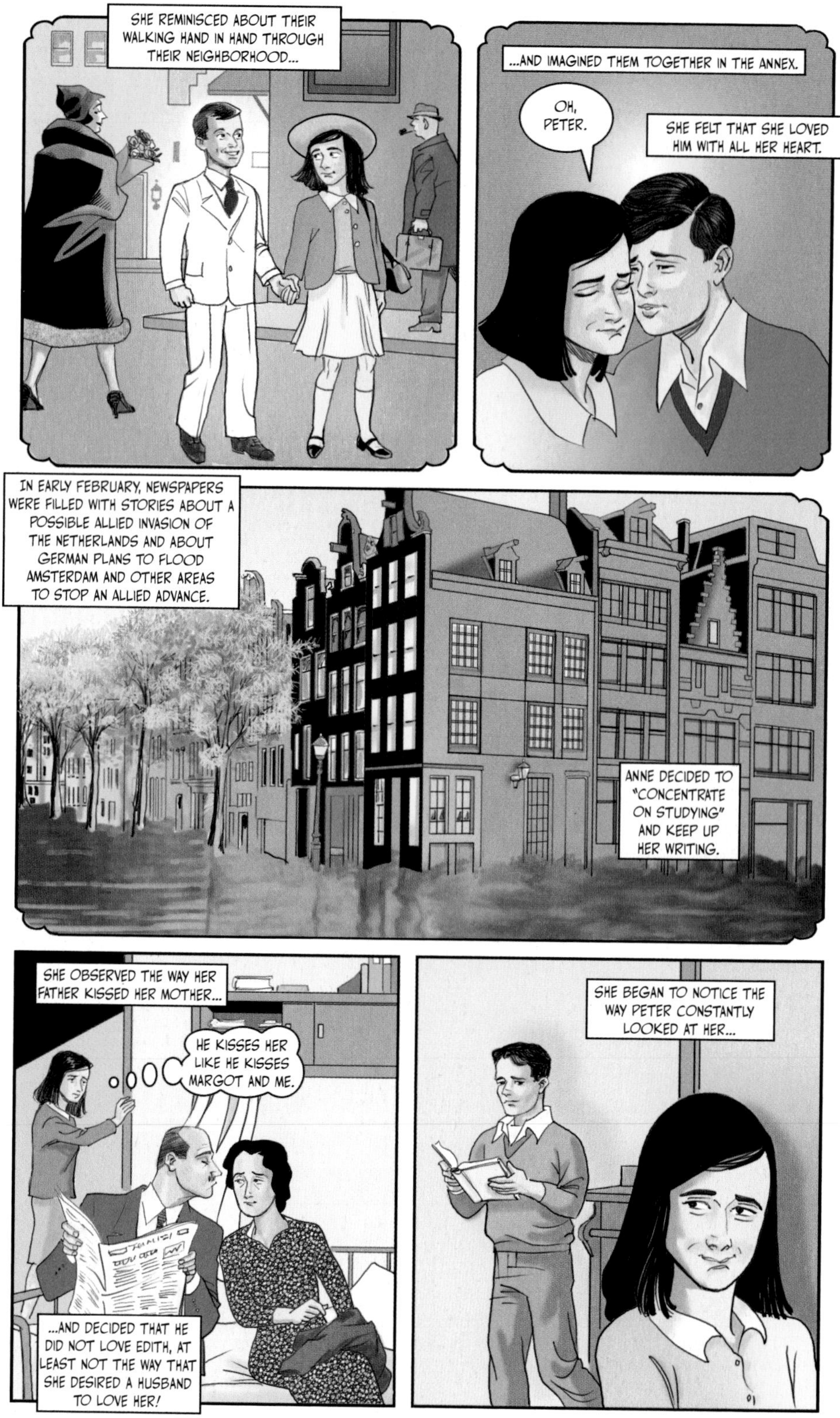
SHE REMINISCED ABOUT THEIR WALKING HAND IN HAND THROUGH THEIR NEIGHBORHOOD...
...AND IMAGINED THEM TOGETHER IN THE ANNEX.
OH, PETER.
SHE FELT THAT SHE LOVED HIM WITH ALL HER HEART.
IN EARLY FEBRUARY, NEWSPAPERS WERE FILLED WITH STORIES ABOUT A POSSIBLE ALLIED INVASION OF THE NETHERLANDS AND ABOUT GERMAN PLANS TO FLOOD AMSTERDAM AND OTHER AREAS TO STOP AN ALLIED ADVANCE.
ANNE DECIDED TO "CONCENTRATE ON STUDYING" AND KEEP UP HER WRITING.
SHE OBSERVED THE WAY HER FATHER KISSED HER MOTHER...
HE KISSES HER LIKE HE KISSES MARGOT AND ME.
...AND DECIDED THAT HE DID NOT LOVE EDITH, AT LEAST NOT THE WAY THAT SHE DESIRED A HUSBAND TO LOVE HER!
SHE BEGAN TO NOTICE THE WAY PETER CONSTANTLY LOOKED AT HER...

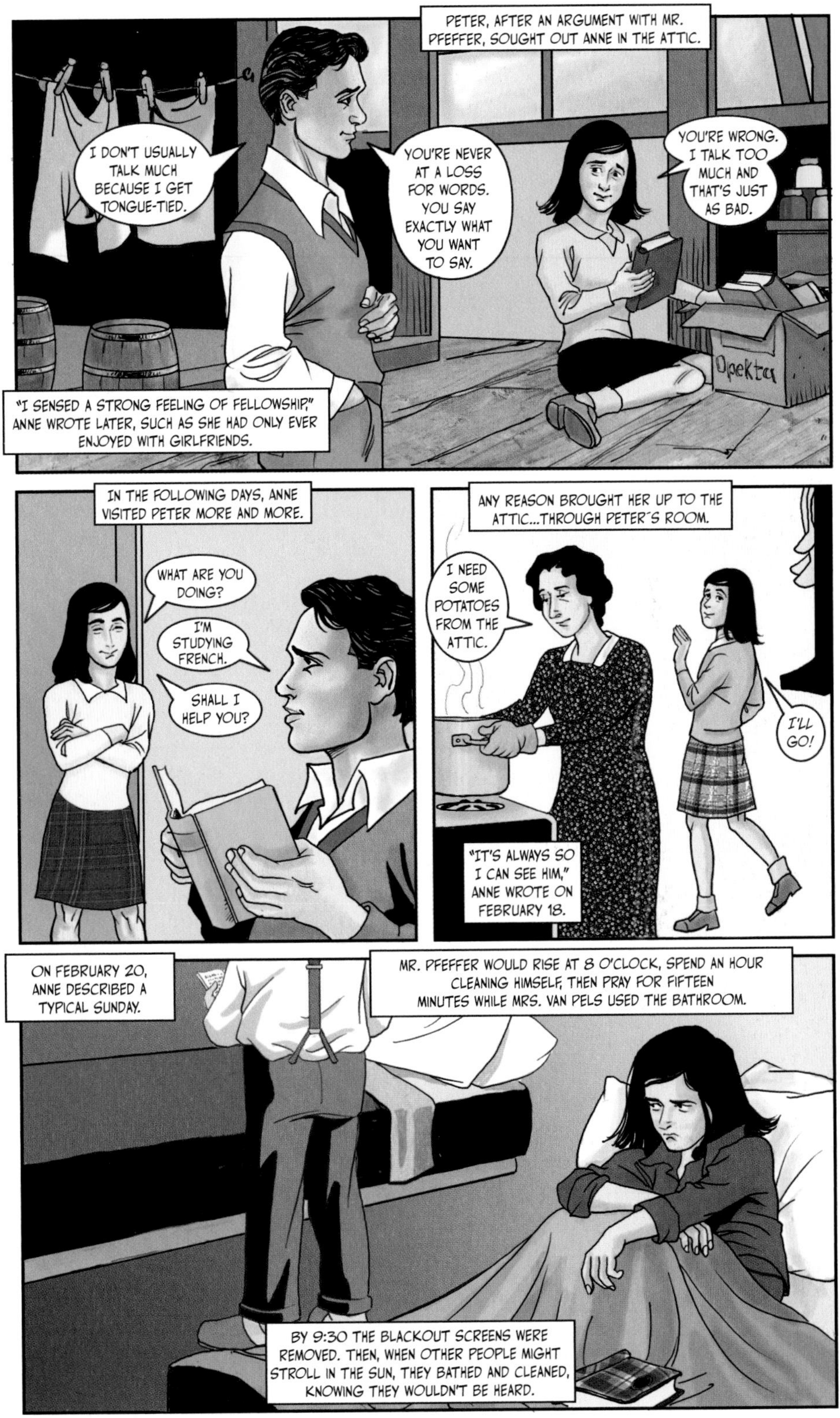
PETER, AFTER AN ARGUMENT WITH MR. PFEFFER, SOUGHT OUT ANNE IN THE ATTIC.
I DON'T USUALLY TALK MUCH BECAUSE I GET TONGUE-TIED.
YOU'RE NEVER AT A LOSS FOR WORDS. YOU SAY EXACTLY WHAT YOU WANT TO SAY.
YOU'RE WRONG. I TALK TOO MUCH AND THAT'S JUST AS BAD.
Opekta
"I SENSED A STRONG FEELING OF FELLOWSHIP," ANNE WROTE LATER, SUCH AS SHE HAD ONLY EVER ENJOYED WITH GIRLFRIENDS.
IN THE FOLLOWING DAYS, ANNE VISITED PETER MORE AND MORE.
WHAT ARE YOU DOING?
I'M STUDYING FRENCH.
SHALL I HELP YOU?
ANY REASON BROUGHT HER UP TO THE ATTIC...THROUGH PETER'S ROOM.
I NEED SOME POTATOES FROM THE ATTIC.
I'LL GO!
"IT'S ALWAYS SO I CAN SEE HIM," ANNE WROTE ON FEBRUARY 18.
ON FEBRUARY 20, ANNE DESCRIBED A TYPICAL SUNDAY.
MR. PFEFFER WOULD RISE AT 8 O'CLOCK, SPEND AN HOUR CLEANING HIMSELF, THEN PRAY FOR FIFTEEN MINUTES WHILE MRS. VAN PELS USED THE BATHROOM.
BY 9:30 THE BLACKOUT SCREENS WERE REMOVED. THEN, WHEN OTHER PEOPLE MIGHT STROLL IN THE SUN, THEY BATHED AND CLEANED, KNOWING THEY WOULDN'T BE HEARD.

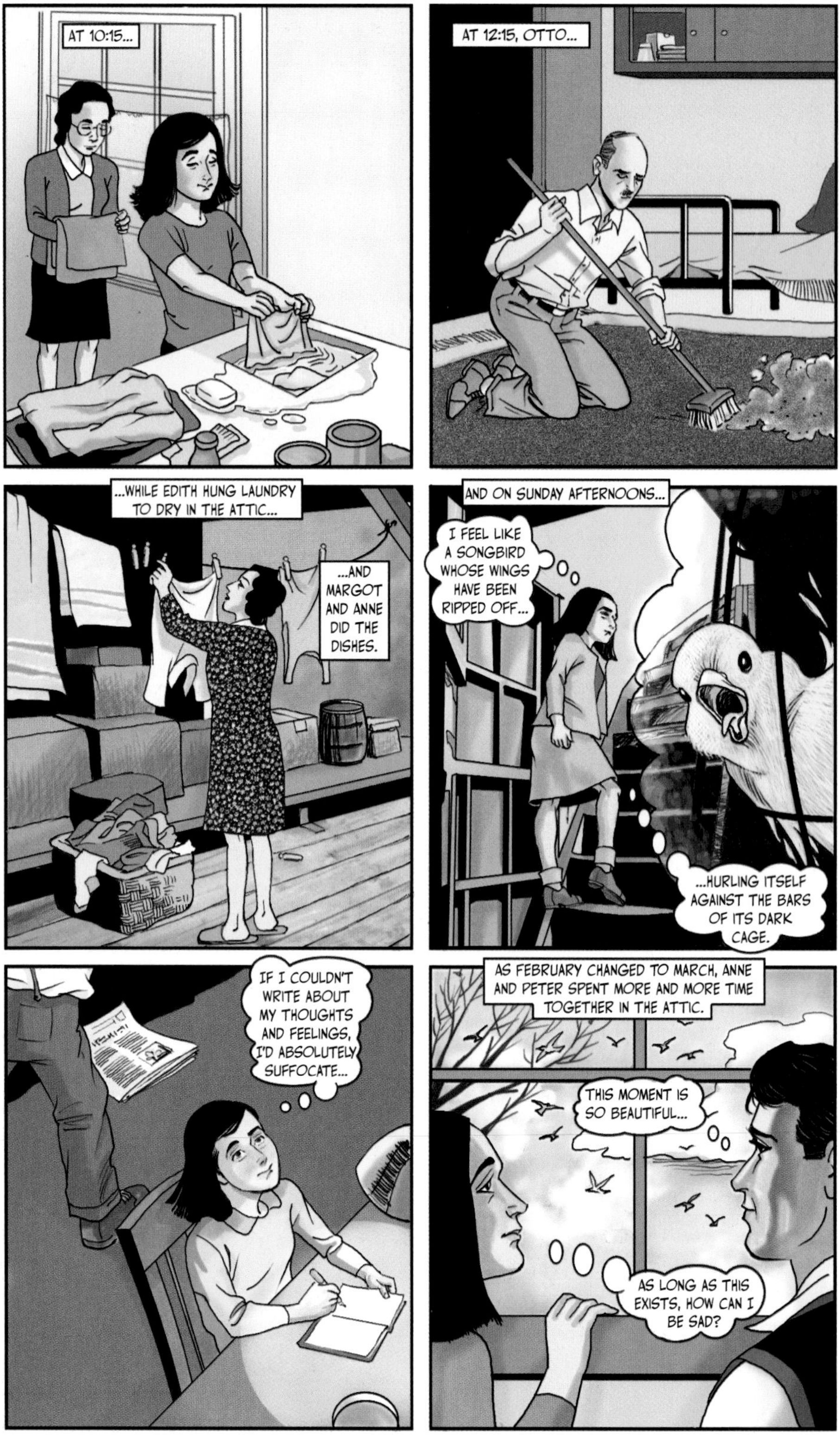
AT 10:15...
AT 12:15, OTTO...
...WHILE EDITH HUNG LAUNDRY TO DRY IN THE ATTIC...
...AND MARGOT AND ANNE DID THE DISHES.
AND ON SUNDAY AFTERNOONS...
I FEEL LIKE A SONGBIRD WHOSE WINGS HAVE BEEN RIPPED OFF...
...HURLING ITSELF AGAINST THE BARS OF ITS DARK CAGE.
IF I COULDN'T WRITE ABOUT MY THOUGHTS AND FEELINGS, I'D ABSOLUTELY SUFFOCATE...
AS FEBRUARY CHANGED TO MARCH, ANNE AND PETER SPENT MORE AND MORE TIME TOGETHER IN THE ATTIC.
THIS MOMENT IS SO BEAUTIFUL...
AS LONG AS THIS EXISTS, HOW CAN I BE SAD?

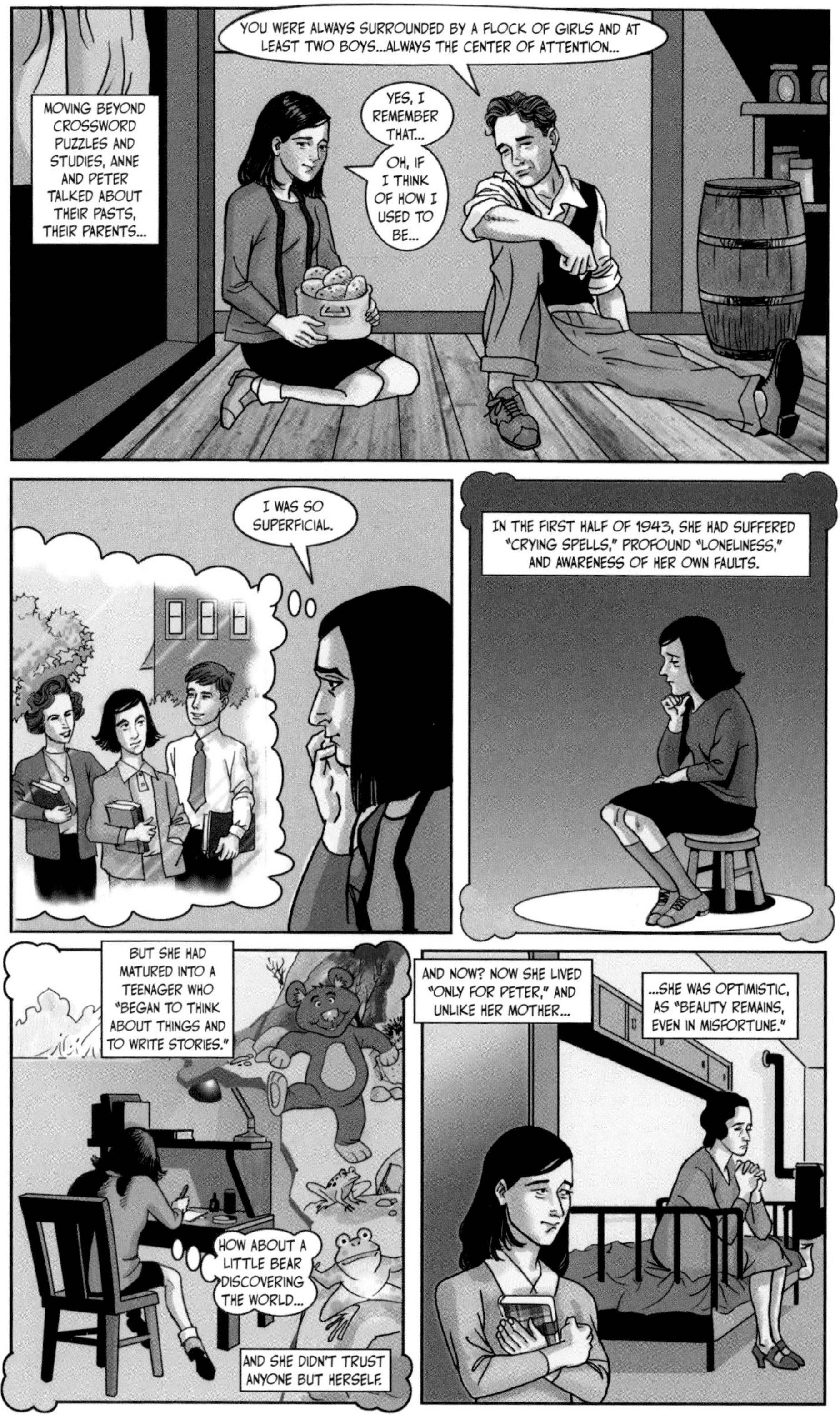
MOVING BEYOND CROSSWORD PUZZLES AND STUDIES, ANNE AND PETER TALKED ABOUT THEIR PASTS, THEIR PARENTS...
YOU WERE ALWAYS SURROUNDED BY A FLOCK OF GIRLS AND AT LEAST TWO BOYS...ALWAYS THE CENTER OF ATTENTION...
YES, I REMEMBER THAT...
OH, IF I THINK OF HOW I USED TO BE...
I WAS SO SUPERFICIAL.
IN THE FIRST HALF OF 1943, SHE HAD SUFFERED "CRYING SPELLS," PROFOUND "LONELINESS," AND AWARENESS OF HER OWN FAULTS.
BUT SHE HAD MATURED INTO A TEENAGER WHO "BEGAN TO THINK ABOUT THINGS AND TO WRITE STORIES."
HOW ABOUT A LITTLE BEAR DISCOVERING THE WORLD...
AND SHE DIDN'T TRUST ANYONE BUT HERSELF.
AND NOW? NOW SHE LIVED "ONLY FOR PETER," AND UNLIKE HER MOTHER...
...SHE WAS OPTIMISTIC, AS "BEAUTY REMAINS, EVEN IN MISFORTUNE."

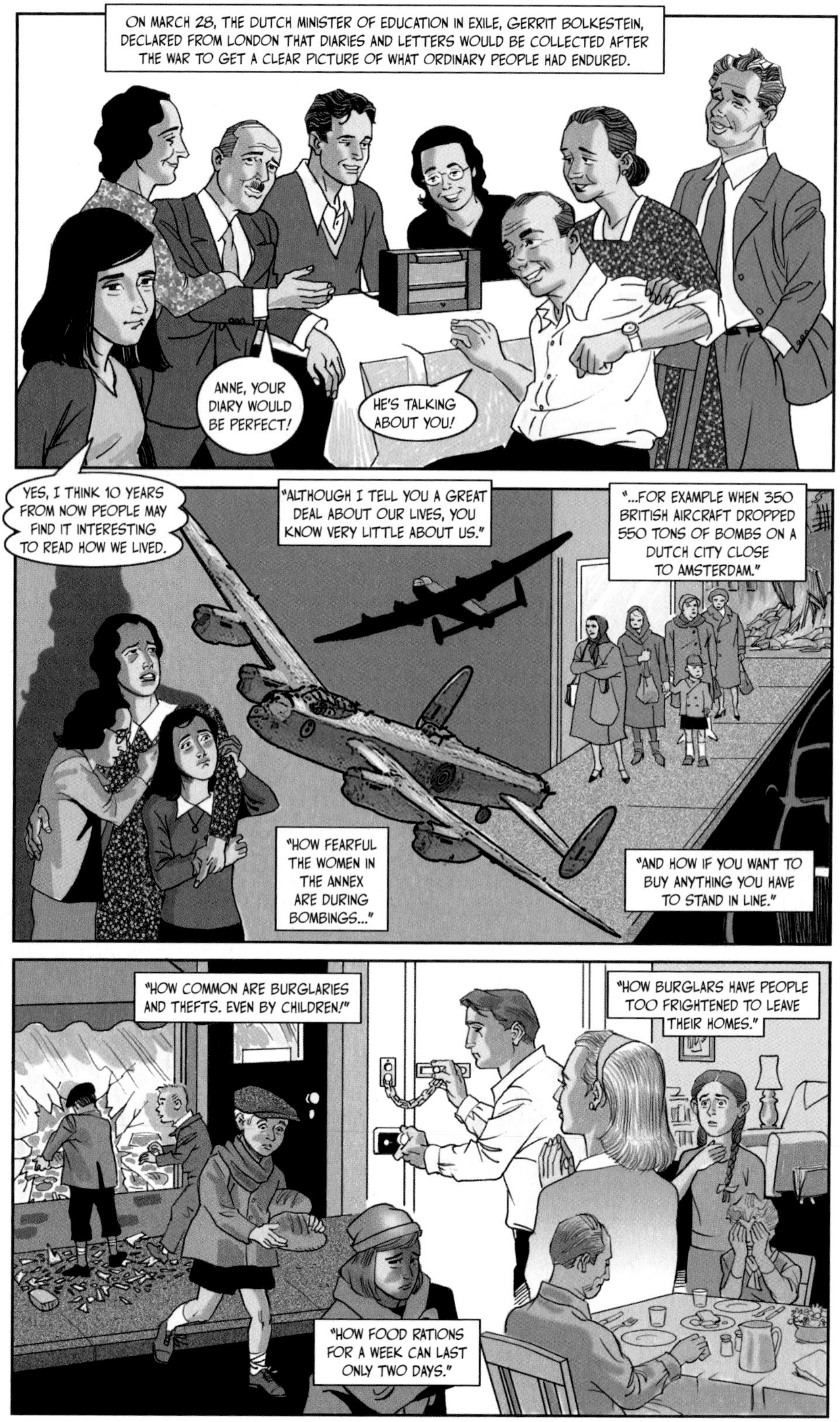
ON MARCH 28, THE DUTCH MINISTER OF EDUCATION IN EXILE, GERRIT BOLKESTEIN, DECLARED FROM LONDON THAT DIARIES AND LETTERS WOULD BE COLLECTED AFTER THE WAR TO GET A CLEAR PICTURE OF WHAT ORDINARY PEOPLE HAD ENDURED.
ANNE, YOUR DIARY WOULD BE PERFECT!
HE'S TALKING ABOUT YOU!
YES, I THINK 10 YEARS FROM NOW PEOPLE MAY FIND IT INTERESTING TO READ HOW WE LIVED.
"ALTHOUGH I TELL YOU A GREAT DEAL ABOUT OUR LIVES, YOU KNOW VERY LITTLE ABOUT US."
"...FOR EXAMPLE WHEN 350 BRITISH AIRCRAFT DROPPED 550 TONS OF BOMBS ON A DUTCH CITY CLOSE TO AMSTERDAM."
"HOW FEARFUL THE WOMEN IN THE ANNEX ARE DURING BOMBINGS..."
"AND HOW IF YOU WANT TO BUY ANYTHING YOU HAVE TO STAND IN LINE."
"HOW COMMON ARE BURGLARIES AND THEFTS. EVEN BY CHILDREN!"
"HOW BURGLARS HAVE PEOPLE TOO FRIGHTENED TO LEAVE THEIR HOMES."
"HOW FOOD RATIONS FOR A WEEK CAN LAST ONLY TWO DAYS."

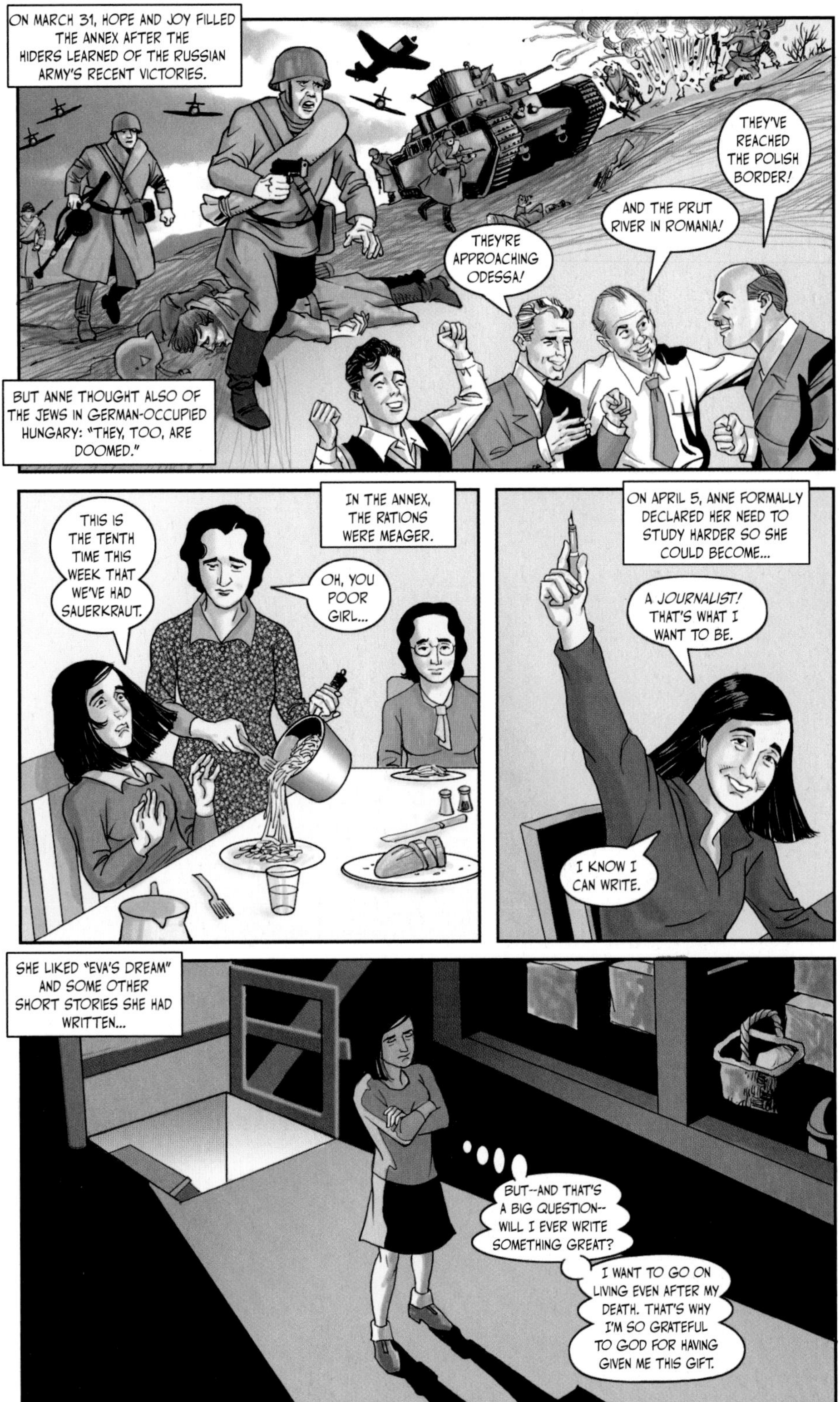

ON MARCH 31, HOPE AND JOY FILLED THE ANNEX AFTER THE HIDERS LEARNED OF THE RUSSIAN ARMY'S RECENT VICTORIES.
THEY'RE APPROACHING ODESSA!
AND THE PRUT RIVER IN ROMANIA!
THEY'VE REACHED THE POLISH BORDER!
BUT ANNE THOUGHT ALSO OF THE JEWS IN GERMAN-OCCUPIED HUNGARY: "THEY, TOO, ARE DOOMED."
IN THE ANNEX, THE RATIONS WERE MEAGER.
THIS IS THE TENTH TIME THIS WEEK THAT WE'VE HAD SAUERKRAUT.
OH, YOU POOR GIRL...
ON APRIL 5, ANNE FORMALLY DECLARED HER NEED TO STUDY HARDER SO SHE COULD BECOME...
A *JOURNALIST!* THAT'S WHAT I WANT TO BE.
I KNOW I CAN WRITE.
SHE LIKED "EVA'S DREAM" AND SOME OTHER SHORT STORIES SHE HAD WRITTEN...
BUT--AND THAT'S A BIG QUESTION--WILL I EVER WRITE SOMETHING GREAT?
I WANT TO GO ON LIVING EVEN AFTER MY DEATH. THAT'S WHY I'M SO GRATEFUL TO GOD FOR HAVING GIVEN ME THIS GIFT.

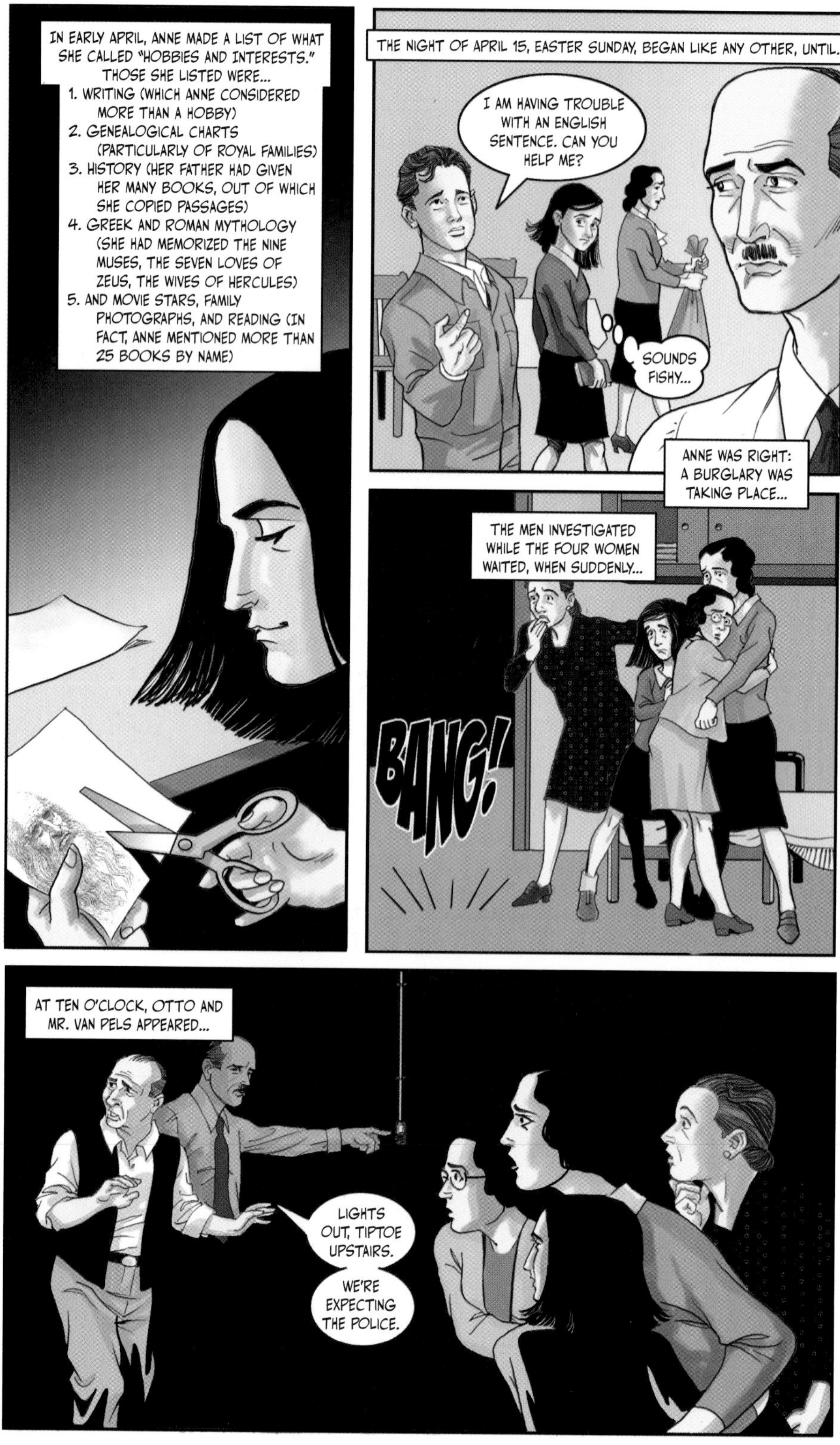
IN EARLY APRIL, ANNE MADE A LIST OF WHAT SHE CALLED "HOBBIES AND INTERESTS." THOSE SHE LISTED WERE...
1. WRITING (WHICH ANNE CONSIDERED MORE THAN A HOBBY)
2. GENEALOGICAL CHARTS (PARTICULARLY OF ROYAL FAMILIES)
3. HISTORY (HER FATHER HAD GIVEN HER MANY BOOKS, OUT OF WHICH SHE COPIED PASSAGES)
4. GREEK AND ROMAN MYTHOLOGY (SHE HAD MEMORIZED THE NINE MUSES, THE SEVEN LOVES OF ZEUS, THE WIVES OF HERCULES)
5. AND MOVIE STARS, FAMILY PHOTOGRAPHS, AND READING (IN FACT, ANNE MENTIONED MORE THAN 25 BOOKS BY NAME)
THE NIGHT OF APRIL 15, EASTER SUNDAY, BEGAN LIKE ANY OTHER, UNTIL...
I AM HAVING TROUBLE WITH AN ENGLISH SENTENCE. CAN YOU HELP ME?
SOUNDS FISHY...
ANNE WAS RIGHT: A BURGLARY WAS TAKING PLACE...
THE MEN INVESTIGATED WHILE THE FOUR WOMEN WAITED, WHEN SUDDENLY...
BANG!
AT TEN O'CLOCK, OTTO AND MR. VAN PELS APPEARED...
LIGHTS OUT, TIPTOE UPSTAIRS.
WE'RE EXPECTING THE POLICE.

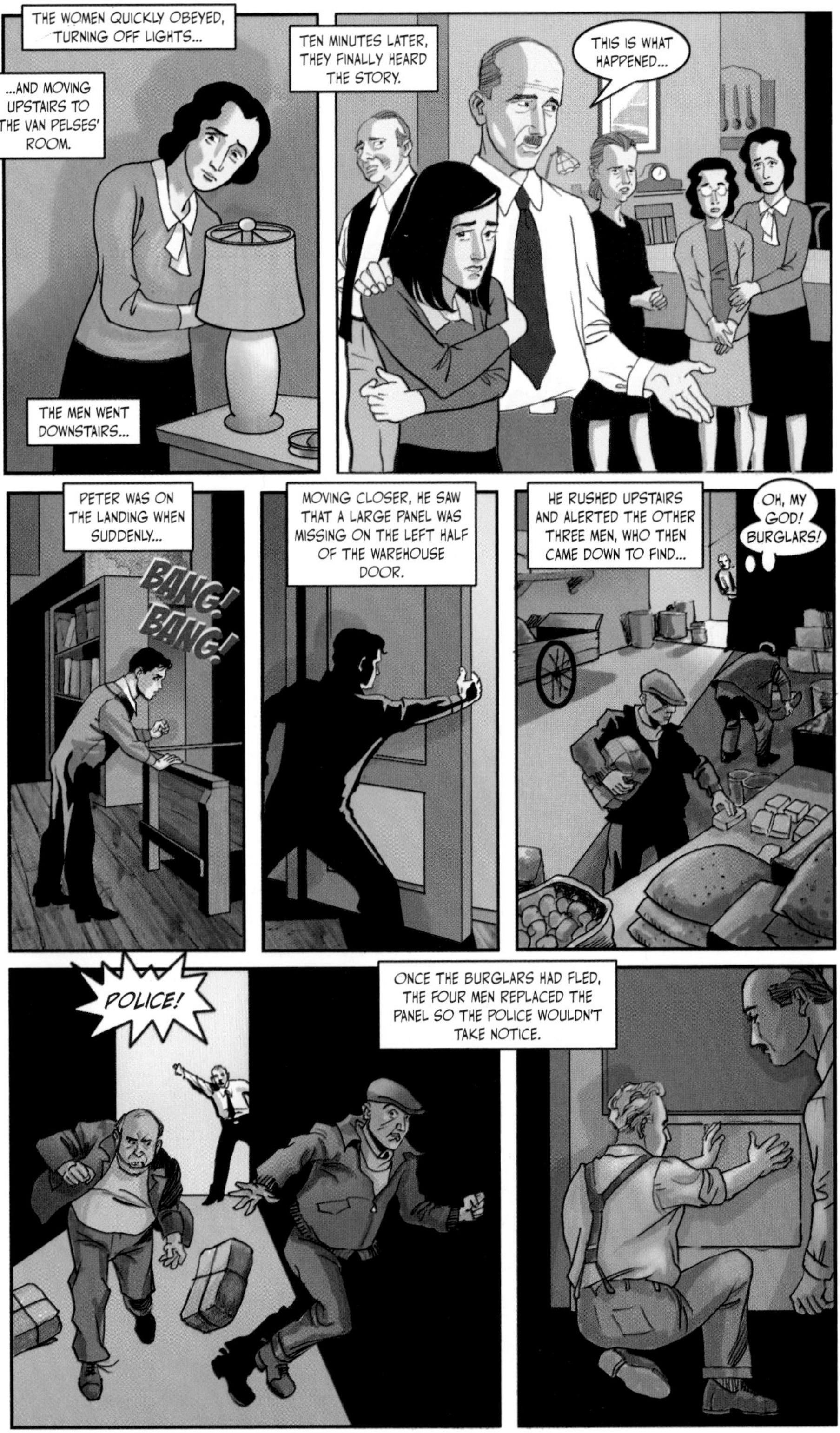
THE WOMEN QUICKLY OBEYED, TURNING OFF LIGHTS...
...AND MOVING UPSTAIRS TO THE VAN PELSES' ROOM.
THE MEN WENT DOWNSTAIRS...
TEN MINUTES LATER, THEY FINALLY HEARD THE STORY.
THIS IS WHAT HAPPENED...
PETER WAS ON THE LANDING WHEN SUDDENLY...
BANG! BANG!
MOVING CLOSER, HE SAW THAT A LARGE PANEL WAS MISSING ON THE LEFT HALF OF THE WAREHOUSE DOOR.
HE RUSHED UPSTAIRS AND ALERTED THE OTHER THREE MEN, WHO THEN CAME DOWN TO FIND...
OH, MY GOD! BURGLARS!
POLICE!
ONCE THE BURGLARS HAD FLED, THE FOUR MEN REPLACED THE PANEL SO THE POLICE WOULDN'T TAKE NOTICE.

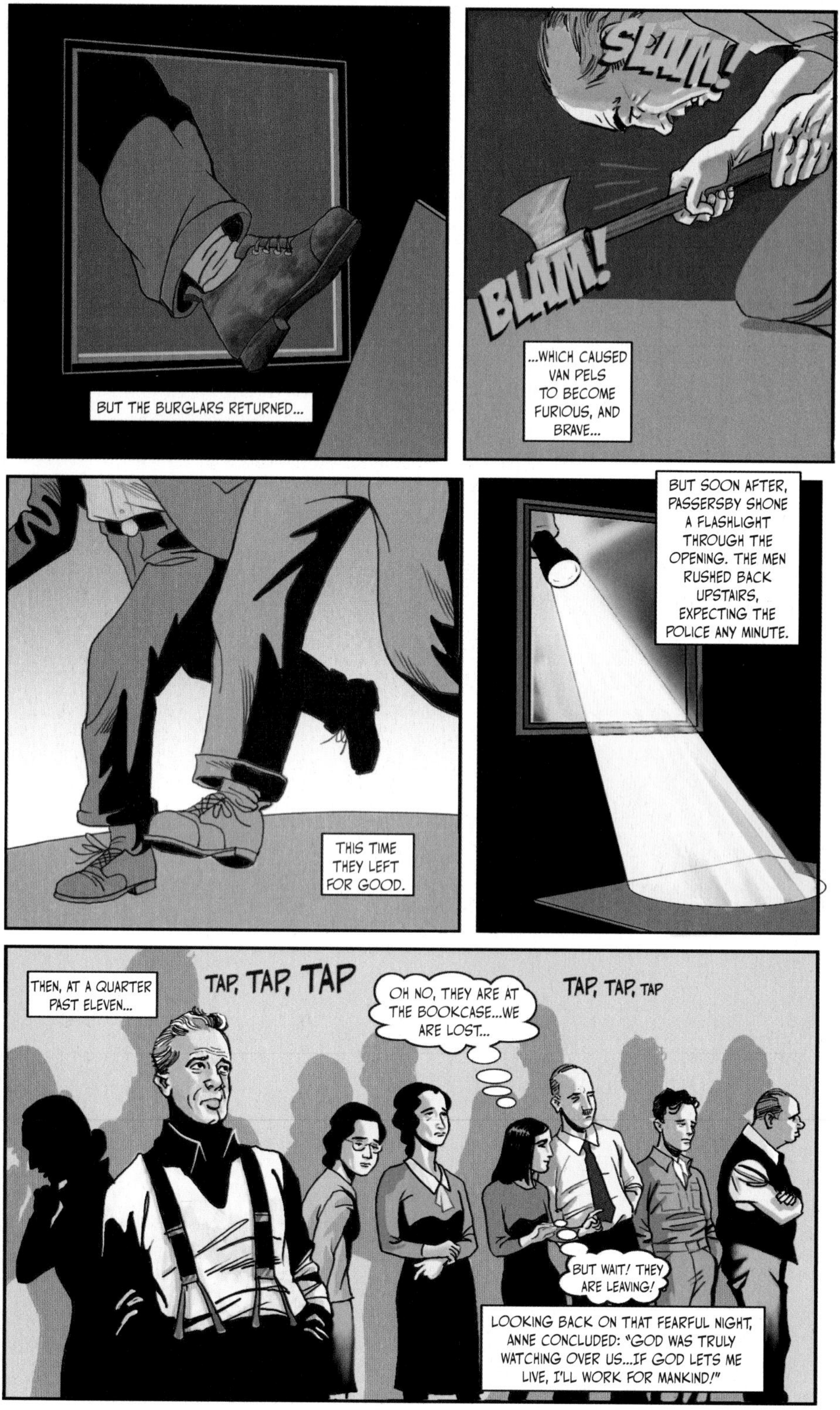
BUT THE BURGLARS RETURNED...
SLAM!
BLAM!
...WHICH CAUSED VAN PELS TO BECOME FURIOUS, AND BRAVE...
THIS TIME THEY LEFT FOR GOOD.
BUT SOON AFTER, PASSERSBY SHONE A FLASHLIGHT THROUGH THE OPENING. THE MEN RUSHED BACK UPSTAIRS, EXPECTING THE POLICE ANY MINUTE.
THEN, AT A QUARTER PAST ELEVEN...
TAP, TAP, TAP
OH NO, THEY ARE AT THE BOOKCASE...WE ARE LOST...
TAP, TAP, TAP
BUT WAIT! THEY ARE LEAVING!
LOOKING BACK ON THAT FEARFUL NIGHT, ANNE CONCLUDED: "GOD WAS TRULY WATCHING OVER US...IF GOD LETS ME LIVE, I'LL WORK FOR MANKIND!"

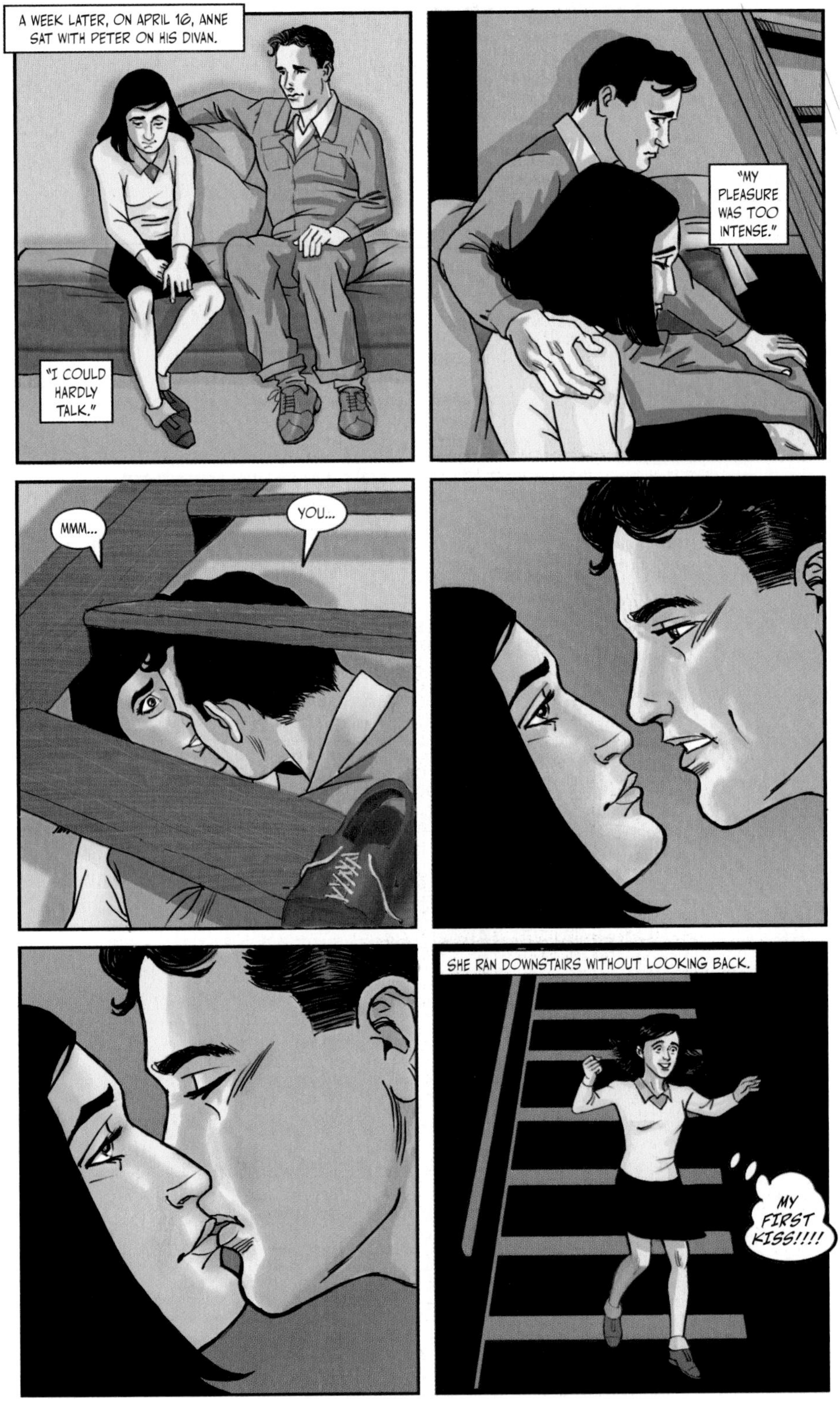
A WEEK LATER, ON APRIL 16, ANNE SAT WITH PETER ON HIS DIVAN.
"I COULD HARDLY TALK."
"MY PLEASURE WAS TOO INTENSE."
MMM...
YOU...
SHE RAN DOWNSTAIRS WITHOUT LOOKING BACK.
MY FIRST KISS!!!!

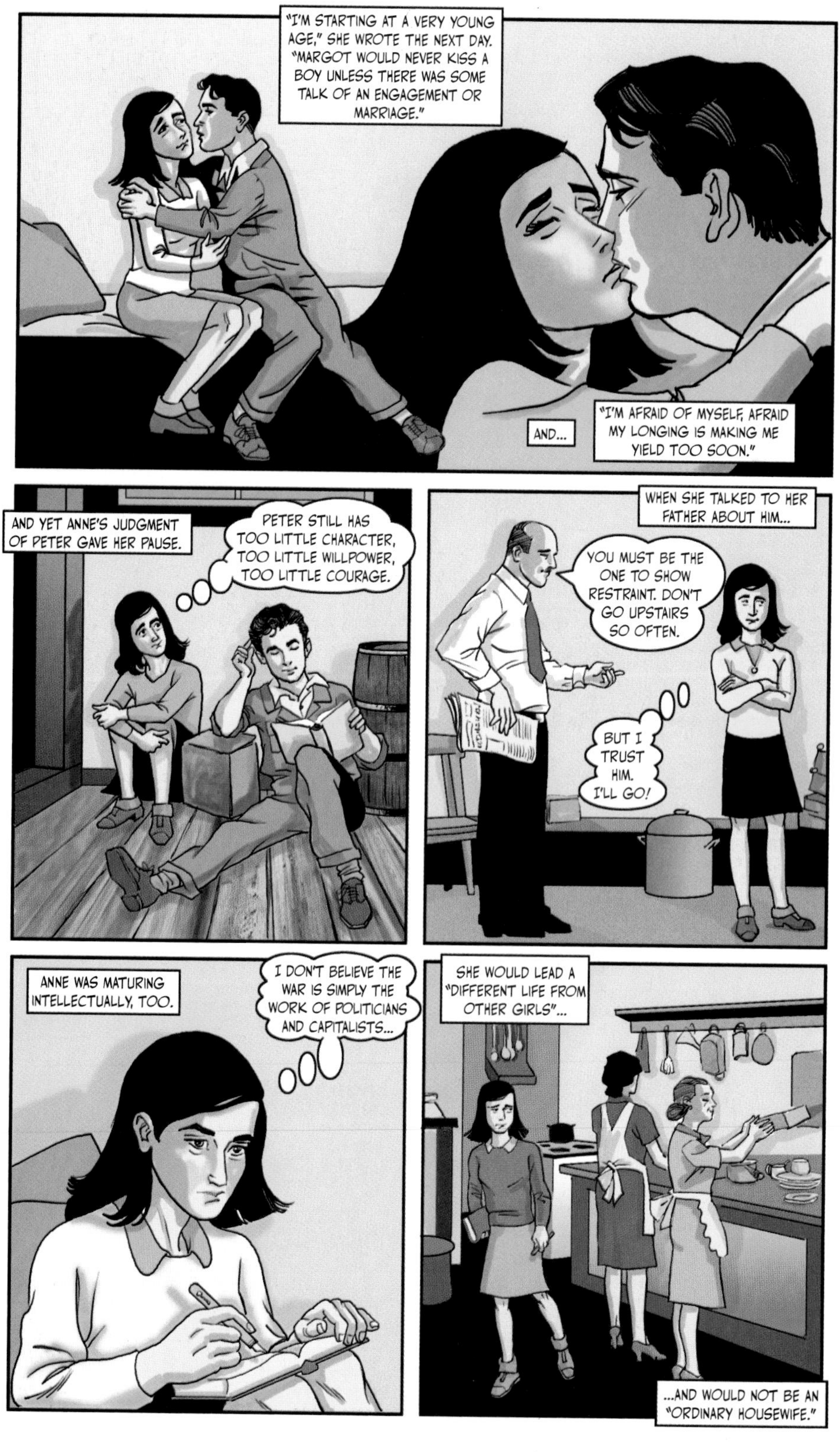
"I'M STARTING AT A VERY YOUNG AGE," SHE WROTE THE NEXT DAY. "MARGOT WOULD NEVER KISS A BOY UNLESS THERE WAS SOME TALK OF AN ENGAGEMENT OR MARRIAGE."
AND...
"I'M AFRAID OF MYSELF, AFRAID MY LONGING IS MAKING ME YIELD TOO SOON."
AND YET ANNE'S JUDGMENT OF PETER GAVE HER PAUSE.
PETER STILL HAS TOO LITTLE CHARACTER, TOO LITTLE WILLPOWER, TOO LITTLE COURAGE.
WHEN SHE TALKED TO HER FATHER ABOUT HIM...
YOU MUST BE THE ONE TO SHOW RESTRAINT. DON'T GO UPSTAIRS SO OFTEN.
BUT I TRUST HIM. I'LL GO!
ANNE WAS MATURING INTELLECTUALLY, TOO.
I DON'T BELIEVE THE WAR IS SIMPLY THE WORK OF POLITICIANS AND CAPITALISTS...
SHE WOULD LEAD A "DIFFERENT LIFE FROM OTHER GIRLS"...
...AND WOULD NOT BE AN "ORDINARY HOUSEWIFE."

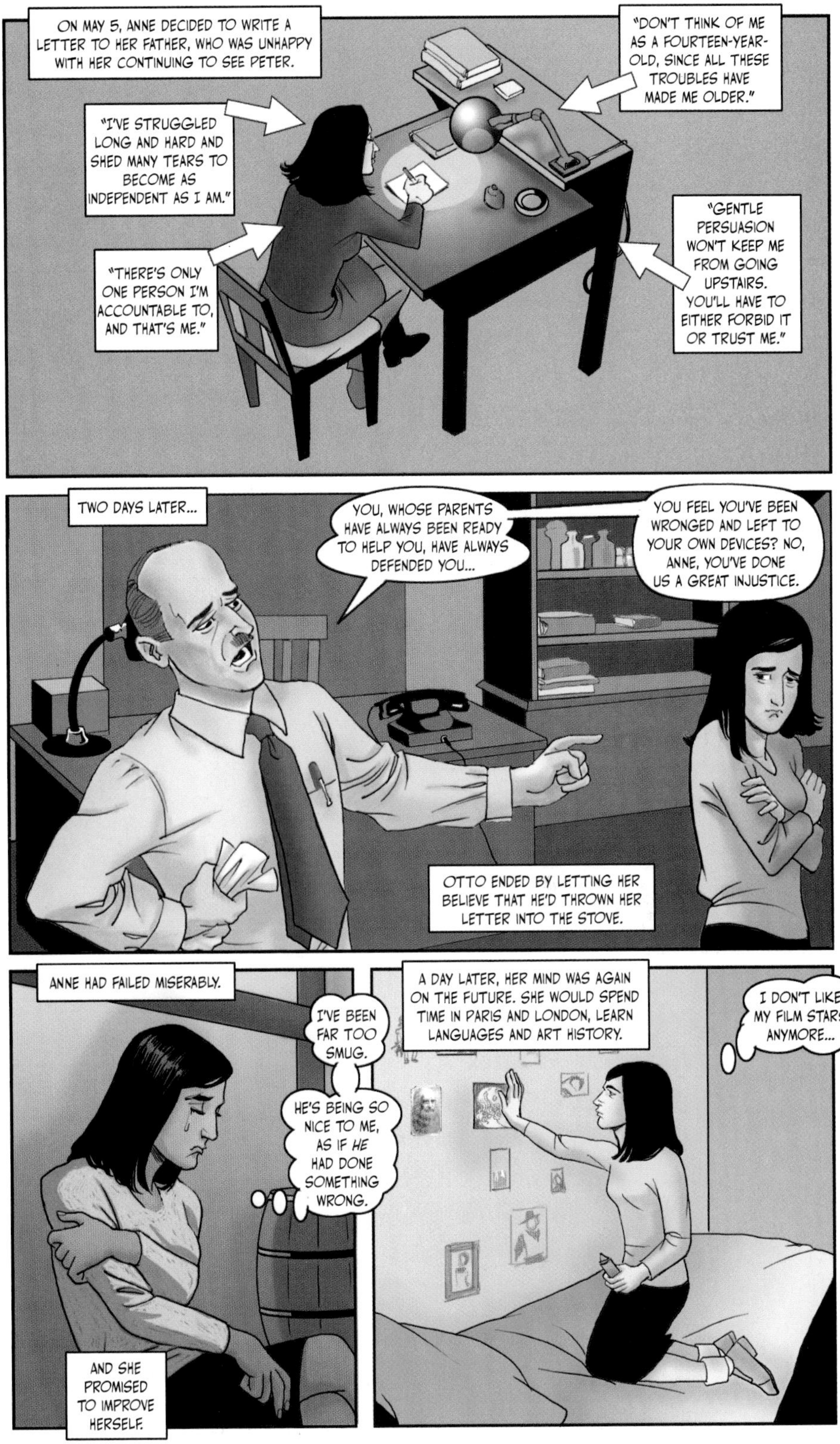
ON MAY 5, ANNE DECIDED TO WRITE A LETTER TO HER FATHER, WHO WAS UNHAPPY WITH HER CONTINUING TO SEE PETER.
"I'VE STRUGGLED LONG AND HARD AND SHED MANY TEARS TO BECOME AS INDEPENDENT AS I AM."
"THERE'S ONLY ONE PERSON I'M ACCOUNTABLE TO, AND THAT'S ME."
"DON'T THINK OF ME AS A FOURTEEN-YEAR-OLD, SINCE ALL THESE TROUBLES HAVE MADE ME OLDER."
"GENTLE PERSUASION WON'T KEEP ME FROM GOING UPSTAIRS. YOU'LL HAVE TO EITHER FORBID IT OR TRUST ME."
TWO DAYS LATER...
YOU, WHOSE PARENTS HAVE ALWAYS BEEN READY TO HELP YOU, HAVE ALWAYS DEFENDED YOU...
YOU FEEL YOU'VE BEEN WRONGED AND LEFT TO YOUR OWN DEVICES? NO, ANNE, YOU'VE DONE US A GREAT INJUSTICE.
OTTO ENDED BY LETTING HER BELIEVE THAT HE'D THROWN HER LETTER INTO THE STOVE.
ANNE HAD FAILED MISERABLY.
I'VE BEEN FAR TOO SMUG.
HE'S BEING SO NICE TO ME, AS IF *HE* HAD DONE SOMETHING WRONG.
AND SHE PROMISED TO IMPROVE HERSELF.
A DAY LATER, HER MIND WAS AGAIN ON THE FUTURE. SHE WOULD SPEND TIME IN PARIS AND LONDON, LEARN LANGUAGES AND ART HISTORY.
I DON'T LIKE MY FILM STARS ANYMORE...

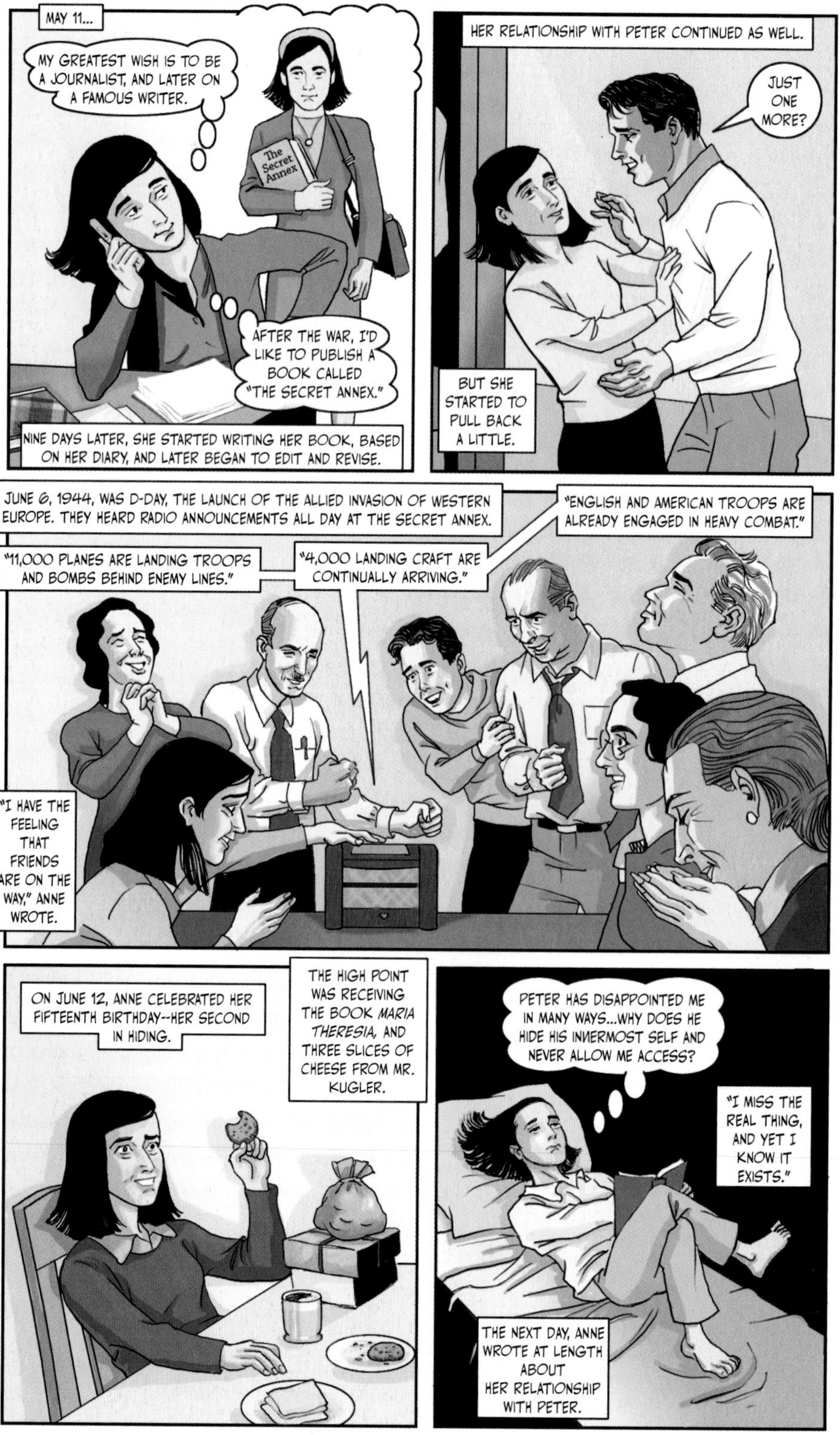
MAY 11...
MY GREATEST WISH IS TO BE A JOURNALIST, AND LATER ON A FAMOUS WRITER.
The Secret Annex
AFTER THE WAR, I'D LIKE TO PUBLISH A BOOK CALLED "THE SECRET ANNEX."
NINE DAYS LATER, SHE STARTED WRITING HER BOOK, BASED ON HER DIARY, AND LATER BEGAN TO EDIT AND REVISE.
HER RELATIONSHIP WITH PETER CONTINUED AS WELL.
JUST ONE MORE?
BUT SHE STARTED TO PULL BACK A LITTLE.
JUNE 6, 1944, WAS D-DAY, THE LAUNCH OF THE ALLIED INVASION OF WESTERN EUROPE. THEY HEARD RADIO ANNOUNCEMENTS ALL DAY AT THE SECRET ANNEX.
"ENGLISH AND AMERICAN TROOPS ARE ALREADY ENGAGED IN HEAVY COMBAT."
"11,000 PLANES ARE LANDING TROOPS AND BOMBS BEHIND ENEMY LINES."
"4,000 LANDING CRAFT ARE CONTINUALLY ARRIVING."
"I HAVE THE FEELING THAT FRIENDS ARE ON THE WAY," ANNE WROTE.
ON JUNE 12, ANNE CELEBRATED HER FIFTEENTH BIRTHDAY--HER SECOND IN HIDING.
THE HIGH POINT WAS RECEIVING THE BOOK *MARIA THERESIA,* AND THREE SLICES OF CHEESE FROM MR. KUGLER.
PETER HAS DISAPPOINTED ME IN MANY WAYS...WHY DOES HE HIDE HIS INNERMOST SELF AND NEVER ALLOW ME ACCESS?
"I MISS THE REAL THING, AND YET I KNOW IT EXISTS."
THE NEXT DAY, ANNE WROTE AT LENGTH ABOUT HER RELATIONSHIP WITH PETER.

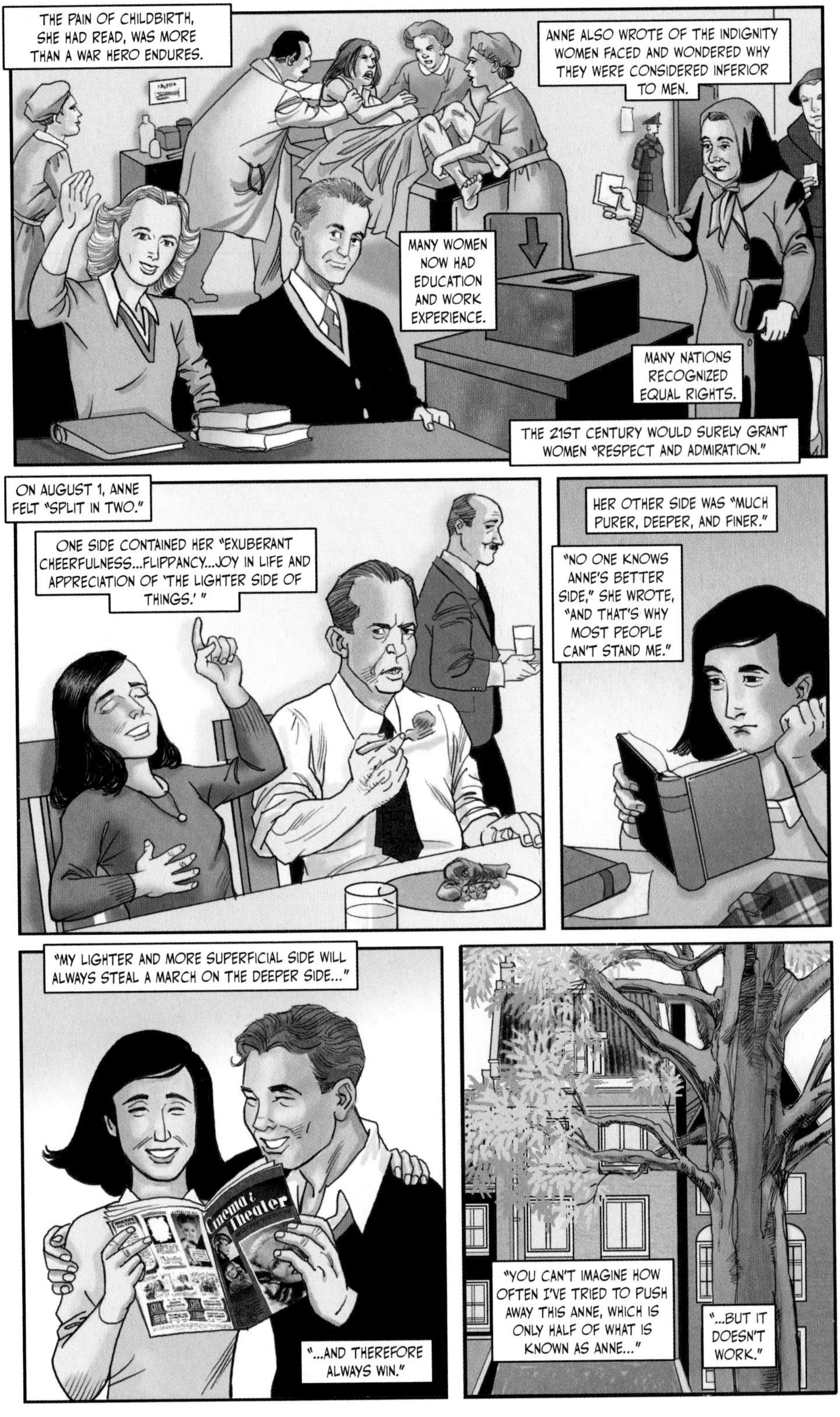
THE PAIN OF CHILDBIRTH, SHE HAD READ, WAS MORE THAN A WAR HERO ENDURES.
ANNE ALSO WROTE OF THE INDIGNITY WOMEN FACED AND WONDERED WHY THEY WERE CONSIDERED INFERIOR TO MEN.
MANY WOMEN NOW HAD EDUCATION AND WORK EXPERIENCE.
MANY NATIONS RECOGNIZED EQUAL RIGHTS.
THE 21ST CENTURY WOULD SURELY GRANT WOMEN "RESPECT AND ADMIRATION."
ON AUGUST 1, ANNE FELT "SPLIT IN TWO."
ONE SIDE CONTAINED HER "EXUBERANT CHEERFULNESS...FLIPPANCY...JOY IN LIFE AND APPRECIATION OF 'THE LIGHTER SIDE OF THINGS.' "
HER OTHER SIDE WAS "MUCH PURER, DEEPER, AND FINER."
"NO ONE KNOWS ANNE'S BETTER SIDE," SHE WROTE, "AND THAT'S WHY MOST PEOPLE CAN'T STAND ME."
"MY LIGHTER AND MORE SUPERFICIAL SIDE WILL ALWAYS STEAL A MARCH ON THE DEEPER SIDE..."
Cinema & Theater
"...AND THEREFORE ALWAYS WIN."
"YOU CAN'T IMAGINE HOW OFTEN I'VE TRIED TO PUSH AWAY THIS ANNE, WHICH IS ONLY HALF OF WHAT IS KNOWN AS ANNE..."
"...BUT IT DOESN'T WORK."

CHAPTER 9
Discovery

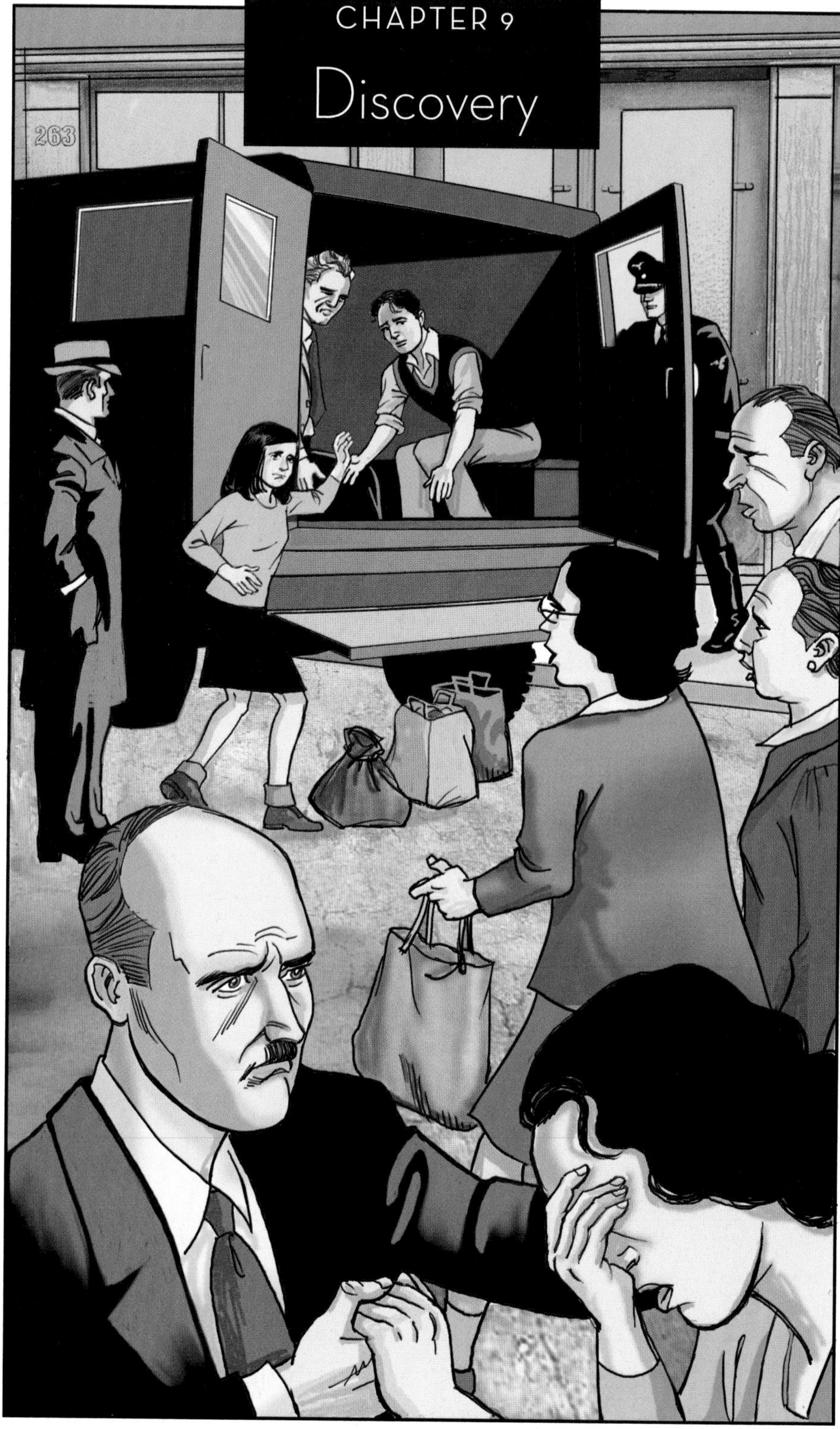
263

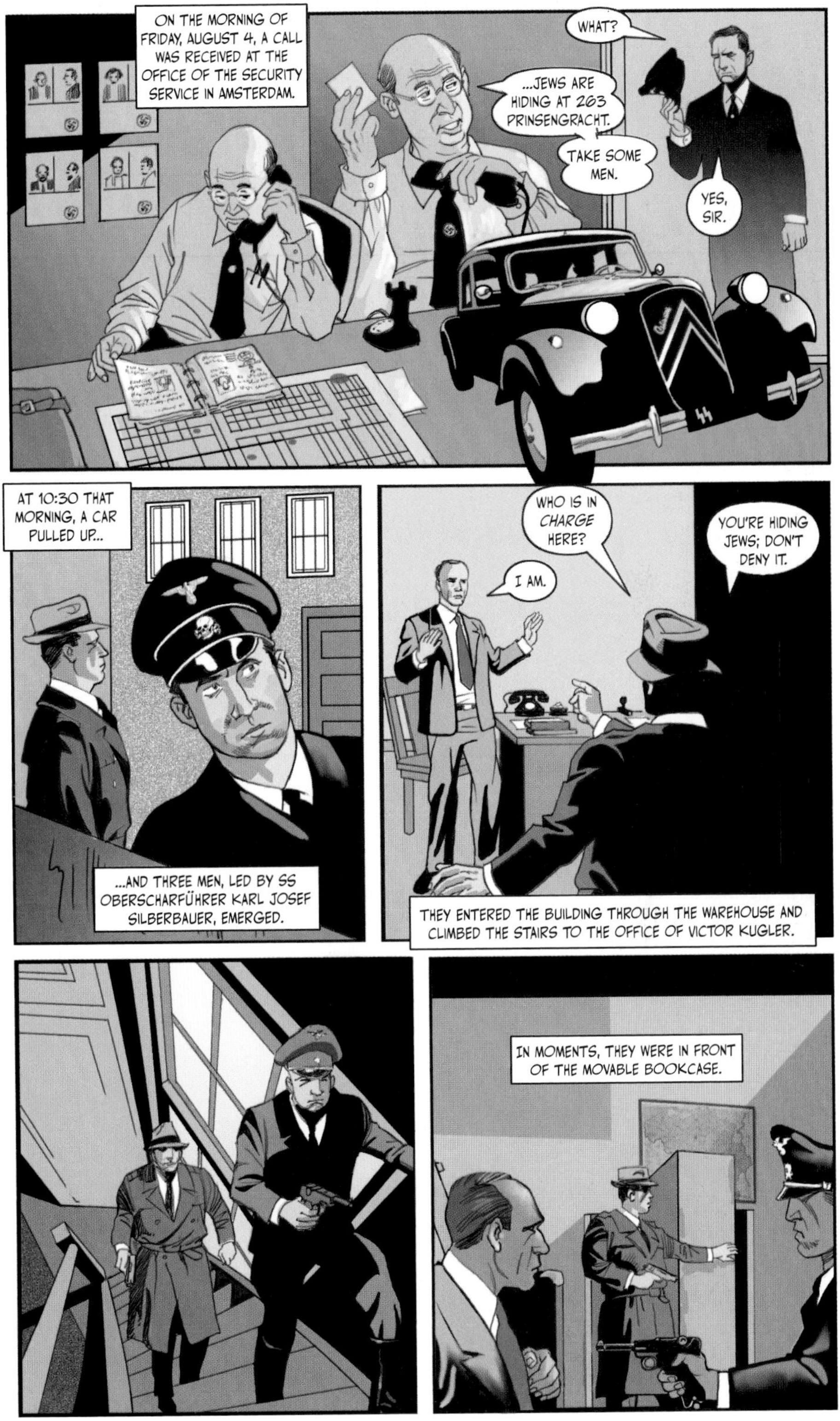
ON THE MORNING OF FRIDAY, AUGUST 4, A CALL WAS RECEIVED AT THE OFFICE OF THE SECURITY SERVICE IN AMSTERDAM.
WHAT?
...JEWS ARE HIDING AT 263 PRINSENGRACHT.
TAKE SOME MEN.
YES, SIR.
AT 10:30 THAT MORNING, A CAR PULLED UP...
...AND THREE MEN, LED BY SS OBERSCHARFÜHRER KARL JOSEF SILBERBAUER, EMERGED.
WHO IS IN *CHARGE* HERE?
I AM.
YOU'RE HIDING JEWS; DON'T DENY IT.
THEY ENTERED THE BUILDING THROUGH THE WAREHOUSE AND CLIMBED THE STAIRS TO THE OFFICE OF VICTOR KUGLER.
IN MOMENTS, THEY WERE IN FRONT OF THE MOVABLE BOOKCASE.

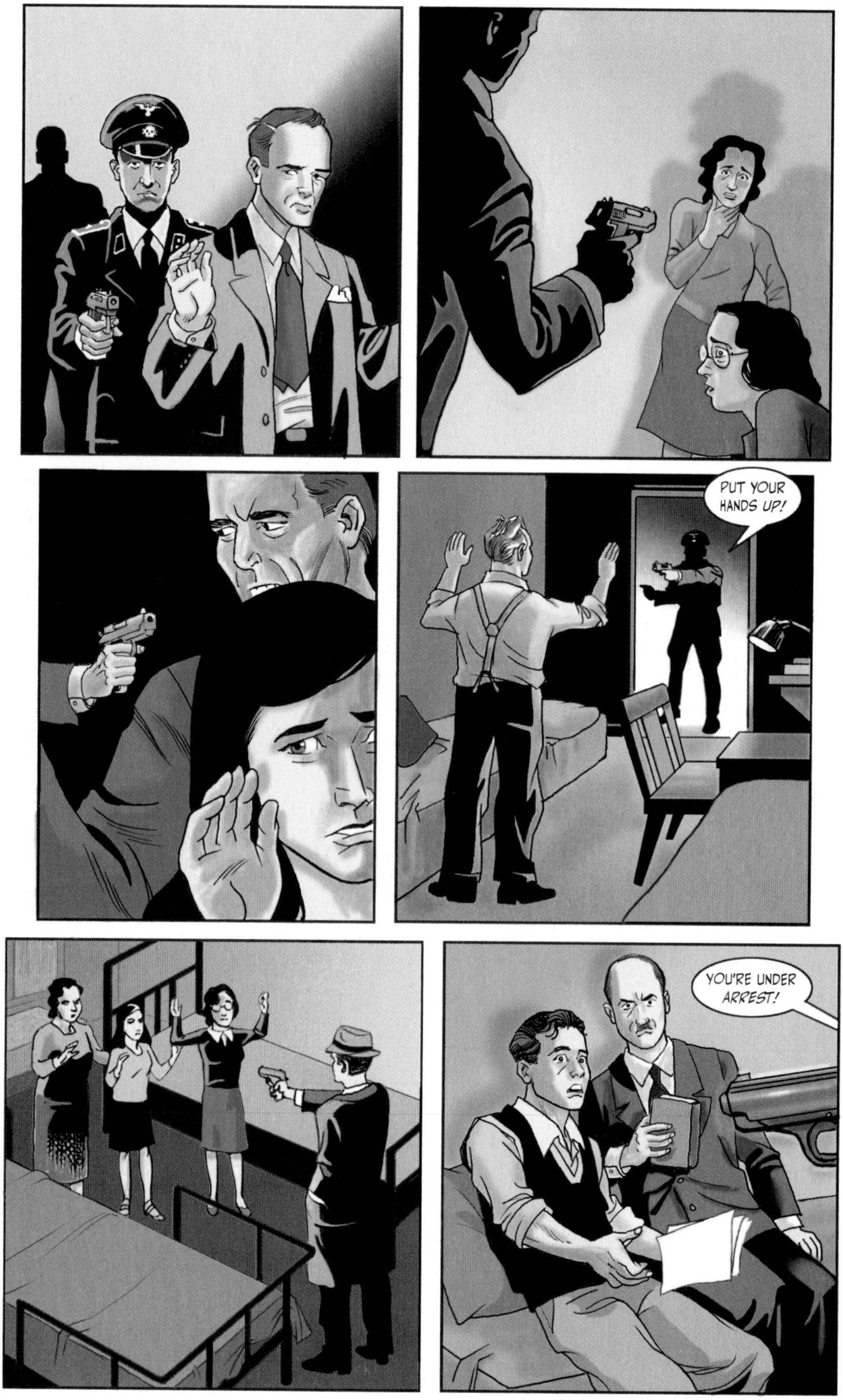
PUT YOUR HANDS UP!
YOU'RE UNDER ARREST!

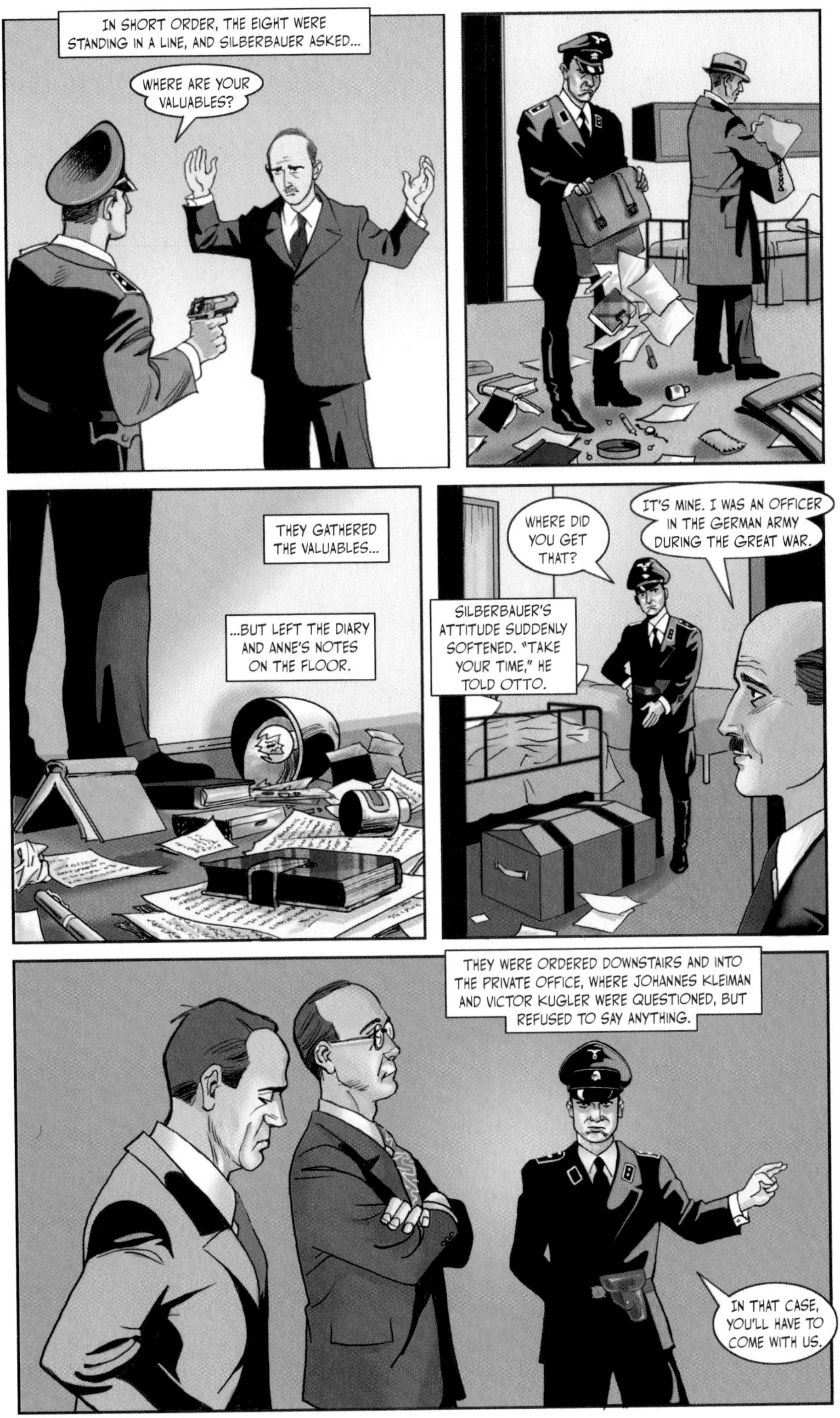
IN SHORT ORDER, THE EIGHT WERE STANDING IN A LINE, AND SILBERBAUER ASKED...
WHERE ARE YOUR VALUABLES?
THEY GATHERED THE VALUABLES...
...BUT LEFT THE DIARY AND ANNE'S NOTES ON THE FLOOR.
WHERE DID YOU GET THAT?
IT'S MINE. I WAS AN OFFICER IN THE GERMAN ARMY DURING THE GREAT WAR.
SILBERBAUER'S ATTITUDE SUDDENLY SOFTENED. "TAKE YOUR TIME," HE TOLD OTTO.
THEY WERE ORDERED DOWNSTAIRS AND INTO THE PRIVATE OFFICE, WHERE JOHANNES KLEIMAN AND VICTOR KUGLER WERE QUESTIONED, BUT REFUSED TO SAY ANYTHING.
IN THAT CASE, YOU'LL HAVE TO COME WITH US.

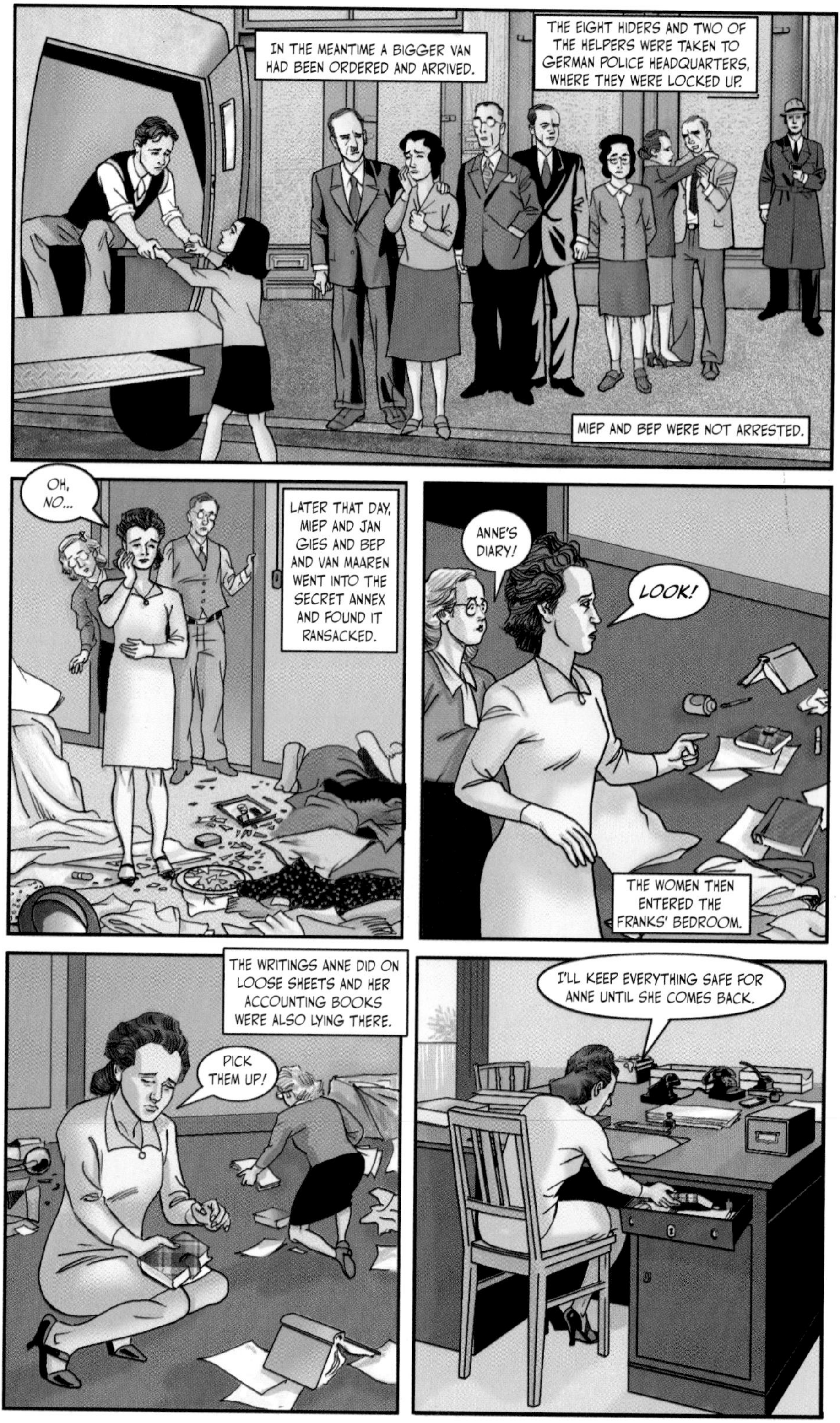

IN THE MEANTIME A BIGGER VAN HAD BEEN ORDERED AND ARRIVED.
THE EIGHT HIDERS AND TWO OF THE HELPERS WERE TAKEN TO GERMAN POLICE HEADQUARTERS, WHERE THEY WERE LOCKED UP.
MIEP AND BEP WERE NOT ARRESTED.
OH, NO...
LATER THAT DAY, MIEP AND JAN GIES AND BEP AND VAN MAAREN WENT INTO THE SECRET ANNEX AND FOUND IT RANSACKED.
ANNE'S DIARY!
LOOK!
THE WOMEN THEN ENTERED THE FRANKS' BEDROOM.
THE WRITINGS ANNE DID ON LOOSE SHEETS AND HER ACCOUNTING BOOKS WERE ALSO LYING THERE.
PICK THEM UP!
I'LL KEEP EVERYTHING SAFE FOR ANNE UNTIL SHE COMES BACK.

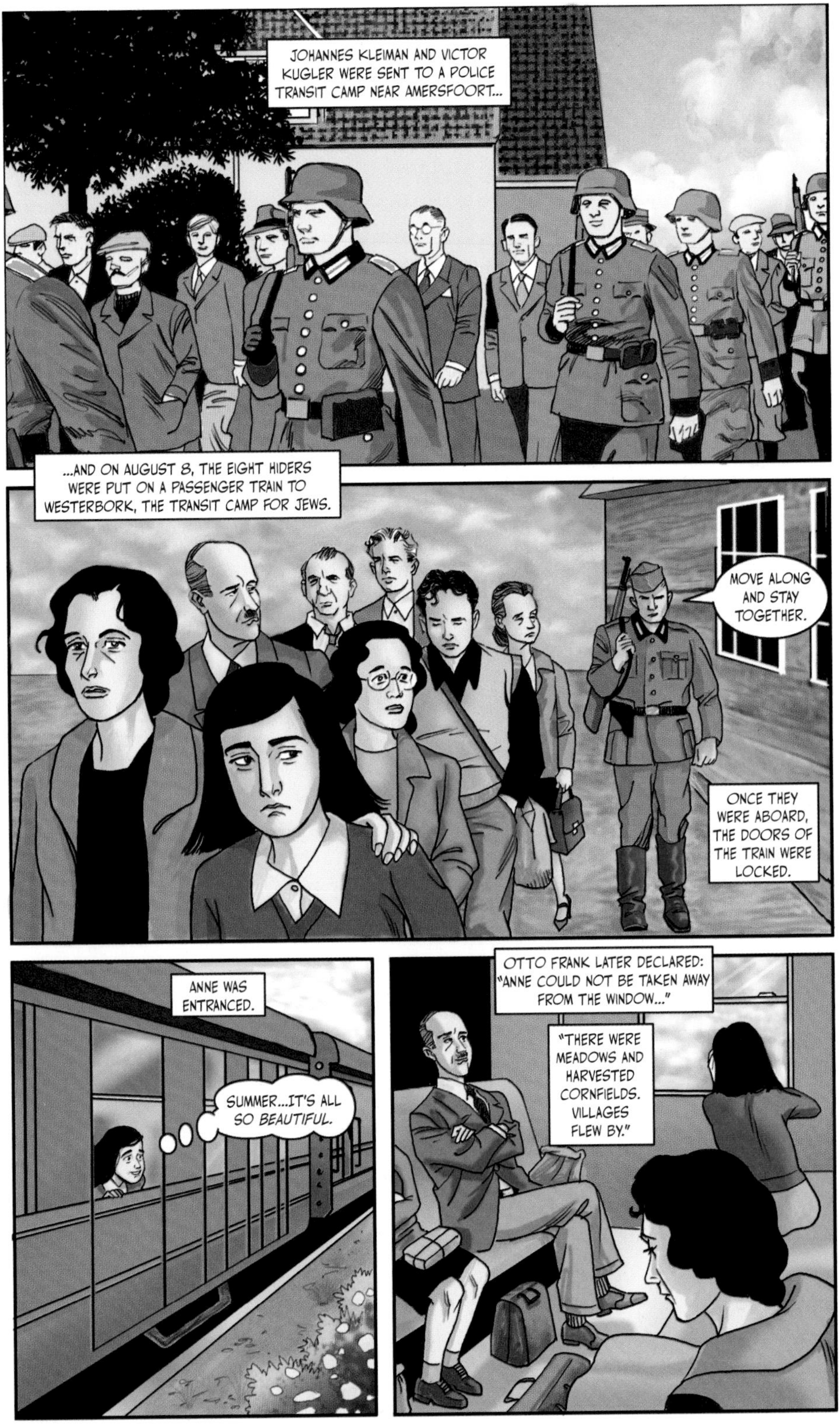
JOHANNES KLEIMAN AND VICTOR KUGLER WERE SENT TO A POLICE TRANSIT CAMP NEAR AMERSFOORT...
...AND ON AUGUST 8, THE EIGHT HIDERS WERE PUT ON A PASSENGER TRAIN TO WESTERBORK, THE TRANSIT CAMP FOR JEWS.
MOVE ALONG AND STAY TOGETHER.
ONCE THEY WERE ABOARD, THE DOORS OF THE TRAIN WERE LOCKED.
ANNE WAS ENTRANCED.
SUMMER...IT'S ALL SO *BEAUTIFUL.*
OTTO FRANK LATER DECLARED: "ANNE COULD NOT BE TAKEN AWAY FROM THE WINDOW..."
"THERE WERE MEADOWS AND HARVESTED CORNFIELDS. VILLAGES FLEW BY."

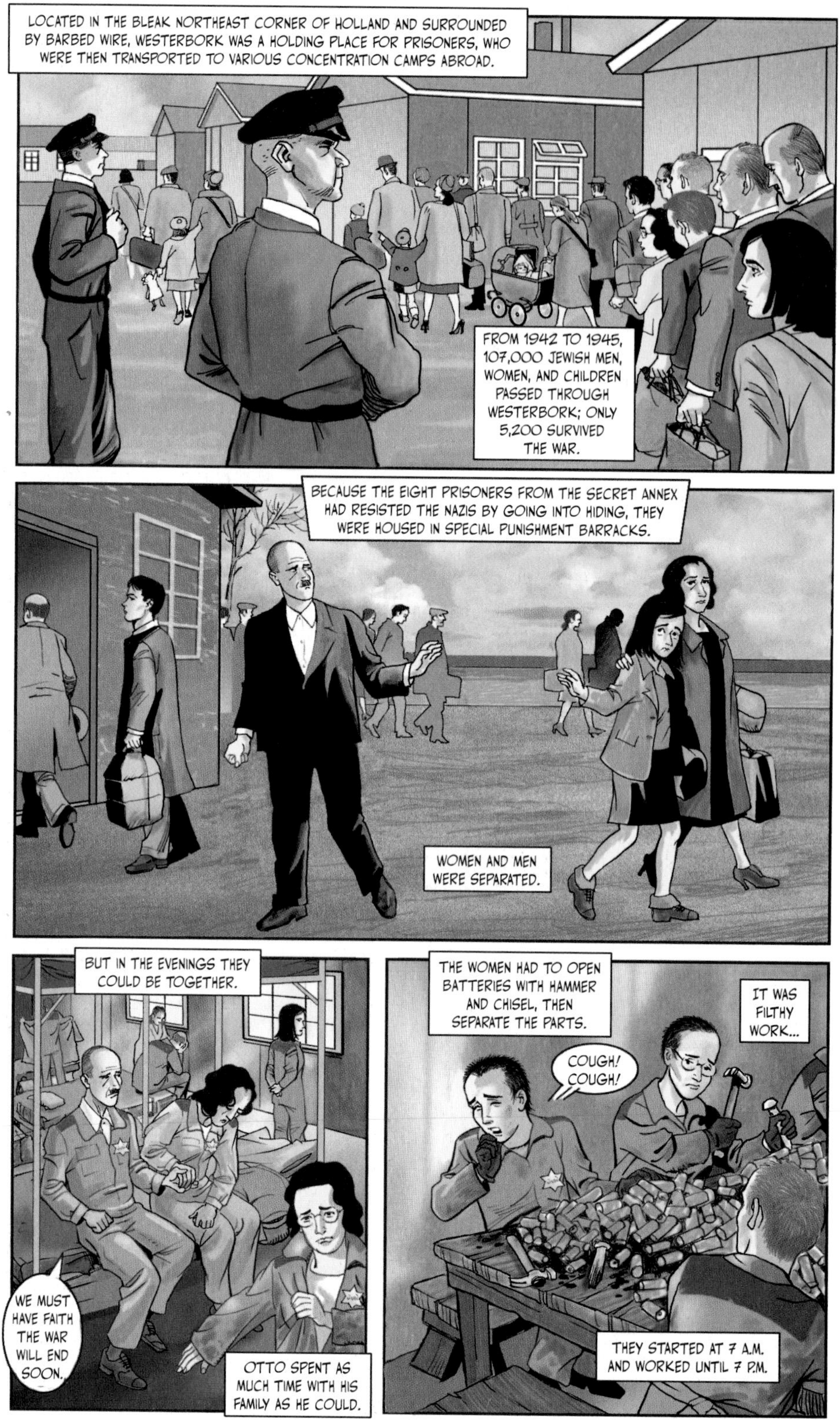
LOCATED IN THE BLEAK NORTHEAST CORNER OF HOLLAND AND SURROUNDED BY BARBED WIRE, WESTERBORK WAS A HOLDING PLACE FOR PRISONERS, WHO WERE THEN TRANSPORTED TO VARIOUS CONCENTRATION CAMPS ABROAD.
FROM 1942 TO 1945, 107,000 JEWISH MEN, WOMEN, AND CHILDREN PASSED THROUGH WESTERBORK; ONLY 5,200 SURVIVED THE WAR.
BECAUSE THE EIGHT PRISONERS FROM THE SECRET ANNEX HAD RESISTED THE NAZIS BY GOING INTO HIDING, THEY WERE HOUSED IN SPECIAL PUNISHMENT BARRACKS.
WOMEN AND MEN WERE SEPARATED.
BUT IN THE EVENINGS THEY COULD BE TOGETHER.
WE MUST HAVE FAITH THE WAR WILL END SOON.
OTTO SPENT AS MUCH TIME WITH HIS FAMILY AS HE COULD.
THE WOMEN HAD TO OPEN BATTERIES WITH HAMMER AND CHISEL, THEN SEPARATE THE PARTS.
IT WAS FILTHY WORK...
COUGH! COUGH!
THEY STARTED AT 7 A.M. AND WORKED UNTIL 7 P.M.

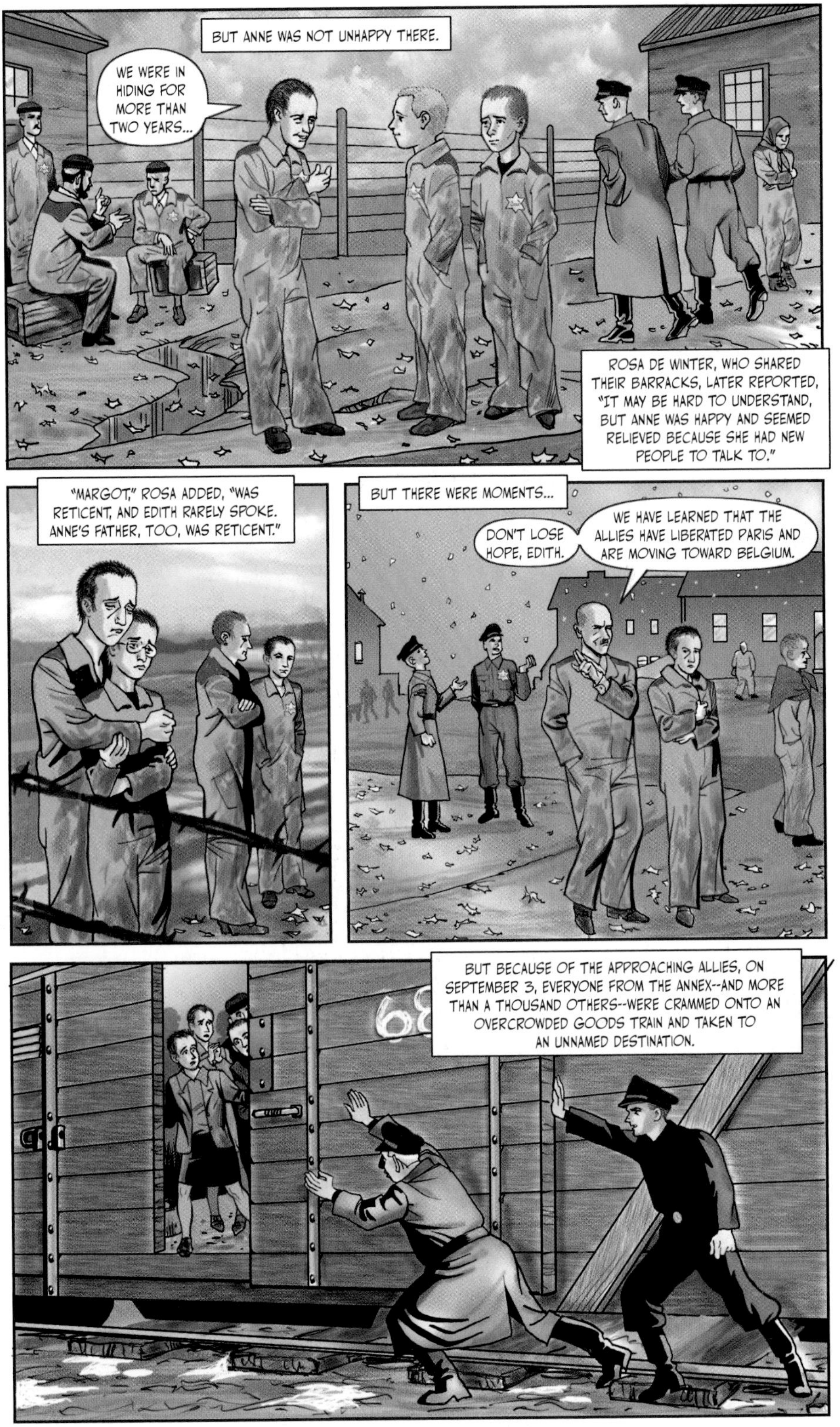
BUT ANNE WAS NOT UNHAPPY THERE.
WE WERE IN HIDING FOR MORE THAN TWO YEARS...
ROSA DE WINTER, WHO SHARED THEIR BARRACKS, LATER REPORTED, "IT MAY BE HARD TO UNDERSTAND, BUT ANNE WAS HAPPY AND SEEMED RELIEVED BECAUSE SHE HAD NEW PEOPLE TO TALK TO."
"MARGOT," ROSA ADDED, "WAS RETICENT, AND EDITH RARELY SPOKE. ANNE'S FATHER, TOO, WAS RETICENT."
BUT THERE WERE MOMENTS...
DON'T LOSE HOPE, EDITH.
WE HAVE LEARNED THAT THE ALLIES HAVE LIBERATED PARIS AND ARE MOVING TOWARD BELGIUM.
BUT BECAUSE OF THE APPROACHING ALLIES, ON SEPTEMBER 3, EVERYONE FROM THE ANNEX--AND MORE THAN A THOUSAND OTHERS--WERE CRAMMED ONTO AN OVERCROWDED GOODS TRAIN AND TAKEN TO AN UNNAMED DESTINATION.

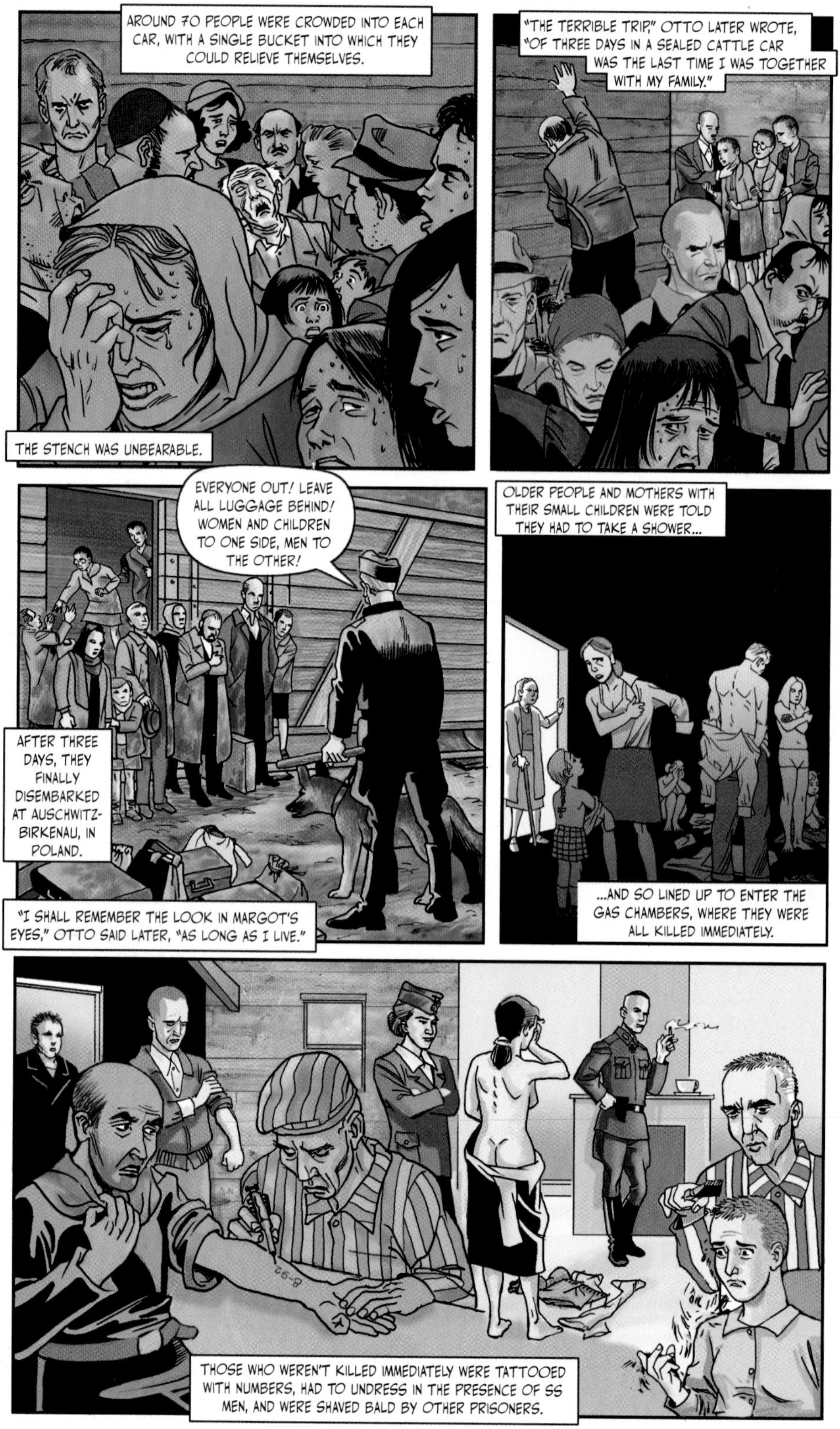
AROUND 70 PEOPLE WERE CROWDED INTO EACH CAR, WITH A SINGLE BUCKET INTO WHICH THEY COULD RELIEVE THEMSELVES.
THE STENCH WAS UNBEARABLE.
"THE TERRIBLE TRIP," OTTO LATER WROTE, "OF THREE DAYS IN A SEALED CATTLE CAR WAS THE LAST TIME I WAS TOGETHER WITH MY FAMILY."
EVERYONE OUT! LEAVE ALL LUGGAGE BEHIND! WOMEN AND CHILDREN TO ONE SIDE, MEN TO THE OTHER!
AFTER THREE DAYS, THEY FINALLY DISEMBARKED AT AUSCHWITZ-BIRKENAU, IN POLAND.
"I SHALL REMEMBER THE LOOK IN MARGOT'S EYES," OTTO SAID LATER, "AS LONG AS I LIVE."
OLDER PEOPLE AND MOTHERS WITH THEIR SMALL CHILDREN WERE TOLD THEY HAD TO TAKE A SHOWER...
...AND SO LINED UP TO ENTER THE GAS CHAMBERS, WHERE THEY WERE ALL KILLED IMMEDIATELY.
THOSE WHO WEREN'T KILLED IMMEDIATELY WERE TATTOOED WITH NUMBERS, HAD TO UNDRESS IN THE PRESENCE OF SS MEN, AND WERE SHAVED BALD BY OTHER PRISONERS.

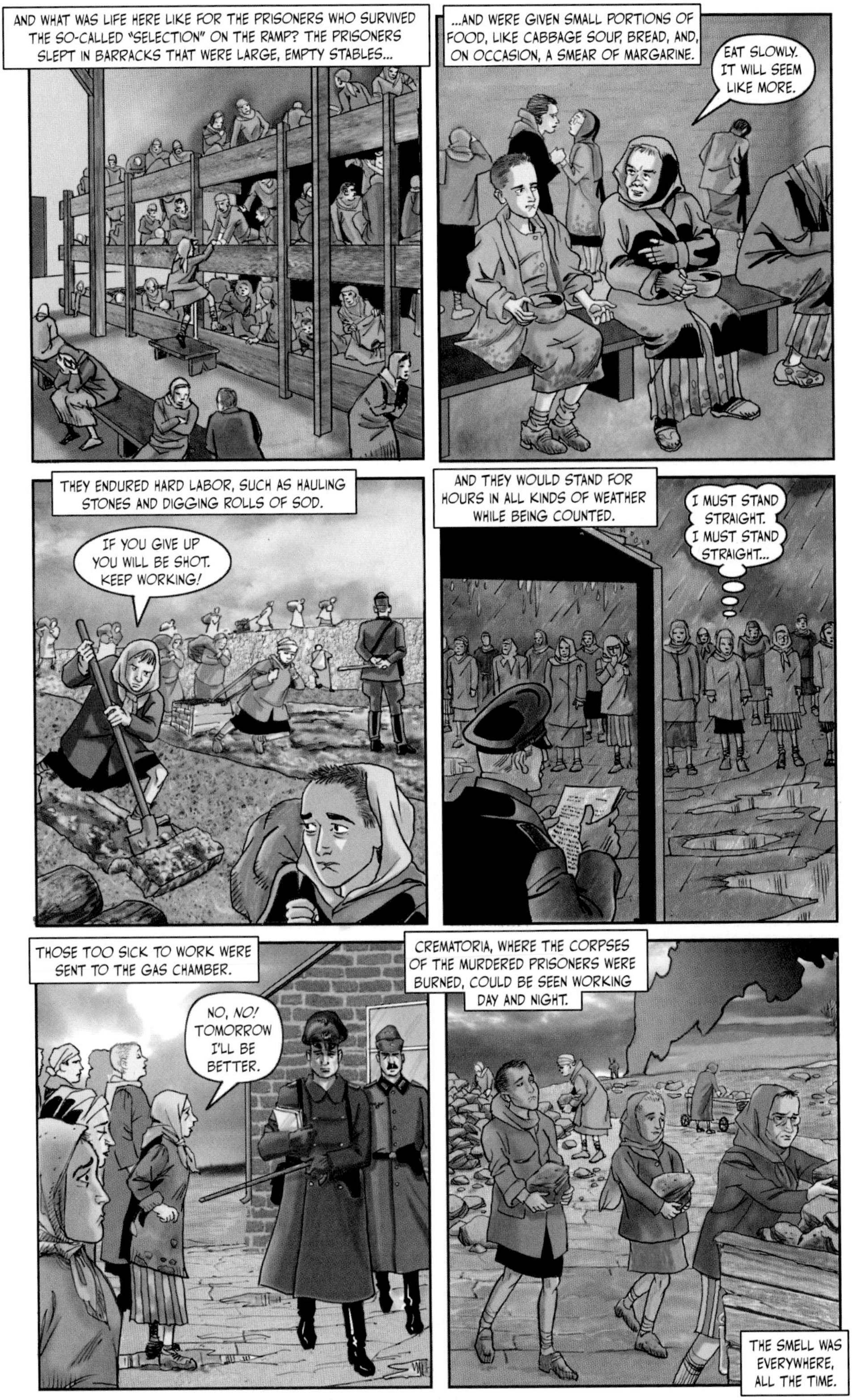
AND WHAT WAS LIFE HERE LIKE FOR THE PRISONERS WHO SURVIVED THE SO-CALLED "SELECTION" ON THE RAMP? THE PRISONERS SLEPT IN BARRACKS THAT WERE LARGE, EMPTY STABLES...
...AND WERE GIVEN SMALL PORTIONS OF FOOD, LIKE CABBAGE SOUP, BREAD, AND, ON OCCASION, A SMEAR OF MARGARINE.
EAT SLOWLY. IT WILL SEEM LIKE MORE.
THEY ENDURED HARD LABOR, SUCH AS HAULING STONES AND DIGGING ROLLS OF SOD.
IF YOU GIVE UP YOU WILL BE SHOT. KEEP WORKING!
AND THEY WOULD STAND FOR HOURS IN ALL KINDS OF WEATHER WHILE BEING COUNTED.
I MUST STAND STRAIGHT. I MUST STAND STRAIGHT...
THOSE TOO SICK TO WORK WERE SENT TO THE GAS CHAMBER.
NO, NO! TOMORROW I'LL BE BETTER.
CREMATORIA, WHERE THE CORPSES OF THE MURDERED PRISONERS WERE BURNED, COULD BE SEEN WORKING DAY AND NIGHT.
THE SMELL WAS EVERYWHERE, ALL THE TIME.

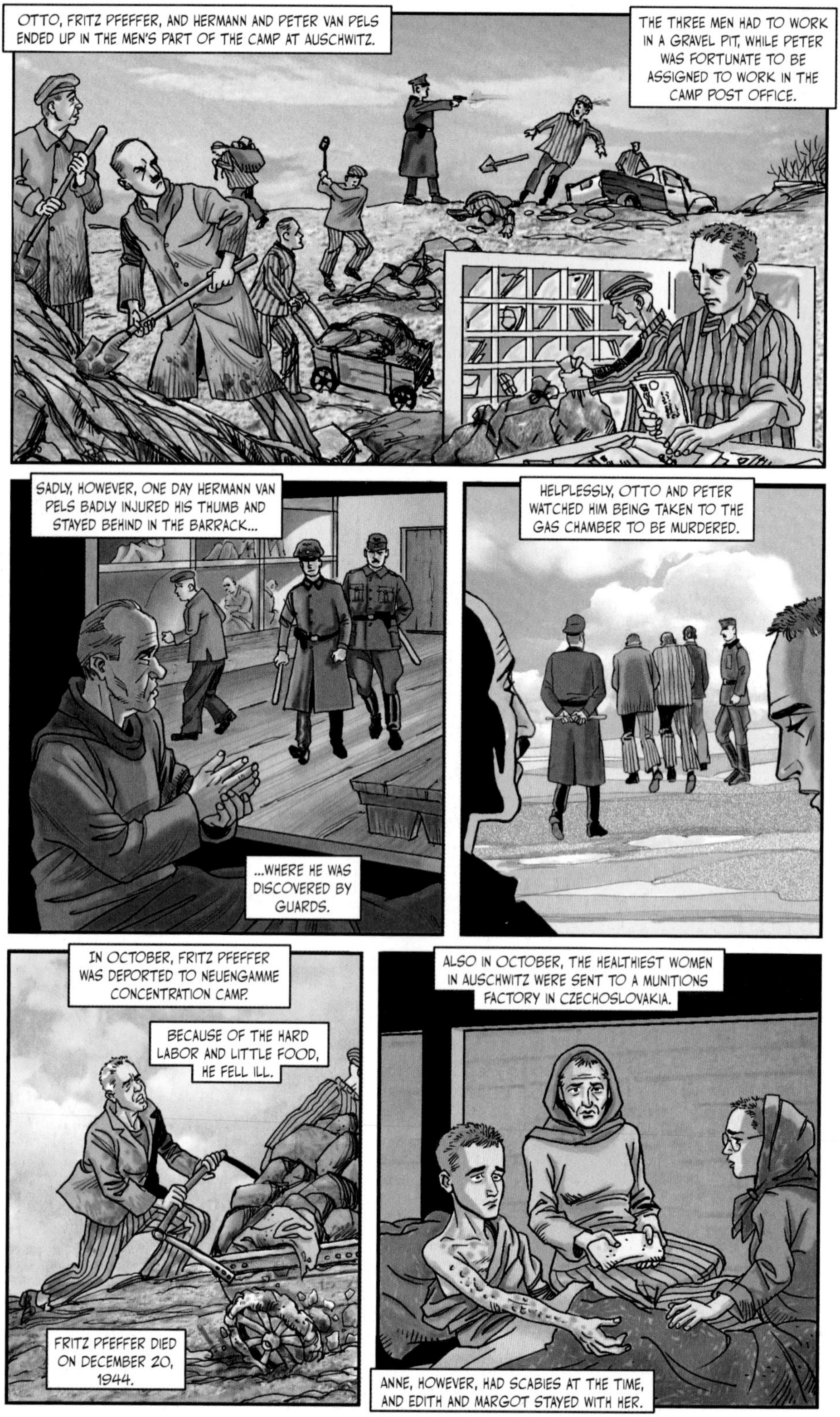
OTTO, FRITZ PFEFFER, AND HERMANN AND PETER VAN PELS ENDED UP IN THE MEN'S PART OF THE CAMP AT AUSCHWITZ.
THE THREE MEN HAD TO WORK IN A GRAVEL PIT, WHILE PETER WAS FORTUNATE TO BE ASSIGNED TO WORK IN THE CAMP POST OFFICE.
SADLY, HOWEVER, ONE DAY HERMANN VAN PELS BADLY INJURED HIS THUMB AND STAYED BEHIND IN THE BARRACK...
...WHERE HE WAS DISCOVERED BY GUARDS.
HELPLESSLY, OTTO AND PETER WATCHED HIM BEING TAKEN TO THE GAS CHAMBER TO BE MURDERED.
IN OCTOBER, FRITZ PFEFFER WAS DEPORTED TO NEUENGAMME CONCENTRATION CAMP.
BECAUSE OF THE HARD LABOR AND LITTLE FOOD, HE FELL ILL.
FRITZ PFEFFER DIED ON DECEMBER 20, 1944.
ALSO IN OCTOBER, THE HEALTHIEST WOMEN IN AUSCHWITZ WERE SENT TO A MUNITIONS FACTORY IN CZECHOSLOVAKIA.
ANNE, HOWEVER, HAD SCABIES AT THE TIME, AND EDITH AND MARGOT STAYED WITH HER.

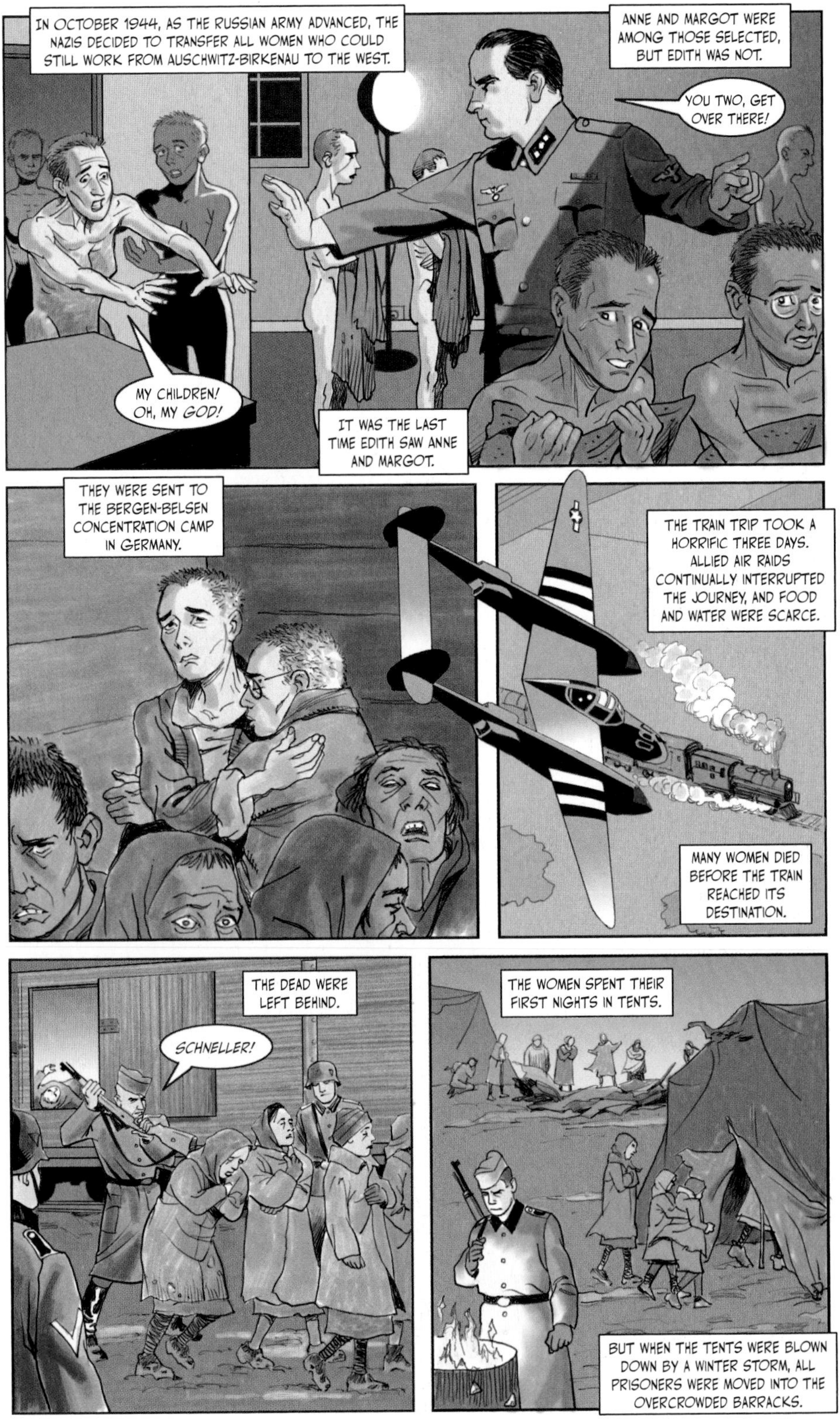
IN OCTOBER 1944, AS THE RUSSIAN ARMY ADVANCED, THE NAZIS DECIDED TO TRANSFER ALL WOMEN WHO COULD STILL WORK FROM AUSCHWITZ-BIRKENAU TO THE WEST.
ANNE AND MARGOT WERE AMONG THOSE SELECTED, BUT EDITH WAS NOT.
YOU TWO, GET OVER THERE!
MY CHILDREN! OH, MY *GOD!*
IT WAS THE LAST TIME EDITH SAW ANNE AND MARGOT.
THEY WERE SENT TO THE BERGEN-BELSEN CONCENTRATION CAMP IN GERMANY.
THE TRAIN TRIP TOOK A HORRIFIC THREE DAYS. ALLIED AIR RAIDS CONTINUALLY INTERRUPTED THE JOURNEY, AND FOOD AND WATER WERE SCARCE.
MANY WOMEN DIED BEFORE THE TRAIN REACHED ITS DESTINATION.
THE DEAD WERE LEFT BEHIND.
SCHNELLER!
THE WOMEN SPENT THEIR FIRST NIGHTS IN TENTS.
BUT WHEN THE TENTS WERE BLOWN DOWN BY A WINTER STORM, ALL PRISONERS WERE MOVED INTO THE OVERCROWDED BARRACKS.

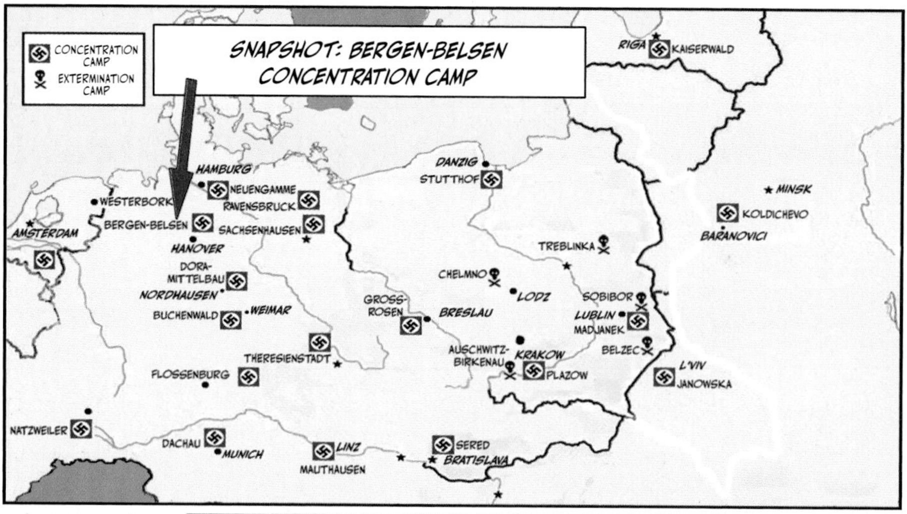
SNAPSHOT: BERGEN-BELSEN CONCENTRATION CAMP
CONCENTRATION CAMP
EXTERMINATION CAMP
RIGA
KAISERWALD
DANZIG
STUTTHOF
HAMBURG
NEUENGAMME
RAVENSBRUCK
WESTERBORK
BERGEN-BELSEN
SACHSENHAUSEN
AMSTERDAM
HANOVER
MINSK
KOLDICHEVO
BARANOVICI
TREBLINKA
DORA-MITTELBAU
NORDHAUSEN
CHELMNO
LODZ
SOBIBOR
LUBLIN
MADJANEK
BUCHENWALD
WEIMAR
GROSS-ROSEN
BRESLAU
AUSCHWITZ-BIRKENAU
KRAKOW
PLAZOW
BELZEC
THERESIENSTADT
FLOSSENBURG
L'VIV
JANOWSKA
NATZWEILER
DACHAU
MUNICH
LINZ
MAUTHAUSEN
SERED
BRATISLAVA

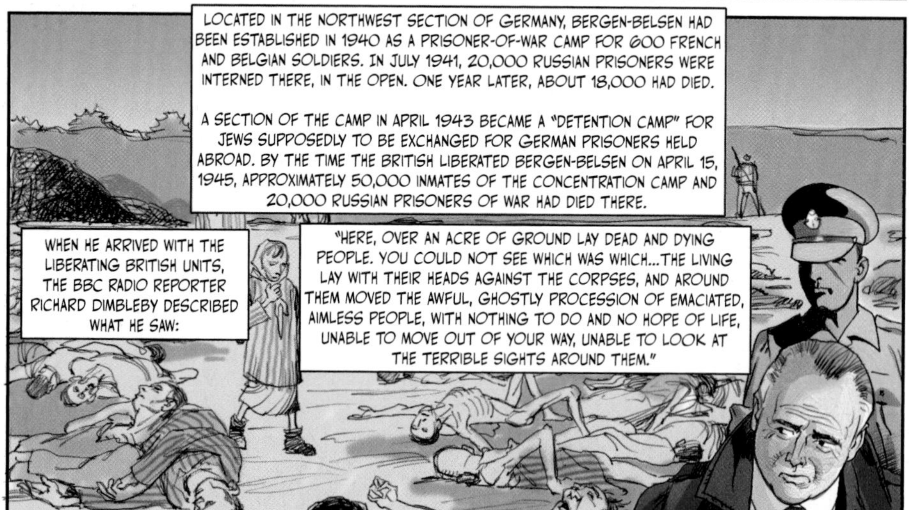
LOCATED IN THE NORTHWEST SECTION OF GERMANY, BERGEN-BELSEN HAD BEEN ESTABLISHED IN 1940 AS A PRISONER-OF-WAR CAMP FOR 600 FRENCH AND BELGIAN SOLDIERS. IN JULY 1941, 20,000 RUSSIAN PRISONERS WERE INTERNED THERE, IN THE OPEN. ONE YEAR LATER, ABOUT 18,000 HAD DIED.
A SECTION OF THE CAMP IN APRIL 1943 BECAME A "DETENTION CAMP" FOR JEWS SUPPOSEDLY TO BE EXCHANGED FOR GERMAN PRISONERS HELD ABROAD. BY THE TIME THE BRITISH LIBERATED BERGEN-BELSEN ON APRIL 15, 1945, APPROXIMATELY 50,000 INMATES OF THE CONCENTRATION CAMP AND 20,000 RUSSIAN PRISONERS OF WAR HAD DIED THERE.
WHEN HE ARRIVED WITH THE LIBERATING BRITISH UNITS, THE BBC RADIO REPORTER RICHARD DIMBLEBY DESCRIBED WHAT HE SAW:
"HERE, OVER AN ACRE OF GROUND LAY DEAD AND DYING PEOPLE. YOU COULD NOT SEE WHICH WAS WHICH...THE LIVING LAY WITH THEIR HEADS AGAINST THE CORPSES, AND AROUND THEM MOVED THE AWFUL, GHOSTLY PROCESSION OF EMACIATED, AIMLESS PEOPLE, WITH NOTHING TO DO AND NO HOPE OF LIFE, UNABLE TO MOVE OUT OF YOUR WAY, UNABLE TO LOOK AT THE TERRIBLE SIGHTS AROUND THEM."

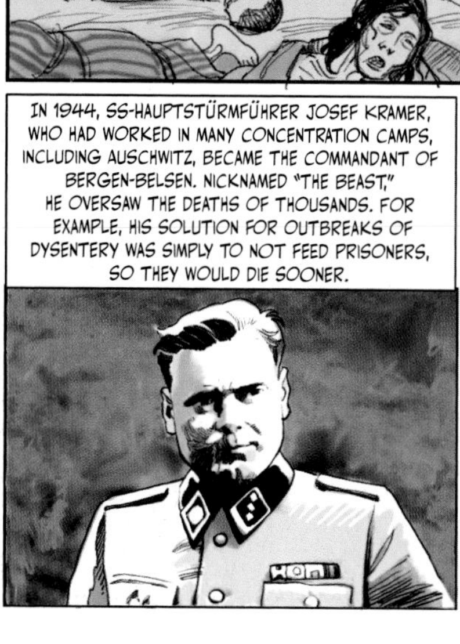
IN 1944, SS-HAUPTSTÜRMFÜHRER JOSEF KRAMER, WHO HAD WORKED IN MANY CONCENTRATION CAMPS, INCLUDING AUSCHWITZ, BECAME THE COMMANDANT OF BERGEN-BELSEN. NICKNAMED "THE BEAST," HE OVERSAW THE DEATHS OF THOUSANDS. FOR EXAMPLE, HIS SOLUTION FOR OUTBREAKS OF DYSENTERY WAS SIMPLY TO NOT FEED PRISONERS, SO THEY WOULD DIE SOONER.

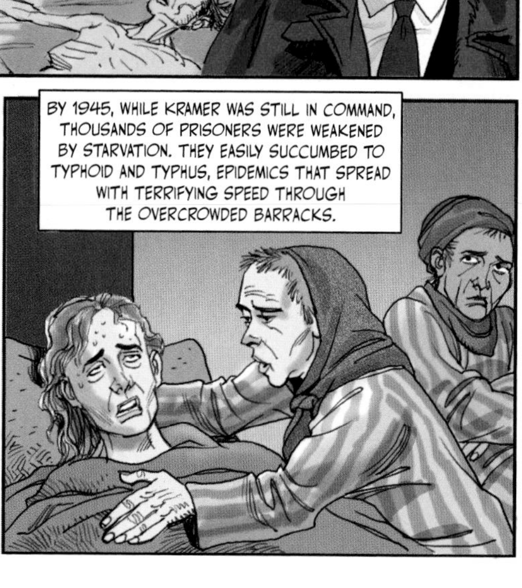
BY 1945, WHILE KRAMER WAS STILL IN COMMAND, THOUSANDS OF PRISONERS WERE WEAKENED BY STARVATION. THEY EASILY SUCCUMBED TO TYPHOID AND TYPHUS, EPIDEMICS THAT SPREAD WITH TERRIFYING SPEED THROUGH THE OVERCROWDED BARRACKS.

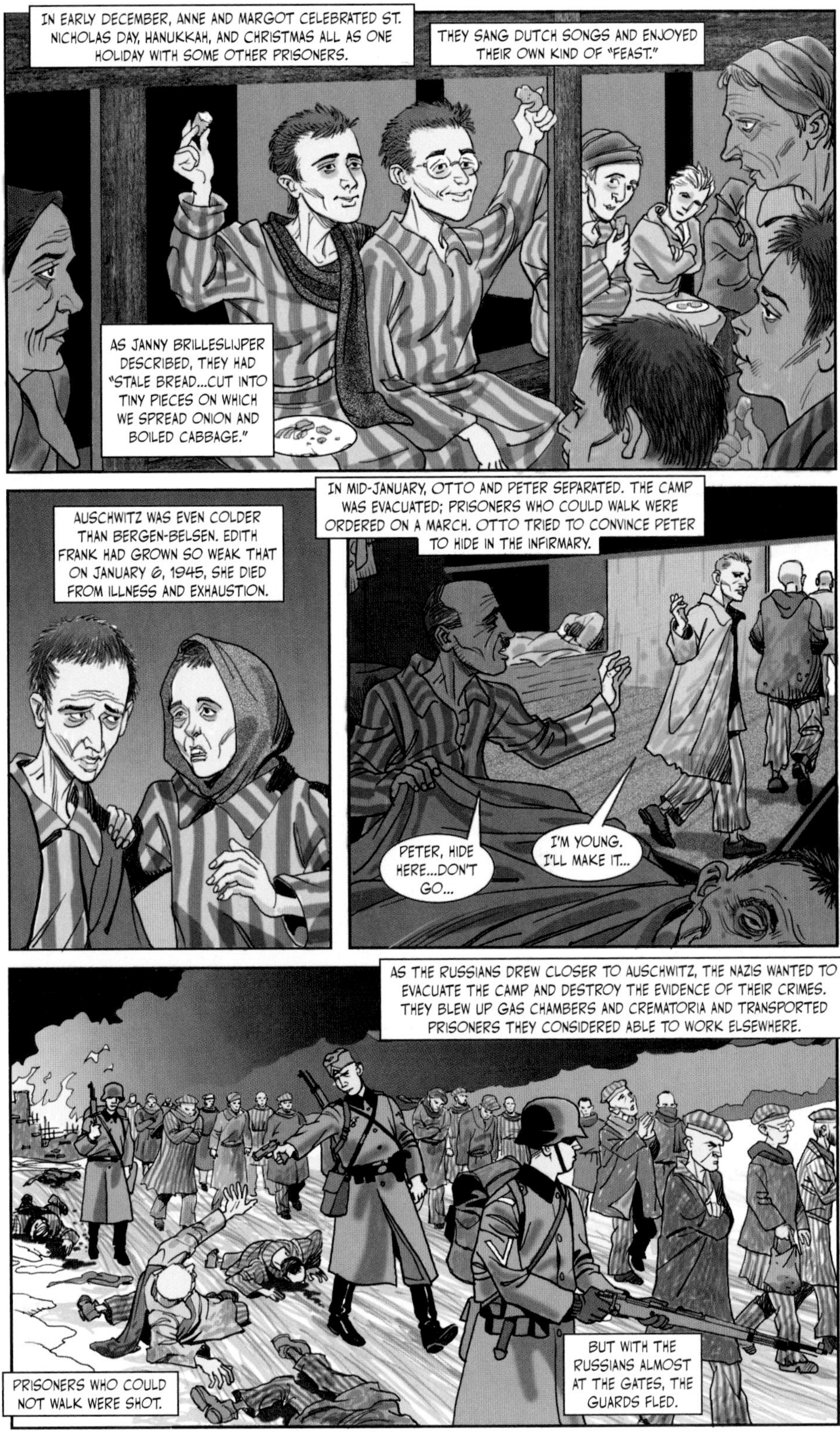

IN EARLY DECEMBER, ANNE AND MARGOT CELEBRATED ST. NICHOLAS DAY, HANUKKAH, AND CHRISTMAS ALL AS ONE HOLIDAY WITH SOME OTHER PRISONERS.
THEY SANG DUTCH SONGS AND ENJOYED THEIR OWN KIND OF "FEAST."
AS JANNY BRILLESLIJPER DESCRIBED, THEY HAD "STALE BREAD...CUT INTO TINY PIECES ON WHICH WE SPREAD ONION AND BOILED CABBAGE."
AUSCHWITZ WAS EVEN COLDER THAN BERGEN-BELSEN. EDITH FRANK HAD GROWN SO WEAK THAT ON JANUARY 6, 1945, SHE DIED FROM ILLNESS AND EXHAUSTION.
IN MID-JANUARY, OTTO AND PETER SEPARATED. THE CAMP WAS EVACUATED; PRISONERS WHO COULD WALK WERE ORDERED ON A MARCH. OTTO TRIED TO CONVINCE PETER TO HIDE IN THE INFIRMARY.
PETER, HIDE HERE...DON'T GO...
I'M YOUNG. I'LL MAKE IT...
AS THE RUSSIANS DREW CLOSER TO AUSCHWITZ, THE NAZIS WANTED TO EVACUATE THE CAMP AND DESTROY THE EVIDENCE OF THEIR CRIMES. THEY BLEW UP GAS CHAMBERS AND CREMATORIA AND TRANSPORTED PRISONERS THEY CONSIDERED ABLE TO WORK ELSEWHERE.
PRISONERS WHO COULD NOT WALK WERE SHOT.
BUT WITH THE RUSSIANS ALMOST AT THE GATES, THE GUARDS FLED.

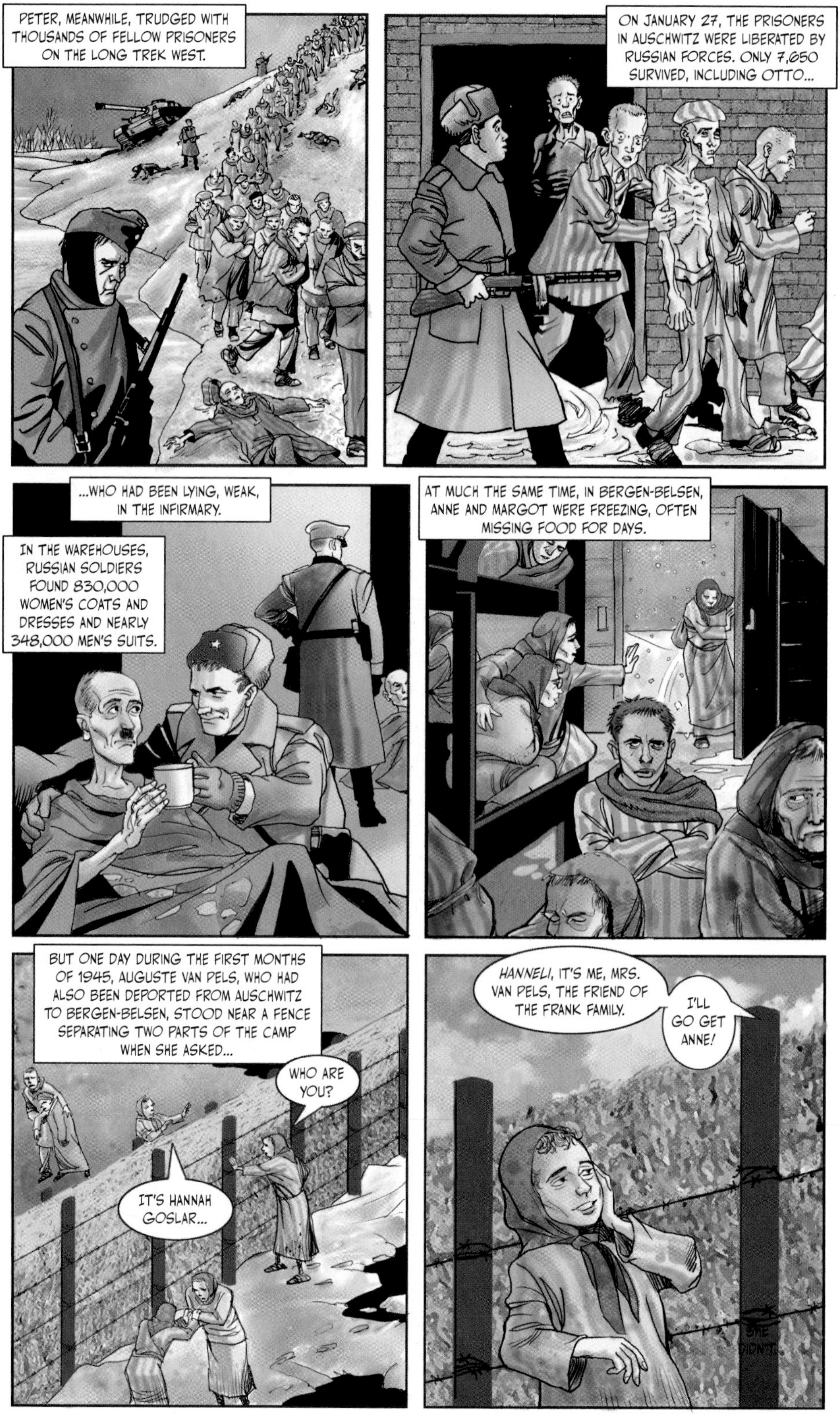
PETER, MEANWHILE, TRUDGED WITH THOUSANDS OF FELLOW PRISONERS ON THE LONG TREK WEST.
ON JANUARY 27, THE PRISONERS IN AUSCHWITZ WERE LIBERATED BY RUSSIAN FORCES. ONLY 7,650 SURVIVED, INCLUDING OTTO...
...WHO HAD BEEN LYING, WEAK, IN THE INFIRMARY.
IN THE WAREHOUSES, RUSSIAN SOLDIERS FOUND 830,000 WOMEN'S COATS AND DRESSES AND NEARLY 348,000 MEN'S SUITS.
AT MUCH THE SAME TIME, IN BERGEN-BELSEN, ANNE AND MARGOT WERE FREEZING, OFTEN MISSING FOOD FOR DAYS.
BUT ONE DAY DURING THE FIRST MONTHS OF 1945, AUGUSTE VAN PELS, WHO HAD ALSO BEEN DEPORTED FROM AUSCHWITZ TO BERGEN-BELSEN, STOOD NEAR A FENCE SEPARATING TWO PARTS OF THE CAMP WHEN SHE ASKED...
WHO ARE YOU?
IT'S HANNAH GOSLAR...
HANNELI, IT'S ME, MRS. VAN PELS, THE FRIEND OF THE FRANK FAMILY.
I'LL GO GET ANNE!
SHE DIDN'T.

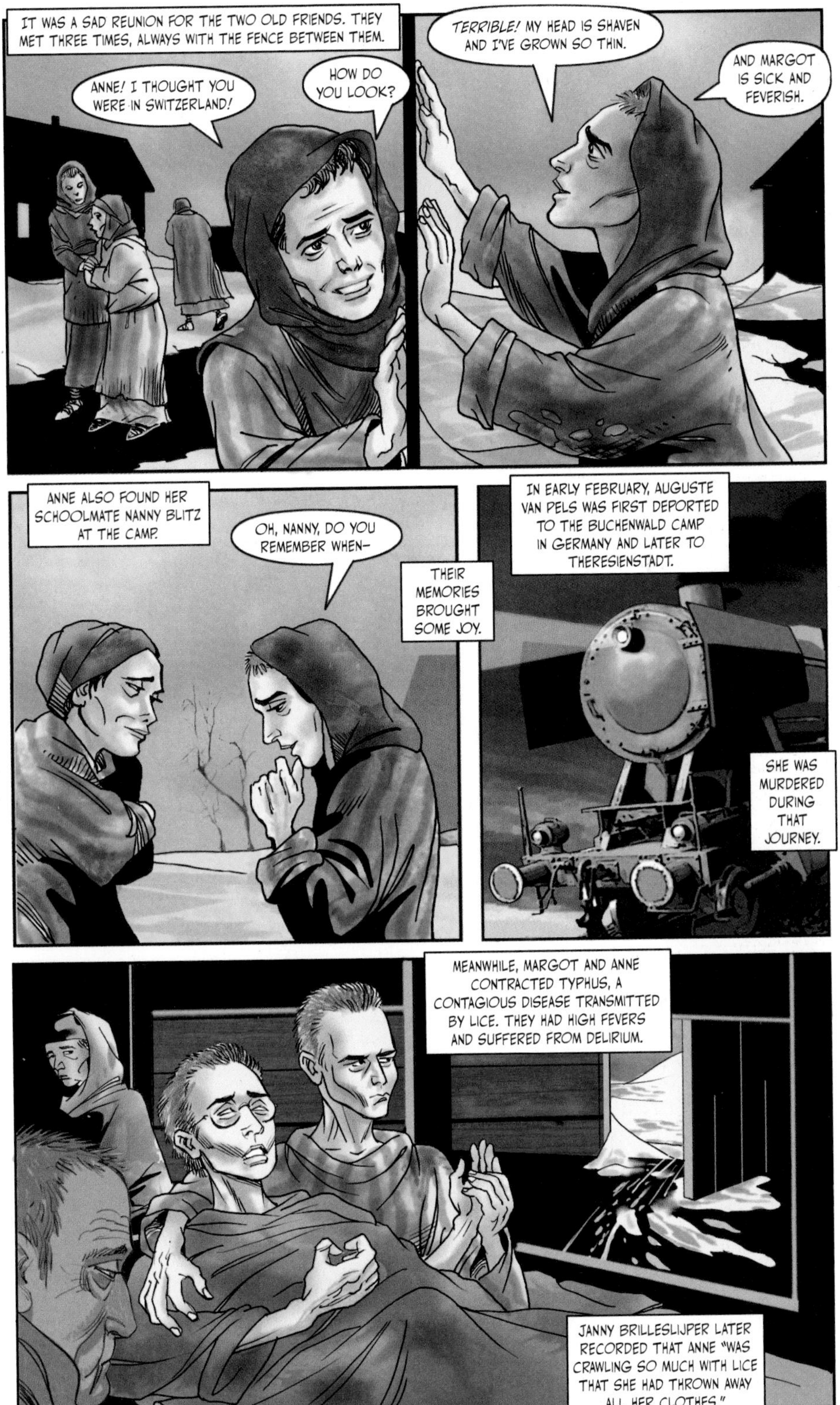
IT WAS A SAD REUNION FOR THE TWO OLD FRIENDS. THEY MET THREE TIMES, ALWAYS WITH THE FENCE BETWEEN THEM.
ANNE! I THOUGHT YOU WERE IN SWITZERLAND!
HOW DO YOU LOOK?
TERRIBLE! MY HEAD IS SHAVEN AND I'VE GROWN SO THIN.
AND MARGOT IS SICK AND FEVERISH.
ANNE ALSO FOUND HER SCHOOLMATE NANNY BLITZ AT THE CAMP.
OH, NANNY, DO YOU REMEMBER WHEN–
THEIR MEMORIES BROUGHT SOME JOY.
IN EARLY FEBRUARY, AUGUSTE VAN PELS WAS FIRST DEPORTED TO THE BUCHENWALD CAMP IN GERMANY AND LATER TO THERESIENSTADT.
SHE WAS MURDERED DURING THAT JOURNEY.
MEANWHILE, MARGOT AND ANNE CONTRACTED TYPHUS, A CONTAGIOUS DISEASE TRANSMITTED BY LICE. THEY HAD HIGH FEVERS AND SUFFERED FROM DELIRIUM.
JANNY BRILLESLIJPER LATER RECORDED THAT ANNE "WAS CRAWLING SO MUCH WITH LICE THAT SHE HAD THROWN AWAY ALL HER CLOTHES."

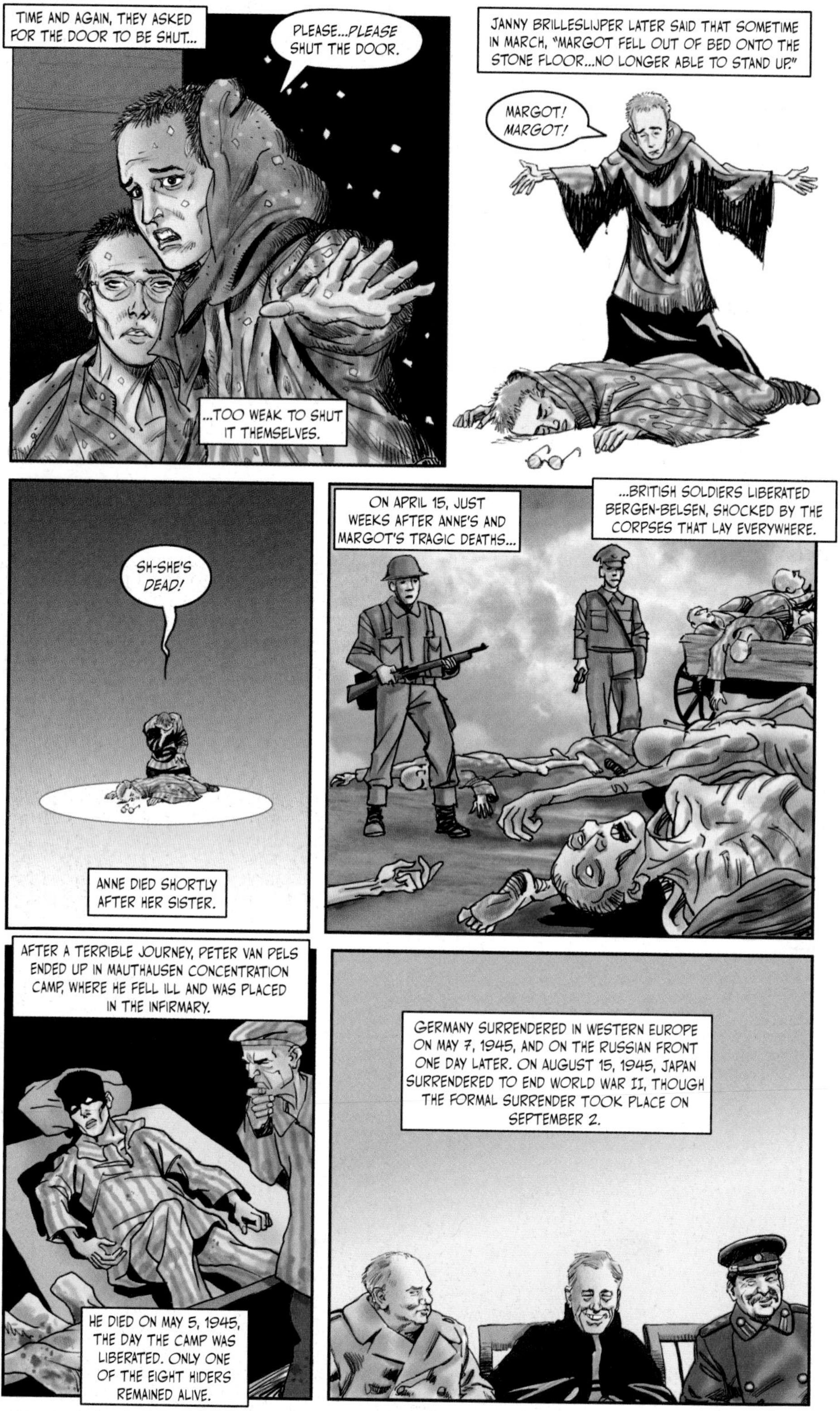
TIME AND AGAIN, THEY ASKED FOR THE DOOR TO BE SHUT...
PLEASE...*PLEASE* SHUT THE DOOR.
...TOO WEAK TO SHUT IT THEMSELVES.
JANNY BRILLESLIJPER LATER SAID THAT SOMETIME IN MARCH, "MARGOT FELL OUT OF BED ONTO THE STONE FLOOR...NO LONGER ABLE TO STAND UP."
MARGOT! MARGOT!
SH-SHE'S *DEAD!*
ANNE DIED SHORTLY AFTER HER SISTER.
ON APRIL 15, JUST WEEKS AFTER ANNE'S AND MARGOT'S TRAGIC DEATHS...
...BRITISH SOLDIERS LIBERATED BERGEN-BELSEN, SHOCKED BY THE CORPSES THAT LAY EVERYWHERE.
AFTER A TERRIBLE JOURNEY, PETER VAN PELS ENDED UP IN MAUTHAUSEN CONCENTRATION CAMP, WHERE HE FELL ILL AND WAS PLACED IN THE INFIRMARY.
HE DIED ON MAY 5, 1945, THE DAY THE CAMP WAS LIBERATED. ONLY ONE OF THE EIGHT HIDERS REMAINED ALIVE.
GERMANY SURRENDERED IN WESTERN EUROPE ON MAY 7, 1945, AND ON THE RUSSIAN FRONT ONE DAY LATER. ON AUGUST 15, 1945, JAPAN SURRENDERED TO END WORLD WAR II, THOUGH THE FORMAL SURRENDER TOOK PLACE ON SEPTEMBER 2.

CHAPTER 10

The Story Lives On

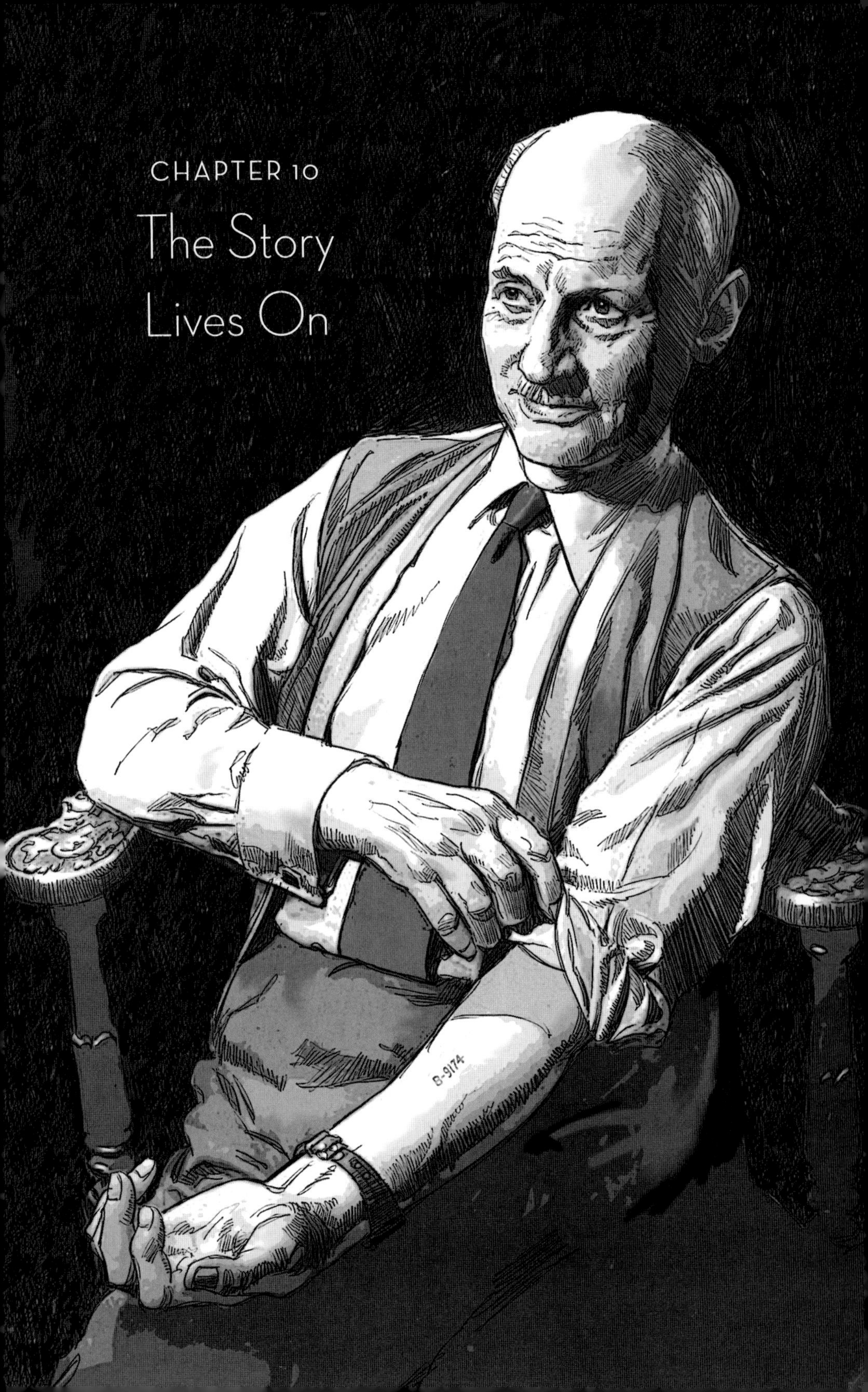
B-9174

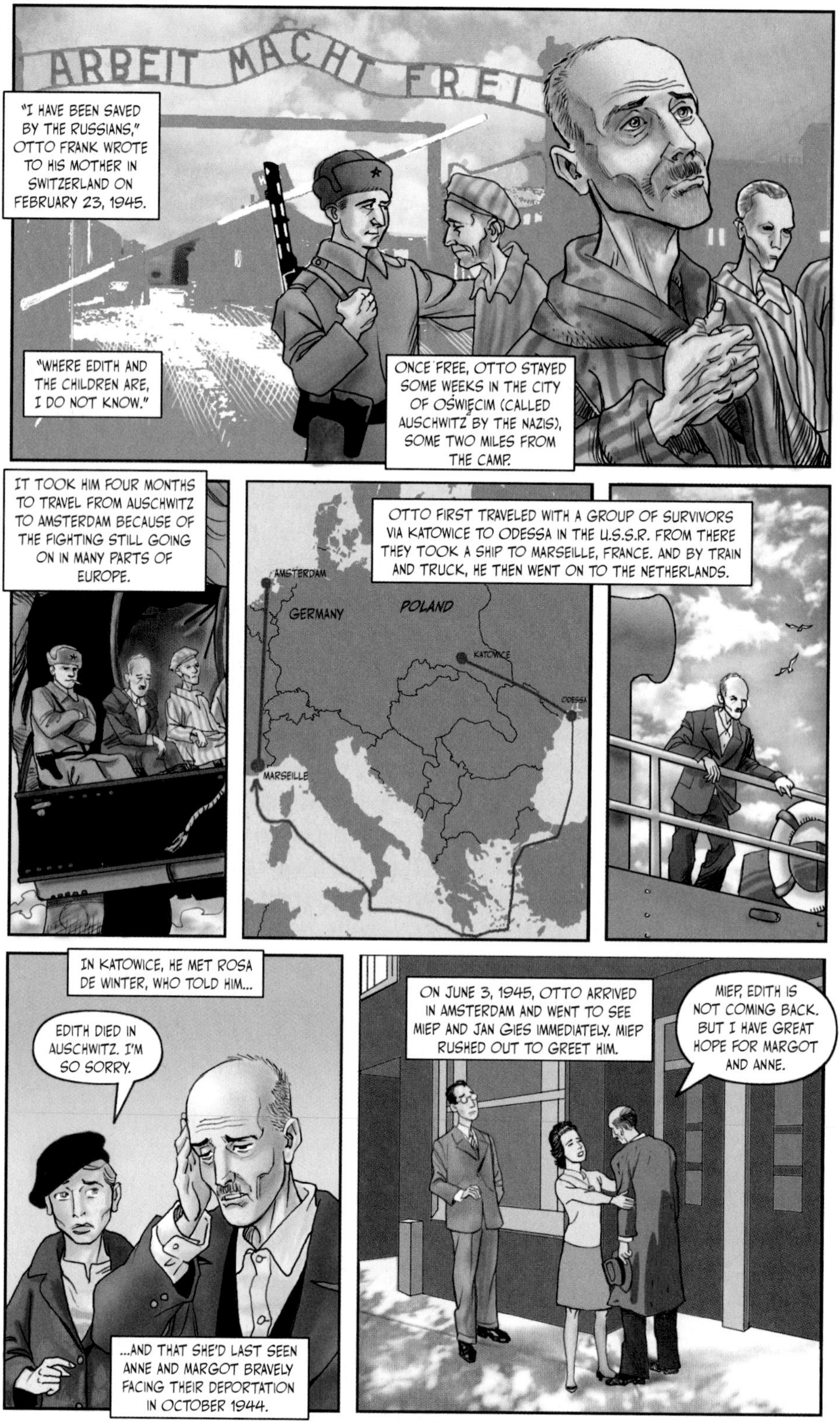
ARBEIT MACHT FREI
"I HAVE BEEN SAVED BY THE RUSSIANS," OTTO FRANK WROTE TO HIS MOTHER IN SWITZERLAND ON FEBRUARY 23, 1945.
"WHERE EDITH AND THE CHILDREN ARE, I DO NOT KNOW."
ONCE FREE, OTTO STAYED SOME WEEKS IN THE CITY OF OŚWIĘCIM (CALLED AUSCHWITZ BY THE NAZIS), SOME TWO MILES FROM THE CAMP.
IT TOOK HIM FOUR MONTHS TO TRAVEL FROM AUSCHWITZ TO AMSTERDAM BECAUSE OF THE FIGHTING STILL GOING ON IN MANY PARTS OF EUROPE.
OTTO FIRST TRAVELED WITH A GROUP OF SURVIVORS VIA KATOWICE TO ODESSA IN THE U.S.S.R. FROM THERE THEY TOOK A SHIP TO MARSEILLE, FRANCE. AND BY TRAIN AND TRUCK, HE THEN WENT ON TO THE NETHERLANDS.
AMSTERDAM
GERMANY
POLAND
KATOWICE
ODESSA
MARSEILLE
IN KATOWICE, HE MET ROSA DE WINTER, WHO TOLD HIM...
EDITH DIED IN AUSCHWITZ. I'M SO SORRY.
...AND THAT SHE'D LAST SEEN ANNE AND MARGOT BRAVELY FACING THEIR DEPORTATION IN OCTOBER 1944.
ON JUNE 3, 1945, OTTO ARRIVED IN AMSTERDAM AND WENT TO SEE MIEP AND JAN GIES IMMEDIATELY. MIEP RUSHED OUT TO GREET HIM.
MIEP, EDITH IS NOT COMING BACK. BUT I HAVE GREAT HOPE FOR MARGOT AND ANNE.

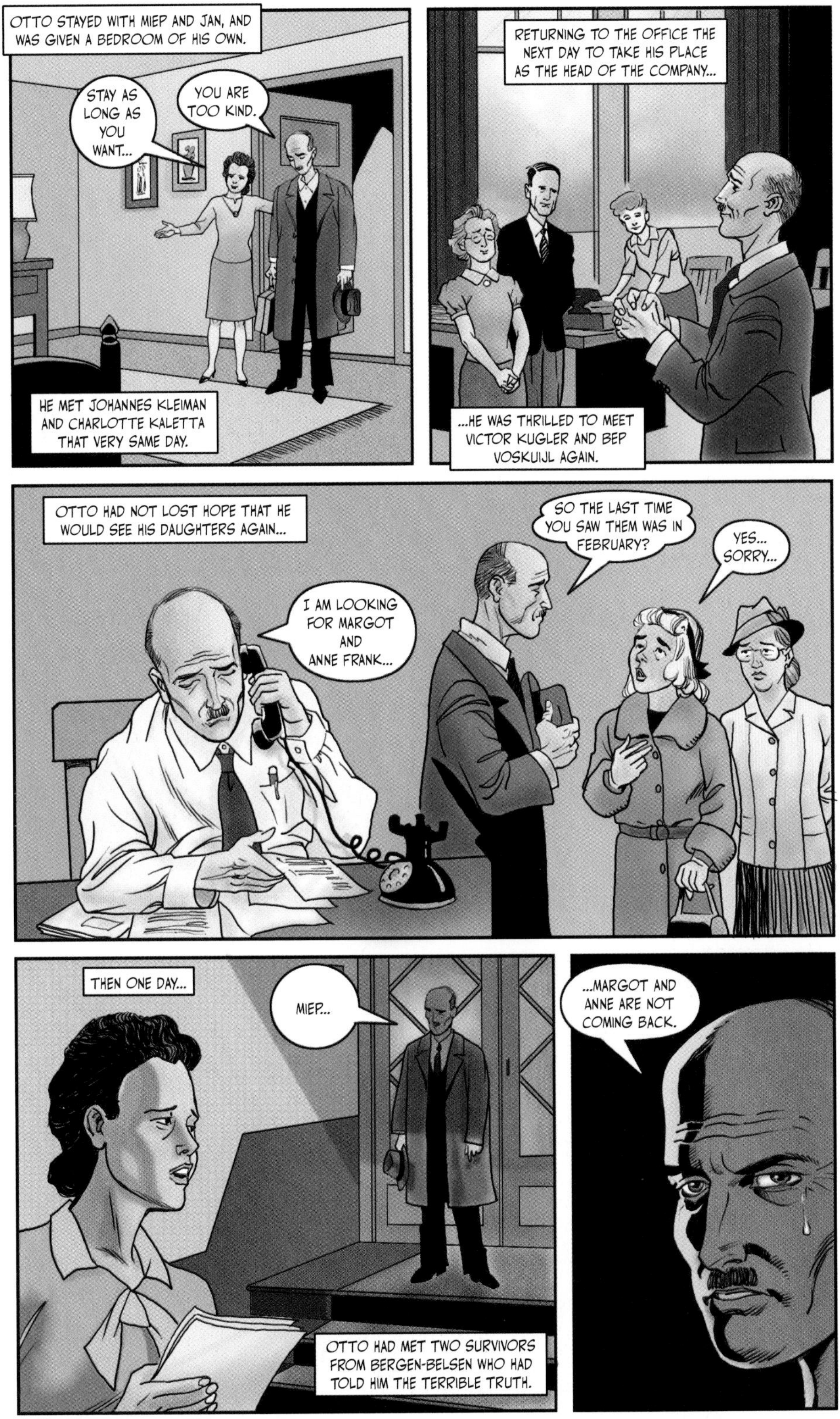
OTTO STAYED WITH MIEP AND JAN, AND WAS GIVEN A BEDROOM OF HIS OWN.
STAY AS LONG AS YOU WANT...
YOU ARE TOO KIND.
HE MET JOHANNES KLEIMAN AND CHARLOTTE KALETTA THAT VERY SAME DAY.
RETURNING TO THE OFFICE THE NEXT DAY TO TAKE HIS PLACE AS THE HEAD OF THE COMPANY...
...HE WAS THRILLED TO MEET VICTOR KUGLER AND BEP VOSKUIJL AGAIN.
OTTO HAD NOT LOST HOPE THAT HE WOULD SEE HIS DAUGHTERS AGAIN...
I AM LOOKING FOR MARGOT AND ANNE FRANK...
SO THE LAST TIME YOU SAW THEM WAS IN FEBRUARY?
YES... SORRY...
THEN ONE DAY...
MIEP...
...MARGOT AND ANNE ARE NOT COMING BACK.
OTTO HAD MET TWO SURVIVORS FROM BERGEN-BELSEN WHO HAD TOLD HIM THE TERRIBLE TRUTH.

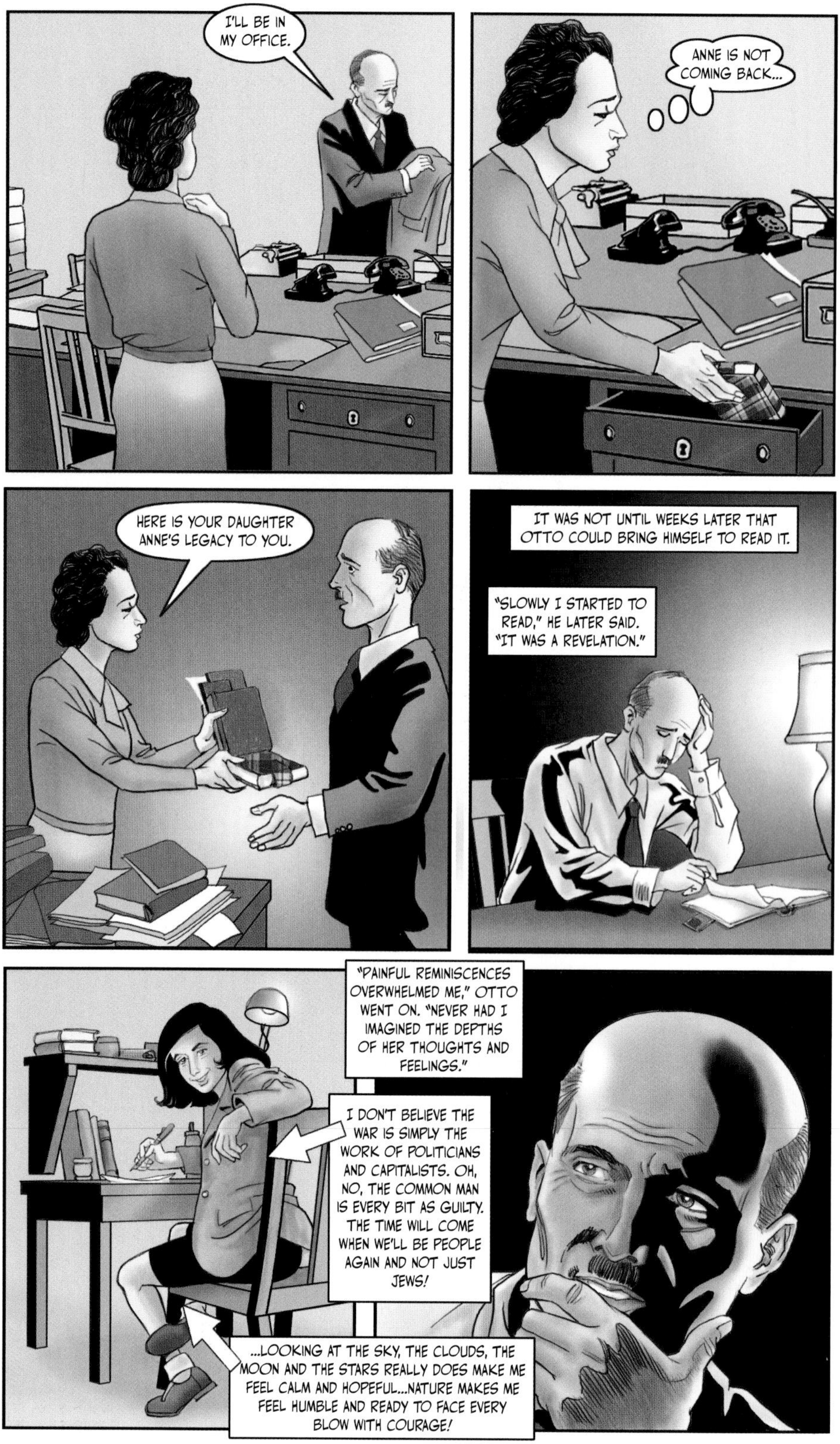
I'LL BE IN MY OFFICE.
ANNE IS NOT COMING BACK...
HERE IS YOUR DAUGHTER ANNE'S LEGACY TO YOU.
IT WAS NOT UNTIL WEEKS LATER THAT OTTO COULD BRING HIMSELF TO READ IT.
"SLOWLY I STARTED TO READ," HE LATER SAID. "IT WAS A REVELATION."
"PAINFUL REMINISCENCES OVERWHELMED ME," OTTO WENT ON. "NEVER HAD I IMAGINED THE DEPTHS OF HER THOUGHTS AND FEELINGS."
I DON'T BELIEVE THE WAR IS SIMPLY THE WORK OF POLITICIANS AND CAPITALISTS. OH, NO, THE COMMON MAN IS EVERY BIT AS GUILTY. THE TIME WILL COME WHEN WE'LL BE PEOPLE AGAIN AND NOT JUST JEWS!
...LOOKING AT THE SKY, THE CLOUDS, THE MOON AND THE STARS REALLY DOES MAKE ME FEEL CALM AND HOPEFUL...NATURE MAKES ME FEEL HUMBLE AND READY TO FACE EVERY BLOW WITH COURAGE!

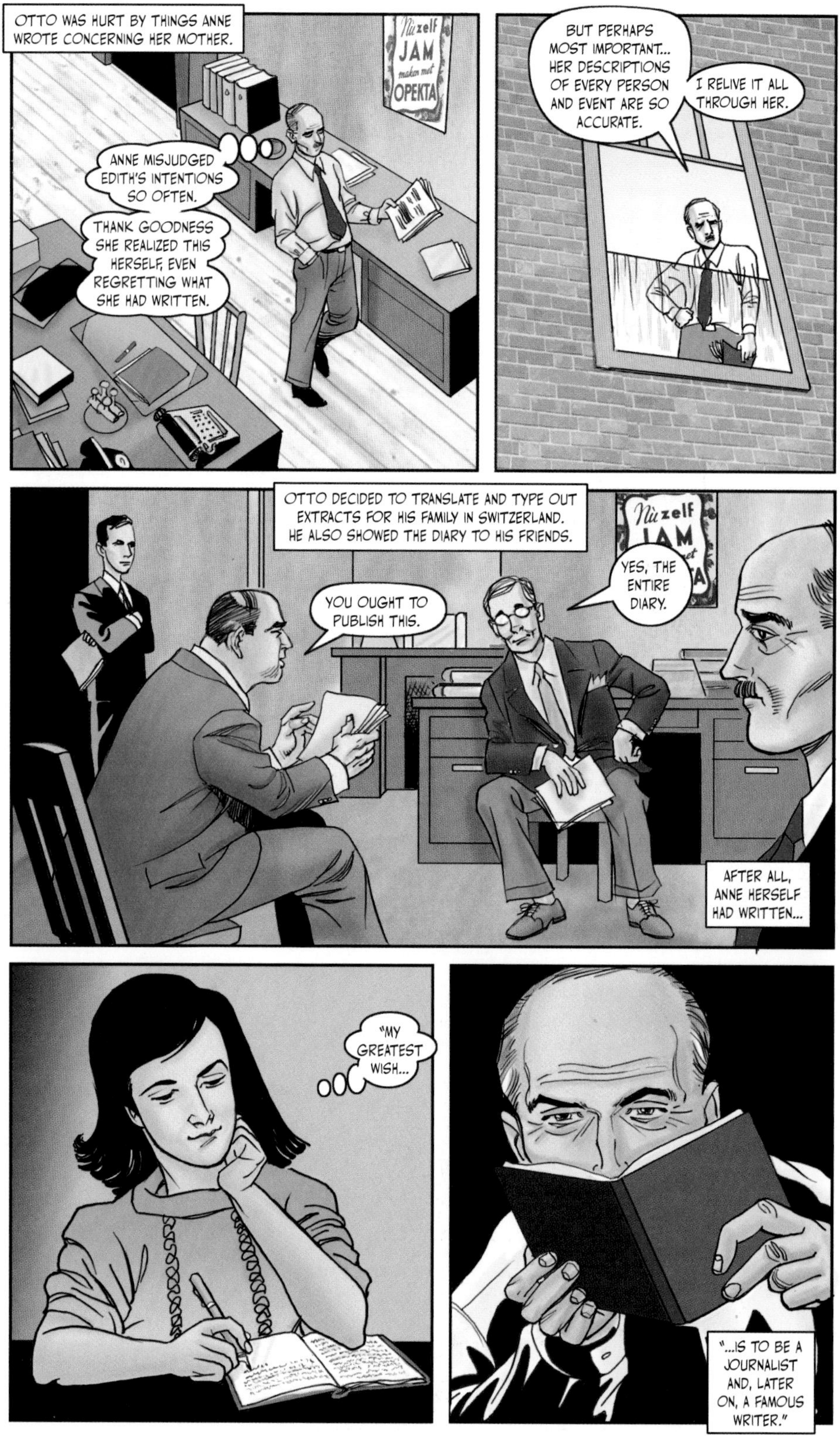
OTTO WAS HURT BY THINGS ANNE WROTE CONCERNING HER MOTHER.
Nü zelf JAM maken met OPEKTA
ANNE MISJUDGED EDITH'S INTENTIONS SO OFTEN.
THANK GOODNESS SHE REALIZED THIS HERSELF, EVEN REGRETTING WHAT SHE HAD WRITTEN.
BUT PERHAPS MOST IMPORTANT... HER DESCRIPTIONS OF EVERY PERSON AND EVENT ARE SO ACCURATE.
I RELIVE IT ALL THROUGH HER.
OTTO DECIDED TO TRANSLATE AND TYPE OUT EXTRACTS FOR HIS FAMILY IN SWITZERLAND. HE ALSO SHOWED THE DIARY TO HIS FRIENDS.
YOU OUGHT TO PUBLISH THIS.
YES, THE ENTIRE DIARY.
AFTER ALL, ANNE HERSELF HAD WRITTEN...
"MY GREATEST WISH...
"...IS TO BE A JOURNALIST AND, LATER ON, A FAMOUS WRITER."

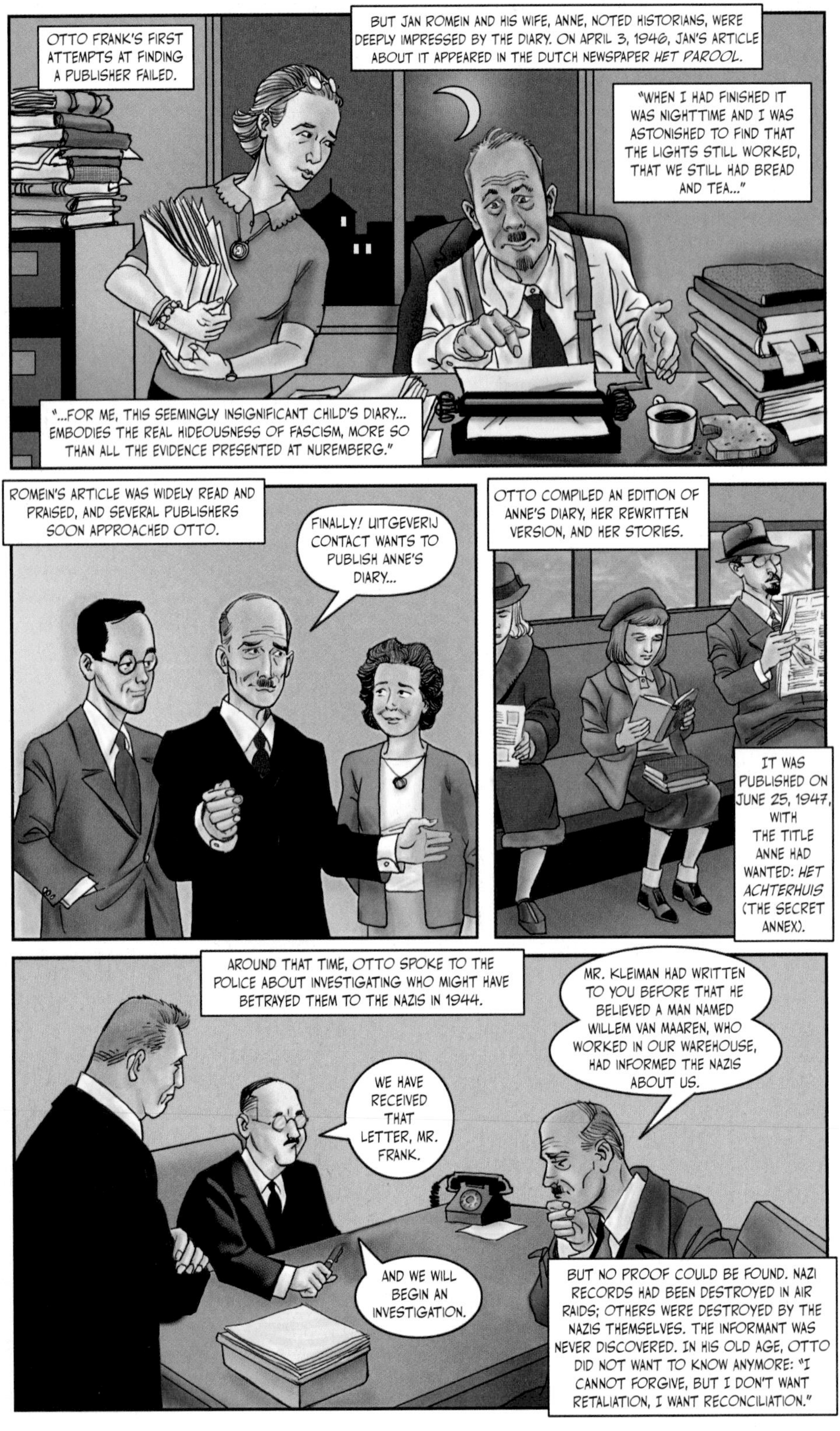

OTTO FRANK'S FIRST ATTEMPTS AT FINDING A PUBLISHER FAILED.
BUT JAN ROMEIN AND HIS WIFE, ANNE, NOTED HISTORIANS, WERE DEEPLY IMPRESSED BY THE DIARY. ON APRIL 3, 1946, JAN'S ARTICLE ABOUT IT APPEARED IN THE DUTCH NEWSPAPER *HET PAROOL*.
"WHEN I HAD FINISHED IT WAS NIGHTTIME AND I WAS ASTONISHED TO FIND THAT THE LIGHTS STILL WORKED, THAT WE STILL HAD BREAD AND TEA..."
"...FOR ME, THIS SEEMINGLY INSIGNIFICANT CHILD'S DIARY... EMBODIES THE REAL HIDEOUSNESS OF FASCISM, MORE SO THAN ALL THE EVIDENCE PRESENTED AT NUREMBERG."
ROMEIN'S ARTICLE WAS WIDELY READ AND PRAISED, AND SEVERAL PUBLISHERS SOON APPROACHED OTTO.
FINALLY! UITGEVERIJ CONTACT WANTS TO PUBLISH ANNE'S DIARY...
OTTO COMPILED AN EDITION OF ANNE'S DIARY, HER REWRITTEN VERSION, AND HER STORIES.
IT WAS PUBLISHED ON JUNE 25, 1947, WITH THE TITLE ANNE HAD WANTED: *HET ACHTERHUIS* (THE SECRET ANNEX).
AROUND THAT TIME, OTTO SPOKE TO THE POLICE ABOUT INVESTIGATING WHO MIGHT HAVE BETRAYED THEM TO THE NAZIS IN 1944.
MR. KLEIMAN HAD WRITTEN TO YOU BEFORE THAT HE BELIEVED A MAN NAMED WILLEM VAN MAAREN, WHO WORKED IN OUR WAREHOUSE, HAD INFORMED THE NAZIS ABOUT US.
WE HAVE RECEIVED THAT LETTER, MR. FRANK.
AND WE WILL BEGIN AN INVESTIGATION.
BUT NO PROOF COULD BE FOUND. NAZI RECORDS HAD BEEN DESTROYED IN AIR RAIDS; OTHERS WERE DESTROYED BY THE NAZIS THEMSELVES. THE INFORMANT WAS NEVER DISCOVERED. IN HIS OLD AGE, OTTO DID NOT WANT TO KNOW ANYMORE: "I CANNOT FORGIVE, BUT I DON'T WANT RETALIATION, I WANT RECONCILIATION."

ONCE PUBLISHED, *THE SECRET ANNEX* TOOK ON A LIFE OF ITS OWN.

IN 1950, TRANSLATIONS APPEARED IN GERMANY AND FRANCE, AND IN 1952, IN GREAT BRITAIN AND THE UNITED STATES. IT HAS SINCE BEEN TRANSLATED INTO MORE THAN 70 LANGUAGES.

ON NOVEMBER 10, 1953, OTTO MARRIED ELFRIEDE MARKOVITS-GEIRINGER, A SURVIVOR OF AUSCHWITZ LIKE HIMSELF.

THEY HAD MET IN 1945 AS BOTH RETURNED TO AMSTERDAM FROM AUSCHWITZ.

THE DIARY'S SUCCESS CONTINUED.

PLAYWRIGHTS ALBERT HACKETT AND FRANCES GOODRICH CAME TO AMSTERDAM. THEY WERE WRITING A PLAY BASED ON THE DIARY.

"INSPIRED THEATRE!"
KERMIT BLOOMGARDEN present
JOSEPH SCHILDKRAUT
The Diary of Anne Fra

THE DIARY OF ANNE FRANK OPENED ON BROADWAY ON OCTOBER 5, 1955, AND RECEIVED EXCELLENT REVIEWS. IT POWERFULLY AFFECTED ITS AUDIENCES, AND RAN FOR 717 PERFORMANCES.

IT WON THE PRESTIGIOUS TONY AWARD AS THE YEAR'S BEST PLAY AND A PULITZER PRIZE FOR ITS TWO PLAYWRIGHTS.

OTTO FRANK COULD NOT BRING HIMSELF TO ATTEND THE OPENING OF THE PLAY.

IN A LETTER TO THE DIRECTOR AND ACTORS, HE WROTE, "THE IDEA THAT MY WIFE AND CHILDREN AS WELL AS I WILL BE PRESENTED ON THE STAGE IS A PAINFUL ONE FOR ME. THEREFORE, IT IS IMPOSSIBLE FOR ME TO COME AND SEE IT."

AND HE NEVER DID...

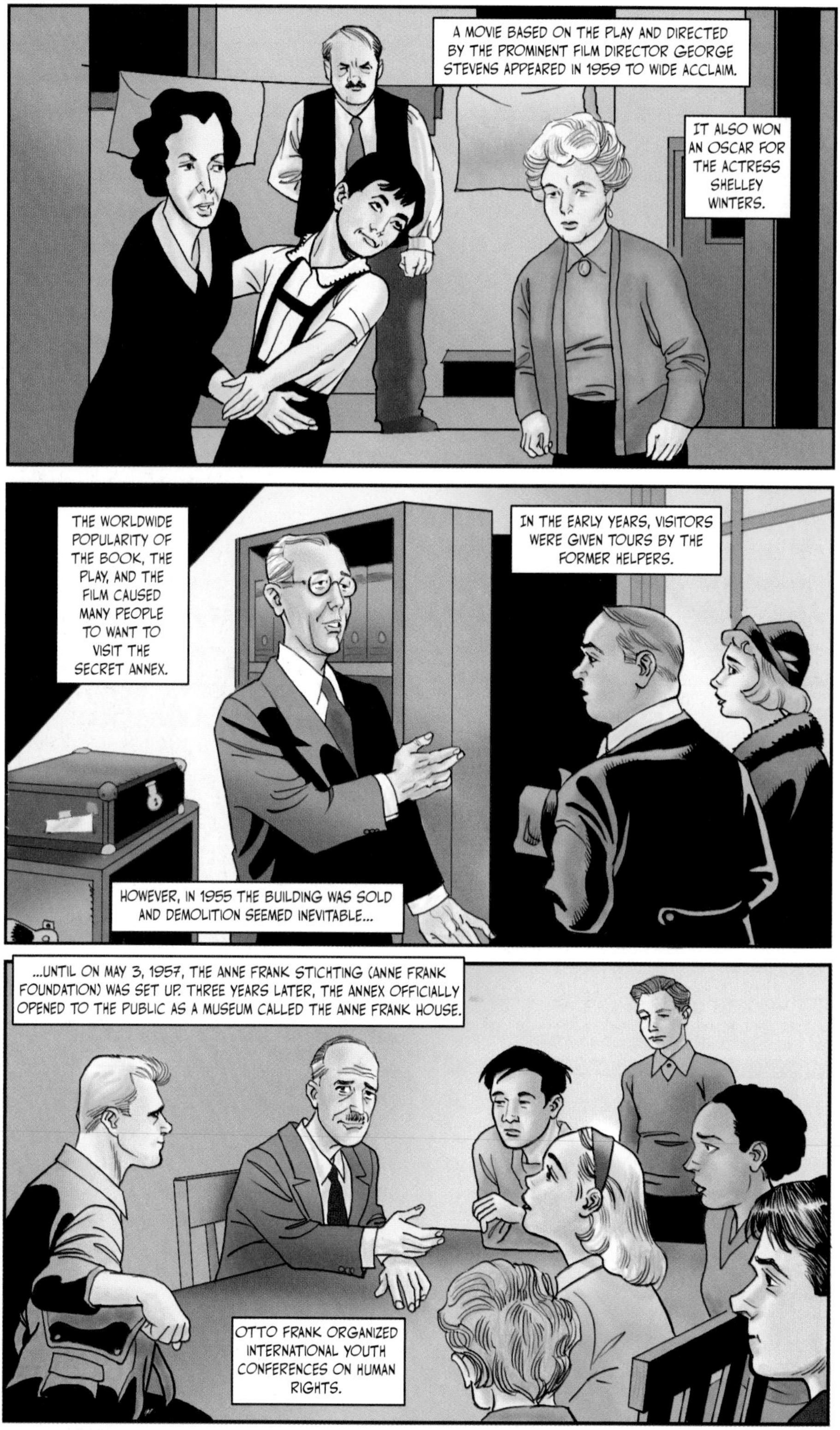
A MOVIE BASED ON THE PLAY AND DIRECTED BY THE PROMINENT FILM DIRECTOR GEORGE STEVENS APPEARED IN 1959 TO WIDE ACCLAIM.
IT ALSO WON AN OSCAR FOR THE ACTRESS SHELLEY WINTERS.
THE WORLDWIDE POPULARITY OF THE BOOK, THE PLAY, AND THE FILM CAUSED MANY PEOPLE TO WANT TO VISIT THE SECRET ANNEX.
IN THE EARLY YEARS, VISITORS WERE GIVEN TOURS BY THE FORMER HELPERS.
HOWEVER, IN 1955 THE BUILDING WAS SOLD AND DEMOLITION SEEMED INEVITABLE...
...UNTIL ON MAY 3, 1957, THE ANNE FRANK STICHTING (ANNE FRANK FOUNDATION) WAS SET UP. THREE YEARS LATER, THE ANNEX OFFICIALLY OPENED TO THE PUBLIC AS A MUSEUM CALLED THE ANNE FRANK HOUSE.
OTTO FRANK ORGANIZED INTERNATIONAL YOUTH CONFERENCES ON HUMAN RIGHTS.

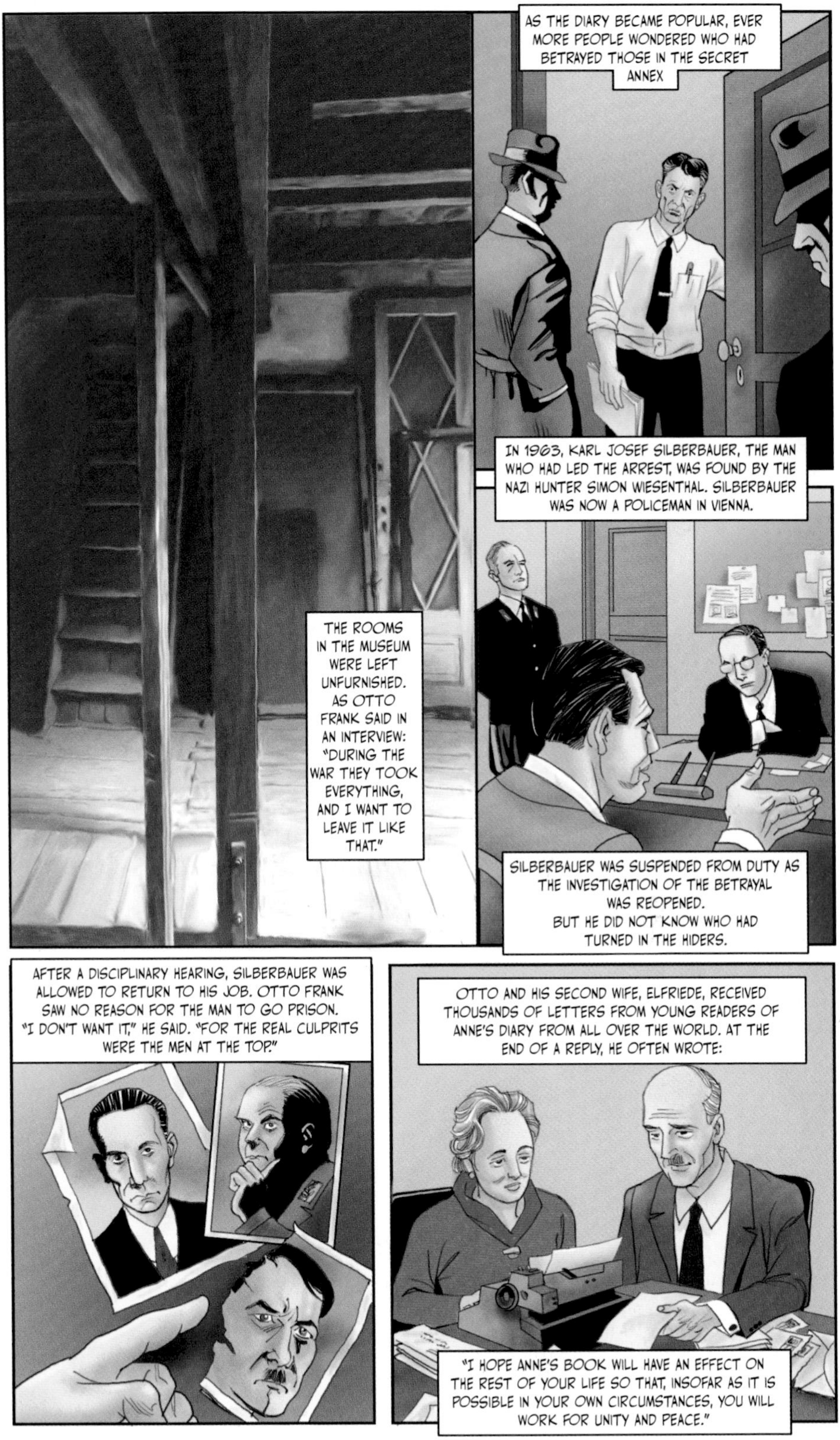
THE ROOMS IN THE MUSEUM WERE LEFT UNFURNISHED. AS OTTO FRANK SAID IN AN INTERVIEW: "DURING THE WAR THEY TOOK EVERYTHING, AND I WANT TO LEAVE IT LIKE THAT."
AS THE DIARY BECAME POPULAR, EVER MORE PEOPLE WONDERED WHO HAD BETRAYED THOSE IN THE SECRET ANNEX
IN 1963, KARL JOSEF SILBERBAUER, THE MAN WHO HAD LED THE ARREST, WAS FOUND BY THE NAZI HUNTER SIMON WIESENTHAL. SILBERBAUER WAS NOW A POLICEMAN IN VIENNA.
SILBERBAUER WAS SUSPENDED FROM DUTY AS THE INVESTIGATION OF THE BETRAYAL WAS REOPENED. BUT HE DID NOT KNOW WHO HAD TURNED IN THE HIDERS.
AFTER A DISCIPLINARY HEARING, SILBERBAUER WAS ALLOWED TO RETURN TO HIS JOB. OTTO FRANK SAW NO REASON FOR THE MAN TO GO PRISON. "I DON'T WANT IT," HE SAID. "FOR THE REAL CULPRITS WERE THE MEN AT THE TOP."
OTTO AND HIS SECOND WIFE, ELFRIEDE, RECEIVED THOUSANDS OF LETTERS FROM YOUNG READERS OF ANNE'S DIARY FROM ALL OVER THE WORLD. AT THE END OF A REPLY, HE OFTEN WROTE:
"I HOPE ANNE'S BOOK WILL HAVE AN EFFECT ON THE REST OF YOUR LIFE SO THAT, INSOFAR AS IT IS POSSIBLE IN YOUR OWN CIRCUMSTANCES, YOU WILL WORK FOR UNITY AND PEACE."

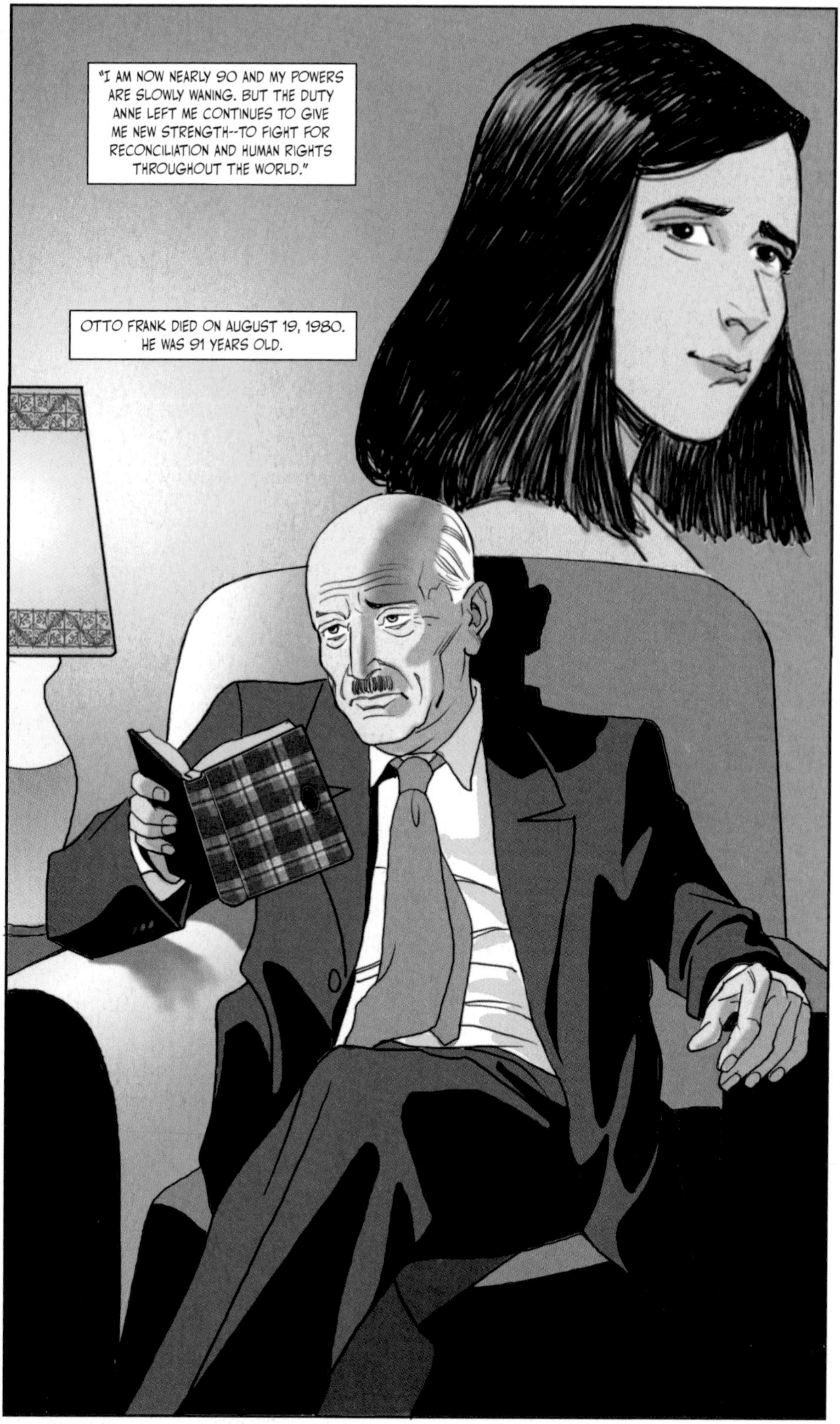
"I AM NOW NEARLY 90 AND MY POWERS ARE SLOWLY WANING. BUT THE DUTY ANNE LEFT ME CONTINUES TO GIVE ME NEW STRENGTH--TO FIGHT FOR RECONCILIATION AND HUMAN RIGHTS THROUGHOUT THE WORLD."
OTTO FRANK DIED ON AUGUST 19, 1980. HE WAS 91 YEARS OLD.

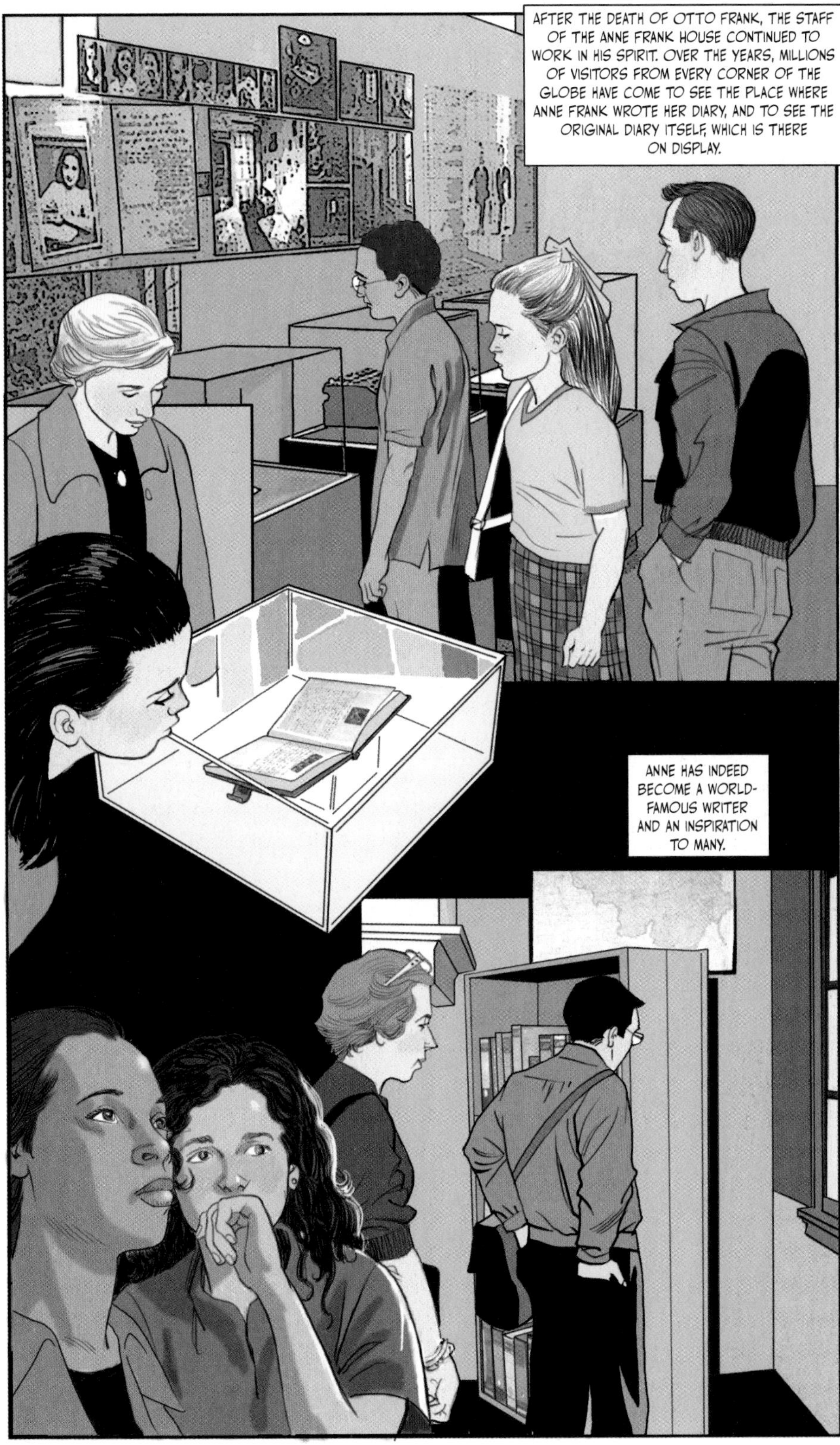
AFTER THE DEATH OF OTTO FRANK, THE STAFF OF THE ANNE FRANK HOUSE CONTINUED TO WORK IN HIS SPIRIT. OVER THE YEARS, MILLIONS OF VISITORS FROM EVERY CORNER OF THE GLOBE HAVE COME TO SEE THE PLACE WHERE ANNE FRANK WROTE HER DIARY, AND TO SEE THE ORIGINAL DIARY ITSELF, WHICH IS THERE ON DISPLAY.
ANNE HAS INDEED BECOME A WORLD-FAMOUS WRITER AND AN INSPIRATION TO MANY.

CHRONOLOGY

"When most of the people of my country, Germany, turned into hordes of nationalistic, cruel, anti-Semitic criminals, I had to face the consequences, and though this did hurt me deeply, I realized that Germany was not the world and I left forever."

—OTTO FRANK

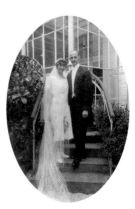

- Otto Frank and Edith Holländer marry in Aachen, Germany (May 12, 1925).
- Volume 1 of Adolf Hitler's book *Mein Kampf* is published (July 18, 1925).
- Margot Frank is born in Frankfurt am Main, Germany (February 16, 1926).

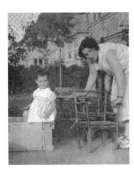

- Anne Frank is born in Frankfurt am Main, Germany (June 12, 1929).
- Black Tuesday descends upon the New York Stock Exchange. Prices collapse amid panic selling, and thousands of investors are ruined as a worldwide economic crisis begins (October 29, 1929).

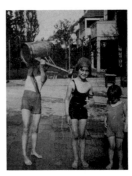

- Adolf Hitler becomes chancellor, the leader of the German government (January 30, 1933).
- Hitler's government organizes a boycott of Jewish shops, doctors, and lawyers. The Nazis say that "real" Germans must not buy from Jews (April 1, 1933).

Deutsche!
Wehrt Euch
Kauft nicht bei Juden!

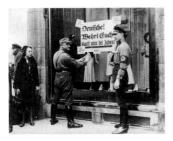

- Hitler's government bans all other political parties. Now Hitler and his party are in total command. Germany has become a dictatorship (July 14, 1933).
- Otto Frank sets up the Opekta company in Amsterdam (September 15, 1933).

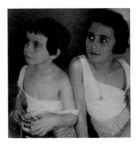

- Alice Frank-Stern, Otto's mother, moves from Frankfurt to Switzerland (October 1933).
- Edith and Margot Frank move to Amsterdam (December 1933).

"In the Netherlands, after those experiences in Germany, it was as if our lives were restored to us. Our children went to school and at least at the beginning our lives proceeded normally. In those days it was possible for us to start over and to feel free."

—OTTO FRANK

- Margot's first day of school in Amsterdam (January 4, 1934).

- Anne Frank is brought to Amsterdam by her uncles Julius and Walter Holländer (February 16, 1934).

- Anne's first day of kindergarten in Amsterdam (April 1934).

- Hitler's government introduces race laws. German Jews have their rights taken away from them. Jews and non-Jews are no longer allowed to get married (September 1935).

- The Nazis destroy Jewish synagogues, shops, and homes throughout Germany. More than 30,000 Jewish men are arrested, and more than 100 Jews are murdered. Later, this night becomes known as Kristallnacht, the "Night of Broken Glass" (November 9, 1938).

- Walter and Julius Holländer immigrate to the Netherlands (Walter in December 1938; Julius in March 1939) and manage to continue their journey to the United States.

Ehefrau

Unterschrift des Paßinhabers

und seiner Ehefrau

Es wird hiermit bescheinigt, daß der Inhaber die durch das obenstehende Lichtbild dargestellte Person ist und die darunter befindliche Unterschrift eigenhändig vollzogen hat.

den

PERSONENBESCHREIBUNG

Ehefrau

Beruf ohne

Geburtsort Schwalbach

Geburtstag

Wohnort

Gestalt mittel

Gesicht oval

Farbe der Augen grau

Farbe des Haares grau

Besond. Kennzeichen trägt Brille

KINDER

Name	Alter	Geschlecht

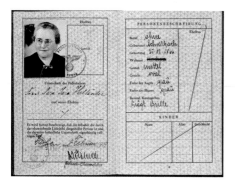

- Fritz Pfeffer and Charlotte Kaletta flee Germany for Amsterdam (December 1938).

- Rosa Holländer-Stern, Anne's grandmother, flees to the Netherlands (March 1939).

- Germany invades Poland. Britain and France declare war on Germany. This is the beginning of the war in Europe (September 1, 1939).

"When I think back to those times during which the occupying forces in Holland introduced regulation after regulation which made life very difficult for us, I have to say that my wife and I did all we could to hide our concerns from the children as far as possible, so that they had a relatively worry-free time."

—OTTO FRANK

- German forces attack and occupy the Netherlands (May 10, 1940). The country surrenders on May 15, and from that date the Netherlands is considered occupied. The royal family and government escape to England.

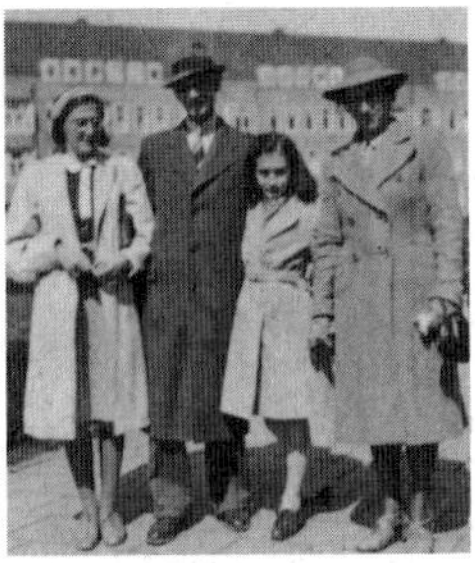

- Otto Frank's company moves to 263 Prinsengracht in Amsterdam (December 1940).

- Anne and Margot are no longer allowed to go to school with non-Jewish children. They have to go to the Jewish high school in Amsterdam (October 1941).

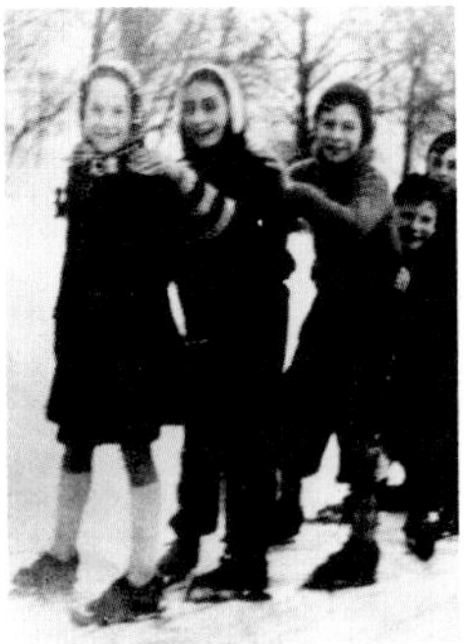

- Japan bombs the American fleet at Pearl Harbor (December 7, 1941). The next day, America declares war on Japan, as does Britain. Germany supports Japan with a declaration of war against the United States.

- High-ranking Nazis come together in a secret meeting in Berlin. They discuss how to carry out a decision that Hitler had already made in 1941: to kill all 11 million Jews in Europe (January 20, 1942).

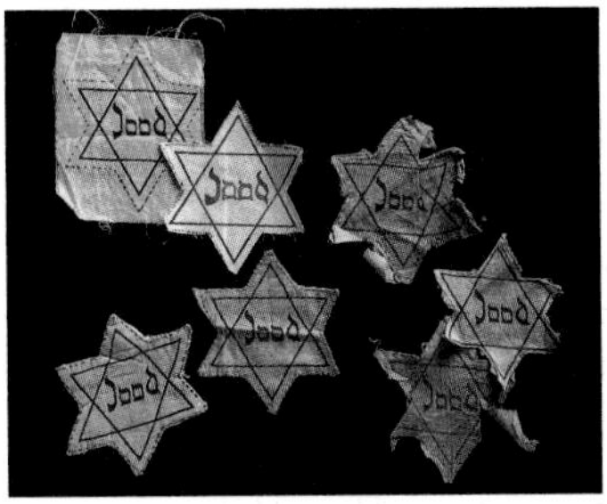
Jood
Jood
Jood
Jood
Jood
Jood
Jood

- All Jews in the Netherlands age six and older have to wear a star with the word "Jood" (Jew) on their clothes (May 3, 1942).

- Anne's thirteenth birthday. Her favorite present is a diary (June 12, 1942).

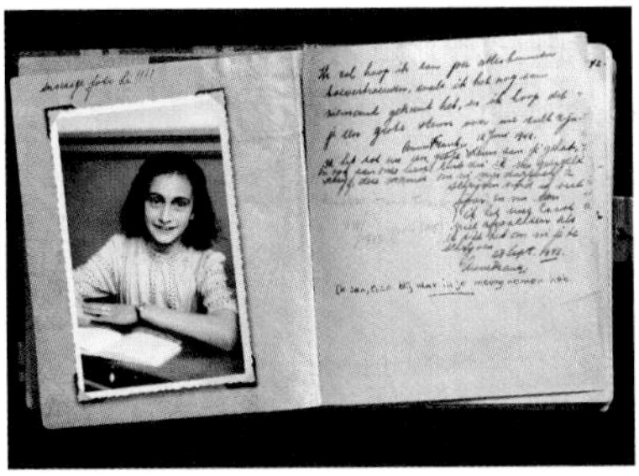

- Margot Frank and many other Jews receive a call-up notice. They have to report for a "work camp" in Germany (July 5, 1942).

"Only by adopting a timetable from the start, and each of us having specific duties, were we able to adapt to the situation. In particular, the children needed enough books for reading and studying. Nobody wanted to contemplate how long this voluntary imprisonment might last."

—OTTO FRANK

- The Frank family goes into hiding in the annex at 263 Prinsengracht in Amsterdam (July 6, 1942).

- The van Pels family goes into hiding in the annex (July 13, 1942).

- Fritz Pfeffer goes into hiding in the annex (November 16, 1942).

- The German army surrenders at Stalingrad, Russia, after a battle lasting five months (February 2, 1943).

- Italy surrenders (September 8, 1943).

- D-Day: Allied armies land in northern France as Operation Overlord begins the liberation of Europe (June 6, 1944).

- Anne turns fifteen, her second birthday in the annex (June 12, 1944).

"There is still much I cannot talk about, even today. Many things I do not want to talk about anymore. About my feelings, for example, when my family was pulled apart on the ramp in Auschwitz."

—OTTO FRANK

- The Frank family, the other people in hiding, and two helpers are betrayed, arrested, and taken to prison (August 4, 1944).
- The people from the hideaways are taken to Westerbork camp (August 8, 1944).
- The people from the hideaways arrive at Auschwitz (September 5–6, 1944).
- Hermann van Pels is killed in the gas chamber (October 1944).
- Anne and Margot are deported from Auschwitz to Bergen-Belsen (October/November 1944).

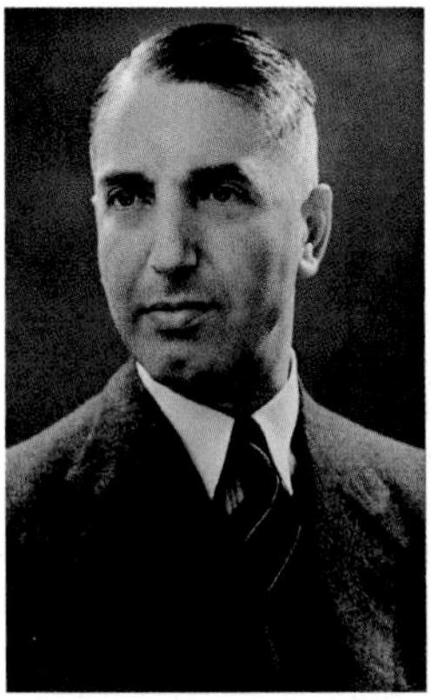

- Fritz Pfeffer dies in Neuengamme (December 20, 1944).
- Edith Frank dies in Auschwitz (January 6, 1945).

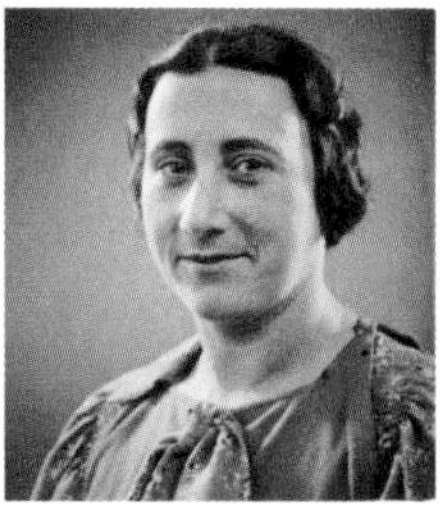

- The Nazis begin the evacuation of Auschwitz. Peter van Pels has to go on a transport. Otto Frank stays behind (January 1945).
- The Russian army liberates Auschwitz, where Otto Frank is being held (January 27, 1945).
- Anne and Margot Frank die in Bergen-Belsen (March 1945).
- Auguste van Pels dies (April 1945).

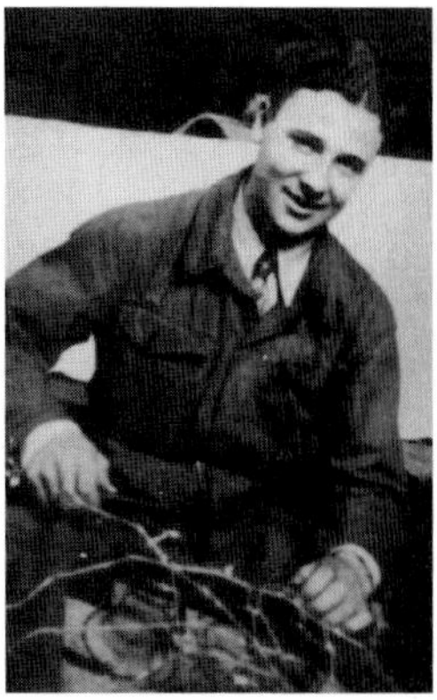

- Peter van Pels dies in Mauthausen concentration camp (May 5, 1945).
- Europe is liberated from Nazi Germany. This day is known as VE Day, the day of victory in Europe (May 8, 1945).
- Otto Frank returns to Amsterdam. He is the only one of the eight people from the annex to have survived the Holocaust (June 3, 1945).

"Little by little, small groups of survivors returned from the various camps, and from these I tried to find out something about Margot and Anne. Finally I found two sisters who had been together with them in Bergen-Belsen, and who told me about the last sufferings and the death of my children. Both had been so weakened through the deprivations that they had succumbed to the raging typhus. My friends, who had been hoping with me, were now mourning with me."

—OTTO FRANK

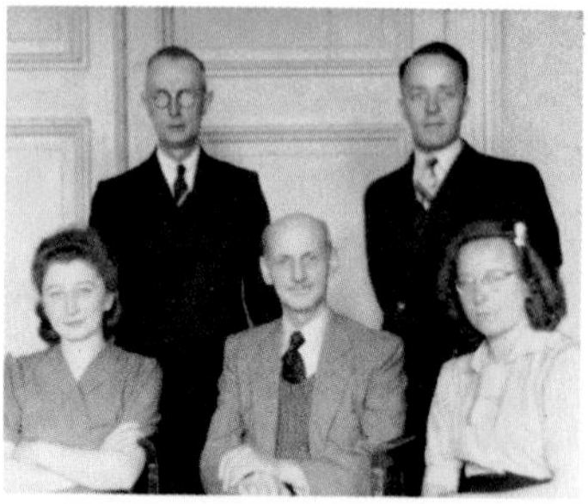

- Otto Frank hears that Anne and Margot have died in Bergen-Belsen. Miep hands him Anne's diary (July 18, 1945).

- Leading Nazis are brought to trial in Nuremburg, Germany. Some are sentenced to death, others to long prison sentences (November 20, 1945).

- The first edition of Anne Frank's manuscript, as compiled and edited by Otto Frank, is published in the Netherlands as *Het Achterhuis* (June 25, 1947).

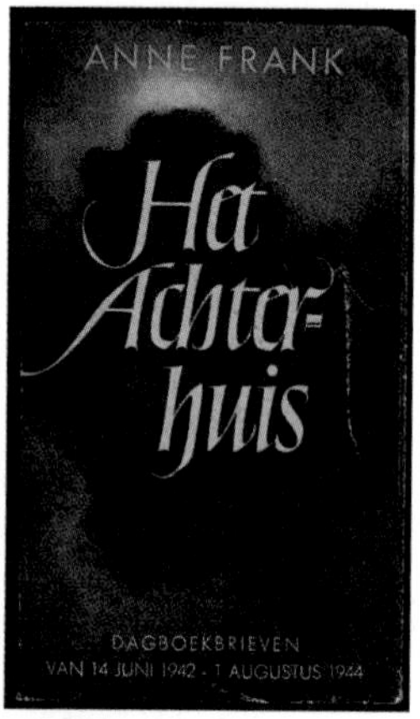
ANNE FRANK
Het Achterhuis
DAGBOEKBRIEVEN
VAN 14 JUNI 1942 - 1 AUGUSTUS 1944

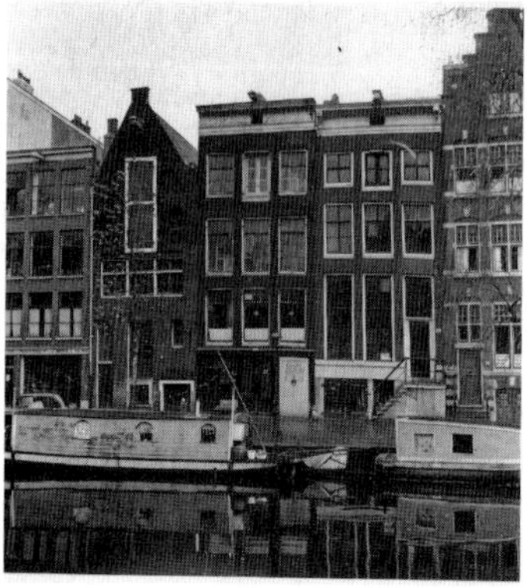

- In 1952, Otto Frank moves to Basel, Switzerland, and marries Elfriede (Fritzi) Markovits (November 10, 1953).

- 263 Prinsengracht opens as a museum, which is named the Anne Frank House (May 3, 1960).

- Otto Frank dies in Basel, Switzerland (August 19, 1980).

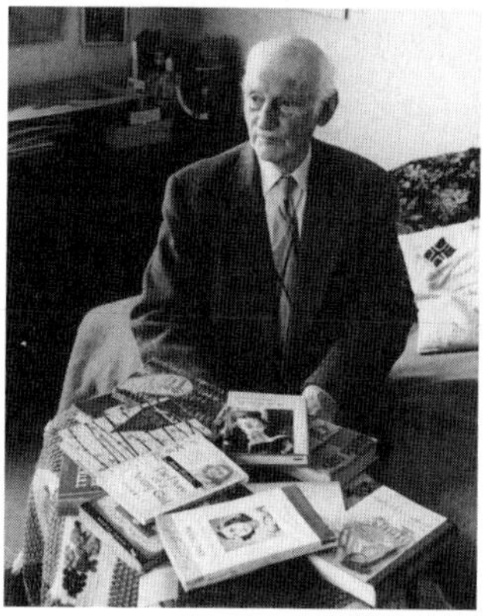

SUGGESTIONS FOR FURTHER READING

Anne Frank's diary is available in a translation made by Susan Massotty and published in the United States by Doubleday, a division of Random House, Inc. If you have not read the diary, we urge you to do so: it is one of the most beautiful books to come out of World War II.

Frank, Anne. *Anne Frank's Tales from the Secret Annex*. New York: Bantam, 2003.

Gies, Miep, with Alison Leslie Gold. *Anne Frank Remembered: The Story of the Woman Who Helped to Hide the Frank Family*. New York: Simon and Schuster, 2009.

Gold, Alison Leslie. *Hannah Goslar Remembers: A Childhood Friend of Anne Frank*. London: Bloomsbury, 1999.

Lindwer, Willy. *The Last Seven Months of Anne Frank*. New York: Anchor, 1992.

Müller, Melissa. *Anne Frank: The Biography*. Translated by Rita and Robert Kimber. New York: Picador, 1999.

Prose, Francine. *Anne Frank: The Book, the Life, the Afterlife*. New York: HarperCollins, 2009.

Van Maarsen, Jacqueline. *My Name Is Anne, She Said, Anne Frank: The Memoirs of Anne Frank's Best Friend*. San Francisco: Arcadia Books, 2008.

Westra, Hans. *Inside Anne Frank's House: An Illustrated Journey Through Anne's World*. New York: Overlook Press, 2004.

ONLINE

www.annefrank.org

www.annefrankguide.net

www.annefrank.org/achterhuis

ACKNOWLEDGMENTS

There are so many people we'd like to acknowledge and thank for their help in the creation of this book. First, and as it seems always, our editor and publisher, Thomas LeBien, for his untiring editing and consistent leadership. Enough can never be said for what he has meant to us. And his assistant, Dan Crissman, has always been there to help during this complicated process. Thanks to Eric van Rootselaar, for the cross-section drawing of 263 Prinsengracht on page 51, and to Joris Fiselier, for his corrections of some of the historical maps. Special thanks to Michael Allen for his help in coloring. He was professional, talented, and an important part of the team.

Several people from the Anne Frank House must be specially acknowledged, though everyone there deserves our thanks. Chantal d'Aulnis, publisher, who first brought this project to us, has been a blessing from the moment she first showed us the tiny space in which Anne and her family lived for those tumultuous years. Menno Metselaar, senior editor, cannot be thanked enough for making sure both the story and the art were as authentic and true as was its incredible heroine. He helped make the book better with each comment and suggestion, and brought Anne Frank deeper into our hearts. Teresien de Silva, director of the Anne Frank Collection, did a fantastic job fact-checking our work. Hans Westra, CEO, and Kleis Broekhuizen, COO/CFO, threw their support behind this transatlantic coproduction, offering us gracious hospitality at the museum in Amsterdam and valuable guidance on several visits to the States.

Yes, this book has given us nearly two years of demanding and often difficult work. But it has rewarded us with a glorious adventure that will never be forgotten. And that, perhaps more than anything, is what we'd like to acknowledge.

The research for the drawings was partially based on the "online hiding place," part of the virtual museum offered by the Anne Frank House. In the 3-D online hiding place, visitors can explore the building as it was during the hiding period. Each room offers extra information—for example, notes about the people who lived there and about the things they used in everyday life. You can find it at www.annefrank.org.

PHOTOGRAPHS REPRODUCED IN THE TEXT COURTESY OF

bildarchiv preussischer kulturbesitz (pages 16, 23, 142)
bildarchiv preussischer kulturbezitz / Bayerische Staatsbibliothek / Archiv Heinrich Hoffmann (page 38)
Bundesarchiv Bild 183-L23001 (page 49)
Beeldank WO2/Nederlands Instituut voor Oorlogsdocumentatie (page 52)
United States Holocaust Memorial Museum, courtesy of Robert A. Schmuhl (page 53)
AFS/Allard Bovenberg (pages 74, 145)
United States Holocaust Memorial Museum (page 126)
Maria Austria Institute (pages 131, 137, 147)
akg-images / Hans Asemissen (page 143)
ullstein bild (page 145)
Anne Frank family photographs © Anne Frank Stichting, Amsterdam / ANNE FRANK–Fonds, Basel